D1346119

LEGAL PROBLEMS OF CREDIT AND SECURITY

AUSTRALIA
Law Book Co.—Sydney

CANADA and **USA**
Carswell—Toronto

HONG KONG
Sweet & Maxwell Asia

NEW ZEALAND
Brookers—Wellington

SINGAPORE and **MALAYSIA**
Sweet & Maxwell Asia
Singapore and Kuala Lumpur

LEGAL PROBLEMS OF CREDIT AND SECURITY

THIRD EDITION

Roy Goode

LONDON
SWEET & MAXWELL
2003

First edition 1982
Second edition 1988

Published in 2003 by
Sweet & Maxwell Limited of
100 Avenue Road, London NW3 3PF
Typeset by J&L Composition, Filey, North Yorkshire
Printed in Great Britain by MPG Books, Bodmin

No natural forests were destroyed to make this product;
only farmed timber was used and replanted

A CIP catalogue record for this book is available from the British Library

ISBN 0421 47150 6

© Roy Goode 2003

PREFACE

To my astonishment it is now 15 years since the appearance of the second edition of this little book. In that time much has happened. There have been a great many decisions on security interests, from the High Court to the House of Lords. Issues of characterisation, to which much space was devoted in the previous editions, have continued to feature prominently as courts wrestle with the question whether the contractual arrangements have created a security interest and, if so, whether it is in the nature of a fixed charge or a floating charge. An illuminating example is the series of decisions in the *Cosslett* case culminating in *Smith (Administrator of Cosslett (Contractors) Ltd.) v Bridgend County Borough Council* [2002] 1 A.C. 336. Happily the clarity of *Re Brightlife* [1987] Ch. 200, temporarily blurred by decisions such as *Re New Bullas Trading Ltd.* [1993] B.C.L.C. 1389, has been restored by the decision of the Privy Council in *Agnew v Commissioners of Inland Revenue* [2001] 2 A.C. 710. Priority issues also remain a regular feature of case law, throwing up a division of judicial opinion as to whether a negative pledge clause in a charge affects subsequent incumbrancers or is purely contractual in effect and continuing debate as to the resolution of the circularity problem which arises where a company that has given a fixed charge expressed to be subordinate to a floating charge goes into liquidation owing preferential debts. There have also been some significant cases on the effect of an assignment in breach of a no-assignment clause, in particular the decision of the House of Lords in *Linden Gardens Trust Ltd. v Lenesta Sludge(Disposals) Ltd.* [1994] 1 A.C. 85.

The legislature has not been idle either, with further restrictions on the enforcement of security given by a small company where the directors obtain an automatic moratorium under the Insolvency Act 2000 by filing prescribed documents with the court and, more dramatically, the almost total abolition of the institution of administration receivership, as well as the elimination of what remained of Crown preference, by the Enterprise Act 2002, though both of these sets of provisions are more relevant to the companion volume in this series, *Principles of Corporate Insolvency Law* (2nd ed.), than to the present volume.

This shift in the balance of power from secured creditors to general creditors and the potential beneficiaries of reorganisations of insolvent companies appears to represent a belated reflection of the sympathies of the incomparable Ambrose Bierce, whose *Enlarged Devil's Dictionary* defines a (secured?) creditor as:

"One of a tribe of savages dwelling beyond the Financial Straights and dreaded for their desolating incursions",

while "debtor" receives the beneficent definition of:

"A worthy person, in whose interest the national debt should be so managed as to depreciate the national currency."

This seems particularly appropriate for inclusion in a preface written on Budget day!

A subject that has assumed enormous importance in recent years is the taking of security and quasi-security interests in corporate investment securities. The move from paper-based to electronic issue and transfer systems (*e.g.* CREST) and, even more significantly, from directly held investment securities to securities held through accounts with intermediaries, has thrown up a complex of problems which in the United States have been largely resolved in the revised Article 8 of the Uniform Commercial Code but with which English law has yet to grapple, including such basic questions as the nature of an account holder's rights in securities credited to his account and whether an account holder can look through his own intermediary to assert claims against higher-tier intermediaries. Of great significance also is the warmly welcomed 2002 EC Directive on Financial Collateral Arrangements, which is designed to protect financial collateral against various possible grounds of avoidance under insolvency law. Finally, in December 2002 there was concluded the Hague Convention on the law applicable to certain rights in respect of securities held with an intermediary, addressing an important conflict of laws question, yet one on which there has hitherto been no reported English case. These developments have led me to provide a substantial new chapter on security interests in investment corporate securities, which I hope will shed some light on dark places. In addition to the above matters I have taken the opportunity to examine the characterisation of transactions such as repos and sell/buy-backs and stock loans.

Apart from these developments, the interval since the second edition has given me time for further reflection on a number of issues, leading to a substantial revision and expansion of the text, including a treatment of security interests by attornment and novation and a rewriting of the chapters on set-off and guarantees. And in relation to charge-backs, the hare which I started in the first edition has now run its course and I have felt compelled to accept that conceptual purity must give way to commercial needs and practices! But my modest suggestion way back in 1982 that charge-backs were conceptually impossible has at least served to stimulate jurisprudential debate, engaging the attention of numerous academic and practising specialists here and abroad and leading to the decision of a High Court judge (now in the Lords), who adopted the suggestion, *obiter dicta* by judges in two Court of Appeal cases (in one of which serious doubt was expressed as to the earlier ruling while the other, which supported the ruling, was on behalf of a court which included the quondam High Court judge himself) and an *obiter dictum* of the

House of Lords disapproving of the *obiter dictum* of the second Court of Appeal! How the doctrine of *stare decisis* is to be applied in this situation remains unclear!

I have benefited over the years from many helpful discussions with fellow academics, practitioners and students. I am indebted in particular to a number of friends and colleagues mentioned below for their assistance. The new chapter on security interests in investment securities was considerably improved as the result of comments by Philip Wood, Catherine Beahan and Nick Segal of Allen and Overy, Guy Morton of Freshfields, Professor Dan Prentice of Pembroke College, Oxford, Professor Jim Rogers of Boston College, Jack Wiener, managing director and deputy general counsel of The Depository Trust and Clearing Corporation, Kristen Geyer, managing director and general counsel, and Diego Devos, director and deputy general counsel, of Euroclear. Robert Stevens of Lady Margaret Hall, Oxford, and Richard Hooley, currently at Fitzwilliam College, Cambridge, but shortly to take up his appointment to a chair at King's College, London, were kind enough to read through the proofs and saved me from a number of errors and omissions. I should also like to express my thanks to my former research assistants, Rafal Zakrzewski and Bushra Razaq, for their help with literature searches. My last but not least expression of appreciation is to Kate Hayes, Senior Publishing Editor, and Melanie Pepper, Senior Project Editor, of Sweet & Maxwell, for all their expertise and support in the production of this new edition, which I hope will be found of assistance both to practising lawyers and to students.

Roy Goode
Oxford
April 9, 2003

PREFACE TO THE SECOND EDITION

This book began as a series of public lectures delivered at the Centre for Commercial Law Studies, Queen Mary College, in 1982, the purpose of which was to explore a range of fundamental legal concepts relating to security and quasi-security interests, with particular reference to security in personal property. The large attendance at those lectures and the kind welcome given both by academic and by practising lawyers to the first edition of this book revealed a widespread recognition of the practical value of a conceptual approach in this complex field, and an awareness of the problems that can result from a purely mechanical application of a set of detailed rules.

This new edition is not merely a technical update but is in many respects a new book. I have now devoted two distinct chapters to the nature and forms of consensual security and concepts of attachment and perfection. The treatment of negative pledges has been substantially expanded, an analysis offered of the legal nature of sub-participations in loan agreements and the chapter on priorities has been enlarged to include an examination of twelve typical priority problems and their solution. I have elaborated the discussion of the vexed question whether a bank can take a charge over its own customer's credit balance, reinforcing the negative view expressed in the first edition which received judicial vindication in *Re Charge Card Services Ltd.* [1986] 3 All E.R. 289. The chapter on set-off has been totally rewritten and substantially extended. Dr. Rory Derham's excellent new book *Set off*, which I had the pleasure of evaluating as an external examiner when it was presented in its earlier form as a doctoral thesis at Cambridge University, reached me too late to be reflected in the above chapter except by way of footnote reference. It is the first modern monograph on the subject and is required reading for anyone interested in set-off.

By concentrating on fundamentals rather than on the minutiae of English law I have sought to provide a text which will be of assistance to lawyers throughout the Commonwealth. In this new edition I have drawn on many Commonwealth decisions, particularly those from courts in Australia, Canada and New Zealand, which have shed light on a number of complex issues and which will, I believe, be as helpful to judges in this country as their own decisions are to courts elsewhere in the Commonwealth.

I am indebted to all those who over the past few years have helped to clarify my thinking or have drawn my attention to cases and problems of which I might otherwise have remained unaware. They are too numerous to mention by name but include my academic colleagues, my students and friends in the practising profession. I owe a particular debt to Philip Wood of Allen and Overy, who has allowed me freely to draw on his encyclopaedic knowledge of finance and security in general and of set-off in particular; to David Weed of Victor Mishcon & Co., who helped me with a practical point on searches in the Companies Registry; and to the various banks and firms of City solicitors who invited me to present in-house seminars on *Charge Card* and related problems and helped me to sharpen the argument, even at the expense to them of an inconvenient conclusion! I should also like to express my thanks to the editorial team at Sweet & Maxwell, and to Sheila Aked for preparing the index. Finally, I am indebted to Queen Mary College for granting me sabbatical leave to complete a new edition of this and other works.

The law is stated on the basis of the materials available to me at February 1, 1988.

Centre for Commercial Law Studies,   R. M. Goode
Queen Mary College,
London.
February 17, 1988

PREFACE TO THE FIRST EDITION

My purpose in delivering the lectures reproduced in this book has been to explore some of the fundamental legal conceptions underlying the more important types of commercial security and to suggest that a number of conventional propositions relied on in everyday practice are conceptually unsound. In some cases the analysis leads to the conclusion that a particular form of security is less effective than previously supposed. Examples are the provision for equal and rateable security in negative pledge clauses; agreements purporting to create a charge in favour of a bank over its customer's credit balance; the registration of details of restrictions in a floating charge; and the use of automatic crystallisation clauses on the mistaken assumption that crystallisation necessarily establishes priority over a subsequent security interest. In other cases, my task has been the more agreeable one of seeking to show that apparent weaknesses in a creditor's security do not in fact exist—for example, the so-called "flawed" asset created when restrictions are imposed on the withdrawal of a deposit; the use of a provision in a guarantee which, far from prohibiting the surety from proving in competition with the creditor, requires him to do so and to hold any dividends on trust for the creditor.

That the practitioner is keenly interested in legal theory, however abstract, affecting commercial transactions was amply demonstrated by the large number of lawyers, bankers and businessmen who attended these lectures. I am indebted to my audience for several thought-provoking questions and illuminating comments, and in preparing the written text I have revised and slightly expanded the material to take account of some of the more important points made. I have also taken the opportunity to update the treatment of the law, which is believed to be correctly stated as at September 14, 1982.

Centre for Commercial Law Studies,   R. M. Goode
Queen Mary College,
London.
1982.

CONTENTS

VII. Set-Off, Netting and Abatement

VIII. Some Aspects of Suretyship Law

TABLE OF CASES

TABLE OF STATUTES

TABLE OF STATUTORY INSTRUMENTS

TABLE OF EC INSTRUMENTS

TABLE OF INTERNATIONAL CONVENTIONS AND TREATIES

I

The Nature and Forms of Consensual Security

1. THE PURPOSES OF SECURITY

reasons of taking security

A financier taking security for an advance[1] is concerned to see that if the **1–01** debtor's assets are insufficient to meet the claims of all his creditors the financier will at least be able to look to his security to obtain total or partial payment. So the primary purpose of security is to reduce credit risk and obtain priority over other creditors in the event of the debtor's bankruptcy or liquidation. However, there is no necessary connection between security and priority. For policy reasons the law allows certain classes of unsecured claim priority over certain classes of secured claim. For example, in a winding up preferential creditors have priority over a floating charge,[2] while the secured claims of directors of a company may in certain circumstances be subordinated to the claims of general unsecured creditors.[3] Nevertheless it remains the general principle that a secured creditor has priority over an unsecured creditor.

A secondary, but important, consideration is that security gives the creditor a certain measure of influence or control over events. This is particularly true of a creditor holding a fixed and floating charge covering substantially the whole of a debtor company's assets. The priority enjoyed by the chargee is likely to deter unsecured creditors from precipitate enforcement action which might inhibit the orderly reorganisation of the company or the sale of the company as a going concern or effective realisation of its assets. Moreover, a creditor holding a charge of the kind described above has until now had as one its most powerful remedies the appointment of an

---

[1] The term "security" should not be confused with "securities" in the sense of investment securities such as shares and bonds. It would be preferable to adopt the term "collateral" for the former, widely used in international finance, at the risk of offending traditionalists who do not care to see English adjectives converted into American nouns! However, the terms are not entirely interchangeable, since in relation to dealings in investment securities the provision of collateral is taken to include sale and repurchase agreements because these serve a security function even though not constituting security agreements in law. See below, para.6–20.

[2] Insolvency Act 1986, s.175(2)(b).

[3] For example, one of the sanctions for fraudulent or wrongful trading by a director of a company in liquidation is subordination of his debt, wholly or in part, to all other debts of the company (Insolvency Act 1986, s.215(4)).

administrative receiver, empowered to assume the management of the company in place of its directors, to carry on the business with a view to sale, hiving down of the company to a newly formed subsidiary, or disposal of the assets. The administrative receiver is agent of the company, not of the creditor who appoints him, so that the creditor is not responsible for the receiver's acts unless it intervenes in the conduct of the receivership.[4] But the creditor needs to be careful not to exercise direct control of the company's affairs, as this may make the creditor a shadow director,[5] with potential liabilities if the company becomes insolvent.[6] Administrative receivership, a widely used mode of enforcing security, is shortly to be abolished as regards future transactions,[7] with certain exceptions related to the capital and financial markets.

1–02   There are other reasons too for taking security. The holding of security is relevant to the risk-weighting of capital for capital adequacy purposes under the Basel Accord 1988 and the EC Capital Adequacy Directive[8]; and where the collateral consists of investment securities held with a right of "use" (including sale) this enhances the creditor's ability to raise funds itself and engage in market operations.

From the viewpoint of the borrower, the ability to furnish security may give it access to funds which might not otherwise be available or might be offered on more expensive terms.

Historically the most important subjects of security were tangible assets: land and goods. With the development of documentary intangibles[9] the pledge could be extended to embrace documents of title to goods, negotiable instruments and negotiable securities. Pure intangibles, such as receivables, also became increasingly important as security, a move sharply accentuated when the volume of paper in issue threatened to overwhelm securities systems and paper-based securities became increasingly replaced by electronic securities and direct holdings from the issuer by indirect holdings through a securities account with a bank or other securities intermediary.[10] The position now is that intangible property is far and away the most significant form of collateral, and in the securities field alone some billions of pounds of value are transferred every day. Yet physical collateral continues to play a significant role in finance, and this is particularly true of cross-border dealings in mobile equipment of high unit value or economic importance. Hence the potentially huge impact of the 2001 Cape Town Convention on International Interests in Mobile Equipment, which provides an international regime

---

[4] Insolvency Act 1986, s.44(1). See further R.M. Goode, *Principles of Corporate Insolvency Law* (2nd ed.), pp.215, 261.

[5] A shadow director is a person in accordance with whose directions or instructions the directors of a company are accustomed to act (Companies Act 1985, s.741(2); Insolvency Act 1986, s.251.

[6] *e.g.*, liability for wrongful trading under s.214 of the Insolvency Act 1986: see s.214(7).

[7] By s.72A of the Insolvency Act inserted by s.250 of the Enterprise Act 2002. See below, para.4–61.

[8] Directive 93/6 as amended.

[9] See below, para.1–44.

[10] See below, para.6–02.

governing security, title retention and leasing interests in aircraft objects, space assets and railway rolling stock.[11]

The secured creditor's protection against competing interests predicates at least three distinct legal facts: first, that his security has *attached*, in the sense that it has fastened on the asset so as to give the creditor rights over the asset *vis-à-vis* the debtor; secondly, that it has been *perfected*, *i.e.* all steps have been taken to preserve its validity against third parties; thirdly, that it will have *priority* under the relevant priority rules.

2. THE CONCEPT OF SECURITY

The steps necessary for attachment and perfection of a security interest are discussed in the next chapter. But first we must explore the different kinds of security and the legal nature of a security interest. The ingenuity of financiers and their legal advisers has given rise to many forms of agreement which are intended to provide security but do not in law create a security interest. Among such quasi-security devices are the reservation of title under a contract of sale, the contractual set-off and the imposition of restrictions on the withdrawal of a cash deposit.   **1–03**

The problem is to distinguish true security from quasi-security, a matter on which legal opinion is at some points acutely divided. The problem is not purely of theoretical interest, for where an agreement creates a security interest in law the debtor has a right to redeem and an interest in any surplus resulting from repossession and sale by the creditor, the security agreement may be registrable by statute and the tax and accounting treatment of the transaction may turn on the fact that it constitutes a security transaction.

The very concept of security varies widely from jurisdiction to jurisdiction, depending as it does on concepts of ownership and possession which are inherently fluid. It appears to be recognised everywhere that a security interest involves the grant of a right in an asset which the grantor owns or in which he has an interest, but legal systems differ in their concept of ownership for this purpose. The most fundamental divide is between the formal and the functional approach. The formal approach is one which sharply distinguishes the grant of security from the retention of title under conditional sale, hire-purchase and leasing agreements, on the basis that the buyer, hirer or lessee has merely a possessory interest, subject to which the seller, owner or lessor continues to enjoy absolute ownership by virtue of the agreement between the parties. The functional approach treats a conditional buyer, a   **1–04**

---

[11] For a comprehensive analysis, see Roy Goode, *Convention on International Interests in Mobile Equipment and Protocol Thereto on Matters Specific to Aircraft Equipment: Official Commentary*. The significance of the Convention and Protocol has recently been dramatically underlined by the press release issued in February 2003 by Ex-im Bank—the Export-Import Bank of the United States—offering a reduction of one-third in its exposure fee on the financing of large US aircraft for all buyers in foreign countries that ratify and implement the Cape Town Convention.

lessee with an option to purchase and, in many cases, a lessee under a finance lease, as the owner and the interest of the conditional seller or lessor as limited to a security interest, so that the reservation of title is equated with a purchase-money chattel mortgage. The functional approach is that adopted throughout the United States under Article 9 of the Uniform Commercial Code,[12] throughout Canada under Personal Property Security Acts based on Article 9,[13] and in New Zealand under its Personal Property Securities Act 1999,[14] which came into force in 2002. The legal systems of other countries, including the United Kingdom,[15] and legal systems belonging to the common law family outside North America and New Zealand[16] and to the civil law family, adhere to the formal approach.[17]

This does not mean that English law looks always to the form of a transaction and not to the substance. If, for example, a documents is a sham designed to disguise the true nature of the agreement reached by the parties, the court will look behind the document to ascertain the real character of the transaction.[18] Again, if the document is a true record of the agreement but its terms indicate that its legal character is not that ascribed to it by the parties—as where a transaction described as a lease is in fact a conditional sale—the court will disregard the label attached by the parties and look to the legal substance. The nature of the rights intended to be conferred by the parties is to be ascertained from the terms of their agreement; the characterisation of

---

[12] Though Art.9 has undergone radical changes over the years, the classic text remains Grant Gilmore's two-volume *Security Interests in Personal Property*.

[13] There are two basic models: the Ontario Personal Property Security Act and the Model Personal Property Security Act of the Canadian Conference on Personal Property Security Law adopted, with local variations, by the Western Provinces. For a penetrating treatment of the whole subject in the context of the Ontario Act, see Jacob S. Ziegel and David L. Denomme, *The Ontario Personal Property Security Act: Commentary and Analysis*.

[14] As amended in 2001. For a very lucid analysis see Linda Widdup and Laurie Mayne, *Personal Property Securities Act: A Conceptual Approach* (2nd ed.).

[15] There are, however, marked differences between English law and Scots law.

[16] For an illuminating treatment of the concept of security and the classification of security interests in Australia, see Edward I. Sykes and Sally Walker, *The Law of Securities* (5th ed.) Ch.1, much of which is either drawn on or equally applicable to English law.

[17] The Crowther Committee on Consumer Credit recommended the enactment of legislation along the lines of Art.9 See the *Report of the Committee on Consumer Credit* (Cmnd 4506, 1971), Ch.5.5. This recommendation was endorsed by the Insolvency Law Review Committee in its report *Insolvency Law and Practice* (Cmmd 8558, 1982), paras 1620–1623 and by the report of Professor Aubrey Diamond, *A Review of Security Interests in Property* (1989). So far, no steps have been taken to implement the proposal. However, the Company Law Review Steering Group recommended in its Final Report adoption of the notice-filing concept embodied in Art.9 and changes in the registration rules so as to make registration a priority point, not merely a perfection requirement, and in consequence dispense with the need to register a charge within 21 days or any other specified time. The Group also recommended that following inter-departmental consultation the Law Commission be asked to examine the system for registering company charges and security and quasi-security generally over property other than land by non-corporate debtors. See *Modern Company Law for a Competitive Economy: Final Report*, Vol.I, Ch.12. The Law Commission has since received a reference for such work and has issued a major consultation paper, *Registration of Security Interests: Company Charges and Property other than Land* (Cons. Paper No. 164, July 2002). See below, para.2–31.

[18] See *Welsh Development Agency v Export Finance Co. Ltd.* [1994] 1 W.L.R. 409; and, for an exhaustive analysis, W.J. Gough, *Company Charges* (2nd ed.), Ch.21.

such rights is a matter of law and is to be determined by the court.[19] But it is the *legal* substance to which the court has regard, not the *economic* effect. English law recognises that the parties are free to structure their transaction as they wish, and that there is nothing objectionable to their selecting, say, conditional sale or hire-purchase instead of a purchase-money chattel mortgage in order to avoid the application of the Bills of Sale Acts.[20] So in determining the substance of the transaction the court looks to what the parties have actually agreed.[21]

There is also a divergence between legal families in the concept of possession. In common law systems possession denotes either physical possession or control through a physical possessor or means of physical access such as a key, so that pure intangibles cannot be given in pledge as this requires the delivery of possession. Civil law systems likewise require possession for a pledge but by a legal construct treat intangibles as notionally delivered if certain formalities are complied with, for example, registration in a public register. A striking example is the fact that most securities issued in France in dematerialised form are characterised by French law as bearer securities.

3. THE CLASSIFICATION OF SECURITY

The only forms of consensual security known to the law are the mortgage, **1–05** which is a security transfer of ownership, the pledge, which creates a limited legal interest by the delivery of possession, and the contractual lien, which differs from the pledge only in that the creditor's possession was acquired otherwise than for the purpose of security, as where goods are deposited for repair and the repairer then asserts a lien for unpaid repair charges. Except in the case of land, where statute provides for a charge by way of legal mortgage,[22] all charges are equitable.

Security may be classified in a number of different ways.

Real and personal security

Real security means security in an asset, whether of the debtor or of a third **1–06** party. The asset may be tangible or intangible. Real security is to be contrasted with personal security, that is, security in the form of a personal undertaking which reinforces the debtor's primary undertaking to give payment or other performance. Typically the personal undertaking is given by a third party, for example, as a surety under a suretyship guarantee or a

---

[19] *ibid.*; and see the decision of the Privy Council in *Agnew v Commissioners of Inland Revenue* [2001] 2 A.C. 710, below, para.1–33.
[20] *i.e.* the Bills of Sale Acts 1878–91.
[21] *McEntire v Crossley Brothers Ltd.* [1895] A.C. 457, *per* Lord Herschell L.C. at 462–463.
[22] Law of Property Act 1925, s.85(1); Land Registration Act 2002, s.51.

guarantor under a demand guarantee.[23] But the debtor too can provide a personal undertaking in a stronger or more easily assignable form than his primary undertaking, as, for example, by giving a negotiable instrument as security for payment. The greater part of this book, including the present chapter, is concerned with real security. However, there are separate chapters on set-off, which is a form of quasi-security,[24] and guarantees.[25]

Tangible and intangible security

1-07   Real security may be over tangible or intangible property.[26] The major difference between the two relates to the mode of creation, in that possessory security (the pledge and the contractual lien) may only be taken over tangibles. Security over pure intangibles[27] may be created only by way of mortgage or equitable charge. A mortgage may be effected by assignment, novation or negotiation, depending on the type of intangible[28]; an equitable charge may be created by agreement with the debtor or by trust.[29]

Possessory and non-possessory security

1-08   Where the security relates to tangible property, it may be either possessory or non-possessory. There are two forms of possessory security, the pledge and the contractual lien.[30] The pledgee or lienee has a limited legal interest in the asset.[31] Pure intangibles do not lend themselves to possession. By contrast documentary intangibles are treated as goods and may be pledged in the same way.[32] Events may result in a posessory security becoming converted into a non-possessory security. For example, where documents of title pledged to a bank are released to the pledgor to enable the goods to be sold and a sale takes place, the proceeds become subject to an equitable charge.[33] Similarly if a pledgee in possession of bearer securities has them converted into registered securities, he becomes a mortgagee or chargee.[34]

---

[23] A demand guarantee is one which, though intended as between the account party (or principal) and the beneficiary to be called only upon the account party's default, is not dependent on default, only on presentation of a written demand and other specified documents. In other words, the requirement of default is confined to the internal relationship between account party and beneficiary and does not constitute a term of the guarantee itself.

[24] Ch.VII.

[25] Ch.VIII.

[26] Documentary intangibles are equated with tangible property. See below, para.1–44.

[27] That is, intangibles which are not documentary intangibles. See below, para.1–44.

[28] See above, para.1–44.

[29] See below, para.1–53.

[30] See below, paras 1–43 et seq.

[31] See below, para.1–43.

[32] See below, para.1–43.

[33] See below, para.1–67.

[34] See below, para.1–67, n.49.

Security over existing assets and security over future assets

As we shall see,[35] while the common law insisted that security could be given **1–09** only over assets currently owned by the debtor, equity facilitated the grant of security over future property by treating the agreement for security as effective to confer a security interest on the creditor immediately on acquisition of the asset by the debtor, without need of any new act of transfer.

Fixed and floating security (security *in specie* and security in a fund)

Security is of two kinds, fixed and floating. Under a fixed charge the asset is **1–10** appropriated to satisfaction of the debt immediately or upon the debtor acquiring an interest in it. Under a floating charge appropriation is deferred; the chargee's rights attach in the first instance not to specific assets but to a shifting fund of assets, the debtor company being left free to manage the fund in the ordinary course of business. It is only when the debtor's management powers are brought to an end that the charge crystallises and fastens on the specific assets then comprised in the fund or subsequently acquired by the debtor.[36] The floating charge is the only kind of floating security encountered in practice, but there seems no theoretical objection to a floating mortgage, by which the mortgagee acquires ownership of the fund by way of security and, upon crystallisation, ownership of the individual components of the fund. The mortgage would, of course, take effect in equity only, there being no present transfer of ownership of identified assets. There is, however, no such thing as a floating pledge, for a pledge requires actual or constructive possession, which can only be taken of assets *in specie*, not of a fund. The distinction between fixed and floating security has important priority implications both at common law and under the Insolvency Act 1986.[37]

Title transfer and charge

Leaving aside the limited legal interests created by pledge or lien, the grant of **1–11** security may take the form either of a security transfer of title (mortgage) or an encumbrance (charge, or hypothecation) which leaves the debtor as owner but imposes a clog on his ownership in favour of the creditor.[38]

---

[35] See below, para.2–12.
[36] See below, paras 4–07 *et seq.*
[37] See below, paras 4–09 *et seq.*
[38] See below, paras 1–51 *et seq.*

Legal and equitable security

(1) *Nature of the distinction*

1–12   A security interest may be either legal[39] or equitable. We have seen that a limited legal security interest arises from a pledge or a lien. To take effect at law in the hands of the creditor any other form of security interest must be a present transfer of an existing asset, the transfer must be to the creditor himself and must be made in conformity with any statutory formalities and the transferor's title to the asset must be a legal title, not merely an equitable interest. Accordingly a security interest may be equitable for any one of six reasons, namely that (a) it relates to future property; (b) there is no transfer or agreement for transfer at all, merely a charge; (c) there is no present transfer, merely an agreement for transfer or a declaration of trust by the debtor; (d) the transfer is not made in accordance with the formal requirements for the transfer of legal title; (e) the transfer is made not to the creditor but to a third party as trustee for the creditor; or (f) the transferor's title to the asset is equitable, not legal. The essential difference in effect between a legal mortgage and an equitable mortgage or charge is that a legal mortgage has priority over subsequent interests whereas an equitable mortgage or charge may be overreached by a disposition to a bona fide purchaser for value of the legal title without notice of the equitable interest. The significance of the distinction has been substantially reduced by statutory provisions for the registration not only of legal mortgages and charges but also of various categories of equitable mortgage or charge[40] and the principle that registration usually constitutes constructive notice.[41] In such cases registration is in the nature of a statutory perfection requirement[42] and does not affect the characterisation of the security interest as legal or equitable. However, in the case of certain specialist registers, such as those relating to intellectual property rights[43] and ship and aircraft mortgages[44] registration is a prerequisite of legal title and an unregistered interest takes effect only as an equitable interest.

The character of the security interest as legal or equitable is distinct from that of an assignment of the underlying debt. If a debt is secured by an equitable mortgage which is then assigned by way of an equitable sub-mortgage, there is no reason why the assignment of the debt itself should not be a statutory assignment, assuming that it is made in conformity with the formalities prescribed by s.136 of the Law of Property Act 1925, thereby enabling the sub-mortgagee as assignee to sue on the personal covenant in his own name without the need to join the assignor. Similarly, though a security interest in investment securities held by a person through an account with an intermediary is only an equitable security interest, this does not preclude the debtor

---

[39] The word "legal" is also used in a different sense to denote a security interest created by law (*e.g.* a repairer's lien) as opposed to consensual security interest.
[40] See below.
[41] See below, paras 2–23 *et seq.*
[42] See below, para.2–19.
[43] See below, paras 1–13, 2–30.
[44] See below, paras 1–13, 2–30.

from making a statutory assignment of his contractual account rights to the creditor.

(2) *Mode of creating a legal mortgage*

This varies according to the subject matter of the mortgage: **1–13**

(a) A legal mortgage of land may be effected by demise for a term of years absolute (*i.e.* a lease) or by a charge by way of legal mortgage.[45] The mortgage must be by deed[46] and in the case of registered land must be registered in the Land Registry.[47]

(b) A legal mortgage of goods may be created orally[48] but if it is in writing and is given by an individual it must be made by deed and in accordance with the form and in conformity with the other requirements of the Bills of Sale Acts 1878 and 1882,[49] and if by a company it is registrable under s.395 of the Companies Act 1985. Moreover, for certain types of goods the mortgage must be in accordance with a prescribed form and registered in a special register to take effect at law, *e.g.* in the case of registered ships the mortgage must be registered in the register of ship mortgages,[50] in the case of registered aircraft, in the register of aircraft mortgages.[51]

(c) A legal mortgage of registrable intellectual property rights is effected by entry in the relevant register.[52]

(d) A legal mortgage of a debt or other chose in action is effected by assignment in writing under the hand of the assignor and written notice of the assignment to the debtor[53] or alternatively by novation.[54]

(e) A legal mortgage of registered securities is effected by novation through entry of a transfer on the issuer's register[55] and of negotiable

---

[45] Law of Property Act 1925, s.85(1). But as to registered land, see para.1–51, n.73.

[46] *ibid.*, ss.52(1), 85, 86. A registered charge under the Land Registration Act 2002 takes effect as if it were a charge by deed by way of legal mortgage (s.51) and if effected electronically is also to be treated as made by deed (s.91(5)).

[47] Under the Land Registration Act 2002.

[48] *Newlove v Shrewsbury* (1888) 21 Q.B.D. 41; *Flory v Denny* (1852) 7 Exch. 581; *Reeves v Capper* (1838) 5 Bing. NC 136.

[49] See 4(1) *Halsbury's Laws*, paras 620, 658.

[50] Under s.16 of the Merchant Shipping Act 1995.

[51] Under the Mortgaging of Aircraft Order 1972, SI 1972/1268.

[52] *i.e.* the register of patents (Patents Act 1977, s.30), the register of trade marks (Trade Marks Act 1994, s.25), or the register of designs (Registered Designs Act 1949, s.19). There is no registration of copyright.

[53] Law of Property Act 1925, s.136.

[54] See below, para.3–03. A charge of a debt leaves ownership of the debt with the chargor, so that although, as with a mortgage by assignment, notice of the charge must be given to the debtor it is not an assignment, nor is it capable of being made by novation.

[55] It follows that if the holder of an equitable charge with a blank transfer registers the transfer he becomes converted from an equitable chargee into a legal mortgagee. The transferee is

securities and negotiable instruments by endorsement and delivery and by delivery of possession with intent to transfer ownership in the case of bearer securities.

Security for fixed indebtedness and continuing security

1–14   Just as personal security, such as a guarantee, may be given either for a specific advance, so that it terminates on repayment, or as a continuing guarantee, which covers the ultimate debit balance due on closure of the account between debtor and creditor and is not satisfied by any intermediate payment,[56] so also real security, such as a mortgage or charge, may secure a specific debt or be a continuing security for an ultimate debit balance. The latter is the common situation where the credit extended to the principal debtor is revolving credit, such as a bank overdraft. While the quantum of the security can never exceed what is due to the bank at any particular time, the security is not discharged merely because the debit balance is reduced to zero or the account goes into credit. This form of credit is a continuing *facility*, the debtor being free to draw on it as and when he chooses within the terms of the facility, not fixed-sum credit, which is granted at the outset for a specified amount and is discharged when that amount is paid. Security for a continuing facility itself continues at least until such time as the facility is ended and the debtor's ultimate obligation is discharged. In practice, security agreements, like guarantees, frequently prolong the duration of the security to cover the possibility that payments made to the secured creditor are recovered by the debtor's trustee in bankruptcy or liquidator as preferences[57] or on some other ground, so that if the secured creditor has to make a repayment the debt thus revived will continue to be secured.

Security for the debtor's obligation and security for third-party indebtedness

1–15   A person may give an asset in security not only for his own indebtedness but also for that of a third party. For example, A, without itself incurring any personal obligation, may mortgage or charge its property to secure a debt due to the creditor from B. Despite the absence of any personal liability on the part of A, this is considered in law to constitute a guarantee.[58] Not uncommonly the same security agreement secures both the primary indebtedness of a third party and a secondary liability of the debtor. The typical case is that of companies forming part of a corporate group which give cross-guarantees,

---

shown as holder of the securities, not as mortgagee, since no notice of any trust (including a trust of the equity of redemption) may be registered (see para.5–08). Accordingly, in contrast to the position with other registers, there can be only one mortgagee on the register as holder, or joint mortgages, not mortgagees in succession.

[56] See below, para.8–05.

[57] Insolvency Act 1986, ss.239, 238, 240–241.

[58] *Re Conley* [1938] 2 All E.R. 127.

each guarantee covering the indebtedness of other members of the group and being secured over property of the guarantor which also directly secures the indebtedness of the other companies. Here the security agreement has a dual aspect, in that it secures both the primary obligation of the other companies and the secondary obligation of the grantor of the security as guarantor. This cross-collateralisation is a common feature of modern financing, though it may in certain circumstances be vulnerable as a transaction at an undervalue in the event of the debtor's insolvency.[59]

4. WHAT CONSTITUTES A SECURITY INTEREST

The nature of a security interest

A security interest is a right given to one party in the asset of another party **1–16** to secure payment or performance by that other party or by a third party. A fixed, or specific, consensual[60] security interest possesses the following characteristics:

(1) It is a right given by a debtor to a creditor in an asset[61];

(2) The right is by way of grant of an interest in the debtor's asset, not by way of reservation of title to the creditor[62];

(3) The right is given for the purposes of securing an obligation[63];

(4) The asset is given in security only, not by way of outright transfer[64];

(5) The agreement restricts the debtor's right to dispose of the asset free from the security interest.[65]

There is authority that a debtor cannot give security over its own obligation, so that a bank cannot take a charge over its own customer's credit balance or an issuer of a negotiable instrument over the instrument.[66] The force of

---

[59] See Insolvency Act 1986, ss.238, 240, 241; and Goode, *Principles of Corporate Insolvency Law* (2nd ed.), pp.206 *et seq.*

[60] That is, a security interest created by agreement, as opposed to one conferred by law, such as the unpaid vendor's lien.

[61] See below, para.1–17. The essential ingredients for attachment (*i.e.* creation) of that right and of its perfection to give it efficacy against third parties are examined in Ch.II.

[62] See below, para.1–28.

[63] See below, para.1–33.

[64] See below, para.1–33. Investment securities disposed of under sale and repurchase (repo) or stock lending transactions are usually described as collateral in the securities market because they fulfil the economic function of security. But they are not secured transactions in law since the transfer is absolute and the transferor does not retain an equity of redemption, merely a right of repurchase or retransfer. See further below, para.6–21.

[65] See below, para.1–39.

[66] See below, para.1–40.

this has been weakened by *obiter dicta* of high persuasive force.[67] Moreover, the widespread practice of charge-backs both in this country and overseas indicates that conceptual reasoning, however powerful, must give way to commercial usage.

A floating security, such as a floating charge, differs from a fixed security in that it relates not to a specific asset but to an identifiable fund of assets, the debtor being authorised by the terms of the security agreement to dispose of all or any of the assets comprising the fund free from the security interest.[68]

A fixed security interest is a right given by a debtor to his creditor in an asset

1–17 It is inherent in a security interest that an asset is appropriated to the debt. Where the debtor is to pay out of his general assets, none of which is earmarked to the debt, there can be no security interest. A good example is provided by the decision in *Swiss Bank Corporation Ltd. v Lloyds Bank Ltd.*,[69] in which the House of Lords, affirming the decision of the Court of Appeal,[70] held that a covenant by a borrower in a loan agreement to observe all exchange control requirements, one of which was that the proceeds of the borrower's securities were to be applied in discharge of the loan, did not create a security interest, since the loan agreement did not itself require the loan to be paid out of the proceeds, and the requirement was simply a stipulation by the Bank of England when granting exchange control consent. As Buckley L.J. had pointed out in his judgment in the Court of Appeal,[71] it had been conceded that if the Bank of England had waived or rescinded the requirement the lender would have had no right to require the proceeds to be utilised in discharge of the debt.

Even where the creditor is to be given rights in respect of an asset, it is necessary to distinguish real rights from personal rights. A real right is a right *in* an asset (right *in rem*) as opposed to a personal right *to* an asset (right *ad rem*). A personal claim to delivery or transfer of an asset does not survive the debtor's bankruptcy but becomes converted into a right to prove for a dividend in the debtor's estate in competition with other creditors. By contrast a security interest is a right *in rem*[72] and in principle the secured creditor is entitled to remove the asset from the general body of creditors.[73] In distinguishing

---

[67] See below, para.3–12. See also paras 6–23, 6–46.

[68] See below, paras 4–03 *et seq.*

[69] [1982] A.C. 584.

[70] [1980] 3 W.L.R. 457.

[71] *ibid.*, at 596–597.

[72] More accurately, a particular type of right *in rem*. Rights *in rem* are those available against third parties generally, and include, for example, rights in tort. Civilian writers refer to rights *in re*, or real rights, to distinguish rights in an asset from other *in rem* rights. It is, of course, a necessary prequisite of a security interest that the subject-matter is both identifiable (see below, para.2–05) and capable of being transferred or otherwise given in security (below, paras 2–07, 3–38 *et seq*).

[73] The Insolvency Act 1986, re-enacting the Insolvency Act 1985, now imposes restrictions on the secured creditor's right to enforce his security where a petition has been presented for an administration order or an administration order has been made. See ss.10(1), 11(3).

security interests from personal rights the following deserve particular mention.[74]

(1) *Agreement to give security*

The maxim that equity treats as done that which ought to be done has the **1–18** effect that most agreements to give security in an asset will be treated in equity as if they were actual transfers,[75] thus blurring the distinction between real and personal rights. But equity has special rules for the perfection of uncompleted transfer agreements.[76] Moreover, even in equity a mere agreement for security is not sufficient to create a security interest unless the agreement relates to an asset or fund which at the time of the agreement or on subsequent acquisition by the debtor can be identified as falling within the agreement. So an obligation by the employer under a building contract to set aside as a separate fund retention monies deducted from interim payments as provided in architects' certificates does not make the contractor a secured creditor until the fund has in fact been established. The deductions themselves simply amount to withholding of payment and do not create any *res* to which a security interest can attach, so that if the employer goes into liquidation before the fund has been set up the contract is merely an unsecured creditor and the court will not grant a mandatory injunction to establish the fund after the employer has gone into winding-up.[77]

(2) *Contractual set-off*

A deposits money with B Bank under an agreement which empowers B Bank **1–19** to set off against its deposit liability any claim it has against A on any other account. Exercise of this contractual right of set-off will, of course, result in B Bank being paid its claim up to the amount of the deposit. The set-off thus fulfils an important security function. But is it a security in law? We can answer this question only by going back to fundamentals. A security interest is a real right in the asset given in security. A right of set-off, even if given by contract, is a purely personal right to set one claim against another. The party asserting it never acquires rights in the other's monetary claim at all; he merely asserts a countervailing claim which operates in *pro tanto* extinction

---

[74] For a fuller description, see Roy Goode, *Commercial Law* (2nd ed.), paras 652 *et seq.*

[75] *Tebb v Hodge* (1869) L.R. 5 C.P. 73. The agreement may be express or implied, and in the case of land could at one time be implied from the deposit of title deeds (*Russel v Russel* (1783) 1 Bro. C.C. 269). But following the repeal of the Law of Property Act 1925, s.40, by the Law of Property (Miscellaneous Provisions) Act 1989, a contract for the sale or other disposition of an interest in land must be in writing, otherwise it is wholly void. In consequence, the equitable doctrine of part performance is no longer part of English law (*Firstpost Homes Ltd v Johnson* [1995] 1 W.L.R. 1567, *per* Peter Gibson L.J. at 1571).

[76] See below, para.2–11.

[77] *Re Jartay Developments Ltd* (1983) 22 Build. L.R. 134; *Mac-Jordan Construction Ltd. v Brookmount Erostin Ltd* [1991] B.C.L.C. 350.

of his monetary liability. It follows that a contractual set-off does not create a security interest.[78] However, the distinction between contractual set-off and security has become blurred by the decision of the House of Lords in *Re Bank of Credit and Commerce International SA (No. 8)*[79] to the effect that there is no conceptual barrier to a person charging back to its creditor the obligation owed to it by that creditor. But since the only method of realising the charge is by a book-entry debit to the account recording the chargee's indebtedness, which is the self-same method utilised to effect a contractual set-off, it seems that the only way of distinguishing a charge over the debtor's obligation from a contractual set-off is by the label given to the agreement by the parties, a point to which we shall return.[80]

(3) *Balance on a current account*

1–20 We have seen from the above that a right of set-off does not constitute a security interest. *A fortiori* this is true of an offset effected through the operation of a single current account, since the only credit balance is the ultimate balance on the account, which forms a single indivisible fund. This is well illustrated by the decision of Millett J. in *Re Charge Card Services Ltd.*,[81] where the facts were as follows:

> Charge Card Services Ltd. (the company) entered into an invoice discounting agreement by which it agreed to factor its receivables to Commercial Credit Services Ltd. (the factor). Under clause 3(a) of the agreement the factor could require the company to repurchase any receivable in stated events, *e.g.* the debtor's dispute of liability, and under clause 3(c) Charge Card guaranteed payment by every debtor and agreed to indemnify Commercial Credit against loss resulting from a debtor's failure to pay. Clause 4 provided that the purchase price payable by Commercial Credit for any receivable was to be the gross amount payable by the debtor less any discount allowable to him and less the factor's discount charge calculated in the manner prescribed by standard condition 3. Under clause 6 the factor's obligation to pay was made subject to the right of debits and rights of retention provided by standard condition 3. Standard condition 3(A) required the factor to maintain a current account to which would be credited (*inter alia*) the purchase price of each receivable before deducting the discounting charge and debited (*inter alia*) certain contingent liabilities of the company under the agreement and the discounting charge. By standard condition 3(B) the factor was to remit to the company or its order any balance for the time being standing to the credit of the current account less any amount which the factor in its absolute

---

[78] This passage was cited with approval by the Singapore Court of Appeal in *Electro-Magnetic (S) Ltd. v Development Bank of Singapore Ltd.* [1994] 1 S.L.R. 734.
[79] *Re Bank of Credit and Commerce International SA (No. 8)* [1998] A.C. 214.
[80] Below, para.3–12.
[81] [1987] Ch. 150.

discretion decided to retain as security for claims against the company, any risk of non-payment by a debtor and any amount prospectively chargeable to the company as a debit under standard condition (3A). Clause 10 (read with clause 11) provided that if the company went into liquidation the factor could terminate the agreement and require the company to repurchase any outstanding receivables previously purchased by the factor. The repurchase price was not an item falling to be debited to the current account under standard condition 3(a).

The company went into insolvent liquidation and contended that the factor's right of retention under standard condition 3(B) was taken as security for rights of set-off and constituted a charge on book debts which was void against the liquidator for want of registration under s.95 of the Companies Act 1948 (now s.395 of the Companies Act 1985).

It was held that the amount payable by the factor for a receivable was not the purchase price as such but the balance standing to the credit of the company's account after the relevant debits had been made and subject to the right of retention. Accordingly the case was not one of set-off at all but of account, for there were no mutual but independent obligations capable of set-off, merely a right to payment of a single balance remaining after exercise of the right of retention.[82] It followed that the right of retention was not a charge on money due to the company, for what was due was arrived at after deducting the sum retained, so that there was no relevant property capable of forming the subject matter of the charge.

As regards the factor's right (which had not yet been exercised) to terminate the agreement and require the company to repurchase the outstanding receivables, this was not a matter for debit to the current account, and accordingly constituted a true set-off, not a charge.[83]

(4) Condition of repayment

A security interest is also to be distinguished from a contractual condition of repayment. An example is the so-called "flawed asset" created where company A deposits money with a bank upon terms that the deposit is to be repayable only when company A and company B (which is typically a member of the same group) have discharged their indebtedness to the bank on other accounts. Such an agreement does not of itself constitute a security, for the bank acquires no rights over the deposit,[84] merely a right to withhold **1–21**

---

[82] See further below, para.7–12, as to the distinction between set-off and account.

[83] See (2) above. The judge also held that the agreement could not be characterised as a charge, because it was conceptually impossible for a charge to be given in favour of a debtor over his own indebtedness. On this aspect of the case the situation has changed. See below, para.3–12.

[84] The efficacy of the flawed asset concept was recognised by the Court of Appeal in *Re Bank of Credit and Commerce International SA (No. 8)* [1996] Ch. 245; and, on appeal, by the House of Lords [1998] A.C. 214, *per* Lord Hoffmann at 227.

It is worth making the point that a depositor has no claim to notes or coins *in specie*. His deposit constitutes a loan which transfers to the bank ownership of the cash deposited, the bank becoming a debtor with a personal obligation to repay. There is a widespread

repayment. The case is thus similar to that of contractual set-off except that A's deposit is not extinguished; it remains intact as A's asset but can be withdrawn only on fulfilment of the condition.

(5) Negative pledge

1–22 A negative pledge is an agreement by the debtor not to encumber his assets in favour of a third party, or not to encumber them by way of a security which would rank ahead of or *pari passu* with the security given to the creditor. Since a negative pledge does not confer rights on any asset of the debtor but merely restricts his ability to give security to others it does not constitute a security interest. Negative pledges are dealt with later in the present chapter.[85]

(6) Subordination agreement

1–23 A subordination agreement is an agreement by which a creditor agrees to subordinate his claim against the debtor, or alternatively a security taken by him from the debtor, to the claim or security of another creditor. The characterisation of subordination agreements is discussed later in the present chapter.[86]

(7) Sale of sub-participation in loan assets

1–24 The sale of a sub-participation in a loan or other financial asset does not usually create a security interest.[87]

(8) Lien on sub-freights

1–25 There are several first instance decisions holding that a shipowner's lien on sub-freights is an equitable charge and as such is registrable under what is now s.395 of the Companies Act 1985 either as a charge on book debts or as a floating charge.[88] However, the authority of these decisions is weakened by the statement of Lord Millett in delivering the decision of the Privy Council in *Agnew v Commissioner of Inland Revenue*[89] that the better view, as

---

misconception that "money on deposit" or "cash at bank" constitutes identifiable property of the depositor in much the same way as the deposit of securities for safe custody. The deposit creates no more than a chose in action, a personal right to repayment.

[85] See below, para.1–71.
[86] See below, para.1–79.
[87] See below, para.1–82.
[88] *Re Welsh Irish Ferries Ltd* [1986] Ch. 471; *Itex Itagrani Export SA v Care Shipping Corp* [1990] 2 Lloyd's Rep. 316; *The Annangel Glory* [1988] 1 Lloyd's Rep. 45.
[89] [2001] 2 A.C. 710.

expressed by Dr Fidelis Oditah some years previously,[90] is that a lien on sub-freights is not a charge at all, merely a personal right to intercept freight before it is paid to the owner, and thus a right analogous to stoppage *in transitu*. This statement was *obiter*, and was made purely to dispose of a passage in the judgment of Fisher J. at first instance giving a lien on sub-freights as an example of a fixed charge defeasible at the will of the chargor. Nevertheless Lord Millett's view is clearly of great persuasive value, and it is thought that for the reasons given by him and previously by Dr Oditah it is the view to be followed in future cases.

(9) *Directions as to the application of proceeds*

Where a person borrows money in order to purchase an asset the loan agreement may provide that if the asset is later sold the proceeds are to be applied in or towards discharge of the debt. There may also be a stipulation that the proceeds are to be paid into a designated bank account in the creditor's name. Suggestions that contractual provisions of this kind are sufficient to confer a security interest on the creditor have usually been robustly rejected by the courts except where the asset from which the proceeds are derived was itself the subject of a security interest in favour of the creditor. Thus in *Palmer v Carey*[91]: **1–26**

> Money was lent to a trader to enable him to purchase goods as stock in trade for his business and the agreement provided that when the goods were sold the proceeds were to be paid to the credit of the lender's account at the lender's bank, and he was to deduct the amount of the loan and one-third of the gross profit and pay the balance to the borrower. Subsequently, the borrower agreed to transfer his unsold stock in trade to the lender in discharge of all obligations under the earlier agreement. The borrower then became bankrupt and in the bankruptcy the transfer of the stock in trade was held void. The lender asserted that if this was the case his rights under the original agreement were restored, and by virtue of that agreement he had an equitable charge over the goods and their proceeds.

The claim was rejected by the Privy Council in the following terms:

> "An agreement for valuable consideration that a fund shall be applied in a particular way may found an injunction to restrain its application in another way. But if there be nothing more, such a stipulation will not amount to an equitable assignment. It is necessary to find, further, that an obligation has been imposed in favour of the creditor to pay the debt out of the fund . . . the money when borrowed is the borrower's money, and the

---

[90] Fidelis Oditah, "The Juridical Nature of a Lien on Sub-Freights" [1989] L.M.C.L.Q. 191.
[91] [1926] A.C. 703, reversing the decision of the High Court of Australia (1924) 34 C.L.R. 380 and restoring the decision of the trial judge.

lender becomes a creditor. The goods when purchased are the borrower's goods. The proceeds of sale when the goods are sold belong to the borrower. They arise from the sale of goods belonging to him. Under art. 3, however, the proceeds are to be paid to the lender's credit at his bank. This gives the lender a most efficient hold to prevent the misapplication of the proceeds, but there is nothing in that article to give him a property by way of security or otherwise in the moneys of the borrower before or after he, the lender, has them in his charge. Art. 6 was not relied on as giving an equitable charge, and it is difficult to see how it could be relied upon for that purpose. It is an article determining the distribution between the parties in manner there defined of a fund which is in the hands of one of them. Their Lordships, therefore, fail to find in the agreement creating, contractually or otherwise, any right of property in either the goods or the proceeds of sale of the goods." [92]

In short, there must be a contractual appropriation of the asset to the debt, which was held to be lacking in *Palmer v Carey*, as it was in the subsequent House of Lords case *Swiss Bank Corporation v Lloyds Bank Ltd*.[93] A diametrically opposite result was reached in the decision of the Court of Appeal in *Re Cosslett (Contractors) Ltd.*,[94] where the facts were as follows:

"The employer under a building contract was given power, on default by the contractor, to take possession of and use plant and machinery on the site belonging to the contractor[95] and to sell it and apply the proceeds towards discharge of the contractor's obligations to the employer. Millett L.J., who gave the leading judgment, held that the provision for possession and use of the plant and machinery did not create a security interest since its purpose was not to provide security but to enable the employer to complete the contract works. By contrast, the power of sale was not attached to any possessory security (*i.e.* a pledge or a lien) but derived solely from the contract and was given for the purpose of security, so that the right of sale and application of the proceeds given to the employer constituted an equitable charge."

---

[92] *Per* Lord Wrenbury at pp.706–707. But see below.

[93] [1982] A.C. 584. See above, para.1–17. See also *Flightline Ltd. v Edwards* [2003] All E.R. (D) 50.

[94] [1998] Ch. 495. The case came before the House of Lords, *sub. nom. Smith (as Administrator of Cosslett) (Contractors) Ltd. v Bridgend County Borough Council* [2001] 3 W.L.R. 1347 in the shape of an appeal from a subsequent, rather startling, decision of a differently constituted appeal court [2000] 1 B.C.L.C. 775 to the effect that failure to register a charge under s.395 of the Companies Act 1985 rendered it void only as against the administrator, not against the company itself. The respondents also contended that contrary to the original Court of Appeal decision the contract did not create a charge or, if it did, that the charge was fixed, not floating, and therefore not registrable. The House of Lords upheld the ruling in the first case, and in particular the judgment of Millett L.J., but reversed the second decision, holding that failure to register rendered an unregistered charge void against the company itself acting by its liquidator or administrator.

[95] There was a provision in the contract deeming such plant and materials to become the property of the employer but this was held not to indicate an intention to transfer actual ownership to the employer.

The significant difference between *Palmer v Carey* and *Re Cosslett (Contractors) Ltd.* is that in the former case the sale was to be effected by the borrower, to whom the goods belonged, so that the proceeds were those of the borrower, whereas in *Cosslett* the plant and materials, though belonging to the contractor, were deemed to have become vested in the employer, who was empowered to sell them, and were in fact sold by the employer, so that not only were the sale and its proceeds at all times under the employer's control but the proceeds emanated from property held to have been appropriated to the employer for the purpose of security and were thus themselves covered by the security interest.

Nevertheless *Palmer v Carey*, which though referred to in argument in the **1-27** Court of Appeal was not mentioned in any of the judgments in *Cosslett* in the Court of Appeal or any of the speeches in the House of Lords, is not an altogether easy case. That decision had been explained in *Re Gillott's Settlement*[96] as turning on the fact that the time of the bankruptcy there was no credit balance in the lender's account, which was substantially overdrawn. This explanation itself is not free from difficulty, for the passage from the opinion of the Privy Council quoted above states that the lender would acquire no security interest in the proceeds even after he had them in his charge in the account. But on this point the reference to moneys in the account can be regarded as *obiter*, since in the absence of such money any question of their appropriation to the debt was moot. The decision could then be explained, as it was in *Re Gillott's Settlement*, on the basis that the only security interest that could be asserted was to the goods themselves, there was no manifested intention to appropriate the goods to the debt, and it was unnecessary to decide whether there was an appropriation of the proceeds.

This seems to be the true *ratio decidendi*. It is significant that in the courts below the claim was merely to the goods, since there were no longer any proceeds in the bank account. The majority decision of the High Court of Australia had been based on the view that a provision for the application of proceeds of an asset in discharge of a debt constitute a charge on the asset. That was plainly wrong, for as will be seen[97] a security interest runs forward from an asset to its proceeds, not backwards from proceeds to the asset. The Privy Council rightly held that no intention had been manifested to create a charge over the goods. That was sufficient to dispose of the case. It was unnecessary to consider whether, independently of any interest in the goods, the lender acquired a charge over moneys in the bank account, because there were no longer any such moneys. If there had been, then it is submitted that they would have been subject to a mortgage in favour of the lender,[98] not because he had any prior charge over the goods which produced the proceeds but because he was plainly given control of the account by way of security, otherwise such control would have served no purpose. The borrower would

---

[96] [1934] Ch. 97, *per* Maugham J. at 109–110.
[97] See below, para.1–68.
[98] Not a mere charge because the account was in the lender's name so that legal title to the claim on the bank was vested in him.

then have had an equitable proprietary right to the return of any part of the fund remaining after discharge of the debt, or to the whole of the fund if the debt was discharged from other sources.[99] If, as the Privy Council accepted, a charge is created when a debtor agrees to pay the creditor from a fund held by the debtor, then *a fortiori* a debtor's conferment on the creditor of a right to withdraw money from a fund under the *creditor's* control should be effective to create a security interest.

At the end of the day, of course, it all comes down to a question of construction of the parties' agreement and the legal effect of what they have agreed.[1] The moral is that the creditor should expressly provide for the creation of a charge or for appropriation of the asset and its proceeds to the debt.

Security is by way of grant of an interest in the debtor's asset, not by way of reservation of title to the creditor

1–28   The debtor cannot give security over an asset in which he has no interest or of which he has no power to dispose. We shall examine in the next chapter what constitutes an interest or power of disposal for this purpose.[2] We have previously noted that, in contrast to legal systems in North America, English law distinguishes reservation of title under a conditional sale, hire-purchase or leasing agreement from a mortgage or charge, treating the conditional seller, owner or lessor as absolute owner subject only to the possessory interest of the conditional buyer, hirer or lessee. It follows that a provision in such an agreement empowering the seller, etc. to repossess upon default by the buyer, does not make the agreement a security agreement, for the seller is not taking rights over an asset of the buyer but is simply reserving the right to recover his own property. Similarly, the lessor's right of re-entry on forfeiture of a lease of land, though sometimes described as designed to secure performance of the tenant's covenants,[3] is not a true security interest, for the lessor is merely reserving the right to re-enter his own property, not taking a security interest in property of the lessee.[4] Expressed in a more general form, the principle is that security in the legal sense derives from grant or declaration of trust by the debtor, not from reservation of title by the creditor. It is for this reason that the reservation of legal title under a sale, hire-purchase or leasing agreement does not constitute a security interest.[5]

---

[99] The mortgage would be by novation, as with other cases of cash collateral, the only difference being that the cash comes from the third-party purchaser, not from the debtor direct.

[1] See, for example, *Palette Shoes Pty. Ltd. v Krohn* (1937) 58 C.L.R. 1; *Federal Commissioner of Taxation v Betro Harrison Constructions Pty Ltd.* (1978) 20 A.L.R. 647.

[2] It may be noted at this point that an agreement to give security over future assets creates an inchoate security interest which attaches automatically upon the debtor's acquisition of the asset and then takes effect as from the time of the agreement. See below, paras 2–12 *et seq.*

[3] See, for example, *Shiloh Spinners Ltd. v Harding* [1973] A.C. 691.

[4] See *Christopher Moran Holdings Ltd. v Bairstow* (also referred to as *Re Park Air Services plc*) [2002] 2 A.C. 172, *per* Lord Millett at 186.

[5] *McEntire v Crossley Bros.* [1895] A.C. 457.

However, English property law does not recognise the possibility of reserving *equitable* ownership whilst transferring the legal title. This is because equitable ownership in one person presupposes legal ownership in another. If legal and beneficial ownership are combined in the same person, he is not the holder of a legal title and a separate equitable interest, he is simply the full owner.[6] It follows that when transferring the legal title he cannot exclude equitable ownership from the transfer for at that stage there is none. An attempt to reserve equitable ownership will be construed as a grant back by the transferee; and if the "reservation" is for the purpose of securing an obligation, it will constitute a security interest.[7]

The distinction between reservation and grant is not always clear-cut. Particular problems have arisen in relation to reservation of title clauses in contracts of sale of goods. Four cases deserve particular examination.

(1) *Simple reservation of title to goods under contract of sale*

S sells goods to B under a contract which reserves title until B has paid the price. As previously stated, no security interest is created in favour of S, for B is not granting rights in an asset in which he has an interest. The effect of the contract is that B does not acquire an interest in the goods until he completes payment. S is simply retaining legal ownership pending payment, and under the Sale of Goods Act the time when the property is to pass from seller to buyer is a matter for agreement between them.[8] **1–29**

(2) *Reservation of title securing other indebtedness*

The character of the transaction is not affected by the fact that the seller's reservation of title is expressed to secure payment not only of the price of the particular goods sold but of the buyer's other indebtedness to the seller under prior or subsequent transactions.[9] **1–30**

(3) *Claims to proceeds of goods supplied under reservation of title*

The position here is a little more complicated. If a person contracts to sell goods, reserving title until payment but giving the buyer the right to resell them on condition that he accounts for the proceeds of sale, does the stipulation as to proceeds constitute merely an undertaking to make over to the seller that which already belongs to him in equity or does it constitute a grant **1–31**

---

[6] *Commissioner of Stamp Duties (Queensland) v Livingston* [1965] A.C. 694, *per* Viscount Radcliffe at 612; *Re Bond Worth Ltd.* [1980] Ch. 228; *Westdeutsche Landesbank Girozentrale v Islington London Borough Council* [1996] A.C. 669, *per* Lord Browne-Wilkinson at 706.
[7] *Re Bond Worth Ltd.*, above.
[8] Sale of Goods Act 1979, s.17.
[9] *Armour v Thyssen Edelstahlwerke AG* [1991] 2 A.C. 339.

by the buyer of rights over proceeds which belong to him? The point is of some practical importance because if in the latter case the grant is construed to be by way of security and the buyer is a company, the security interest will be void against a liquidator, administrator and creditors if not registered as a charge on book debts.[10] In the famous *Romalpa* case[11]:

> "The plaintiffs agreed to sell aluminium foil to the defendants under a contract which provided *(inter alia)* that until payment ownership was to remain with the sellers and that the buyers would keep the goods and any products into which they were made up as fiduciary owner but would be at liberty to make up the goods into new products and to sell the goods and products upon terms that ownership of the products or proceeds should immediately pass to the sellers. It was conceded by counsel for the buyers that they held the goods as bailees. The buyers went into receivership and the question was whether the sellers could assert a proprietary tracing claim to the proceeds of sale received by the company and taken over by the receiver.
>
> The Court of Appeal, upholding the decision of the trial judge, held that the buyers were in a fiduciary relationship with the sellers as their agents and bailees and as such had an equitable obligation to account for the proceeds of sale. Accordingly the sellers were entitled to trace the proceeds and recover them in a proprietary claim. The contractual provision requiring the buyers to account for the proceeds did not constitute a charge on the buyers' book debts, since the proceeds belonged to the sellers in equity and the proceeds clause did no more than require the buyers to make over to the sellers that which in equity was already their property."

Subsequent judicial response to the *Romalpa* decision[12] was unenthusiastic, no doubt because it looked uncomfortably like acceptance of a seller's ability to pull himself up by his own bootstraps. The duty to account arose in equity and the proceeds clause was merely designed to perfect the seller's equitable ownership. But what created the duty to account? The terms of the proceeds clause itself! In later cases, the courts have held that a contractual duty to account for proceeds cannot by itself confer on the seller an equitable right to trace; it must be shown from the language of the contract or the surrounding circumstances that a fiduciary relationship existed between the parties, such as that of principal and agent, bailor and bailee, so that the buyer resells not on his own account but on behalf of the seller, to whom he is accordingly accountable for the proceeds. The proceeds clause then operates not as a substantive

---

[10] Under ss.395 and 396 of the Companies Act 1985.

[11] *Aluminium Industrie Vaassen B.V. v Romalpa Aluminium Ltd.* [1976] 1 W.L.R. 676.

[12] See, for example, *Borden (UK) Ltd. v Scottish Timber Products Ltd.* [1979] 3 All E.R. 961; *Re Bond Worth Ltd.* [1980] Ch. 228; *Hendy Lennox Ltd. v Grahame Puttick Ltd.* [1983] 1 W.L.R. 485; *Re Andrabell Ltd.* [1984] 3 All E.R. 407; *E. Pfeiffer Weinkellerei-Weineinkauf GmbH & Co. v Arbuthnot Factors Ltd.* [1987] B.C.L.C. 522. The trend to limit the impact of *Romalpa* was to some extent reversed by the decision of the Court of Appeal in *Clough Mill Ltd. v Martin* [1984] 3 All E.R. 982, where it was pointed out by Goff L.J. at 985 that in each case much depended on the language of the particular clause, the issue for determination, the way in which the matter was presented to the court and any material concession by counsel.

independent assignment but merely as an ancillary security by which the seller perfects his title to that which in equity already belongs to him.[13]

(4) *Claims to products of goods supplied under reservation of title*

Contracts of sale commonly provide that where goods supplied under reservation of title are commingled with other materials, belonging to the buyer or third party, to form a new product, ownership of the product is to vest in the seller. Such a provision will almost invariably be treated as creating a mortgage or charge,[14] for either the original goods supplied have been consumed in the course of manufacture, destroying the supplier's interest in them,[15] or, though they have simply become commingled without losing their identity,[16] the resultant product embodies materials not previously owned by the seller but contributed by others and can therefore vest in the seller only by way of grant, not by way of reservation.[17]

1–32

The right is given for the purpose of securing an obligation

In characterising any transaction the court has to perform two tasks. The first is to ascertain the intention of the parties from the terms of their agreement. The second is to determine the legal effect of what they have agreed. Whether what they have agreed produces a given legal effect is a matter of law and does not depend on intention. Thus in deciding whether or not an agreement has created a security interest the court looks not to whether that was intended by the parties but whether the nature of the rights they intended their agreement to confer is such as to constitute the agreement an agreement for security. The point was well put by Lord Millett in *Agnew v Inland Revenue Commissioners*,[18] where the dispute was not whether a charge had been created but whether it was a fixed or floating charge:

1–33

---

[13] For an illustration see the decision of Phillips J. in *E. Pfeiffer Weinkellerei-Weineinkauf GmbH & Co. v Arbuthnot Factors Ltd.*, above, n.12. The insistence on the existence of a fiduciary relationship as a prerequisite of the equitable right to trace stems from *Re Diplock* [1948] Ch. 465. It is widely regarded as anomalous. In the context of the present discussion the essential question is surely whether the buyer resells on his own account or on account of the seller. In the latter case the fiduciary duty to account follows from the capacity in which the buyer is required to act.

[14] See *Re Bond Worth Ltd.* [1980] Ch. 228; *Borden (UK) Ltd. v Scottish Timber Products Ltd.* [1979] 3 All E.R. 961, *per* Templeman L.J. at 973; *per* Buckley L.J. at 974–975; *Clough Mill Ltd. v Martin* [1984] 3 All E.R. 982.

[15] *Borden (UK) Ltd. v Scottish Timber Products Ltd.*, above.

[16] See generally Peter Birks, "Mixtures", in Norman Palmer and Ewan McKendrick (eds), *Interests in Goods* (2nd ed.), Ch.9; and Duncan Webb, "Title or Transformation: Who Owns Manufactured Goods?" [2000] J.B.L. 513.

[17] *Re Bond Worth Ltd.*, above; *Clough Mill Ltd. v Martin*, above. In the latter case the court opined that there was no reason in law why the parties should not be free to contract for the seller to take absolute title to the product, as opposed to a security interest, but considered it unlikely that the parties would intend to confer a windfall on the seller as to value added by the buyer. See generally R. M. Goode, *Proprietary Rights and Insolvency in Sales Transactions* (2nd ed.), Ch.V.

"31 The principal theme of the judgment, however [*i.e.* the judgment of Nourse L.J. in the Court of Appeal], was that the parties were free to make whatever agreement they liked. The question was therefore simply one of construction; unless unlawful the intention of the parties, to be gathered from the terms of the debenture, must prevail. It was clear from the descriptions which the parties attached to the charges that they had intended to create a fixed charge over the book debts while they were uncollected and a floating charge over the proceeds. It was open to the parties to do so, and freedom of contract prevailed.

32 Their Lordships consider this approach to be fundamentally mistaken. The question is not merely one of construction. In deciding whether a charge is a fixed charge or a floating charge, the court is engaged in a two-stage process. At the first stage it must construe the instrument of charge and seek to gather the intentions of the parties from the language they have used. But the object at this stage of the process is not to discover whether the parties intended to create a fixed or a floating charge. It is to ascertain the nature of the rights and obligations which the parties intended to grant each other in respect of the charged assets. Once these have been ascertained, the court can then embark on the second stage of the process, which is one of categorisation. This is a matter of law. It does not depend on the intention of the parties. If their intention, properly gathered from the language of the instrument, is to grant the company rights in respect of the charged assets which are inconsistent with the nature of a fixed charge, then the charge cannot be a fixed charge however they may have chosen to describe it. A similar process is involved in construing a document to see whether it creates a licence or tenancy. The court must construe the grant to ascertain the intention of the parties: but the only intention which is relevant is the intention to grant exclusive possession: see *Street v Mountford* [1985] AC 809, 826 per Lord Templeman. So here: in construing a debenture to see whether it creates a fixed or a floating charge, the only intention which is relevant is the intention that the company should be free to deal with the charged assets and withdraw them from the security without the consent of the holder of the charge; or, to put the question another way, whether the charged assets were intended to be under the control of the company or of the charge holder."

When the question is whether a security interest has been created at all, the relevant intention is the intention to confer on the creditor an interest in the debtor's property by way of security which will cease when the debt has been discharged. If that is the intention, the fact that the parties have chosen to characterise the transaction in some other way, for example as an outright transfer, is irrelevant. Conversely, no security interest is created where the asset is made available to the creditor for purposes other than security or is intended to be paid or transferred to the creditor absolutely, so that though it is paid or transferred as "security" for the debt, the debtor is to have merely

---

[18] [2001] 2 A.C. 710 at 725–726.

a personal claim to repayment of any excess received by the creditor over what was due to him.[19] The proposition that a security interest arises from a transaction intended as security in the sense described above has both a positive and a negative aspect. In its positive aspect it means that a transaction intended as security and fulfilling the other criteria specified below for the creation of a security interest will be treated as such by the court even if in form it is an outright transfer. It is a well established rule of mortgage law that the mortgagor's right to redeem at any time before sale or foreclosure cannot be cut off either by contractual provision or by disguising the mortgage as a sale or other transaction. In its negative aspect the proposition signifies that a transaction which is not intended as security in the above sense will not be treated as such by the law even if it may appear at first sight to have an affinity with security.

A good example of assets made available otherwise than for the purpose of security is provided by the decision of the Court of Appeal in *Cosslett*[20] to which reference has already been made.[21] Again, where title to an asset is transferred and the intention is that the transfer shall be absolute, so that the transferor will have neither the right nor the obligation to reacquire it *in specie*, no security interest arises. Four groups of cases deserve particular mention.

(1) *Transfer in or towards reduction of an existing indebtedness*

The assignment of a debt or transfer of another asset in reduction or discharge of the assignor's own indebtedness to the assignee does not constitute a security interest but an outright transfer. The principle was long ago applied in *Ex p. Newitt, in Re Garrud*,[22] where a provision in a building contract entitling the building owner, upon default by the builder, to take the builder's materials towards discharge of the builder's liability for damages was held not to create a security interest, for the materials were taken not as security for the builder's obligation but towards discharge of it. A rather more recent illustration is the decision in *Siebe Gorman & Co. Ltd. v Barclays Bank Ltd.*[23]:

1–34

> "RHM Ltd. owed the plaintiffs £8,707. At the plaintiffs' request RHM made an outright assignment to the plaintiffs of bills of exchange held by RHM totalling £8,417 in value. The assignment was expressed to be 'as security for the aforementioned debt' owed by the assignor. The bills were held by RHM's bank, who collected four of them and, despite notice of the

---

[19] This is discussed below, para.1–35, in the context of the fourth ingredient of security listed above, para.1–16.

[20] *Re Cosslett (Contractors) Ltd.* [1998] Ch. 495. The position was held to be otherwise as regards a power in the same contract to sell the plant and take from the proceeds payment of the sums due to the employer. See above.

[21] See above, para.1–26.

[22] (1881) 16 Ch.D 522. See also *Ashby Warner & Co. Ltd. v Simmons* [1936] 2 All E.R. 697; distinguished in *Coakley v Argent* (1998) June 4, Rimer J.

[23] [1979] 2 Lloyd's Rep. 142; see to the same effect *Carreras Rothman Ltd. v Freeman Mathews Treasure Ltd.* [1985] Ch. 207.

assignment, paid the proceeds to the credit of RHM's overdrawn account. RHM having gone into liquidation, the plaintiffs sued the defendants for recovery of the sums collected on the bills, and the defendants contended that the assignment to the plaintiffs constituted a charge on book debts which was void for want of registration."

It was held by Slade J. that whilst the assignment was not by way of sale it was equally clear that it was not intended as a mortgage either but was an outright transfer towards payment of RHM's indebtedness. The words "as security for the aforementioned debt," though *prima facie* indicating a mortgage or charge, had to be construed in context as denoting an assignment in payment of the debt. The assignment was therefore not registrable.

1–35   In *Siebe Gorman* the value of the bills transferred was less than the assignor's indebtedness to the bank, so that commercially there was no point in the assignor being given a right to redeem the bills. Suppose, however, that the collectable value of the debt due to the intending assignor exceeds what he owes to the intended assignee. In this situation, it is unlikely that the assignor intends to make a gift of the excess to the assignee, and the court will normally infer an intention to mortgage the debt instead of assigning it outright. But let us imagine that the assignor is willing to make an outright transfer of the debt due to him, with no right of redemption, provided that the assignee for his part undertakes to repay the amount by which the sum he collects from the account debtor (the assignor's debtor) exceeds the debt due from the assignor. At first sight this seems a mortgage disguised as an outright assignment to evade the registration requirements for a charge on book debts.[24] However, if it be the case that the assignor is genuinely giving up all his interest in the debts due to him, with no intention to reacquire the debts by paying off his own indebtedness but merely a reliance on the assignee's personal undertaking to repay the excess, the assignment cannot be faulted as a mortgage and escapes the registration provisions. We should see no difficulty in the matter if the subject-matter of the assignment were not debts but a motor car. What causes us to hesitate in the case of assignment of debts is that money is being exchanged for money, and it is a matter of indifference to the assignor whether he mortgages the debts or sells them outright against the assignee's undertaking to pay him the surplus. But such considerations have not in the past led the courts to disregard the distinction between an outright transfer of debts and a loan on the security of debts.[25] Moreover, the outright transfer of the proceeds differs in substance in another way from a mortgage of the proceeds in that the assignor, whose claim to repayment of the excess is a purely personal claim, bears the risk of the assignee's insolvency before repayment has been made.

---

[24] Under the Companies Act 1985, ss.395, 396.
[25] See, for example, *Olds Discount Ltd. v John Playfair Ltd.* [1938] 3 All E.R. 275; *Chow Yoong Hong v Choong Fah Rubber Manufactory* [1962] A.C. 209; *Lloyds and Scottish Finance Ltd. v Cyril Lord Carpet Sales Ltd.* (1979) 129 N.L.J. 366.

In short, the position is exactly the same as that described in case (2) below except that the payment or transfer is made in or towards satisfaction of an existing indebtedness rather than a prospective indebtedness.

(2) *Transfer to cover future indebtedness*

Similar reasoning applies where money is paid not towards discharge of an existing indebtedness but as cash cover for a future indebtedness to the payee. Examples are the payment of margin by an investor to his broker to cover future indebtedness arising from share dealings on the investor's behalf, payment of money by an importer to his bank to cover the bank's prospective liability under letters of credit issued to pay for the goods being imported, and payment of a deposit by the buyer under a contract of sale as security for completion of the purchase or by a tenant as security for dilapidations. In each case the intention is to provide security in the sense of assurance to the payee but it is necessary to distinguish a special-purpose payment which must be held and applied exclusively for the purpose of satisfying any indebtedness of the payer, any surplus being returned and meanwhile being held on trust for the payer, from an outright payment which becomes part of the payee's free assets, so that his only obligation if the sum paid exceeds the later indebtedness is a personal repayment obligation. In the former case the payee is the legal mortgagee of the fund, the payer having an equity of redemption which is not subject to rights of set-off by third parties against the payee[26] or by the payee himself against the debtor in respect of other indebtedness of the debtor,[27] and which can be asserted against the payee's creditors in the event of his insolvency[28]; in the latter there is no security interest at all, and the payment is an outright transfer of funds in which the payer has no equity of redemption. **1–36**

(3) *Sale and lease-back; sale and repurchase*

The third category of outright transfers involves, as an integral part of the transaction, an agreement by the transferor to take the asset back on lease or hire-purchase or to repurchase it. It is well established that so long as the initial transfer is genuinely intended to confer full ownership on the transferee, as opposed to a mere security interest, the transaction will be characterised according to its description and will not be recharacterised as a security agreement. So a genuine sale of land or goods does not constitute a borrowing **1–37**

---

[26] *Re Pollitt, Ex p. Minor* [1893] 1 Q.B. 455.
[27] See below, paras 1–40, 1–69.
[28] *Re City Equitable Fire Insurance Co. Ltd.* [1930] 2 Ch. 293.

on security even if it is followed by a lease back or a letting on hire-purchase,[29] and a sale of debts does not become a mortgage of debts merely because the seller gives recourse.[30] Similarly, the raising of overnight or other short-term funds by the sale and repurchase of investment securities ("repos") does not as a rule involve the grant of a security interest, for the intention is that the original sale shall pass a full title and the buyer has a mere contractual obligation to retransfer the securities. Accordingly the seller runs the risk of the buyer's failure to effect the promised resale, though if the retransfer obligation is collateralised a security interest will then come into existence.[31] Again, stock lending, which involves the transfer of securities upon terms that at a later date the recipient is to retransfer securities of the same kind,[32] does not normally constitute a security agreement, though it is common for the obligations of one or both of the parties to be secured by cash or securities collateral.[33] Hence the commercial treatment of repos and stock loans as collateral reflects the economic rather than the legal effect; the seller or lender transfers outright title, which exposes it to a credit risk, but the risk that the buyer or borrower will not honour its repurchase or reacquisition obligation is covered by contractual provisions which entitle the seller or lender to close out the transactions in the event of default and net the obligations of the parties.[34]

(4) Establishment of common fund as payment mechanism

1–38   Finally, a security agreement must be distinguished by an arrangement in which a fund in common beneficial ownership is established as a means of payment to the beneficial owners of the sums respectively becoming payable to them. An instructive decision is *Lovell Construction Ltd. v Independent Estates plc*[35]:

> "The plaintiffs entered into an agreement with the defendants to carry out certain construction work for them. The parties entered into an escrow agreement by which an escrow account was to be opened on their behalf in

---

[29] *Yorkshire Wagon Co. v Maclure* (1882) 21 Ch.D. 309; *Welsh Development Agency v Export Finance Co. Ltd.* [1992] B.C.C. 270. The position is otherwise where the agreement recording the purported sale and transfer back is a sham, as in *North Central Wagon Finance Co. Ltd. v Brailsford* [1962] 1 All E.R. 502; *Polsky v S. and A. Services* [1951] 1 All E.R. 185, affirmed [1951] 1 All E.R. 1062, n.); or where, though the agreement is genuine, its overall legal effect is that of a security agreement, as in *Re Curtain Dream plc* [1990] B.C.L.C. 925, referred to below, para.???. See generally Roy Goode, *Commercial Law* (2nd ed.), paras 651 *et seq.*; *Hire-Purchase Law and Practice* (2nd ed.), Ch.4.

[30] See cases cited below, para.3–05.

[31] See further Ch.VI.

[32] This differs from the repo in that there is no money consideration for either transfer.

[33] See Ch.VI. The everyday nature of these transactions is amply attested by the widespread use made of standard forms of master repurchase and master securities lending agreement produced by bodies such as the International Swap Dealers Association, the International Securities Market Association and the International Securities Lenders Association.

[34] See further on netting below, paras 6–44, 7–17 *et seq.*

[35] [1994] 1 B.C.L.C. 31.

the names of their solicitors to receive moneys payable by the defendants and third parties. Such moneys were to be deemed impressed with a trust in favour of the plaintiffs, to whom sums would be payable from the account against architects' certificates, while in certain circumstances moneys might be payable to the defendants, *e.g.* for liquidated and ascertained damages for breach of the construction contract. The defendants went into liquidation and the liquidator alleged that the escrow agreement created a registrable charge which was void for want of registration.

Held by Judge Fox-Andrews QC that the escrow account was established not for the purpose of giving security but as a mechanism of payment and created a trust of the moneys paid into the account in which both parties had a beneficial interest. The escrow agreement was therefore not registrable as a charge."

A fixed security interest implies a restriction on the debtor's dominion over the asset

A creditor cannot claim a fixed[36] security interest in an asset and at the same time allow the debtor the right to continue to treat the asset as his own. Hence if a debtor mortgages or charges his stock-in-trade, for example, and is left free to sell items of stock without having to secure his creditor's prior approval, the creditor has no fixed security interest, merely a floating mortgage or charge. It makes no difference that upon sale the debtor is required to pay the proceeds to a blocked account or otherwise hold them separate from his own moneys for the creditor. The creditor may then have a fixed security over the proceeds but his security in the original asset remains a floating security. Where the debtor is not generally permitted to dispose of the asset without the creditor's consent, the security will normally be recognised as a fixed security. However, a particular problem arises in relation to security over debts, for these are extinguished by payment. So if C wishes to obtain from D a fixed security over debts due to D it is not sufficient to prohibit D from disposing of the debts; C must also control their collection. He can do this in one of two ways: by giving notice of assignment to the debtors and collecting the debts in himself, or by appointing D his agent for collection and requiring D to keep the sums collected separate from his own moneys and hold them for C's account. If C not only leaves collection of the debts in D's hands but also allows D to deal with the sums collected as his own, C's security interest, even if labelled as fixed by the terms of the security agreement, will be characterised by the court as a floating security.[37] While the principle is clear, its application by the courts has given rise to considerable controversy and a division of judicial opinion.[38]

1–39

---

[36] For the distinction between fixed and floating security, see Ch.III, below.

[37] *Agnew v Commissioners of Inland Revenue* [2001] 2 A.C. 710; *Re Brightlife Ltd.* [1986] 3 All E.R. 673; *Hart v Barnes* (1982) 7 A.C.L.R. 310. See further below, paras 4–13 *et seq.*

[38] See below, paras 4–13 *et seq.*

The grant of security by a debtor over his own obligation: charge-backs and pledge-backs

1-40   Since a person cannot sue himself, it was until recently thought conceptually impossible for a debtor to take from his creditor a charge or other security over the debtor's own obligation and that a "security" of this kind took effect as a contractual set-off. But the House of Lords has now decided that there is no conceptual impossibility in a debtor taking a charge over his own obligation[39]; and presumably what applies to charge-backs is equally applicable not only to mortgage-backs but also to pledge-backs so as to enable the issuer of securities or negotiable instruments, for example, to take a pledge-back from the holder. The question is examined in later chapters in the context of a charge taken by a bank over its own customer's credit balance or by a securities intermediary over its customer's securities account with that intermediary.[40] Suffice to give a reminder at this stage that the debtor's equity of redemption is a property right, not a mere money entitlement, so that any surplus remaining when the mortgagee has taken what is due to him is not available for set-off against other, unsecured indebtedness of the mortgagor to the mortgagee.[41] So the prudent creditor will reinforce his charge-back with a general set-off clause.

Security in a fund of assets

1-41   Hitherto the discussion has been concerned with specific (or fixed) security, that is, security which attaches to identified or identifiable assets or classes of asset in the sense that there is an immediate appropriation of the assets to satisfaction of the debt and the debtor loses the right to deal with them free from the security interest. However, it is also possible to take security in an identifiable fund of assets by way of a floating mortgage or floating charge which leaves the debtor free to continue managing and dealing with the assets in the ordinary course of business, so that no specific assets are appropriated to the debt until the fund closes through crystallisation of the security. It is also possible to have a floating sub-security in a floating security interest, and this probably occurs more often than is realised. Despite voluminous literature devoted to floating security some of the underlying concepts remain elusive. They are examined in some detail in Chapter IV.

---

[39] *Re Bank of Credit and Commerce International SA (No. 8)* [1998] A.C. 214.
[40] Below, paras 3–12, 6–23, 6–46.
[41] See above, para.1–36; below, para.1–69. It would seem that as regards financial collateral within the scope of the 2002 EC Directive on Financial Collateral Arrangements (2002/47) the position will change, since Art.4(1)(a),(b) requires Member States to ensure that on the occurrence of an enforcement event the collateral taker will be able to realise any financial collateral by, among other things, setting off the value of any financial instruments and the amount of any cash against the relevant financial obligations. See para. 6–41.

5. THE FORMS OF CONSENSUAL SECURITY

The four consensual security devices

There are only four types of consensual security known to English law: the **1-42**
pledge, the contractual lien, the mortgage and the charge.[42] Each of these is
capable of being given in security so as to create a derivative, or sub-security,
interest.[43]

Pledge[44]

(1) *Nature of pledge*

The pledge, the oldest security device, is the actual or constructive delivery of **1-43**
possession of the asset to the creditor by way of security. As possessor the
pledgee enjoys a "special property"[45] or limited legal interest in the asset, but
ownership remains with the pledgor. The pledgee's interest goes beyond a
mere right to detain the asset. It encompasses the right to use the asset at his
own risk so long as this will not impair it; to sell his interest as pledgee or
assign it by way of gift; to deliver the asset to another for safe keeping; to sub-
pledge the asset on the same conditions as he holds it and for a debt no
greater than his own; and to sell the asset in the event of default in payment
by the pledgor.[46]

(2) *Assets susceptible to pledge*

Since a pledge depends on possession, an asset is not pledgeable unless it is **1-44**
reducible to possession. It may still be theoretically possible to have a pledge
of land,[47] but such a security has not been encountered for centuries. In practice, pledges are confined to goods and to documentary intangibles, that is,
documents embodying title to goods, money or securities such that the right

---

[42] This is disputed by some scholars, who maintain that there is no *numerus clausus* of security
interests. This is true in the sense that English law does not formally limit the permissible categories of security interest, but the four categories designated appear to cover every case, and
the critics have not been able to identify any new kind of interest. The proposition in the text,
advanced in successive editions of this work, receives support from the judgment of Millett
L.J. (as he then was) in *Re Cosslett (Contractors) Ltd* [1998] Ch. 495 at 508.

[43] See below, paras 1–58 *et seq.*

[44] See generally Norman Palmer, *Bailment* (2nd ed.), Ch.22.

[45] *Donald v Suckling* (1866) L.R. 1 Q.B. 585, where the nature of the pledge is exhaustively
examined.

[46] See *ibid.* and authorities there cited; *The Odessa* [1916] A.C. 145 at 158–159; and below. The
pledgee is not entitled to foreclosure, for he lacks the ownership which this remedy makes
absolute (*Carter v Wake* (1877) 4 Ch.D. 605).

[47] The pledge was the earliest form of security over land known to English law. See A. W. B.
Simpson, *A History of the Land Law* (2nd ed.), p.141.

to these assets is vested in the holder of the document for the time being and can be transferred by delivery of the document with any necessary indorsement. Put another way, the obligor's delivery or payment obligation is owed not to the original obligee as such but to whoever is the holder of the document and presents it for delivery or payment. Documentary intangibles are thus to be distinguished from pure intangibles, where the entitlement may be evidenced in or recorded in a document but it is not a document which represents the right.[48]

What constitutes a documentary intangible has never been exhaustively determined in English law; indeed, the class is not closed, for it is liable to expansion through mercantile usage. We can say with confidence that a pledge may be taken of bills of lading and other documents of title to goods,[49] and of negotiable instruments[50] and negotiable securities,[51] but that it is not possible to pledge ordinary written contracts such as building contracts or hire-purchase agreements, the production of which is not a condition of the obligor's duty of payment or other performance. Between these are documents and commercial paper which are not negotiable in the ordinary sense but are commonly deposited with banks by way of security. Examples are non-negotiable transport documents, non-negotiable instruments, certificates relating to registered shares and debentures, and insurance policies. Some of these are normally required to be produced before the obligor will perform and to this extent they differ from the documents previously mentioned. However, their possession does not of itself confer rights against the obligor and there is therefore little doubt that they too are non-pledgeable, but they deserve somewhat closer examination.

1–45   (a) *Non-negotiable transport documents* A document of title to goods, such as a bill of lading, embodies an undertaking by the carrier to surrender the goods to whoever is the holder of the document and presents it at the destination. Delays in the arrival of bills of lading have led increasingly to the use of non-negotiable transport documents, such as sea waybills, which constitute a receipt by the carrier and evidence the terms of the contract of carriage but do not require to be produced by the consignee in order to obtain possession of the goods. Delivery of such a document to a bank by way of security does not of itself confer on the bank any right to delivery of the goods. Accordingly it is not effective to create a pledge and at most evinces an intention to create an equitable mortgage or charge.

---

[48] The terms "documentary intangible" and "pure intangible" were coined by the *Report of the Committee on Consumer Credit* (Cmnd. 4596, 1971), App.III, para.3.8.

[49] *e.g.* warehouse and dock warrants or receipts which by statute or custom are negotiable.

[50] The term "negotiable instrument" is here used in its broad sense to denote an instrument capable of transfer by delivery and indorsement, whether or not it is of a kind such that a transferee is capable of taking as a holder in due course free from equities. Among such instruments are bills of exchange, cheques, promissory notes and Treasury bills.

[51] Including bearer shares, share warrants, bearer bonds and debentures and negotiable certificates of deposit.

(b) *Non-negotiable instruments* A bill of exchange marked "Not nego- **1–46** tiable" is incapable of transfer[52] and is thus non-pledgeable. By contrast a cheque crossed "Not negotiable" remains transferable and the only effect of the crossing is that a transferee acquires no better title than his trans- feror and thus takes subject to equities.[53] There is therefore no legal obstacle to the pledge of such a cheque. However, a cheque is not trans- ferable (and therefore not pledgeable) if it is crossed and marked "not transferable."[54] A cheque crossed and bearing the words "account payee" or "a/c payee," either with or without the word "only" was formerly trans- ferable but this is no longer the case,[55] so that a cheque so crossed is no longer capable of being pledged.

(c) *Share and debenture certificates* Whilst share warrants and bearer **1–47** shares and debentures, being transferable by delivery, are clearly capable of being pledged,[56] it would seem that English law does not recognise a pledge of registered securities. A contrary position is taken in the United States, where even registered securities are pledgeable if they are certifi- cated.[57] By contrast, decisions in English cases assume that even where the delivery of the certificate to the creditor is accompanied by a com- pleted or blank transfer the interest of the transferee is purely equitable until the transfer has been registered,[58] and that pending registration he is an equitable mortgagee or chargee, not a pledgee. This assumption accords with commercial realities. In England a certificate relating to reg- istered shares or debentures is not negotiable either in form or in sub- stance. It is made out in favour of a named person, it is not expressed to

---

[52] Bills of Exchange Act 1882, s.8(1).
[53] *ibid.*, s.81.
[54] Bills of Exchange Act 1882, s.8(1).
[55] *ibid.*, s.81A.
[56] And, it would now seem, of being pledged back to the issuer itself. See below, para.6–23.
[57] Uniform Commercial Code, §§ 9–313(a); 8–301. Grant Gilmore, *Security Interests in Personal Property*, §1.3. This reflects the fact that American certificates, unlike English certificates, are printed with a blank transfer form on the reverse and can thus pass from hand to hand by indorsement and delivery. But the modern trend towards dematerialisation of securities or the issue and immobilisation of global notes is gradually reducing the significance of investment securities as pledgeable assets. However, it should be noted that in international finance the term "pledge" is increasingly used as a generic term for the grant of security and thus as encompassing intangibles. The analysis in the text is based on the English law concept of pledge as delivery of possession by way of security.
[58] The decision usually cited as the leading case in *Harrold v Plenty* [1901] 2 Ch. 314, but the judgment is very concise and does not discuss the possible documentary character of a right to shares embodied in a share certificate, merely referring to the fact that a share is a chose in action. There are, however, a number of dicta of high authority to the effect that the transfer of legal title depends on registration, and that the registered holder is trustee for the party ben- eficially entitled. See, for example, *Societe Generale de Paris v Walker* (1885) 11 App. Cas. 20, *per* Earl of Selborne at 28; *Colonial Bank v Hepworth* (1887) 36 Ch.D. 36, *per* Chitty J. at 54; *Hardoon v Belilios* [1901] A.C. 118, *per* Lord Lindley at 123; *Ireland v Hart* [1902] 1 Ch. 522, *per* Joyce J. at 529; *Re Rose* [1952] Ch. 499, *per* Jenkins L.J. at 515. Most textbooks on com- pany law take this position. See, for example, *Gore-Browne on Companies*, §16.4.3; L.C.B. Gower, *Principles of Modern Company Law* (6th ed.), pp.437, 464; *Palmer's Company Law*, para.6.605. For a contrary view see R. R. Pennington, *Company Law* (8th ed.), pp.416–417.

be transferable and it is not indorsed when passed on to an intended trans-feree.[59] Whilst deposit of the certificate and transfer form deprives the transferor of the ability to deal in the security (unless he acts fraudulently) and may confer on the transferee a legal right to be registered as the holder of the shares or debentures, the benefits flowing from an interest in the shares, such as the right to vote, to receive dividends and to participate in a surplus on winding-up, and all other contractual rights against the com-pany depend on registration. Hence a share or debenture certificate lacks the essential quality of a documentary intangible, which is that the docu-ment embodies the underlying entitlement so as to confer on the holder for the time being rights of actions against the obligor, in this case the issuing company. At most, possession of the document and transfer form confer a right to registration; they do not confer the rights stemming from registra-tion. The position is otherwise, however, in the case of documents which are issued by the company, or by a depositary institution holding its shares or debentures, in negotiable form and which, though not themselves con-ferring on the holder the status of a shareholder,[60] entitle him to call for the issue to him of shares to the number or value designated in the document. An example is the American depositary receipt, which is freely negotiable and is accordingly capable of being pledged. Thus the ADR, like the share warrant, is a negotiable document of title to a non-negotiable security—a truly ingenious creation of the business community.

1–48 (d) *Insurance policies* Certain types of insurance policy, such as endow-ment policies, are commonly deposited by way of security. Nevertheless they are not pledgeable, since whilst their production may be called for as a condition of payment their possession does not of itself confer rights against the insurer.[61]

Contractual lien

1–49 Whilst a possessory lien is generally described as a right conferred by law to detain goods until money owed to the detainee has been paid, a possessory lien may also be created by contract. It differs from a pledge in that the goods are deposited not for the purpose of security but for some other purpose, *e.g.* custody or repair. The addition of a contractual power of sale does not convert a contractual lien into an equitable charge.[62]

---

[59] It is this which distinguishes the English from the American share certificate. See n.57 above.

[60] In contrast to share warrants, the holder of which is a shareholder and may also, if the arti-cles of association so provide, exercise some or all of the rights of a member. The holder of the warrant is entitled to exchange it for registered shares.

[61] Again, the position is otherwise in the United States. See *Gilmore, op. cit.*, §1.3.

[62] *Great Eastern Rly. Co. v Lord's Trustee* [1909] A.C. 109; distinguished in *Re Cosslett (Contractors) Ltd.* [1998] Ch. 495, above, para.1–26; *Re Hamlet International plc* [1999] 2 B.C.L.C. 506; following the decision of Richmond J. in *Waitomo Wools (NZ) Ltd v Nelsons (NZ) Ltd* [1974] 1 N.Z.L.R. 484 at 493 in regarding the point as established in *Great Eastern Rail Co v Lord's Trustee* [1909] A.C. 109.

Mortgage

A mortgage is a transfer of ownership of the asset (or of any lesser interest **1–50**
held by the transferor) by way of security upon the express or implied condition that ownership will be re-transferred to the debtor on discharge of his
obligation. A mortgage thus involves the acquisition of an existing interest,
not the creation of a new one, a fact which distinguishes it from an equitable
charge. It does not require the delivery of possession so that any kind of
asset, tangible or intangible, is capable of being mortgaged. Since a mortgage
constitutes a form of appropriation of the asset to the discharge of the debt
it encompasses a charge.[63] A mortgage may be legal or equitable.[64]

Mortgages of intangibles raise distinct considerations in the variety of
forms they may take. A mortgage of almost any kind of intangible may be
effected by assignment[65] or novation[66]; and in the case of documentary intangibles, a further option is negotiation by delivery with any necessary indorsement.[67] These are examined in Ch.IV in the particular context of security
over receivables.

As previously mentioned, a mortgage can, it seems, be granted to a creditor over his own obligation. Thus a deposit account, a negotiable instrument
and a negotiable security can all be given to the bank with which the deposit
account is held or to the issuer of the instrument or security, who thus
becomes its own creditor.[68]

Charge

A good description of the nature of a charge is to be found in the judgment **1–51**
of Atkin L.J. in *National Provincial and Union Bank of England v Charnley*[69]:

"The first question that arises is whether or not this document does create
a mortgage or charge, and to determine that it is necessary to form an idea
of what is meant by a 'charge.' It is not necessary to give a formal definition of a charge, but I think there can be no doubt that where in a transaction for value both parties evince an intention that property, existing or
future, shall be made available as security for the payment of a debt, and
that the creditor shall have a present right to have it made available, there
is a charge, even though the present legal right which is contemplated can
only be enforced at some future date, and though the creditor gets no legal
right of property, either absolute or special, or any legal right to possession, but only gets a right to have the security made available by an order

---

[63] See below, para.1–52.
[64] See above, paras 1–12, 1–13 and below, para.2–04.
[65] See below, para.3–03.
[66] See below, para.3–03.
[67] See above, para.1–13, below, para.2–20.
[68] See above, para.1–40, and, for a discussion of such "charge-backs", below, paras 3–12, 6–23, 6–46.
[69] [1924] K.B. 431 at 449.

of the Court. If those conditions exist I think there is a charge. If, on the other hand, the parties do not intend that there should be a present right to have the security made available, but only that there should be a right in the future by agreement, such as a licence, to seize the goods, there will be no charge."

Thus a charge (also sometimes termed hypothecation) does not depend on either the delivery of possession or the transfer of ownership, but represents an agreement between creditor and debtor by which a particular asset or class of assets is appropriated to the satisfaction of the debt, so that the creditor is entitled to look to the asset and its proceeds to discharge the indebtedness, in priority to the claims of unsecured creditors and junior incumbrancers. The charge does not transfer ownership to the creditor[70]; it is merely an incumbrance, a weight hanging on the asset which travels with it into the hands of third parties other than a bona fide purchaser of the legal title for value and without notice. Thus in contrast to a mortgage, an equitable charge entails the creation of a new interest in the property of the debtor, so that while a mortgagee acquires a right *in re sua* by virtue of the transfer to him the interest of a chargee is a right *in re aliena*. A mere contractual right to take or retain possession, without a right of appropriation, does not constitute a charge.[71] Apart from the special case of the consensual maritime liens such as bottomry bonds and respondentia, which have their roots in Admiralty law, the charge is the creature of equity; there is no such thing as a legal charge, except as provided by statute. Land is a special case, by virtue of the Law of Property Act 1925. In the first place, the Act provides, somewhat confusingly, for a charge by way of legal mortgage.[72] Secondly, a mortgage of land is by demise for a term of years absolute (*i.e.* a lease) or by legal charge, not by assignment.[73]

1–52   Whilst a *mere* charge does not transfer ownership, either at law or in equity, the agreement to appropriate the asset to discharge the debt may be reinforced by an agreement to give a mortgage, which equity treats as itself a mortgage. In such a case the mortgage (which itself entitles the creditor to appropriate the asset in satisfaction of the debt) encompasses the charge. Hence the saying that "every charge is not an equitable mortgage, though every equitable mortgage is a charge."[74] In other words, a mortgage is a right of appropriation (= charge) plus a transfer of ownership, at law or in equity, as security for payment. Since a mortgage is a broader security and includes a charge it is often referred to as a charge, and this is unobjectionable so long as it is borne in mind that the converse is not true. An equitable charge which

---

[70] In consequence it cannot be created by novation. Moreover, the chargee, unlike a mortgagee, has no right to obtain foreclosure, nor can he avail itself of the self-help remedies of sale or appointment of a receiver, though he may apply to the court for one of these remedies or alternatively, in the case of a charge on a debt, for an order directing the chargor to execute an assignment in his favour (*Burlinson v Hall* (1884) 11 Q.B.D. 347, *per* Day J. at 350).

[71] *Re Cosslett (Contractors) Ltd* [1998] Ch.495, *per* Millett L.J. at 507–508.

[72] ss.86(1), 87(1).

[73] s.86(1), (2). A mortgage by demise of registered land will no longer be possible when s.23(1)(a) of the Land Registration Act 2002 has been brought into force.

[74] *Shea v Moore* [1894] I.R.158, *per* Walker L.C. at 168.

is neither created as an incident of a mortgage nor accompanied by an agreement for a mortgage is a mere charge and does not operate to transfer ownership to the creditor either at law or in equity.[75] Whether a security is a mere charge or a charge with a superadded agreement for a mortgage depends on the intention of the parties.

It has to be said that courts and writers have not been consistent in their use of terminology. The terms "charge" and "mortgage" have often been treated as interchangeable or used in combination. This is particularly true in relation to security over a debt or fund. Thus it has been said that a charge on a fund operates as a partial assignment[76] and that a direction by a debtor to a person holding a fund on his behalf to pay a sum from the fund to the creditor amounts to "an equitable assignment by way of charge."[77] The explanation for this rather loose use of language lies in the fact that in contrast to charges on tangibles, under which the creditor looks to the proceeds of the charged asset, a charge on a debt or fund is enforced by collecting payment out of the fund from the fund holder in the same way as under a partial assignment, and in construing the statutory provisions governing the assignment of choses in action[78] the courts focused on the question whether the assignment was to be considered absolute or "by way of charge only," a phrase taken to include partial assignment. Certainly in practical terms the difference between a partial assignment by C to A of a debt owed to C by D and a charge of the debt by C to A is of little significance, since in both cases D is entitled to make payment to A of the sum assigned or charged, in neither case can D safely pay C after notice of A's rights, and in neither case can D be compelled to pay A except in proceedings to which C is a party.

A charge, like a mortgage, can be granted to the creditor over his own obligation.[79]

The trust not an independent security device

The pledge, the contractual lien, the mortgage and the charge encompass all **1–53** the forms of consensual security known to English law. The trust, if created for the purpose of securing an obligation, is not an independent security device, merely a form of equitable mortgage, which may be effected either by the debtor declaring himself to be a trustee of the asset for the creditor or by his transferring the asset to a trustee to hold it on trust for the creditor.

---

[75] In consequence the chargee is not entitled to possession or foreclosure, merely to an order for sale or the appointment of a receiver, with an alternative right to sell or appoint a receiver out of court where the charge is by deed (Law of Property Act 1925, ss.101(1), 205(1)(xvi)). For the position of a debenture holder under a debenture creating a floating charge see below, paras 4–06 *et seq.*

[76] *Colonial Mutual General Insurance Co. Ltd. v ANZ Bank Group (New Zealand) Ltd.* [1995] 1 W.L.R. 1140 at 1144; citing *Durham Bros. v Robertson* [1898] 1 Q.B. 765, where, however, the charge was accompanied by an assignment.

[77] *Walter & Sullivan Ltd. v J. Murphy & Sons Ltd.* [1955] 2 Q.B. 584, *per* Parker L.J. at 588.

[78] Law of Property Act 1925, s.136.

[79] See above, paras 1–12 and 1–13 and below, para.3–12.

Attornment not an independent security device

1–54   We have seen that in the case of goods and documentary intangibles[80] a pledge may be created by the delivery of actual or constructive possession and that a common form of constructive possession is by attornment, where the debtor or a third party agrees to hold the goods or documents for the creditor instead of the debtor. Attornment in relation to goods or documentary intangibles is therefore simply a mode of constructive delivery, not a distinct form of security interest, and thus simultaneously creates and perfects a pledge.

The cases also indicate that where a third party holds a fund, whether of money or of securities, on behalf of the debtor, the third party can attorn to the creditor by agreeing to hold the fund for him instead of for the debtor.[81] But there are important differences between an attornment in respect of goods or documents and an attornment in respect of a fund. Goods and documents are tangibles and are therefore susceptible to pledge, but this requires actual or constructive delivery; mere agreement is not sufficient. Attornment here fulfils the dual function of attachment and perfection of the security interest both of which depend on agreement between debtor and creditor.[82] By contrast, an interest in a fund is intangible and is therefore not susceptible to pledge. Attornment in respect of a fund presupposes that the fund remains the property of the debtor and is therefore consistent only with a charge, not a mortgage. The creation of the charge is not, however, brought about by the attornment but stems from the parties' agreement, which suffices without more. Accordingly attornment in respect of a fund constitutes neither a distinct form of security interest nor a mode of attachment of a charge; its sole function is to perfect a charge previously created by giving the chargee control of the fund, in that the fund holder will act only on the chargee's instructions and the chargee has the right to appropriate the fund to satisfaction of the debt due to him. Though it has been said that "nothing is gained by framing a security as an attornment rather than an assignment,"[83] the concept of perfection through control by an undertaking by the fund holder to comply with instructions by the secured party (in other words, what we would call an attornment) has been developed in America into a powerful mechanism for perfecting security interests in investment securities held with a securities intermediary,[84] commodity contracts held with a commodity intermediary,[85] and even deposit accounts.[86] There seems no reason to deny its efficacy in England in relation to funds held for another.

---

[80] See above, para.1–44.

[81] See below, para.3–34.

[82] See below, paras 2–04, 3–34.

[83] Fidelis Oditah, *Legal Aspects of Receivables Financing*, p.90.

[84] Uniform Commercial Code, §§ 8–106, 9–106(a), 9–314.

[85] *ibid.*, §§ 9–106(b).

[86] *ibid.*, §§ 9–104, 9–314. This probably goes beyond the purview of attornment in English law, where the better view is that it is available only in respect of a fund, not a mere debt, despite the controversial decision in *Shamia v Joory* [1954] 1 Q.B. 448, a decision not followed by the Queensland Supreme Court in *Rothwells Ltd. v Nommack* (1988) 13 A.C.S.R. 421, which preferred the view expressed in Goff and Jones, *Law of Restitution* (currently in the 6th ed.,

6. THE PERMISSIBLE OBJECTS OF SECURITY

We have previously seen that a pledge cannot be taken over pure intangibles.[87]   **1–55**
Subject to this, a security interest may in principle be taken over any kind of
property or class of property, tangible or intangible, present or future,[88] including land, goods, negotiable and non-negotiable instruments, documents of title,
securities (whether held directly from the issuer or through a securities account
with an intermediary),[89] intellectual property rights of various kinds, policies
of insurance, transferable licences and quotas, bank deposits and letters of
credit, drawing rights under facility agreements with banks, subscription agreements with underwriters, rights under construction contracts, transferable
membership rights, and indeed anything which is identifiable[90] and transferable, whether in gross or as appurtenant to land or other property.[91] Moreover,
security interests may themselves be given in security, so that a chargee may
grant a sub-charge and a mortgagee a sub-mortgage or a charge.[92]

As we have seen, the focus has shifted sharply from tangibles to intangibles
as the subject-matter of security in commercial and financial transactions.
There are, however, certain categories of property which, by reason of their
personal nature, considerations of public policy or a contractual prohibition
against assignment, are incapable of transfer, though this will not preclude an
assignment of the income or proceeds received by the assignor.[93] Among
the types of property not capable of being given in security are: contract
rights which are made non-assignable by the terms of the contract[94] or by
rules incorporated into the contract[95]; property and rights which are made
non-assignable by statute, such as future property under a bill of sale,[96] occu-
pational pension rights,[97] social security benefits,[98] various categories of
statutory licence,[99] and the rights of a participating charity in a common
investment scheme which makes no provision for assignment[1]; and rights the

---

para.28–003), that there can not be an attornment to a mere debt. See to the same effect R.M.
Goode, "The Right to Trace and its Impact in Commercial Transactions – I" (1976) 92 L.Q.R.
360 at 387–388. For a contrary view see Oditah, *op. cit.*, p.89.

[87] That is, intangibles not embodied in a negotiable document of title, instrument or security.
[88] Though in the case of future property the security interest is nascent and cannot attach until
the property has been acquired. See below.
[89] See below, Ch.IV.
[90] See below, paras 2–05 *et seq.*
[91] *Swift v Dairywise Farms Ltd* [2000] 1 W.L.R. 1177 (agreement for transfer of milk quota by
way of security and retransfer on redemption). As to legal impediments to assignment, see
below.
[92] See para.1–70, below.
[93] See below, para.3–41.
[94] But see text to n.93 above. See also below, paras 3–40 *et seq.*
[95] For example, the Uniform Customs and Practice for Documentary Credits (UCP 500),
Art.48b, which provides that a credit is transferable only if so designated by the issuing bank.
[96] Bills of Sale Act 1878 (Amendment) Act 1882, s.5.
[97] Pensions Act 1995, s.91.
[98] Social Security Administration Act 1992, s.187.
[99] For example, a consumer credit licence (Consumer Credit Act 1974, s.22(2)).
[1] Charities Act 1993, s.24(6).

assignment of which is contrary to public policy, such as an assignment which would deprive the debtor and his family of all means of support,[2] an assignment of the salary of a public officer,[3] and an assignment of a bare right of litigation.[4] There are also rights which can be assigned in equity but not at law because they are recorded in a register and are transferable at law only by novation, that is, substitution of the creditor for the debtor. These include registered securities and ship and aircraft mortgages.[5] Finally, there are certain categories of mortgage which cannot be effected without judicial or administrative approval. For example, land held by a charity, other than an exempt charity, may not be mortgaged without an order of the court or the Charity Commissioners.[6]

Money, in the sense of a claim on a bank as opposed to notes and coin, may be given in security in two different ways. One way is by assignment of the claim, as where a customer charges his bank deposit account to secure an advance from a third party.[7] The other is by novation, that is, by transfer of funds to the creditor or a third party by way of a special-purpose payment, to be held as a segregated fund and used only to discharge the debt due to the creditor, any balance being returnable to the debtor, whose interest is thus a proprietary interest in the shape of an equity of redemption.[8]

7. ACCRETIONS TO THE SECURITY

1–56 In principle, accretions to the asset given in security, such as fixtures, accessions and improvements, enure for the benefit of the secured creditor. This would seem to apply also to intangibles, such as a bonus issue or rights issue of shares.[9] It is a separate question whether the income from intangibles, such as interest and dividends, forms part of the security or belongs to the debtor.[10]

8. DERIVATIVE SECURITY INTERESTS

1–57 A security interest may be derivative either because it is in an asset derived from other assets as their product or proceeds or because it is a sub-security

---

[2] *King v Michael Faraday & Partners* [1939] 2 K.B. 753; *Horwood v Millar's Timber & Trading Co Ltd* [1917] 1 K.B. 305.

[3] *Palmer v Bate* (1821) 2 B & B 673.

[4] *Trendtex Trading Corp v Credit Suisse* [1982] A.C. 679. See below, para.3–39.

[5] See above, para.1–13 and below, paras 2–16, 2–19 and 2–30.

[6] Charities Act 1993, s.38(1).

[7] Or even from the bank itself. As to such charge-backs, see below, para.3–12.

[8] See below, para.1–69.

[9] If this were not the case, every such issue would diminish the value of the secured creditor's shareholding.

[10] See below, para.1–61.

interest carved out of a larger interest held by a secured creditor of higher degree, as in the case of a sub-mortgage or sub-pledge.

(i) Security in derivative assets

Security in an asset and its product

We have seen that a retention of title to goods which is expressed to carry through to a new product formed by the commingling of those goods with others will almost invariably be treated as creating a mortgage or charge.[11] Security in a product may also arise as a matter of law from the fact that goods over which a security interest has been taken become commingled with the goods of others to form a new product. In such a case the secured creditor will normally have a security interest in the product in the proportion which the value of the original goods bears to the value of the product.[12]

1–58

Security in an asset and in its proceeds[13]

Security in an asset will almost invariably carry through to the proceeds of an unauthorised disposition by the debtor or a third party[14] and will also extend to proceeds of an authorised disposition where it is effected on behalf of the creditor rather than for the debtor's own account.[15] But where the debtor sells subject to the security interest the creditor has no claim to the proceeds, for the subject of the sale is the debtor's equity of redemption, not any asset of the creditor.[16] Proceeds may result not only from the act of the debtor but from other events outside the debtor's control, including exercise by the creditor or another creditor of a power of sale on default.[17]

1–59

The relationship between a security interest in an asset and a security interest in its proceeds has not been fully developed in English law. Numerous issues require examination:

---

[11] See above, para.1–32.

[12] The subject is complex, involving consideration of principles of *confusio, commixtio* and *specificatio* as well as equitable rules governing tracing into mixed substitutions. For penetrating analyses, see Peter Birks, "Mixtures" in *Interests in Goods* (Norman Palmer and Ewan McKendrick, eds); and Lionel Smith, *The Law of Tracing*, Ch.2.

[13] See further Roy Goode, *Commercial Law* (2nd ed.), pp.667–668, 754–755.

[14] Including the proceeds of an asset sold by a chargee when the asset was already subject to a crystallised charge in favour of a prior debenture holder. See *Re Real Meat Co.* [1996] B.C.C. 254.

[15] This statement was approved by the Court of Appeal in *Buhr v Barclays Bank plc* [2001] EWCA Civ. 1223.

[16] See *Buhr v Barclays Bank plc*, above, where the argument that the mortgagors were selling only their equity of redemption was rejected, the purchasers having contracted to buy the full unencumbered title. See also para.5–34.

[17] See below, para.1–61.

(1) *What is the theoretical basis of the claim to proceeds of an unauthorised disposition?*

1–60   Until recently it had been thought that a claim to proceeds of an unauthorised disposition was based on unjust enrichment, not on a pure property right. However, the House of Lords has now held that the interest in proceeds is a pure property right flowing from ownership of the original asset and does not derive from the law of restitution. Such a property right, like other property rights, is determined by fixed principles and is not dependent on the court's discretion or on ideas as to what is fair, just and reasonable.[18] Accordingly the claimant succeeds by virtue of his title and not by way of reversal of unjust enrichment.[19] It is therefore unnecessary for the claimant to show that the defendant has been unjustly enriched, the claimant is entitled to the proceeds as of right, not in exercise of the court's discretion, and defences particular to the law of restitution such as change of position are not available.[20]

Professor Lionel Smith's work on *The Law of Tracing* has done much to clarify both thinking and terminology in this complex subject. First, a distinction is drawn between *following* the original asset and *tracing* its proceeds. Secondly, tracing is not itself a remedy, merely a legal technique to establish that value received by the defendant can be identified as resulting from value formerly held by the claimant. Assuming that this is demonstrated, it is then for the law determine, according to rules of *claiming*, whether the claimant has a proprietary claim to what the defendant received or whether this is barred by an available defence. Thirdly, it is wrong to regard proceeds as the original asset in a changed form, since the original asset continues to exist, and the proceeds represent the exchange value of the asset to the parties to the transaction which produces them. It follows that there is no need to show any physical correlation between the asset the claimant lost and the asset the defendant received, merely a loss of *value* by the claimant and a receipt of *value* by the defendant. Accordingly an improper transfer of value by novation[21] is just as traceable as a transfer of value by assignment. These concepts have now been endorsed by the highest authority.[22]

(2) *What constitutes proceeds?*

1–61   The parties may themselves agree that a security interest in an asset is to carry through to its proceeds, and what constitutes proceeds is then a question of

---

[18] *Foskett v McKeown* [2001] A.C. 102, *per* Lord Millett at 127.

[19] The issue had divided academic writers. See, for example, Peter Birks, [1997] N.Z.L.R. 623, advocating the concept of reversal of unjust enrichment; Ross Granthan and Charles E.F. Rickett, [1997] N.Z.L.R. 668; and Graham Virgo, *The Principles of the Law of Restitution*, p.12, contending that the right of recovery is based on property, not unjust enrichment.

[20] *Foskett v McKeown*, above.

[21] See below, para.3–03.

[22] See *Foskett v McKeown* [2001] 1 A.C. 102, *per* Lord Millett at 128.

construction of the agreement. In other cases the proceeds of an asset are anything which is traceable as a direct or indirect substitute for the asset. Proceeds thus cover money, goods, or anything else received in exchange for the asset and traceable as such into the debtor's hands, as well as the traceable proceeds of proceeds. Whether something is traceable is to be determined by rules of equity which define the conditions in which property held by the defendant can be considered causally linked to property lost by the plaintiff.[23] So if an asset subject to a security interest is wrongfully sold by the debtor, who receives a cheque in payment, the cheque constitutes traceable proceeds. When the cheque is collected and the amount of the cheque is credited to the debtor's account, the resultant claim on the bank constitutes traceable proceeds.

There seems no reason to confine proceeds to the receipts of a disposition by the debtor or a realisation by the creditor.[24] In principle they should include, for example, compensation paid to the debtor on compulsory acquisition of the asset, money received on the redemption of shares, a payment under an insurance policy for loss of or damage to the insured property given in security, damages recovered from a third party for a wrongful act or omission causing loss of or damage to the asset, or, of course, realisation by the creditor himself, or by another creditor having a security interest in the same asset, following default by the debtor.[25] The position in relation to insurance proceeds received by the debtor under a contract of insurance taken out by him is a little more complex than for other forms of proceeds and depends on the extent to which the secured creditor had an interest in the bundle of rights created by the insurance policy itself.[26] Where the debtor insures the asset for its full value and not merely for the value of his interest as represented by his equity of redemption, then while he can recover the full amount insured he must account to the secured creditor for such part of that amount as exceeds the debtor's interest,[27] and meanwhile holds that excess on trust for the creditor.[28] Where, on the other hand, the terms of the policy indicate that the debtor was insuring only for his own interest, then the policy proceeds are attributable only to that interest and are not proceeds that can be reached by the secured creditor.

Proceeds do not include income derived by the debtor from an asset (*e.g.* rentals, share dividends), or natural produce (*e.g.* milk from cows) or natural increase (*e.g.* progeny of livestock), for these are not given in exchange for the asset, which remains in place. Whether, in the absence of agreement to the contrary, they belong to the debtor or the creditor depends on the circumstances. Where the debtor is lawfully in possession of a tangible asset, such as land or goods, it will normally be assumed that the fruits belong to the debtor in the absence of any agreement to the contrary.[29] Income received by the

---

[23] See *ibid.* and, for an extended analysis, Lionel Smith, *Law of Tracing*.
[24] As to which see below.
[25] As to realisation by a creditor and the nature of the interest in surplus proceeds, see below, para.1–69.
[26] See *Foskett v McKeown* [2001] 1 A.C. 102, *per* Lord Millett at 132–133.
[27] *A. Tomlinson (Hauliers) Ltd v Hepburn* [1966] A.C. 451.
[28] In the language of tracing, the case is one of mixed substitution.
[29] See as to livestock *Tucker v Farm & General Investment Trust Ltd* [1966] 2 Q.B. 421.

debtor from an asset given in security to the creditor of which the debtor had no right to possession or had lost such right, or in respect of which he had no right to enter into the transaction producing the income, belongs to the creditor—not, however, as proceeds but as the fruits of the creditor's property.[30] The same applies to income derived from proceeds of the creditor's asset resulting from the debtor's unauthorised disposition.[31] In the case of intangibles, such as bank deposits and investment securities, the same principle should apply. In relation to investment securities market usage considers it fair that dividend income and other distributions should enure for the benefit of the debtor.[32] Since in many cases the securities account is in the name of the creditor it is customary for the agreement between debtor and creditor to provide that so long as the debtor is not in default the creditor will pass over all such benefits.[33]

(3) *Can the creditor enforce a security interest both in the asset and in its proceeds?*

1–62 Suppose that C has taken a specific mortgage of D's motor car and D wrongfully sells the car to E. In the absence of any applicable exception to the *nemo dat* rule C can recover his vehicle from E. Alternatively he can adopt the wrongful sale and treat his security interest as attaching to the proceeds received by D. But can he enforce security in both the car and the proceeds at the same time? No, because the remedies are inconsistent. C's equitable claim to the proceeds rests on his implied adoption of the wrongful sale.[34] He cannot have his cake and eat it. He must elect which right to pursue and having made his election he is bound by it.

(4) *What is C's position prior to his election?*

1–63 Two alternative views have been propounded. The first, advanced by Professor Peter Birks,[35] is that where C still has rights to the original asset he has no vested interest in the proceeds but merely a power, or equity, which crystallises only upon C's electing to take the proceeds rather than the original asset. The alternative view, put forward by Professor Lionel Smith, is

---

[30] The distinction between a claim to proceeds and a claim to fruits is admirably explained by Lionel Smith, *Law of Tracing*, pp.21–24.

[31] Smith, *op. cit.*, pp.23–24, 144.

[32] See Paul Harding and Christian A. Johnson, *Mastering collateral management and documentation*, pp.24–25.

[33] See ISDA Credit Support Deed (1995), para.6(e)(i), (g); TBMA/ISMA Global Master Repurchase Agreement (2000), para.5. Payments so made over to the debtor are known as manufactured dividends, since they are the equivalent of the coupon payments the creditor has received.

[34] *United City Australia Ltd. v Barclays Bank Ltd.* [1941] A.C. 1.

[35] *An Introduction to the Law of Restitution*, pp.70, 92, 393; *Laundering and Tracing* (P.B.H. Birks, ed.), pp.307–311.

that C acquires a vested interest in the proceeds as soon as they come into existence but that he must elect whether to claim the original asset or the proceeds and upon electing for one remedy he loses the other. The two approaches produce different results. Under the former, C's right to the proceeds is displaced if, before he has made his election, the debtor disposes of the proceeds to a bona fide purchaser for value and without notice, even if the purchaser's interest is purely equitable, for this will override a mere equity, whereas under the latter approach C would win since his vested equitable interest is first in time. It would seem from the speech of Lord Millett in *Foskett v McKeown*[36] that the latter approach is correct:

> "A beneficiary of a trust is entitled to a continuing beneficial interest not merely in the trust property but in its traceable proceeds also, and his interest binds everyone who takes the property or its proceeds except a bona fide purchaser for value[37] without notice."[38]

The question of election does not, of course, arise where C loses title to the car by virtue of some exception to the *nemo dat* rule.

(5) One security interest or two?[39]

A question of some importance is whether the effect of the security agreement is to create a single, continuous security interest which moves from asset to proceeds or two entirely distinct security interests, the security in the original asset at the time of the security agreement and the security in proceeds at the time they come into the hands of the defendant. There are compelling reasons for treating the security interest as an indivisible and continuous security interest which moves from the original asset to the proceeds. To treat the security interest in proceeds as a separate security interest coming into existence upon their receipt by the debtor would have implications for the priority of the security interest, while an agreement providing for a security interest in proceeds would be a mere contingent agreement for security and as such not effective to confer rights *in rem* without a post-receipt act of transfer (which in the absence of new consideration would be vulnerable as a preference if the debtor went into liquidation within the statutory preference period[40]) or an agreement for transfer supported by fresh executed consideration.[41] The continuity of the security interest is of particular significance in relation to floating charges and their crystallisation.[42]

1–64

---

[36] [2001] A.C. 102.

[37] *Semble*, a bona fide purchaser of the legal title; on general property principles, the purchaser of an equitable interest is postponed to the holder of a prior equitable interest.

[38] [2001] A.C. 102 at 128.

[39] See Roy Goode, "Charges over Book Debts: A Missed Opportunity", (1994) 110 L.Q.R. 592 at 603–605.

[40] See Insolvency Act 1986, ss.239, 240.

[41] See above, paras 2–11, 2–15.

[42] See below, para.4–29.

(6) *What if C expressly bargains for security both over an asset and over its proceeds?*

1–65   Two situations have to be considered. The first is where the security agreement, in covering both the asset and its proceeds, indicates that the security rights are to apply consecutively rather than concurrently, as where D is authorised to dispose of the asset free from C's security interest, so that this subsists in the goods until sale to E and in the proceeds thereafter. In such a case C, having authorised resale, plainly cannot trace the goods into E's hands. The second situation is where the security agreement, while containing no such authorisation, is expressed to confer on C a security interest in the proceeds concurrently with his security interest in the original asset. Such an agreement cannot of itself entitle C to cumulative remedies so as to avoid the need for him to make an election. The case is not one where the proceeds can also be picked up as original collateral,[43] for they do not fall within a separate category of collateral but are simply whatever results from disposition of the original asset.

It may also be noted that it is not possible to have a concurrent interest in a debt and its proceeds, for upon collection the debt ceases to exist.[44]

(7) *Security in an asset both as proceeds and as original collateral*

1–66   One and the same asset may, however, constitute both proceeds and original collateral where it is covered by a description which is independent of its status as proceeds. Thus:

> "C takes a fixed charge over D's business equipment and book debts to secure an advance. D wrongfully sells equipment for £10,000 to E, who buys with notice of the charge. D has agreed to give E three months' credit. C can assert concurrent security rights over the equipment and the book debt resulting from the sale to E. This does not involve the assertion of mutually inconsistent rights, for C's claim to the book debt does not depend on the right to trace in equity from the equipment to its proceeds but derives from the fact that the book debts are a separate category of collateral under the security agreement."

Proceeds may also be picked up concurrently as original collateral by virtue of an after-acquired property clause in the security agreement:

> "C takes a charge over D's equipment and any equipment D may subsequently acquire. At the time the charge is given D owns a lathe which, in breach of the security agreement, he exchanges for a new lathe. C has a

---

[43] See below.
[44] A point which appears to have been overlooked by the Court of Appeal in its controversial decision in *Re New Bullas Trading Ltd.* [1993] B.C.C. 251, since disapproved by the Privy Council in *Agnew v Commissioners of Inland Revenue* [2001] 2 A.C. 710. See below, paras 4–15 *et seq.*

security interest in the new lathe both as proceeds of the original lathe and as after-acquired equipment."

(8) *Relationship between security in an asset and security in its proceeds*

Where the security interest in the proceeds derives from agreement, there is **1–67** no necessary correspondence between that interest and the interest in the original asset; indeed, as noted above, the agreement may not confer a security interest in the original asset at all.[45] So a creditor may take a floating charge over stock in trade but a fixed charge over proceeds, or a fixed charge over equipment—requiring the chargee's consent to a sale free from the charge—but a floating charge over the proceeds of an authorised sale. There is, however, an exception which derives from the nature of the subject-matter of the charge. In the case of a charge on debts, as opposed to a security interest in tangible assets, it is not possible to have a fixed charge over a debt when the charge over the proceeds is only a floating charge.[46] This is because the effect of leaving the chargor to collect the debts is that the only way in which the chargee can assert his security interest as a fixed interest is through the proceeds, for collection extinguishes the debt, so that the original asset given in security is destroyed.[47]

Where a proprietary interest in proceeds arises by operation of law—for example, on the defendant's wrongful disposal of the claimant's asset—it will not normally be different in *quantum* from the interest enjoyed over the original asset, so that if the interest in the original asset was only a security interest, the interest in the proceeds will likewise be a security interest.[48] However, the *character* of the security interest in proceeds is dependent on the nature of the proceeds and is not necessarily the same as in the original asset. For example, if imported goods are pledged to a bank by deposit of a bill of lading which is then released to the pledgor under a trust receipt by which the pledgor agrees to hold the goods and their proceeds on trust for the bank, then if the pledgor sells the goods and receives payment into his bank account the proceeds, in the form of the pledgor's claim on his bank, are intangible and so cannot be the subject of a pledge but only of a mortgage or charge, which in this case will be equitable in nature.[49]

---

[45] See further para.1–68, below.
[46] See Roy Goode, "Charges over Book Debts: A Missed Opportunity" (1994) 110 L.Q.R. 592, in which this point is developed. Though controversial, it has now been accepted by the Privy Council in *Agnew v Commissioners of Inland Revenue* [2001] 2 A.C. 710. See below, para.4–16.
[47] See below, para.4–16.
[48] See *Foskett v McKeown* [2001] A.C. 102, *per* Lord Millett at 128.
[49] There is a curious dearth of authority as to the metamorphosis undergone by a possessory security interest when tangible property subject to the security interest is converted into intangible property, but there can be no doubt that the erstwhile lienee or pledgee does have a security interest in the proceeds, albeit in a different form. If the position were otherwise, any right of sale given to the holder of a possessory security by agreement or custom (in the case of a lien) and by implication of law (in the case of a pledge) would be valueless.

(9) *Security interests run forward to proceeds, not backwards to the original asset*

1-68   There are dicta which on a superficial reading suggest that an obligation on the debtor to apply the proceeds of his asset towards discharge of the debt, and not for any other purpose, creates an equitable charge not merely over the proceeds but over the asset itself.[50] But the dicta must be taken in context and are not, it is submitted, intended to lay down any such rule, which would cause great confusion. A security interest in an asset carries forward to proceeds; a security interest in proceeds does not run backwards to the asset from which they derive. If it did, a creditor taking a charge over book debts would automatically acquire a charge over the trading stock the sale of which produced the book debts. What is necessary to create a security interest in an asset is that the asset itself, and not merely its proceeds, is appropriated to the debt.[51]

(10) *Surplus proceeds on realisation by a creditor*

1-69   The principal method of enforcing a security interest in the event of the debtor's default is sale of the asset given in security and application of the proceeds in discharge of the debt. Where no other creditor has a security interest in the asset, any surplus proceeds remaining after the creditor has taken what is due to him have to be handed over to the debtor and meanwhile are held on trust for him,[52] so that if the creditor becomes insolvent while the surplus is still in his hands it does not form part of his estate but belongs to the debtor. It follows that the creditor has no right to set off some other debt owed to him by the debtor against the surplus, for a money claim cannot be set off against a property claim.[53] Where the sale is by a junior incumbrancer and takes effect subject to the interest of a prior incumbrancer, the latter has no claim to the surplus proceeds, since his security interest continues in the original asset. By contrast, an incumbrancer ranking after the selling mortgagee has an interest in the surplus ahead of the debtor, and the mortgagee, if having notice of such incumbrancer's rights, is obliged to hold the surplus on trust for him, and to make it over to him.[54] Where the selling mortgagee is a junior incumbrancer

---

[50] See, for example, the judgment of Browne-Wilkinson J. in *Swiss Bank Corporation v Lloyds Bank Ltd.* [1979] Ch. 548 at 566.

[51] See para.1–27 and *Re Sikorski v Sikorski* (1979) 89 D.L.R. (3d) 411.

[52] This is so whether the mortgagee sells under his statutory power (Law of Property Act 1925, s.105) or under the express provisions of the mortgage (*Charles v Jones* (1887) 35 Ch.D 544; *Banner v Berridge* (1881) 18 Ch.D 254). The mortgage instrument may, of course, make express provision for a trust of the surplus proceeds, but if it does not the mortgagee is a constructive trustee (*Banner v Berridge*, above).

[53] See below, para.???. The position is otherwise where the parties have agreed that the mortgagee is to be a mere debtor for the proceeds (or the set-off is against a money claim secured on property (see below paras 7–61, 7–82 and 7–84). See below, para.7–85).

[54] *Charles v Jones*, above. It appears that where there are several mortgages ranking after that of the selling mortgagee, his duty is to hand over the entire surplus to the next in line, leaving it to him to pass over any remaining surplus to the next mortgagee, rather than the selling mortgagee having to distribute the surplus among all junior incumbrancers in order of priority. See Fisher & Lightwood's *Law of Mortgage* (11th ed.), para.20.47.

and the sale is not made subject to the senior incumbrancer's interest, this then attaches to the proceeds of sale and must be satisfied from those proceeds in priority to the claim of the junior incumbrancer.[55]

(ii) Sub-security

The holder of a security interest may himself give that interest in security **1–70** except so far as the security agreement otherwise provides. Thus a mortgagee may grant a sub-mortgage, a chargee a sub-charge and a pledgee a sub-pledge. In each case what is involved is the security transfer of or charge on the security interest coupled with an assignment of the debt secured by that interest. However, the holder of the security interest may not grant a sub-security interest greater than his own. So a chargee under an equitable sub-charge can give a sub-charge but not a sub-mortgage, since he has merely an incumbrance, not ownership. On the other hand, there is nothing to prevent a mortgagee from charging his mortgage interest instead of granting a sub-mortgage. A pledgee cannot sub-pledge for an amount exceeding that secured by the pledge to him.[56]

In general the law governing sub-security is reasonably clear. The main area of difficulty in financial transaction relates to the right of the holder of a security interest in investment securities to deal with them, whether by way of sub-security or otherwise. This is dealt with in Chapter VI.

9. THE NEGATIVE PLEDGE

I now want to turn to a new topic, on which there has been relatively little **1–71** English literature and almost no case law, namely the negative pledge. The most significant discussion of the negative pledge in English law is to be found in one of the volumes of Mr Philip Wood's excellent six-volume work *Law and Practice of International Finance*,[57] in which he discusses in some detail the use of negative pledge clauses in international loan transactions and the typical forms of negative pledge clause. For a detailed conceptual analysis of the negative pledge we have to turn to the works of our American colleagues, and in particular to Ch.38 of the late Professor Grant Gilmore's brilliant book *Security Interests in Personal Property*, which after 37 years remains the *locus classicus* for the legal treatment of security interests. I must express my indebtedness to both these authors for clarifying my thoughts on what must necessarily be a very brief treatment of this subject.

---

[55] See Law of Property Act 1925, ss.105, 107(2).
[56] *Donald v Suckling* (1866) L.R. 1 Q.B. 585.
[57] *International Loans, Bonds and Securities Regulation*, paras 3–10 *et seq*. See also Penn, Shea and Arora, *The Law and Practice of International Banking*, paras 6.37 *et seq*. and literature there cited.

Common forms of negative pledge

(1) *Domestic transactions*

1–72   The typical negative pledge clause in a domestic financing transaction is that which is to be found in the standard form of floating charge, by which the debtor company undertakes that it will not, without the prior written consent of the debenture holder, grant any subsequent security ranking in priority to or *pari passu* with the floating charge. Such a stipulation may also be contained in a fixed charge, though it is not strictly necessary for priority purposes, since a fixed charge has priority over subsequent interests except a bona fide purchaser for value of the legal title without notice. However, the covenant in a fixed charge tends to be more stringent, since it typically prevents the borrower from granting even subordinated security without the consent of the prior lender. Such a covenant goes beyond mere preservation of the first lender's priority; the grant of a subsequent security interest to another financier is a breach of the negative pledge clause and thus a default event attracting various rights and remedies. Whether the covenant not to incumber is restricted or absolute, in domestic transactions the traditional form of covenant does not involve any commitment by the debtor to give security to the first financier, whether on breach of the covenant not to incumber or as a condition of its relaxation.

(2) *International transactions*

1–73   In international loan finance, the negative pledge is commonly taken by an unsecured lender and is often designed to secure equality rather than priority. In such cases the objective is not to prohibit the borrower from giving security to another financier but to ensure that if the debtor does so then the prior (unsecured) lender will either have equal and rateable security over the same asset or be given security over other assets of the debtor to at least the same value. The negative pledge clause may be expressed as a purely negative covenant or as an affirmative covenant. In its negative form the covenant is that the borrower will not give security over the asset without giving equal and rateable security over that asset (or alternatively security over another asset of equal value) to the earlier financier. In the affirmative form of covenant the borrower agrees that if it gives security over an asset it will give equal and rateable security over that asset (or over another asset of equal value) to the same financier. This may seem a distinction without a difference but the effect of the two formulations is not quite the same. In its purely negative form the covenant does not involve a promise by the borrower to give equal and rateable security (or security of equal value); the provision of such security is simply a condition of the borrower's licence to encumber the asset. By contrast the affirmative covenant obliges the borrower to give security to the first financier upon the occurrence of the designated contingency, *i.e.* the grant of security to the second financier.

Juridical nature of the negative pledge

(1) *Covenant not to incumber is not a security interest*

Is the negative pledge a mere contract, an equity or a full-blooded security **1–74**
interest? In attempting an answer to this question so far as English law is concerned I should emphasise that this is necessarily speculative, there being no
case law containing any conceptual analysis of the question. In my view, a
pure negative pledge—that is, a covenant not to incumber, with no requirement to furnish security to the first financier if security is given to another
financier—cannot of itself amount to a security interest, for it does not purport to give the creditor any rights, even contingently, over the debtor's present or future assets.[58] In this respect, it makes no difference whether the
negative pledge is given in favour of a secured or an unsecured creditor.
However, where the creditor holds a floating charge, what the negative pledge
does do is to limit the scope of the debtor company's dealing powers and
thereby ensure the priority of the floating charge, once crystallised, over a
subsequent incumbrancer in favour of a third party taking with notice of the
negative pledge.[59] So in this case the negative pledge, though not a security
interest in itself, firms up the security given by the floating charge, and
constitutes an equity binding a third party with notice.

(2) *Provision for matching security creates no security interest*

Let us now take the case where the negative pledge clause allows the debtor **1–75**
to grant subsequent security provided that matching security is given to the
creditor. Where this covenant is given in negative form the debtor does not
undertake to furnish security to the first creditor on granting security to the
second; the furnishing of security is merely a non-promissory condition of
the debtor's right to incumber the asset.[60] Accordingly the first creditor is not
entitled to security, even if the covenant is broken, as he has not bargained
for it. The position is otherwise in the case of an affirmative covenant; the
debtor undertakes that if an asset is given by way of security to a subsequent
creditor security in another asset of at least equal value will be given to the
first creditor. The occurrence of the stipulated event triggers the debtor's
promise to give security. So the question in this case is not whether, on security being given to the second creditor, the first creditor is entitled to security—for at the very least he has a personal right to call for it—but whether
he acquires a security interest without any further act on the part of the
debtor. The answer to this question is clear. The contention by the first

---

[58] As to the effect of the covenant on a subsequent financier who takes with notice of it where
the covenantee is an unsecured creditor, see below, para.1–78.
[59] See below, para.5–40.
[60] It is, of course, a question of construction whether the covenant is negative or affirmative. A
covenant which appears at first sight to be negative may, when the instrument is construed as
a whole, be read as importing a promise, not simply stating a condition.

creditor that he automatically acquires a security interest falls at the first hurdle, for the assets prospectively offered as future security are not identifiable without an act of appropriation by the debtor after the contingency has occurred. This makes it unnecessary to proceed to the second question, whether a contingent agreement for security constitutes a security in equity so as to attach automatically to an identified asset upon the occurrence of the contingency. Such a question does, however, arise where the covenant is to provide equal and rateable security in *the same* asset.

(3) *Provision for automatic attachment to same asset creates no security interest*

1–76 Where the agreement provides that on the grant of security over an asset a security interest in favour of the earlier creditor shall automatically attach *to that asset* so as to constitute the creditor a secured creditor over the asset equally with the later incumbrancer, the problem of identifiability is removed. The grant of security to the third party fixes the asset to which the negative pledge clause is to apply, without the need for any act of appropriation on the part of the debtor. At first sight, therefore, the creditor's rights attach to the incumbered asset by virtue of the negative pledge clause, and the only question remaining is whether those rights rank equally with those of the incumbrancer or whether the latter has priority.

I hope I shall not cause too much consternation if I advance the proposition that this is all an illusion. In my view, an agreement for automatic attachment of a security interest to an asset upon the debtor subsequently charging this to a third party gives the first creditor nothing at all beyond a mere contract right. At the time the agreement is made it does not constitute even an inchoate security, capable of restrospective attachment later on,[61] for it is merely contingent on the occurrence of a future uncertain event.[62] Nor does the provision for automatic attachment have effect as a security interest at the time when the debtor gives security to the third party. Why not? Because it lacks the essential requirement of *value*. As we shall see, an agreement for security takes effect in equity only if the consideration is executed, by actual advance of the money. For this purpose, the money must be furnished at or after and in consideration of the security. But in the case of a purely contingent agreement for security, the security interest cannot come into existence, even in equity, until the contingency has occurred. Money advanced by the creditor prior to that date does not count as new value; on the contrary, it represents no more than an advance by an unsecured creditor who may, at some unspecified time, be able to call on the debtor for security in the future. So the mere occurrence of the contingency does not produce automatic

---

[61] See below, paras 2–13, 2–15.
[62] See below, para.2–11. The position is otherwise if the security interest is to attach on a specified future date or the expiry of a stated period or the occurrence of some other future event which is bound occur.

attachment; in the absence of a completed transfer (mortgage or pledge) the creditor will obtain a security interest only upon the making of a new agreement and advance and to the extent of that advance.[63] It follows that the later incumbrancer will inevitably acquire priority, whether or not he had notice of the *pro rata* clause in the prior agreement with the first creditor. It follows also that if the debtor were to go into liquidation without making a fresh security agreement or receiving a new advance, the original creditor would remain unsecured. Further, even a fresh security agreement would be vulnerable as a preference if no new value were furnished and the preference were given within the prescribed time prior to the onset of insolvency of the company.[64] Finally, the making of the new agreement or the provision of new value by the creditor after the grant of the incumbrance to the later creditor would bring a charge into existence at that time which would require registration under s.395 of the Companies Act 1985 if falling within one of the registrable categories specified in s.396.

So the *pro rata* clause, in so far as it is designed to produce automatic security, wholly fails to achieve that objective. It merely gives the creditor a contractual right to call for security on the grant of the charge to the third party and may constitute a default event triggering other remedies.

(4) *Provision entitling the first creditor to call for equal and rateable security creates no security interest*

If a stipulation for automatic creation of equal and rateable security in an asset upon its being incumbered by the debtor does not suffice to create a security interest when that event occurs, then *a fortiori* a provision which merely entitles the first creditor to call for equal and rateable security does not give rise to a security interest in equity. Such a provision introduces a second contingency, the demand for security by the first creditor, whose position is thus weaker than under the form of negative pledge previously described.[65] **1–77**

Effect of negative pledge in favour of unsecured creditor

Given that a negative pledge clause is not effective by itself to create a consensual security interest in favour of the original creditor, can he nevertheless invoke any equitable real right against a subsequent incumbrancer who takes **1–78**

---

[63] For a contrary view, see Peter Gabriel, *Legal Aspects of Syndicated Loans*, pp.86–90.

[64] *Re Jackson & Bassford Ltd.* [1906] 2 Ch. 467, a case on what was termed fraudulent preference under the former insolvency legislation. The position under the present law is that a preference may be set aside by the court where it is given in favour of a person connected with the company in the period of two years ending with the onset of insolvency or, where given in favour of any other person, in the period of six months ending with the onset of insolvency.

[65] In *Williams v Burlington Investments Ltd.* (1977) 121 S.J. 424 it was argued that an agreement for the execution of a charge on demand by the creditor gave rise to an equitable security when the demand was made. The House of Lords, while not finding it necessary to rule on the point, appears to have treated the proposition with appropriate scepticism.

his security with notice of the negative pledge? The matter does not appear to have been the subject of any reported case in England, and in such few cases as have surfaced in the United States the courts have been divided.[66] Considerable ingenuity has gone into devising alternative causes of action against the incumbrancer. Thus in *Kelly v Central Hanover Bank and Trust Co.*,[67] a company issued unsecured debentures containing a negative pledge clause in negative form and subsequently gave some of its assets in security to the defendant. The plaintiff, a debenture holder, alleged that the grant of the security was a breach of the negative pledge clause and that the defendant had notice of the negative pledge. On this basis the plaintiff contended:

(1) that it had an equitable lien[68] on all the assets of the debtor company;

(2) that the covenants created "something in the nature of an equitable servitude"[69];

(3) that the defendant, having participated in the debtor's breach of trust or knowingly and unjustifiably interfered with the plaintiff's rights as debenture holder, held the security as constructive trustees for the plaintiff;

(4) that the plaintiff had a right of equitable reparation against the defendant for knowingly invading the plaintiffs right to continued performance of its contract by the debtor.

The claim was dismissed both on the facts and on the law.[70]

There is little doubt that if such contentions were advanced before an English court they would meet a similar fate. Quite apart from doctrinal objections to the notion of covenants running with negotiable securities,[71] it is clear that the party invoking the negative pledge cannot be put in a better position than he would have had if the covenant had not been broken. This alone is sufficient to exclude the possibility of equitable security in the debtor's assets, whether directly or as beneficiary under a constructive trust of the security taken by the subsequent creditor. If the claimant is himself unsecured and thus has no real rights in the debtor's assets, what meaning, in property terms, is to be given to the proposition that the subsequent creditor

---

[66] See the cases referred to by Gilmore, *op. cit.*, Ch.38.

[67] 11 F.Supp. 497 (1935), reversed 85 F.2d 61 (1936).

[68] In English law terms, an equitable charge.

[69] By analogy with the doctrine in *Tulk v Moxhay* (1848) 2 Ph. 774.

[70] The decision was subsequently set aside in an extremely brief decision of the Second Circuit and remitted for determination of certain facts. The case was later settled. Gilmore clearly favours the reasoning at first instance. See *op. cit.*, pp.1006–1007.

[71] A subject that has generated much debate over the years, rekindled by the decision of Browne-Wilkinson J. in *Swiss Bank Corp. v Lloyds Bank Ltd.* [1979] Ch. 548 on the application of the principle in *De Mattos v Gibson* (1859) 4 De G. & J. 276. The decision in the *Swiss Bank* case was subsequently reversed by the Court of Appeal [1980] 3 W.L.R. 457 on the inference of fact. A further appeal to the House of Lords [1982] A.C. 584 was dismissed. See *Simon Gardner* (1982) 98 L.Q.R. 279; *Andrew Tettenborn* (1982) 41 C.L.J. 58; Nili Cohen-Grabelsky (1982) 45 M.L.R. 241.

takes his security subject to the negative pledge? Such a proposition surely has significance only where the claimant holds a floating charge and the negative pledge is used to secure priority for that charge over a subsequent incumbrance.[72] The most the claimant can hope for is an injunction to restrain breach of the negative covenant or damages for the tort of inducing breach of contract. The former remedy depends for its efficacy upon the creditor becoming aware of the intended breach in time.[73]

10. THE SUBORDINATION AGREEMENT

A party to whom money is owed may accept subordination either of a security interest he holds or of unsecured indebtedness owed to him.[74] A creditor holding security may agree to subordinate his security interest to that of a third party over whom he would otherwise have priority; an unsecured creditor may agree with a third party not to take payment from the debtor until any debts owed by the debtor to the third party have been paid. Does either of these forms of subordination constitute the grant of a security interest by the subordinated creditor to the party in whose favour the subordination is made? **1-79**

Subordination of security

The holders of successive security interests are free to vary the priority of their interests *inter se* without the consent of the debtor, who has no right to insist on the order in which successive mortgage debts are satisfied.[75] This does not result in an exchange of the security interests, which could affect the ranking of the subordinated interest in relation to an intermediate security interest in favour of a third party. All that happens is that the *priorities* are reversed—so that if the subordinated creditor enforces his security he holds what he receives on trust for the senior creditor up to the amount due to the latter or any lower sum fixed by the subordination agreement—but that in other respects each of the two mortgagees retains exactly the same interest as he had before. No exchange of security interest is intended to result from the subordination and none is effected. It follows that if there are successive mortgages in favour of M1, M2 and M3, and M1 agrees to subordinate his security interest to M3, this does not give M3 priority over M2, for M3 is not taking over M1's mortgage in exchange for his own, merely acquiring a **1-80**

---

[72] See below, para.5–40.

[73] A mandatory injunction to undo a breach already committed is unlikely to be granted. For two Australian cases on the availability of negative injunctions, see *Pullen v Abelcheck Pty. Ltd.* (1930) 20 N.S.W..L.R. 732; *Bond Brewing v National Australia Bank* (1990) 1 A.C.S.R. 445; Jonathan R.C. Arkins, [2000] J.I.B.L. 198.

[74] See generally Philip R. Wood, *The Law of Subordinated Debt*; W.J. Gough, *Company Charges* (2nd ed.), Ch.40; Bruce MacDougall, "Subordination Agreements," (1994) 32 Osgoode Hall L.J. 225. Subordination may also be by agreement between debtor and junior creditor.

[75] *Cheah v Equitcorp Finance Group Ltd.* [1992] 1 A.C. 472.

priority over M1.[76] Subordination differs, of course, from release of the asset to the debtor in that the subordinated interest retains its priority against interests other than that to which the subordination relates, and when the latter is discharged attaches to any surplus. Contractual subordination also differs from waiver in that the former is given for consideration whereas the latter is voluntary. Subject to this, subordination produces the same consequences as waiver in constituting an equity in favour of the senior creditor[77] which will bind an assignee from the junior creditor who takes with notice of it or without giving value.[78]

Subordination of unsecured debt

1–81 A creditor who merely agrees to subordinate his unsecured claim to that of another creditor by not collecting his debt or any dividend payable in the debtor's liquidation until the senior debt has been paid does not, on the face of it,[79] give security over anything. His subordination (commonly termed a contractual subordination) is a particular form of negative covenant, *i.e.* a covenant not to collect the debt due to him before the senior creditor has been paid. The question is whether, if he collects payment in breach of that covenant, he holds the amount collected on trust for the senior creditor. If so, then indirectly his covenant is secured. It is thought that subordination of this kind gives the senior a purely personal contractual right to require an accounting, not a proprietary claim. The position is not analogous to, say, the assignor of a debt who collects it on behalf of the assignee and holds it on trust for the assignee,[80] for what the assignor collects belongs to the assignee, who has bought it, whereas the subordinated debt belongs to the subordinated creditor. In the case of the "turnover" subordination, where the subordinated creditor expressly agrees to account for collections, it is a question of construction whether this is a purely personal undertaking or a declaration of trust.[81] The most common form of turnover subordination is the subordination trust, in which the junior creditor expressly undertakes to hold on trust for the senior creditor payments received in respect of the junior debt.[82] The parties should be careful not to provide for turnover of the entire amount of the junior debt received where this exceeds the amount of the senior debt, for since it would not normally be the intention that the senior

---

[76] There appears to be no English authority on the point, but it is well-established in pre-Uniform Commercial Code decisions in the United States. See, for example, *AmSouth Bank NA v J & D Financial Corp.* 679 So 2d 695 (1996); *Shaddix v National Security Co.*, 221 Ala 268, 128 So 220 (1930).

[77] *i.e.* the creditor in whose favour the subordination is given.

[78] See below, para.5–56.

[79] Where the subordination is not immediate but is triggered only by specified events, such as default in payment of the senior debt or the debtor's winding-up, it is commonly referred to as contingency subordination.

[80] See para.3–36.

[81] See further Roy Goode, *Commercial Law* (2nd ed.), pp.664–666. As to the validity of a subordination agreement on the liquidation of the debtor company, see below, para.5–59.

[82] Wood, *op. cit.*, para.2.4.

creditor should retain any surplus for his own benefit such an arrangement risks being characterised as a charge on book debts,[83] the charge being given to secure a third-party indebtedness. But turnover limited to the amount of the senior debt is an outright assignment of part of the debt due to the subordinated creditor, not a charge.[84]

11. SALE OF PARTICIPATION IN LOAN ASSETS

As part of the process of disintermediation[85] that began many years ago in the financial markets, both in England and overseas, banks and other financial institutions have become extensively engaged in the securitisation[86] of financial assets. There are three main methods for "selling" financial assets: assignment, novation and sub-participation. An assignment is a transfer by the lender to a third party of the whole or part of his rights under the loan agreement. Unless otherwise provided by the loan agreement this may be done without the borrower's consent. A novation is the substitution of a third party as lender under the loan agreement, the original lender giving up his rights and being relieved of his obligations. This requires the assent of the borrower unless provided for in the loan agreement.[87] A funded sub-participation[88] involves an agreement by a third party (known as the buyer or

1–82

---

[83] *ibid.*, para.5.3.

[84] See above, para.1–34, as to outright assignments in or towards discharge of a debt.

[85] Disintermediation is the inelegant term given to the process by which banks and other holders of financial assets (receivables due from borrowers, lessees, etc. whether secured or unsecured) move out of borrowing and on-lending by way of loans held to maturity and instead of acting as intermediate parties between borrowers and lenders adopt ancillary roles such as brokerage, underwriting, initiation and disposal of loan agreements. Several factors have brought about this process, in particular, the discovery by commercial borrowers that they could obtain funds more cheaply than from banks by issuing commercial paper directly to the market, and by investors that they could obtain a greater return on their funds than from deposits with the banks, and the desire of banks to reduce their financial assets, and thus remove them from the balance sheet, in order to reduce exposure and to avoid having to inject more capital to meet increasingly stringent capital to primary assets ratios introduced by regulatory authorities.

[86] That is, the packaging of receivables of a given class (which may be secured or unsecured) and their sale to a special-purpose vehicle, the price being either borrowed from banks or raised by issue of a bond or note on the securities market, repayment being secured on the purchased assets. It is important to bear in mind the distinction between "security" in the sense of conferment of rights in assets as security for payment and "securities," a term used to denote stocks, shares, debentures, notes, etc. issued on a market. "Securitisation" refers to the conversion of non-marketable into marketable financial assets; it does not denote security for payment, though as stated above the obligations of the purchaser are secured.

[87] The mechanism for novation can be agreed in advance, *e.g.* by an agreement that registration of an executed transferable loan certificate will result in an automatic substitution of the new lender.

[88] Also termed a participation, a term which is avoided here because it is also used to embrace any arrangement by which the lender disposes of an interest in his financial assets, whether by assignment, novation or otherwise. The term "sub-participation" helps to make the essential point that the agreement between lead bank and sub-participant is a sub-agreement, that is, a back to back (and non-recourse) transaction not legally derived from the underlying loan agreement with the borrower.

sub-participant) to deposit with the original lender (known as the seller, or lead bank) a sum of money representing an agreed proportion of the amount advanced or to be advanced by the lead bank, the sub-participant acquiring in exchange the right to receive from the lead bank a sum equal to the same proportion of the amount repaid by the borrower. Sub-participation agreements usually make it clear that the sub-participant's relationship is solely with the lead bank and that he acquires no interest in the underlying loan, whether by assignment or otherwise. Hence the "sale" of a participation refers not to the transfer of an interest in the loan as such but to the conferment on the sub-participant of a right to payment from the lead bank measured by the agreed proportion of its receipts from the borrower. It follows that under such an agreement there is no trust in favour of the sub-participant who bears the double risk of insolvency of the borrower and of the lead bank, and in either case is merely an unsecured creditor, with no right *in rem* either to sums payable by the borrower or to sums received by the lead bank.[89]

It is, of course, possible to set up a sub-participation agreement as either an outright purchase of a proportionate interest in the loan and of its proceeds or a sub-loan on the security of such an interest. In the typical form of sub-participation agreement the relationship between sub-participant and lead bank is not that of sub-lender and sub-borrower, for the sub-participant's entitlement is measured not by what he has paid but by what the lead bank receives. To put it another way, the lead bank does not *repay* a sub-loan, it *pays* a sum equal to the agreed proportion of what it receives. The sub-participant does not lend; he buys a claim on the lead bank. The lead bank could declare itself a trustee of the loan and for proceeds as security for performance of its obligations to the sub-participant but in the absence of such a declaration the court would require evidence of the intention to create a trust, and in relation to the proceeds it would also be necessary for the sub-participant to establish that the lead bank was under a duty to keep the proceeds as a distinct fund separate from its own moneys and that such fund was still identifiable when the lead bank became insolvent.[90]

---

[89] *Lloyds TSB Bank plc v Clarke* [2002] 2 All E.R. (Comm) 992. See also Philip R. Wood, *International Loans, Bonds and Securities Regulation*, Ch.7.

[90] See *Hibernian National Bank v Federal Deposit Insurance Co.*, 733 F.2d 1403 (1984). Thus if the lead bank collects payment by exercise of a right of set-off no trust claim can be asserted to the sum paid for there is not fund to which the trust can attach, merely the extinction *pro tanto* of the lead bank's countervailing obligation to the borrower. For a Canadian case where a trust was held established, see *Re Canadian Commercial Bank* [1986] 5 W.W.R. 531.

II

Attachment and Perfection of a Security Interest: General Considerations[1]

Priority rules governing fixed and floating security cannot be properly under- **2–01** stood without a grasp of the concept of attachment. As we shall see, this apparently straightforward concept possesses a number of subtleties which we ignore at our peril. A mechanical application of priority rules which takes no account of the manner in which a security interest attaches or the time from which attachment takes effect is likely to lead to erroneous solutions. So it is with attachment that I propose to begin.

1. PRINCIPLES OF ATTACHMENT

The concept of attachment

Attachment denotes the creation of the security interest as between debtor **2–02** and creditor. The effect of attachment is that the security interest fastens on the asset so as to give the creditor rights *in rem* against the debtor himself, though not necessarily against third parties. Attachment of a security interest is thus to be distinguished from perfection of a security interest, the latter usually involving a further step (possession, registration, notice, or attornment) which constitutes notice of the security interest to third parties and must be taken if they are to be bound.[2]

There is admittedly something odd in the notion of a right *in rem* available only against the debtor, for that which distinguishes real rights from personal rights is supposed to be that the former affect not only the obligor but the world at large. True, we can speak of the secured party's right *vis-à-vis* the debtor to restrict the debtor's use or disposition of the goods, to take possession or to sell, but precisely the same rights could be exercised by mere

---

[1] See generally Roy Goode, *Commercial Law* (2nd ed.), Ch.23. For attachment and perfection of security interests in non-documentary receivables see Ch.III; and incorporate investment securities, Ch.IV.

[2] The conversion of an equitable interest into a legal interest may also be regarded as an aspect of perfection in that it confers stronger rights against third parties, but some further act of perfection such as registration may still be required.

contract. The fact is that a real right enforceable only against the debtor is scarcely distinguishable in its effects from a mere personal right. A similar conundrum is posed by the sub-heading to Pt III of the Sale of Goods Act 1979, which speaks of "transfer of property as between seller and buyer." What sort of transfer can it be that is effective solely *inter partes*?

In fact, of course, even an unperfected security interest, like a transfer of property "as between seller and buyer," is likely to bind at least some categories of third party, in particular an unsecured non-insolvency creditor. The purpose of the concept is to demonstrate that the debtor cannot dispute the conferment of real rights on the creditor, and the consequent restriction on the debtor's own dominion over the asset, but that the same is not necessarily true of third parties, some of whom may, in the absence of perfection, be able to contend that the grant of the security has no impact on them.

The rules governing attachment apply equally whether the security interest is being granted to the creditor himself or a trustee on his behalf. The only difference in legal effect is that the legal owner (in the case of a legal mortgage) is the trustee, not the creditor, who is the beneficial owner of the mortgage and thus an equitable mortgagee. Mortgages and charges to secure an issue of bonds, notes or debentures (typically in the context of a securitisation) are invariably made in favour of security trustees for the holders, who hold their entitlements subject to the terms of the trust deed. This has the effect of co-ordinating the holders' fractional interests so that while they are the legal owners of the securities registered in their name their rights are enforced by the security trustee pursuant to the irrevocable authority conferred by the trust deed, not by the holders directly.

The ingredients of attachment

2–03 In order for a security interest to attach otherwise than by operation of law the following conditions must co-exist:

(1) There must be an agreement for security conforming to statutory formalities;

(2) The asset to be given in security must be identifiable;

(3) The debtor must have an interest in the asset or a power to give it in security;

(4) There must be some current obligation of debtor to creditor which the asset is designed to secure;

(5) Any contractual conditions for attachment must have been fulfilled;

(6) In the case of pledge, actual or constructive possession must be given to the creditor.

Each of these elements will now be examined in turn.

(1) *Agreement for security conforming to statutory formalities*

Mere unilateral action by the creditor against the asset does not suffice to **2–04** give him a security interest. There must be an agreement to create a security interest. The agreement may be to create a pledge, which as we will see requires delivery of actual or constructive possession, or a mortgage (which is a security transfer of ownership or of such lesser interest as the transferor possesses), or an equitable charge, where there is a mere incumbrance on the debtor's continuing ownership. Leaving aside pledge for the moment,[3] we can say that so long as the agreement is valid it suffices to create a security interest in equity so long as conditions (2) to (5) are fulfilled. If a mortgage is to take effect as a legal mortgage there must be an actual transfer by way of security[4] and compliance with any statutory requirements as to form, but these are not conditions of attachment of a security interest, merely additional steps needed to convert an equitable security into a legal security. An equitable charge, not being a transfer of ownership, rests in contract; there is therefore no distinction between a charge and an agreement for a charge.[5] The essential point is that there must be an agreement for security. A debtor who deposits deeds or documents of title with his bank by way of safe custody does not thereby create a charge, or any other form of security, in favour of his bank to secure his indebtedness, nor does he by implication confer on the bank the right to take unilateral action to bring a security interest into existence.[6] The creation of security by actual transfer is relatively simple; and in the case of intangibles the transfer may be effected in one of several different ways, depending on the nature of the intangible.[7] But where the creditor relies not on an actual transfer but on a mere agreement for security—as in the case of an equitable charge or an agreement for a mortgage—equity requires certain conditions to be satisfied before it will recognise the contract as giving rise to real rights. So we shall shortly return to the efficacy of the security agreement itself constituting an equitable security. This is not possible in the case of pledge, which depends on actual or constructive possession; mere agreement is not sufficient.[8] Nor can a contractual lien subsist without possession as against the debtor.[9]

An equitable charge or mortgage may be reinforced by a document or book entry which enables the chargee or mortgagee to perfect his security interest. For example, an equitable mortgage or charge of paper-based shares

---

[3] See section (6), below, para.2–10.
[4] Again, land is a special case. See above, para. 1–51.
[5] The position is otherwise in the case of a charge of land by way of legal mortgage. See below, para.1–51.
[6] The bank may, of course, have a lien by operation of law. A deposit of title deeds or a land certificate by way of security is no longer valid in the absence of an agreement in writing signed by or on behalf of both parties. See above, para.1–18, n.75.
[7] In particular, whether it is a documentary or a pure intangible. See para.1–44.
[8] See section (6), below, para.2–10.
[9] See section (6), below, para.2–10.

is usually accompanied by execution of a blank transfer in favour of the chargee or mortgagee which enables him, in the event of default, to be registered as the holder, whilst in the CREST system for dematerialised securities the same effect is produced by transfer into an escrow account which is a sub-account of the mortgagor under the control of an escrow agent.[10] But the blank transfer and the escrow account are not constitutive elements of the equitable mortgage or charge, which takes effect solely by virtue of the agreement.

A security interest cannot attach unless the agreement providing for it is valid and enforceable agreement.[11] So an agreement for a mortgage of land is devoid of legal effect, and thus incapable of creating a security interest in the land, unless it is in writing and the document incorporates all the agreed terms and is signed by or on behalf of both parties.[12] There is a similar requirement for a mortgage of a patent[13] or a registered trade mark,[14] However, an agreement for security which is fully binding but requires only that the consideration be executed[15] before it can be enforced is an inchoate security which, upon the consideration being executed, as by the making of the advance, becomes attached as from the time of the agreement.[16]

(2) *Identifiability of the subject matter*

2–05 A security interest cannot exist in an asset which is neither identified at the time of the security agreement nor identifiable as subsequently falling within its terms. The point may seem an obvious one but it is regularly overlooked.

The requirements for identification of the subject matter of tangible security are the same as those for the identification of goods as the subject of a contract of sale.[17] The asset to be given in security must either be identified

---

[10] See below, para.6–29.

[11] It is, of course, possible to have an agreement which is valid and unenforceable and thus a security interest which is valid and unenforceable, but with the enactment of the Law of Property (Miscellaneous Provisions) Act 1989, s.2 (see below, n.12) this is rarely likely to arise. In any event, we include enforceability as an element of attachment since a security interest which cannot be enforced in any manner is a theoretical abstraction. It is not without interest that Art.9 of the American Uniform Commercial Code requires as a condition of attachment that the security interest is enforceable against the debtor, which requires (*inter alia*) that the security agreement be in writing or otherwise authenticated. See §§ 9–203(b)(3)(a), – 102(7).

[12] Law of Property (Miscellaneous Provisions) Act 1989, s.2. Previously the agreement was merely required to be evidenced in writing signed by or on behalf of the party to be charged and, if not, was merely unenforceable, not wholly void. (Law of Property Act 1925, s.40), and even this requirement could be dispensed with if there was a sufficient act of part performance, an equitable doctrine abolished by the 1989 Act. See above, para.1–18, n.75.

[13] Patents Act 1977, s.30(6).

[14] Trade Marks Act 1994, s.24(3).

[15] See below, para.2–13.

[16] Whether this gives the secured creditor priority over a subsequent incumbrancer who acquired his interest while the first security interest was still inchoate is a separate question discussed below, para.2–13. See also Roy Goode, *Commercial Law* (2nd ed.), pp. 683–684.

[17] See Goode, *op. cit.*, pp. 214 *et seq.*, 246–247; *Benjamin's Sale of Goods* (6th ed.), paras 5–059 *et seq.*

by the security agreement or, in the case of fungibles,[18] ascertained subsequently as the result of an unconditional act of appropriation of the asset to the agreement. So a purported mortgage of 100 tons of potatoes amounts to no more than an agreement for a mortgage, and until a particular group of potatoes is earmarked to the agreement the creditor has no security interest of any kind. The same is true of an agreement to give security in an unidentified part of an identified bulk. A purported pledge of 12 cases of 1966 Chateau Montrose wine from a larger quantity of such wine in a warehouse is a mere agreement for a pledge, for without an act of appropriation we could not tell which cases are the subject matter of the security,[19] nor is the position altered where several creditors each hold purported pledges of undivided interests in a bulk to a quantity totalling the entirety of the bulk.[20]

However, in the case of contracts of sale the position was altered by the Sale of Goods (Amendment) Act 1995, which introduced new provisions into the Sale of Goods Act 1979 to make the prepaying buyer of goods forming part of a bulk a proportionate co-owner of the bulk.[21] One effect of this is to enhance the security of banks advancing money against bills of lading. Bulk cargo, such as oil and grain, is frequently shipped under a multiplicity of bills of lading without segregation as between one bill and another; indeed, such segregation would in most cases both be unnecessary and impracticable. Hence all that the bank as holder of an individual bill of lading previously acquired against the carrier was a personal right to delivery of a given quantity or volume of the cargo upon its arrival at the port of destination. Now, its advance of the purchase price results in the buyer becoming a co-owner of the bulk, so that the bank acquires a valid pledge of the buyer's share of the bulk. The provisions do not apply (and are not needed) where the contract itself identifies the goods, for which purpose a contract of sale of a given share of the bulk (as opposed to a stated number of units of the bulk) suffices at common law.

Security in intangible property remains governed by the common law **2–06** requirement of identification. It is, however, necessary to bear in mind that the problem of identification, whether in relation to tangibles or intangibles, arises only where the subject-matter of the transaction is susceptible to division into units capable in law of being separately owned and transferred.[22] In the case of goods this depends on whether they are capable of physical segregation. A charge of a share in a racehorse is a charge of a single, identified asset, for a racehorse cannot be divided without loss of identity and it is impossible to hold a share in a racehorse otherwise than by co-ownership of the racehorse itself. In the case of intangibles the test is not whether they are

---

[18] That is, consisting of two or more units which, in terms of the delivery or transfer obligation, are legally interchangeable.

[19] *Re London Wine Co. (Shippers) Ltd.* [1986] P.C.C. 121; also reproduced in R.M. Goode, *Proprietary Rights and Insolvency in Sales Transactions* (2nd ed.), Appendix.

[20] *ibid.*

[21] See Sale of Goods Act 1979, ss.20A and 20B.

[22] See Roy Goode, "Are Intangibles Fungible?" in *Themes in Comparative Law* (Peter Birks and Arianna Pretto, eds), pp. 97 *et seq*, to be reproduced with revisions [2003] L.M.C.L.Q. August.

capable of physical division (obviously they are not) but whether are legally divisible into units capable of separate ownership, as opposed to ownership in common. Much of the criticism of the decision of the Court of Appeal in *Hunter v Moss*[23] stems from a failure to appreciate that shares of the same issue are no more than fractions of a single asset, namely the share capital of the issuing company, and that on a sale or trust of the shares it is not possible to segregate the shares of the subject of the sale or trust from an interest in the remainder of the issuer. In short, such shares are not fungibles at all, they represent co-ownership of a single, identified asset.[24] The same applies to a credit balance in a bank account. The argument advanced by some writers that an assignment of £100 forming part of a £500 credit balance in the assignor's account is void for want of identification, is misconceived, because there is only one, indivisible asset, the credit balance, and the sole effect of the partial assignment is to make the assignee co-owner of the credit balance with the assignor. The widely misunderstood nature of fungibility in relation to shares is examined in more detail later.[25]

Precise identification of the asset at the time of the agreement is not required; it suffices that it is or becomes identifiable as falling within the terms of the security agreement. So a debtor can effectively charge *all* his existing and future book debts[26] or, indeed, all his assets.[27]

(3) *Debtor's interest or power to dispose*

2–07   The second prerequisite of attachment is that the debtor has a present interest in the asset intended to comprise the security or alternatively has, by virtue of some exception to the *nemo dat* rule, a present power to dispose of the asset or grant a charge over it. The debtor cannot normally give a valid security over someone else's asset, though there are exceptions to this rule, both at common law (*e.g.* where the owner has held out the debtor as having a power of disposal) and by statute (*e.g.* where the debtor is a mercantile agent).[28] But whilst the grant of security over future property does not create a security interest until the debtor has acquired an interest in the property, the security agreement does create an inchoate interest which is legally significant. This is one of the subtleties to which I have referred and it merits closer consideration. I shall return to it later.

It is not necessary for the debtor to be the owner of the asset given in security. Any interest suffices, including a security interest granted by the debtor's own debtor (so that the debtor is giving a sub-security to his own creditor),

---

[23] [1994] 1 W.L.R. 452, affirming the decision at first instance [1993] 1 W.L.R. 934.
[24] See further below, para.6–09.
[25] See below, para.6–09, and Goode, *loc.cit.*, above, n.22.
[26] *Tailby v Official Receiver* (1888) 13 App.Cas. 523.
[27] *Re Kelcey* [1899] 2 Ch. 530; *Syrett v Egerton* [1957] 3 All E.R. 331. The last case left open the question whether an assignment of all future property would be held contrary to public policy if its effect was to deprive the debtor of all means of support.
[28] Factors Act 1889, s.2. For non-assignable rights, see above, para.1–55.

and a possessory interest, for example, that enjoyed by a lessee in possession under an equipment lease. Of course, in the absence of some applicable exception to the *nemo dat* rule the debtor cannot grant by way of security an interest greater than that which he himself holds.

(4) *Subsistence of current obligation*

No security interest can exist in an asset at any time when there is no current obligation of debtor to creditor which is secured on the asset. Security may be given for a past advance, and can then attach on the making of the agreement for security, but if it is for an advance to be made after execution of the security agreement then until it has been made the creditor has merely an inchoate security interest, of much the same kind as that of a purchaser of land on exchange of contracts who has not yet paid the purchase price, the interest relating back to the time of the agreement once payment has been made.[29] As a corollary, a security interest can never be greater in quantum than the value of the debtor's current obligation. Suppose that the debtor company mortgages its premises to secure a loan of £10,000. The premises may be worth £500,000, but the creditor's security interest is still no more than £10,000, for on payment of this sum (if we ignore interest) the debtor is entitled to have the mortgage discharged. The same applies to a charge to secure a fluctuating balance, *e.g.* an overdraft. Unless there is a debit balance on the account, the chargee, even if holding a charge by way of legal mortgage, has no security interest.

2–08

(5) *Fulfilment of contractual conditions for attachment*

Attachment does not take place unless the conditions for attachment specified in the security agreement have been fulfilled. This does not, however, imply that the parties may, consistently with the equitable rules for creation of a security interest by agreement, stipulate any event they choose as producing attachment. On the contrary, where the designated event is a mere contingency—an event which may or may not occur—then unless the contingency is simply the debtor's acquisition of an interest in the asset the agreement will not by itself be effective to create a security interest, even on the occurrence of the contingency.[30] The rule is otherwise where the agreement provides for the grant of security on a specified date or after the lapse of a stated period or on the occurrence of some other future event which is bound to occur, or on the debtor's acquisition of property falling within the description in the security agreement, for in all these cases attachment of the

2–09

---

[29] *Rayner v Preston* (1881) 18 Ch.D 1, *per* James L.J. at 13; *Shaw v Foster* (1872) L.R. 5 H.L. 322; *Lysaght v Edwards* (1876) 2 Ch.D 499.
[30] See above, para.1–76; below, para.2–15.

security interest is not dependent on a contingency other than (in the case of security in future property) the debtor's acquisition of the property.

The rule concerning contingent interests does not apply to a provision in an agreement for the conversion of a floating security, such as a floating charge, into a fixed security; the parties are free to designate any event they choose as causing the charge to crystallise and fasten on the assets then owned or subsequently acquired by the chargor. This is because a floating charge is not a mere contract for future security; on the contrary it creates a present security in a fund of assets.[31]

(6) *In the case of pledge or contractual lien, delivery of possession*

2–10   The sixth requirement for attachment is confined to pledges and contractual liens. A pledge requires delivery of possession; an agreement for a pledge which is not accompanied or followed by delivery of possession is a mere contract conferring no real right on the intended pledgee.[32] The delivery of possession to the creditor may be actual or constructive. A pledge of goods may be created by delivery to the creditor of the documents of title to the goods.[33] Another common form of constructive possession arises where a third party holding physical possession on behalf of the debtor agrees to attorn to (*i.e.* hold possession for) the creditor instead. There is authority to indicate that even the debtor in possession may create an effective pledge by declaring that he holds the goods to the creditor's order,[34] in which case his possession is in law the creditor's possession. Though this was never accepted in case law in the United States,[35] it is consistent with long-established case law on delivery and receipt in the sale of goods[36] and with decisions upholding continuance of a pledge where the pledgee redelivers the goods to the pledgor to hold on the pledgee's behalf, *e.g.* under a trust receipt.[37]

A third party in physical possession may agree to attorn to the creditor subject to discharge of a lien or other interest held by the third party itself. For example, where the debtor's goods are held in a warehouse and on the debtor's instructions the warehouseman undertakes to the creditor to hold them on the latter's behalf subject to discharge of the warehouseman's lien for warehousing charges, the pledge is inchoate and becomes operative as soon as the lien is discharged. In such a case the debtor's bankruptcy before discharge of the lien does not affect the efficacy of the pledge, for the goods

---

[31] See below, para.4–03.
[32] *Dublin City Distillery Ltd. v Doherty* [1914] A.C. 823.
[33] See Roy Goode, *Commercial Law* (2nd ed.) p. 700.
[34] *Martin v Reid* (1862) 11 C.B.N.S. 730; M*eyerstein v Barber* (1866) L.R. 2 C.P. 38; *Dublin City Distillery Co. Ltd. v Doherty* [1914] A.C. 823, *per* Lord Parker of Waddington C.J. at 852; *Askrigg Pty. Ltd. v Student Guild of the Curtin University of Technology* (1989) 18 N.S.W.L.R. 738. However, in policy terms the US approach is preferable.
[35] See Grant Gilmore, *Security Interests in Personal Property*, §14.2.21
[36] *Michael Gerson (Leasing) Ltd. v Wilkinson* [2001] Q.B. 514; *Marvin v Wallace* (1856) E. & B. 726.
[37] *North Western Bank v Poynter* [1895] A.C. 56; *Re David Allester Ltd.* [1922] 2 Ch. 211.

have been subject to a continuous possessory interest, first in favour of the warehouseman and then, without any interval, in favour of the pledgee.[38]

Similar considerations apply to a contractual lien, which differs from a pledge only that it arises from the creditor's possession of goods which were delivered to him for some purpose other than security.[39]

The security agreement

We must now look more closely at the first of the prerequisites of attach-   **2–11**
ment, a security transfer or agreement. If the security has actually been given, by pledge or mortgage, no problem arises. My concern is with the effect of an agreement for security. At this point, it will occur to the property lawyer to ask: how can a mere *agreement* for security, as opposed to an actual transfer by way of security, give rise to an immediate security interest? The answer at common law was quite clear: it could not. The creation of proprietary rights, whether absolute or by way of security, required a completed transfer, by deed or delivery of possession, except where the contract was for the sale of goods[40] or related to potential property, such as future crops or identified, future young of identified livestock, etc.[41] Save in these cases a mere agreement to transfer constituted at best a contract, creating a mere obligation, not a proprietary right.

Equity, however, treating as done that which ought to be done, considers that the agreement to give security takes effect as an immediate security interest if this is consistent with the agreement between the parties and the subject-matter is identifiable. This is subject to the qualification that the security interest remains inchoate, or incomplete, until the consideration is executed. That is to say, the creditor cannot enforce his security against the debtor, or assert it against third parties, until he has actually advanced his money; his commitment to advance it does not suffice, for equity does not decree specific performance of a contract to borrow or lend money[42] and the court will therefore not treat the debtor as one who could be compelled to execute the security instrument.[43] But once the creditor has advanced his money the contract ceases to be executory and equity treats the transfer as perfected, so that the matter is no longer considered to rest in contract and specific performance

---

[38] The same principle applies to a buyer's rights to identified goods subject to a lien. See R.M. Goode, *Proprietary Rights and Insolvency in Sales Transactions* (2nd ed.), pp. 13–14.

[39] See above.

[40] This common law exception, now embodied in s.17 of the Sale of Goods Act 1979, is of long standing. See *Cochrane v Moore* (1890) 25 Ch.D. 57, *per* Fry L.J. at 70–71.

[41] *Grantham v Hawley* (1615) Hob. 132.

[42] *Rogers v Challis* (1859) 27 Beav. 175.

[43] It is only in this sense that the susceptibility of the contract to specific performance—a requirement described in somewhat infelicitous terms by Lord Westbury in *Holroyd v Marshall* (1862) 10 H.L.Cas. 161 and subsequently explained away in *Tailby v Official Receiver*, above— is relevant to the recognition of the security interest.

in its narrow sense[44] is unnecessary. Perfection of the transfer by making of the advance takes effect as from the date of the security agreement,[45] in much the same way as a charge over future property has retrospective effect once the property has been acquired.[46]

In order for the existence of the security interest to be consistent with the agreement between the parties the following conditions must be satisfied:

(a) The agreement must manifest an intention to confer a security interest on the creditor, not a mere contractual right[47];

(b) It must reflect the intention of the parties that the interest should attach to the asset immediately or on the debtor's acquisition of an interest in it or at an agreed time or on the occurrence of some future event which is certain to occur, and that attachment is not to be dependent on some contingent event (other than the debtor's acquisition) such as the execution of a security instrument on demand by the creditor[48];

(c) The asset over which the security is claimed must be shown to fall within the description in the security agreement—a not very stringent requirement, amounting, as we have seen, to little more than that ascertainment of the subject matter of the security must be apparent from the terms of the security agreement itself and must not be made to depend on some act of appropriation by the debtor.

Security over future property

2–12 At common law, an agreement to give security over future property created no proprietary rights even after acquisition of the property by the debtor. This was consistent with the common law rule that only an immediate transfer would do. The common law therefore usually required some new act of transfer, after acquisition by the debtor, to vest a proprietary interest in the creditor.

---

[44] *i.e.* an order compelling performance of an executory contract. Though secured in equity because the contract has become executed, the creditor whose debtor has promised to execute a security instrument is entitled to specific performance in its broader sense of compelling performance of any contractually stipulated act, even though it is not necessary for the establishment of his proprietary rights but merely perfects rights already acquired in equity. See Jones and Goodhart, *Specific Performance* (2nd ed.), p.1, n.1, and, for the two meanings of specific performance, I.C.F. Spry, *Equitable Remedies* (6th ed.), p. 51.

[45] See *Rayner v Preston* (1881) 18 Ch.D. 1, *per* James L.J. at 13, when discussing the position of the purchaser under a contract of sale of land.

[46] See below, para.2–13.

[47] *Palmer v Carey* [1926] A.C. 703; *Swiss Bank Corp. Ltd. v Lloyd's Bank Ltd.* [1980] 2 All E.R. 419, affirmed [1981] 2 All E.R. 449. See further above, para.1–76.

[48] See above, para.1–76 and below, para.2–18.

Had the common law rule retained its full vigour, financing against future assets would have remained seriously inhibited, for the creditor has no ready way of knowing that his debtor has acquired a new asset, and the debtor may become insolvent before the creditor has the chance of obtaining the performance of the required new act of transfer.

Fortunately, equity came to the rescue. In the great case of *Holroyd v Marshall*,[49] machinery in a mill was mortgaged upon terms requiring the mortgagor to hold the machinery for the mortgagee, with liberty to substitute new machinery, which would then itself become subject to the mortgage, together with any additional machinery brought on to the premises. It was held that the mortgage attached to new and additional machinery from the moment of its acquisition by the debtor, without any new act of transfer, and had priority over the claims of an execution creditor. Though the principle had been established well before, the authoritative effect of *Holroyd v Marshall* as a decision of the highes tribunal has been to place a most powerful security device in the hands of a creditor, who can literally secure a monopoly of the debtor's non-purchase-money financing[50] by taking security over all his property, present and future. Since it is a common misunderstanding that security over future property is necessarily a floating security, it is worth emphasising that the interest upheld in *Holroyd v Marshall* was a fixed security interest, not a floating mortgage.

As from what time does a security interest in future property attach?

We now come to the crucial question, when does the security interest in future property attach? This seems clear enough. We have already seen—indeed, it is almost too obvious to require stating—that a security interest cannot attach in an asset before the debtor has acquired an interest in it (we exclude for this purpose cases where the debtor has a power to give security over someone else's property). In addition, *Holroyd v Marshall* tells us that, unless the arrangement otherwise provides, the debtor's acquisition is sufficient without more. For example, a debtor executes a charge in favour of X over future property on April 1 and acquires a new asset on August 1. The charge attaches on August 1. There appears to be no problem. But suppose that on May 1 the debtor had executed a second charge, in favour of Y, over the same classes of future asset. Who wins, X or Y? The answer is simple enough: X wins, as he is the first in time. The problem is to know how this result is arrived at, because, of course, the security interest does not attach until the debtor has acquired the asset, so that the competing interests of X and Y attach simultaneously. How, then, does X get priority?

2–13

---

[49] (1862) 10 H.L.Cas. 191.
[50] The position is otherwise as to purchase-money finance, where the second financier who proceeds in proper order can usually be sure of obtaining priority for his purchase-money security interest even though it is later in time. See below, paras 5–62 *et seq*.

Here we have a striking example of the intellectual subtlety of the common law. In a number of cases the courts have ruled that whilst, in a sense, an agreement for security over after-acquired property cannot attach to that property prior to acquisition, yet the agreement constitutes a *present* security.[51] In other words, it creates an inchoate security interest which is waiting for the asset to be acquired so that it can fasten on to the asset but which, upon acquisition of the asset, *takes effect as from the date of the security agreement*. Acquisition of the asset produces the situation in which the security is deemed to have continuously attached to the asset from the time of execution of the security agreement. This may seem metaphysical but has its counterpart in other branches of law. Take the case of the unborn child. Until birth, a child has no separate legal existence and no action can be brought on its behalf. But once born it acquires the right to sue even for injuries caused to it before birth.[52] Legal existence is, so to speak, attached to the child at birth as from the moment of its conception.[53] So also with a security interest in future property.

A corollary is that once value has been given for the grant of the security, each asset coming in under the after-acquired property clause is deemed to have been given for new value. Let us take an extreme case. A lends B £1 and takes security over B's after-acquired property. B acquires a new asset to the value of £1,000. A has security over that asset for the £1 advance. B acquires a further asset, to the value of £100,000. The further asset is likewise deemed to have been charged to A for new value. A can go on stacking up more and more security without injecting any additional funds. Indeed, the expansion of his security is not halted even by B's bankruptcy. A new asset falling in after the commencement of B's bankruptcy becomes instantly caught by A's security interest,[54] provided that the consideration for the security was already executed before the commencement of the bankruptcy.[55] Indeed, we can go further. Even the debtor's discharge from bankruptcy does not affect the force and priority of the after-acquired property clause. However, the value of the security interest can never exceed £1 and accrued interest.

2–14   A good example of the principle, and of the underlying conceptual rationale, is *Re Lind*[56]:

"L assigned his expectant share in his mother's estate to the N. Society by way of mortgage to secure an advance, and subsequently executed a further mortgage of the same expectancy to A, subject to the first mortgage. L later became bankrupt, and eventually received his discharge. He then assigned the same expectant share to the I. Syndicate. His mother then

---

[51] See *Holroyd v Marshall*, above, *per* Lord Chelmsford at 220; *Tailby v Official Receiver* (1888) 13 App.Cas. 523, *per* Lord Watson at 533.
[52] *Watt v Rama* [1972] V.R. 353. There is no reported English decision, but the right of action is expressly given by the Congenital Disabilities (Civil Liabilities) Act 1976.
[53] *Kelly v Gregory*, 125 N.Y.S. (2d) 696 (1953).
[54] *Re Reis* [1904] 2 K.B. 769; *Re Lind* [1915] 2 Ch. 345.
[55] *Re Collins* [1925] Ch. 556.
[56] See above.

died. It was held that the first two mortgages were unaffected by the bankruptcy or the discharge and therefore had priority over the third mortgage, even though the asset had not fallen into possession until after the discharge."

Particularly significant are the words of Bankes, L.J.:

"It is true that the security was not enforceable until the property came into existence, but nevertheless the security was there, the assignor was the bare trustee of the assignee to receive and hold the property for him when it came into existence."[57]

This principle of continuous existence applies equally to the winding up of a company. So an after-acquired property clause in a charge given by a company is effective to catch property coming into the company's hands after the commencement of the winding up of the company despite s.127 of the Insolvency Act 1986. That section (re-enacting prior legislation) renders void any disposition of a company's property made after the commencement of the winding up. If security in future property had no inchoate existence prior to the acquisition of the asset, then a post-liquidation acquisition would fall foul of s.127. But once it is seen that the security interest relates back to the time of the security agreement, any problem with s.127 disappears. I should add the cautionary comment that to the best of my knowledge this point has not yet arisen for decision by the courts.[58] Nevertheless, the conclusion must, in my view, follow from the principle.

Re Lind, and the earlier decision in Re Reis[59] which it applied, have been trenchantly criticised by Mr Paul Matthews, who argues that it runs counter to the policy of bankruptcy law.[60] In so far as the principle in Re Lind allows the chargee to increase his security margin during the six months run-up to liquidation, the point is in my view well taken, and supports the criticism which I have myself expressed elsewhere.[61] But an enhancement of the security margin outside this period seems to be unobjectionable. The creditor bargained at the outset for security over future property; he ought not to be deprived of the basis of his bargain. He is entitled to say that in asserting security rights over future property without putting in fresh value he is not taking out of the estate a penny more than he put into it, for without the debtor's acceptance of the after-acquired property clause the money would never have been advanced in the first place.

---

[57] [1915] 2 Ch. 345 at 374.
[58] It is, however, well established that exercise of a power of sale by a mortgagee or receiver after commencement of the winding up does not contravene the section, for to the extent that the asset is subject to the security interest it is not the property of the company at all. See *Sowman v David Samuel Trust Ltd.* [1978] 1 All E.R. 616, *per* Goulding J. at 623; *Re Margaret Pty. Ltd.* (1984) 9 A.C.L.R. 269.
[59] [1904] 2 K.B. 769.
[60] The effect of bankruptcy upon mortgages of future property [1981] 1 L.M.C.L.Q. 40.
[61] "The Death of Insolvency Law" (1980) 1 Co. Law 123 at 125–126.

Equitable security distinguished from mere contract

2–15   An agreement for a mortgage or charge is treated in equity as a security interest only if it is not subject to any contingency other than the debtor's acquisition of an interest in the asset.[62] An agreement to give security on any other contingency, whether the contingency be a demand by the creditor to do so, default by the debtor or the occurrence of some other uncertain event, is a mere contract, not an equitable charge.[63] Even on the occurrence of the designated event the security interest will not attach in equity merely by virtue of the earlier agreement, for in order to be specifically enforceable so as to constitute an equitable security the agreement must be supported by an executed consideration, *i.e.* the making of the advance; whereas an unqualified agreement for security over future property creates an inchoate security, so that a payment made on or after the agreement constitutes value in equity, an agreement for security contingent on a future uncertain event is a mere contract. It follows that a security interest cannot attach by virtue of that agreement even on the occurrence of the designated event. There must be either a completed security transaction, by pledge or mortgage, or a new security agreement accompanied or followed by the payment of money; and in the latter case, the security interest will be limited to the amount so paid. It is for this reason that provisions for equal and rateable security in negative pledge clauses are of little value as security devices.[64]

The floating charge is a special case, standing midway between a mere contract for future security and an attached security interest. The floating charge is a present security, not a mere agreement for security on a contingency,[65] but it is security in a shifting fund of assets, not in the specific assets from time to time comprising the fund.[66]

---

[62] See above, para.1–76 and below.

[63] *Re Jackson & Bassford Ltd.* [1906] 2 Ch. 467; *Re Gregory Love & Co. Ltd.* [1916] 1 Ch. 203; *Williams v Burlington Investments Ltd.* (1977) 121 S.J. 424. It is therefore not registrable under s.395 of the Companies Act 1985. In general a contingent agreement for security, being a mere contract and not a security interest, has no priority effect, and a subsequent incumbrancer whose interest is created after the contingent agreement and before the grant of security pursuant to that agreement has priority. However, an agreement to give a charge over unregistered land if so requested by the creditor is registrable as an estate contract under the Land Charges Act 1972, and the House of Lords has held that this suffices to give a subsequent charge made pursuant to the agreement priority over an intervening incumbrance even though the agreement, being for contingent security, does not itself create a security interest (*Williams v Burlington Investments Ltd.*, above).

[64] See above, para.1–77. In *Williams v Burlington Investments Ltd.*, above, it was argued that an agreement for the execution of a charge on demand by the creditor gave rise to an equitable security when the demand was made. The House, while not finding it necessary to rule on the point, appears to have treated the proposition with appropriate scepticism.

[65] *The Annangel Glory* [1988] 1 Lloyd's Rep. 45. In the light of the view expressed by Lord Millett in *Re Cosslett (Contractors) Ltd.* [1998] Ch. 495 that a lien on sub-freights is merely a personal right to divert the sub-freights to the lienee (see above, para.1–25), the actual decision in *The Annangel Glory* is now open to question. But it correctly applies the principle that a floating charge is a present security, not a mere agreement to provide security upon a contingency.

[66] See above, para.1–10; below, para.4–03.

2. PERFECTION OF A SECURITY INTEREST

Nature of perfection

When a security interest attaches it becomes enforceable against the debtor **2–16** himself. But the existence of the security interest will not necessarily be known to a third party who is himself proposing to acquire an interest in the asset. To safeguard such a third party the law usually requires the secured party to perfect his security by some form of public notice or other act (*e.g.* possession) designed to bring the security interest to the notice of subsequent purchasers or incumbrancers. Perfection is not a necessary step to render the security enforceable against the debtor himself, for of course as the grantor of the security interest he needs no notice of it.[67]

The concept of perfection as rooted in notice is somewhat blurred by the distinction which English law draws between legal and equitable interests. The latter may be displaced by transfer of the legal title to a bona fide purchaser for value without notice. Thus the conversion of an equitable interest into a legal interest does represent an aspect of perfection, though not displacing any separate perfection requirement such as registration. But in the case of certain types of asset, notably registrable ship and aircraft mortgages and intellectual property rights, a legal interest is obtained only by registration,[68] which thus simultaneously elevates the status of the quondam equitable interest and perfects it as fully as it can be perfected.

Perfection does not guarantee priority over subsequent incumbrancers; that is a matter to be resolved by priority rules we shall examine later. All that perfection of a security interest does is to give maximum efficacy to the security interest. So an unperfected security interest will usually be invalid against subsequent incumbrancers and against unsecured execution and insolvency creditors regardless of any other priority rule; and a perfected security interest will bind subsequent incumbrancers and execution and insolvency creditors unless displaced by a particular priority rule.

There are no fewer than six (sometimes overlapping) modes of perfection **2–17** of a security interest, namely:

(1) attachment without further act;

(2) in the case of goods and documents,[69] possession;

(3) registration of the security interest as such[70] in one or more statutory registers;

---

[67] A remarkable exception to this rule is to be found in the Bills of Sale Act (1878) Amendment Act 1882, s.8 of which renders an unregistered security bill of sale void as to the security even as against the debtor himself.

[68] See above, para.1–12 and below, para.2–30.

[69] *i.e.* documents of title, negotiable instruments and negotiable securities.

[70] As opposed to registration of securities transfers. See para.2–19.

(4)   in the case of a security assignment or charge of a debt or of a beneficial interest in a fund,[71] notice of the security interest to the account debtor[72] or trustees or other legal owners of the fund;

(5)   in the case of a mortgage of securities or of a debt or fund,[73] novation by registration of the mortgagee as holder of the securities as through the transfer of the debt or fund to an account in the name of the mortgagee; and

(6)   in the case of security over a fund, attornment by the fund holder.

Mode (3) applies both to tangibles and to intangibles. Modes (4) to (6) are confined to intangibles. These raise special considerations and are not discussed further in the present chapter but are examined in Chapter III in relation to receivables and in Chapter VI in relation to investment securities.

At this stage we shall concern ourselves only with perfection by mere attachment and perfection by registration and possession. In certain cases it may be necessary to perfect by more than one method. So while possession is usually an alternative to registration of a security interest in goods[74] there are some cases in which even a possessory security interest has still to be perfected by registration.[75] Similarly where a company mortgages its book debts, the perfection by notice of assignment to the debtors does not dispense with the need for registration under s.395 of the Companies Act 1985. Again, company charges which are registrable in specialist registries concerned with particular kinds of asset, such as land, ships and aircraft, will usually be registrable also in the Companies Registry.[76]

Perfection by mere attachment

2–18   There are various cases in which attachment suffices by itself to perfect a security interest without any further step. Typically this arises where the debtor is a company and the security interest is outside (1) the *numerus clausus* of security interests prescribed by s.396 of the Companies Act 1985; and (2) the scope of the rule in *Dearle v Hall* dealing with the priority of

---

[71] If the mortgage or charge is not by a beneficiary of his beneficial interest but is a mortgage or charge of the fund itself by the trustees or other legal owners of the fund, notice must be given to the bank or other person with whom the fund is held.

[72] *i.e.* the debtor's debtor.

[73] *i.e.* by the trustees or other legal owners of the fund. It would be unusual for the mortgage of a beneficial interest to take place by novation.

[74] *i.e.* as a bill of sale where the security interest is granted by an unincorporated debtor or as a charge registrable under s.395 of the Companies Act 1985 where the chargor is a company.

[75] For example, a first legal mortgage of land protected by deposit of the title deeds (Land Registration Act 2002, s.4(1)(g)) or a pledge of goods established by the debtor's written attornment (see above, para.2–10), which, if the pledge is given by an individual, is registrable under the Bills of Sale Acts 1878 and 1882 and, if given by a company, is registrable under s.396(1)(c) of the Companies Act 1985 as a charge created or evidenced by an instrument which, if created by an individual, would be registrable as a bill of sale.

[76] See below.

successive assignments of a chose in action. Into this category of perfection by attachment fall, for example:

(1) oral fixed[77] mortgages or charges of goods other than ships or aircraft[78];

(2) fixed charges on shares in a company, even where it is a subsidiary of the debtor;

(3) fixed charges on imported goods (other than ships or aircraft) which if granted by an individual would be exempt from registration as a bill of sale;

(4) "charge-backs", *e.g.* mortgages or charges of a bank deposit in favour of the bank itself (which have now been held conceptually possible)[79] since the bank, by virtue of being its own debtor, controls the account, so that nothing further needs to be done to perfect its interest.[80]

There is a further case where the same act suffices for attachment and perfection, namely the pledge, where the delivery of possession required to produce attachment of the security interest[81] also perfects it. But possession is also an independent mode of perfecting an unregistered non-possessory mortgage or charge.[82]

Perfection by registration

Various categories of charge created by companies are registrable under s.395 **2–19** of the Companies Act 1985.[83] Perfection by registration is sometimes complicated by the need to perfect in a specialist register in addition to registration under the Companies Act.[84] Thus, any charge by a company must be registered both in the Companies Registry and in the Land Charges Registry as a Class C(i) mortgage where it is over unregistered land and is a puisne mortgage, that is, one which is not protected by deposit of the title deeds[85]

---

[77] A floating charge constitutes a distinct category of registrable security under s.396 of the Companies Act 1985.

[78] Charges over ships and aircraft constitute distinct heads of registrable charge within s.396.

[79] See above, para.1–40; below, para.3–12.

[80] The bank may exercises various interim remedies, such as segregating the account or placing a stop on it and withholding payment to the customer, but since the bank can neither sue itself nor sell a right to do so the only way of obtaining payment from the security is by a transfer from the deposit account to the account recording the indebtedness of the debtor or a third party for whose liability the cash collateral was given as security. This involves the same mechanism as a contractual set-off. See further below, para.3–12.

[81] See above, paras 1–43 *et seq.*, 2–10.

[82] See below.

[83] See below paras 2–21 *et seq.*

[84] As to the specialist registers, see below, para.2–30.

[85] Land Charges Act 1972, s.2(4)(i).

or in the Land Registry where it is a charge over registered land[86] or is a first legal mortgage of an unregistered estate protected by deposit of the title deeds[87]; and a charge by a company over a ship or aircraft must be registered both in the Companies Registry and the ship's port of registry[88] or the registry of aircraft mortgages,[89] as the case may be.[90]

Entirely distinct from the statutory regimes for registration of charges is the requirement for transfers of shares in a company to be registered in the company's register, or in the case of uncertificated securities, in the CREST register,[91] for legal title to pass. The register is a membership and shareholding register, not an ownership register, though entry on it is the best *prima facie* evidence of ownership and is a prerequisite of legal title. It follows that a person is not registered as mortgagee; indeed, the company is neither obliged nor empowered to receive notice of any assignment or trust, which includes the trust of an equity of redemption.[92] The mortgagee, on registration of the transfer to him, is simply shown as the new member of the company and holder of the shares. This perfects his title as legal mortgagee by novation. A mere chargee, not being a transferee, cannot get on to the register except by converting himself into a mortgagee by transfer. Charges and off-register mortgages take effect in equity only.

Perfection by possession

2–20　This mode of perfection is, of course, available only where the subject matter of the security is capable of possession, *i.e.* pledgeable. Where a security interest has been perfected by possession but the creditor later loses possession the security interest becomes unperfected unless it has meanwhile been perfected by another means, *e.g.* registration. For example, a written chattel mortgage may normally be perfected by possession without registration under the Bills of Sale Acts,[93] but if possession is later lost before registration of the bill of sale[94] the interest becomes unperfected and therefore vulnerable to a competing security interest. A pledge or mortgage of rights embodied in a document of title, a negotiable instrument or a negotiable security is per-

---

[86] Land Registration Act 2002, s.4.
[87] *ibid.*
[88] Merchant Shipping Act 1894, s.33.
[89] Civil Aviation Act 1982, s.86; Mortgaging of Aircraft Order 1972 (SI 1972/1268, as amended SI 1981/611 and SI 1986/2001), made under s.16 of the Civil Aviation Act 1968 but having effect under the 1982 Act by virtue of s.17(2)(b) of the Interpretation Act 1978.
[90] The Law Commission has issued a consultation paper proposing that registration under s.395 of the Companies Act 1985 should cease to be a perfection requirement as regards security interests registrable in these specialist registries. See *Registration of Company Charges and Security Intersts over Property other than Land*, paras 4–199 *et seq.*
[91] See below, para.6–05.
[92] Companies Act 1985, s.360. See below, para.5–08, n.21.
[93] But see above.
[94] By which time the seven days allowed for registration is likely to have expired, necessitating an application for an extension of time.

fected by negotiation, that is, delivery with any necessary endorsement, and the debtor or other obligor may disregard a notice of assignment.[95]

3. REGISTRATION UNDER S.395 OF THE COMPANIES ACT 1985

Registrable charges

S.396 of the Companies Act 1985 lists the categories of charge by a company   **2-21**
which require registration under s.395.[96] The list includes charges on land, book debts,[97] ships and aircraft; floating charges; and charges created or evidenced by an instrument which, if executed by an individual, would require registration as a bill of sale. The time allowed for lodgement of the documents is 21 days from the date of creation of the charge, *i.e.* 21 days from execution of the charge instrument, regardless whether there is at that time any property to which it can attach.[98]

I do not wish to spend more than a moment or two discussing what is registrable, for with a few qualifications the list is fairly self-explanatory.[99] There are, however, four important points to be made about registrability. First, even leaving aside the fact that only charges, not title reservation agreements, are registrable, the list is seriously inadequate, omitting as it does numerous important categories of collateral, including debts other than book debts,[1] charges over future income under PFI projects, insurance policies, and contingent debts. Secondly, charges by an English company are registrable even if created outside the United Kingdom and comprising property situated outside the United Kingdom. Thirdly, the effect of s.409 is that a charge by an oversea company on property in England is registrable under s.395 if the company has an established place of business in England, even if in breach of the Act the place of business has not been registered. This is one of the many important points established by *Slavenburg's* case,[2] in which Lloyd J., also held that even if the overseas company has no assets in England at the

---

[95] *Bence v Shearman* [1898] 2 Ch. 582.
[96] See generally Gerard McCormack, *Registration of Company Charges*.
[97] But see below, para.3–25, text and n.62, below.
[98] *Esberger & Son v Capital & Counties Bank* [1913] 2 Ch. 366; *Independent Automatic Sales Ltd. v Knowles & Foster* [1962] 3 All E.R. 27.
[99] For a detailed examination see R. R. Pennington, *Company Law* (8th ed.), pp. 604, *et seq.*; and the Law Commission's Consultation Paper, *Registration of Security Interests: Company Charges and Property other than Land* (Law Com. Cons. Paper No. 164, June 2002), paras 2.26, 3.12–3.15.
[1] Usually a charge on a bank deposit will not be considered a book debt (*Re Brightlife Ltd.* [1987] Ch. 200; *Re Permanent Houses (Holdings) Ltd* [1988] B.C.L.C. 563; *Northern Bank Ltd. v Ross* [1991] B.C.L.C. 504), though this is not necessarily true in every case (*Re Permanent Houses (Holdings) Ltd.*, above. As to shares, see below, paras 6–28, 6–80.
[2] *NV Slavenburg's Bank v Intercontinental Natural Resources Ltd.* [1980] 1 All E.R. 955. For a comment on the case and on the memorandum by the Law Society's Standing Committee on Company Law, see A.J. Boyle (1981) 2 Co. Law. 218.

time it grants the charge, its subsequent acquisition of an asset in England within the scope of the charge renders the charge retrospectively registrable within the prescribed 21–day period (which may by then have run out!) or such further period as may be allowed by the court. The difficulties created by the *Slavenburg* decision, and the defects in what is now s.409 of the Companies Act 1985 (formerly s.106 of the Companies Act 1948) which that decision highlights, were admirably set out in a paper by the Law Society's Standing Committee on Company Law[3] and have since been examined in detail by the Company Law Review Steering Group as part of its reviews of the legislative treatment of oversea companies[4] and by the Law Commission.[5] I shall not say any more about them here. Fourthly, there is considerable doubt about the application of the registration provisions to charges granted by a trustee company. One view is that these are not registrable at all: not against the trustee company, since it is not the beneficial owner of the charged assets, and not against the beneficial owner, since it has not created the charge. Reinforcing this conclusion is the fact in relation to unsecured creditors in a winding up the sanction of invalidity for non-registration has no meaning, since the charged assets, being trust assets, could not be claimed by the liquidator anyway. Another view is that a trustee company, which unlike a bare trustee has management powers, is to be considered the full owner of the charged assets and that the charge should therefore be registered against it. In practice, chargees usually do register against the trustee company *ex abundante cautela*. The Law Commission has provisionally proposed legislative provisions requiring registration against the trustee company but with a note in the register that it holds the charged property as trustee.[6]

What I do want to discuss at this point are a number of questions relating to the effect of registration of charges in general and floating charges in particular.

Registration is a perfection requirement

2–22   At the risk of restating the obvious, I should like to emphasise that registration is a *perfection* requirement, which has to be complied with in order to make the charge effective against a liquidator, administrator[7] and creditors.

---

[3] Reproduced in (1981) 78 L.S.Gaz. 921.

[4] *The Strategic Framework*, Ch.5.6; *Reforming the Law Concerning Oversea Companies*; *Modern Company Law for a Competitive Economy: Final Report*, Vol. I.

[5] *Registration of Company Charges and Security Interests over Property other than Land*, paras 3.33 *et seq.* See also, for a critical review of the present law, Gerard McCormack, *Registration of Company Charges*, Ch.8. Companies House maintains a "Slavenburg" register of unregistered companies that have a registered place of business in England, Wales and Scotland.

[6] *loc. cit.*, above, n.5, paras 5.65, 5.75.

[7] *i.e.* an administrator appointed under an administration order made pursuant to Pt II of the Insolvency Act 1986.

By "creditors" is meant subsequent creditors[8] having an interest in the charged assets, and thus a *locus standi* to complain of want of perfection, *i.e.* secured and execution creditors and lienees and, if but only if the company has gone into liquidation or administration, unsecured creditors. Registration is not a requirement for *attachment*; an unregistered charge is good against the company itself, so long as it is not in winding up or administration. Nor is registration a priority point.[9] Priority of competing charges is governed by the common law rules previously described, not by the order of registration. So an intending lender who advances money to a company in reliance on a clear search should not assume that he is protected; there may well be an earlier charge granted within the preceding 21 days that has not yet been registered. Unfortunately there is no provision in the Companies Act comparable to that of the property legislation by which protection is given to one who makes a pre-completion search and then completes his own transaction within 14 days. Similarly, registration does not guarantee priority against subsequent interests. This is so even where registration constitutes notice of the charge, for notice is not in all cases a determinant of priority.[10]

Registration as notice[11]

It is commonly said that registration of a charge constitutes notice to the out-   **2–23**
side world. But this formulation raises three questions: notice of what? by what means? and to whom?

Of what facts does registration constitute notice?

(1) *Registration of a charge is not notice of its contents*

It is well established that registration of a charge, though notice of the exis-   **2–24**
tence of the charge,[12] is not notice of the contents of the instrument of charge,[13] despite the fact that a party searching the register and obtaining details of a registered charge is then entitled to inspect a copy of the charge

---

[8] Prior creditors are obviously not prejudiced by want of registration and it is submitted that they are not entitled to invoke s.395 even if having an interest in doing so, *e.g.* where their security ranks after the unregistered charge. There is no English authority on the point but the proposition is supported by an old American case. See *United States v New Orleans and Ohio Railroad Co.* 79 U.S. (12 Wall) 362, 365; 20 L. Ed. 434, 436 (1871).

[9] However, failure to register may have priority effects. See below, paras 3–30, 5–25.

[10] See below, paras 2–30, 5–15 and 5–39.

[11] For an exhaustive treatment of this subject, see John de Lacy, "Constructive Notice and Company Charge Registration" (2001) 65 Conv. 122.

[12] This is now generally accepted as the result produced by the authorities, though the historical antecedents are not as strong as has generally been supposed. See John de Lacy, above, n.70, and W.J. Gough, *Company Charges* (2nd ed.), Ch.32.

[13] *English & Scottish Mercantile Investment Co. v Brunton* [1892] 2 Q.B. 700; *Wilson v Kelland* [1910] 2 Ch. 306; *Siebe Gorman & Co. Ltd. v Barclays Bank Ltd.* [1979] 2 Lloyd's Rep. 142.

instrument at the company's registered office.[14] English law has never sub-scribed to the view that to fix a third party with notice of the terms of a secu-rity agreement it is sufficient to put him on the trail leading to the instrument itself. As a matter of fact, the mechanism for getting details of the instrument is decidedly inconvenient. All the interested party is entitled to do is to inspect the copy of the charge instrument at the debtor company's registered office and to write out his own copy. He has no right to demand a copy either from the company or from the chargee. Whether the provision of such a right would have affected the attitude of the court is a matter for speculation. As the law now stands, the rule is clear: registration is not notice of the terms of the security agreement.

This rule has little impact on the rights of a fixed chargee. In the case of a fixed charge, the debtor has neither actual nor ostensible authority to dispose of the charged asset free from the charge. Hence notice of the existence of the charge suffices to preserve the chargee's priority over a subsequent legal mortgagee. The position is otherwise in the case of a floating charge, where a third party dealing with the debtor company is entitled to assume that it has freedom to dispose of its assets, in the absence of notice of restrictions on the debtor's powers of disposition. So for a floating chargee the mechanics of giving such notice may be of paramount importance. I shall return to this point shortly, because it arises in connection with the separate question whether, even if registration is not notice of the contents of the security agreement as such, it might constitute notice of terms customarily found in an instrument of the same type as that registered.

(2) *Particulars to be filed*

2–25 It is clear that as regards all particulars which are required to be filed under the Companies Act, the filing of those particulars constitutes notice of them, at any rate as regards third parties who could reasonably be expected to make a search.[15] The required particulars are the date and description of the instru-ment creating the charge, the name of the company and particulars of the

---

[14] Companies Act 1985, s.408.

[15] This is subject to one qualification. s.395 is complied with by delivering particulars for reg-istration in Form M.395, together with the charge instrument. Until the Companies Registry records the particulars (and sometimes particulars are mislaid), it will not be discoverable by a search and third parties will therefore not have notice of it. The same difficulty arises where the Registrar of Companies wrongly refuses to register a charge. In such cases, if the application for registration was made in due time and was in order, the applicant is protected and will have priority over a third party advancing funds under a subsequent charge in reliance on a clear search. There is a further pitfall for searchers in that registration is a per-fection requirement, not a priority point, so that registration after a clear search does not guarantee priority. See above, para.2–22. Searches may be made at Companies House or online. Security documents are not retained but are returned after being examined against the registered particulars.

persons entitled to the charge, the amount secured by it,[16] short particulars of the property charged and particulars of any commission paid in connection with the transaction.[17]

Suppose that the chargee omits some of the prescribed particulars or files inaccurate particulars. This does not vitiate the registration, for the Act provides that the issue of a certificate of registration by the Registrar of Companies is conclusive evidence that the registration requirements have been complied with, and the court has held that this remains the case even if the filed particulars omit a category of property covered by the charge[18] or misstate the date of execution of the charge instrument[19] or the amount secured by it.[20] But these cases were concerned with the validity of registration, not with notice for the purpose of fixing priorities; and my view is that registration does not constitute notice as regards those particulars which ought to have been filed and were not, and that a searcher is entitled to rely on the accuracy of the particulars filed. So if he is misled by the omission of a part of the security or by any other material mis-description of the assets comprising the security, he is not fixed with notice of the matters omitted or misstated.

(3) *Particulars filed voluntarily*

(a) *No constructive notice* Where a floating charge creates restrictions on **2–26** the debtor's powers of disposal—typically, by providing that the debtor shall not create any subsequent charge ranking in priority to or *pari passu* with the floating charge or sell any of its assets outside the ordinary course of business—it has long been customary to record brief details of these restrictions in the filed particulars. It is clear that, subject to a point about notice raised by Professor Farrar which I shall discuss in a moment, the absence of reference to such restrictions in the filed particulars entitles a third party acquiring an interest in the asset without notice of the restrictions to ignore them.[21] But is the technique of including details of the restrictions in the filed particulars effective? As regards those who search the register there is, of course, no problem, for they have actual notice. The matter is otherwise as regards those who do not search. Restrictions on a charger's dealing powers are not among the details which the Act requires to be filed. A searcher is therefore entitled to say

---

[16] It is generally considered that this does not have the effect of requiring the charge instrument to specify a stated amount secured, and that it is perfectly in order for the instrument to secure "all moneys from time to time outstanding to the chargee" and to register this accordingly.

[17] Companies Act 1985, s.395(1); Companies (Forms) Regulations 1985 (SI 1985/854), Sch.3, form 395. As to debentures issued in a series, see s.397.

[18] *National Provincial and Union Bank of England v Charnley* [1924] 1 K.B. 431.

[19] *Re Eric Holmes (Property) Ltd.* [1965] Ch. 1052; *Re C. L. Nye Ltd.* [1971] Ch. 442.

[20] *Re Mechanisations (Eaglescliffe) Ltd.* [1966] Ch. 20. Even if the charge should never have been accepted for registration at all, the certificate is conclusive and cannot be attached by way of judicial review (*R. v Registrar of Companies, Ex p. Central Bank of India* [1986] 2 W.L.R. 177).

[21] See cases cited n.13, above.

that, so far as the scheme of registration under the Act is concerned, he has no reason to suppose that those particulars will be on file. Put another way, filing is constructive notice as regards those matters for which it is required but not as regards optional extras.

2–27   (b) *Inferred knowledge at common law?* However, Professor Farrar, whilst accepting this proposition, has argued powerfully that such restrictive provisions are now so common that a third party has inferred knowledge of them at common law once he has acquired notice of the existence of the floating charge.[22] At first sight, the argument is attractive. Every well drafted floating charge contains restrictions on the debtor company's powers to create subsequent incumbrances; surely a reasonable third party ought to be sufficiently alerted by this general practice to make further enquiry?

There are, however, powerful arguments against this conclusion. In the first place, it runs counter to all the authorities over a period of nearly a century, the latest being the *Siebe Gorman* case previously mentioned; and a decision of the Irish Supreme Court at about the same time[23]; and whilst Professor Farrar argues that these cases turned on constructive notice in equity, not inferred knowledge at law, it is hard to believe that the common law principle would not have been applied had it been regarded as relevant. Secondly, English law has never adopted a concept of notice based on generalised knowledge but has always insisted that there must be something specific to the transaction under consideration. So the mere fact that goods are commonly supplied on hire-purchase does not fix an innocent purchaser of hired goods with inferred knowledge of a hire-purchase agreement affecting them. Even in equity, an intending purchaser or mortgagee has no duty to investigate documents the existence of which is disclosed or discovered unless from the information given it is apparent that those documents will *necessarily* affect the title.[24] Thirdly, inferred knowledge at common law requires not merely a knowledge of facts which would put a reasonable man on enquiry but a wilful shutting of one's eyes to those facts, knowing or suspecting what the result of the enquiry would be.[25]

---

[22] J. H. Farrar, *Floating Charges and Priorities* (1974) 38 Conv. (N.S.) 315, at 319 *et seq.*

[23] *Welch v Bowmaker (Ireland) Ltd.* [1980] I.R. 251.

[24] *Jones v Smith* (1841) 1 Hare 43, affirmed (1843) 1 Ph. 244; *English & Scottish Mercantile Investment Co. v Brunton* [1892] 2 Q.B. 700. See also below, para.116.

[25] See *English & Scottish Mercantile Investment Co. v Brunton*, above, *per* Lord Esher, M.R., at 708.

How should notice be given?

If particulars of restrictions do not, by virtue of filing, constitute notice to a 2–28
third party making a search, how is notice to be given? The short answer is,
by embodying details of the restrictions in a document which does have to be
filed, such as a special or extraordinary resolution of the company.[26] In some
cases this will be practicable, in others it will not. In the latter event, the
debenture holder taking a floating charge will have to chance his arm. After
all, if he is going to leave the debtor free to manage its assets, he must be
expected to assume some risks.

To whom is registration notice?

Even as regards those matters of which registration constitutes notice—*i.e.* 2–29
the existence of the charge and those obligatory particulars which are in fact
filed—it does not follow that the whole world is affected. It has been held in
several cases that the doctrine of constructive notice does not apply to chattels or to commercial transactions.[27] But those decisions must be read in their
context and should not be taken to lay down any absolute rule. In particular,
a distinction must be drawn between those buying goods from a supplier selling in the ordinary course of business and those lending money on the security of goods or other assets. What can be said with some confidence, having
regard to the underlying purpose of the doctrine of notice, is that registration
is notice only to those who could reasonably be expected to search. This
would normally exclude a buyer in the ordinary course of business,[28] for it
would be quite impracticable to expect a purchaser from a manufacturer or
dealer to search in the Companies Registry every time he wishes to consum-
mate a purchase; and since the buyer of goods comprised in a floating charge
is not bound by the charge merely because he knows of it, but only if he is on
notice that the sale to him is in breach of the terms of the charge, such a
buyer will usually take free from the chargee's rights regardless of any
restriction on dealing noted in the file in the Companies Registry.

4. THE SPECIALIST REGISTERS

Apart from the register maintained by the Companies Registry for charges by 2–30
companies falling within ss.395 and 396 of the Companies Act 1985 there are
at least 10 specialist registers providing for registration of security interests in

---

[26] See Companies Act 1985, s.380.
[27] *Manchester Trust v Furness* [1895] 2 Q.B. 539; *By Appointment (Sales) Ltd. v Harrods Ltd.*
[1977], unreported CA (Bar Library transcript no. 465); *Feuer Leather Corp. v Frank Johnstone
& Sons* [1981] Comm. L.R. 251.
[28] *Feuer Leather Corp. v Frank Johnstone & Sons*, above.

particular types of asset, namely registers for bills of sale,[29] charges over registered land,[30] charges over unregistered land,[31] agricultural charges,[32] ship mortgages over registered ships or shares therein,[33] aircraft mortgages over registered aircraft,[34] mortgages of patents,[35] trade marks,[36] and registered designs,[37] and charges granted by an industrial and provident society.[38] When granted by a company most of these categories of charge are concurrently registrable under the Companies Act 1985 and if not so registered will be void against subsequent secured creditors and against a liquidator or administrator and creditors generally in a winding-up.[39]

Certain features common to a number of these specialist registers may be noted. First, in most cases a mortgage or charge on an asset is registrable only if ownership of the asset has been registered. Secondly, though a security interest can still be created without registration it will generally take effect in equity only. Thirdly, registration is usually not merely a perfection requirement but a priority point, so that priority is determined by the order of registration. This is not changed by notice of the prior interest or by the fact that the security interest is also registrable under the Companies Act, where the order of registration is irrelevant to priorities.

5. PROPOSALS FOR REFORM

2–31 In line with the recommendations of the Company Law Review,[40] the Law Commission has proposed that registration be made a priority point, not merely a perfection requirement.[41] This would have several advantages. First, it would remove the problem of the invisibility period and makes the grant of security transparent. Secondly, it would obviate the need to require registration within a stated period,[42] and the consequent expense of obtaining leave to register out of time; a secured creditor would have every incentive to reg-

---

[29] Established under the Bills of Sale Acts 1878 and 1882 and located in the Filing Department of the Royal Courts of Justice. These provide for registration of both absolute and security bills of sale (written chattel mortgages) and also require a general assignment of book debts by an unincorporated trader to be registered as it were a bill of sale.

[30] *i.e.* land registered under the Land Registration Acts 1925 and 1972, shortly to be replaced by the Land Registration Act 2002.

[31] Maintained in the Land Charges Registry under the Land Charges Act 1972.

[32] Which must be registered in the Land Registry under the Agricultural Credits Act 1928, s.9.

[33] Merchant Shipping Act 1995, Sch.1.

[34] Maintained under the Mortgaging of Aircraft Order 1972, SI 1972/1268.

[35] Patents Act 1977, s.33.

[36] Trade Marks Act 1994, s.25.

[37] Registered Designs Act 1949, s.19.

[38] Registrable in the central office established under the Industrial and Provident Societies Act 1896, s.1 and exempt from the Bills of Sale Acts if an application is lodged within 14 days (Industrial and Provident Societies Act 1965, s.1).

[39] Companies Act 1985, s.395(1)

[40] See above, para.2–19, n.90.

[41] *Registration of Security Interests: Company Charges and Property other than Land*, para.14.13.

[42] A requirement the Law Commission logically proposes should be abolished (*ibid.*, para.4.75).

ister as quickly as possibly in order to avoid the risk of subordination to another secured creditor who registered first. Indeed, the proposals go further and advocate[43] the adoption of the "notice filing" system embodied in Art.9 of the Uniform Commercial Code, which dispenses with the filing of transaction documents and even the need for transaction details and permits the filing of a simple financing statement specifying the asset or description of asset in which the registrant has acquired or may acquire a security interest.[44] In contrast to the system under s.395 of the Companies Act 1985, notice-filing is not transaction-based; a single filing can cover all future secured transactions between the parties,[45] obviating the need for a separate filing for each security interest. A consequential feature of Art.9 of the Uniform Commercial Code and of the Canadian and New Zealand Personal Property Security Acts, which are modelled on Art.9, is that the steps to perfection (agreement, value, filing) can be taken in any order, so that a financing statement may be filed before the security agreement has been concluded and no further filing is required when the agreement has been made and value given. Priority goes back to the time of filing, so that a subsequent secured creditor who took and perfected his security interest first will nevertheless be on notice from the financing statement that his priority is liable to be displaced.

A further, important recommendation is that a security interest registrable in a specialist register[46] should not be registrable under s.395 of the Companies Act.[47] This removes a long-standing trap for the unwary as well as avoiding conflicts between the priority effect of non-registration under s.395 and the priority rules governing the specialist registers.

---

[43] *ibid.*, para.4.12.
[44] The form of financing statement provided by UCC §9–521 does not contain any statement that the registrant has acquired or may acquire a security interest in the collateral described. This is implicit in the financing statement and the rules covering it, including the provision that it may be filed before a security agreement is made or a security interest otherwise attaches (§9–502(d)).
[45] Including sales under reservation of title, which are treated as creating security interests.
[46] See below.
[47] *ibid.*, above, n.41, para.4.200.

III

Attachment, Perfection and Effects of Fixed Security in Non-Documentary Receivables

1. INTRODUCTION

Intangible property is today the most valuable object of security for the financier, and pure intangibles[1] possess several advantages over tangible assets. They are not susceptible to physical loss, damage or deterioration; they can be stored on and transferred by computer and turned over in huge volumes without constraints of size or physical delivery requirements; and they may be notionally shifted from one country to another at the press of a button. This does not mean that they are free from risk. Intellectual property rights may be attacked as invalid or lose their value because of superior competing products; debtors may become insolvent; and supposed debtors may assert against a mortgagee or chargee defences based on non-performance or defective performance by the mortgagor or chargor or rights of set-off in respect of cross-claims against the mortgagor or chargor.[2] But the ease with which intangibles may be given in security makes them an ideal form of collateral.

3–01

Intangibles are also distinctive in that, depending on their nature, they may be mortgaged in up to three different ways: by assignment, by novation, and by negotiation.[3]

The particular form of intangible examined in the present chapter is the account receivable (abbreviated to "receivable"), by which I mean the right to payment of a sum of money, whether presently or in the future, for goods supplied, services rendered or facilities made available, being a right not embodied in a negotiable instrument.[4] The discussion is concerned with attachment and perfection of fixed security interests. Floating charges, and

---

[1] As distinguished from documentary intangibles. See above, para.1–44.

[2] The subject of set-off is discussed in Ch.III.

[3] See below, paras 3–03 *et seq.* as to assignment and novation.

[4] In other words, debts. But "receivables" is a convenient term, first, because it makes it clear that the perspective is that of the creditor, not the debtor, and secondly, because it avoids confusion with book debts, which constitute a narrower category. For a comprehensive treatment of the subject, see Fidelis Oditah, *Legal Aspects of Receivables Financing.* As to documentary intangibles, which are susceptible to pledge as well as mortgage or charge, see above, para.1–44.

the particular problems of distinguishing a fixed charge of receivables from a floating charge, are analysed in Chapter IV. Priority issues are the subject of Chapter V. The special problems arising in connection with security interests in investment securities, and particularly in investments securities held indirectly with an intermediary, are examined in Chapter VI.

3–02   Receivables financing cannot be viewed in isolation but must be seen in the context of a life cycle of assets. Money is invested in raw materials which are made up into the finished product, becoming stock in trade. The stock is sold, producing receivables. The receivables crystallise into cash which is reinvested in new raw materials. Security may be taken over an asset at any stage in its life cycle—from chrysalis to butterfly—and since, as we have seen,[5] security in an asset carries through to products resulting from commingling of the proceeds, it not uncommonly happens that one party lays claim to a receivable as original security—*i.e.* security in the form in which he bargained for it at the outset—whilst another claims security rights over it as the product or proceeds of another asset featuring earlier in the cycle. For example, a manufacturer sells goods to a distributor, reserving title until payment but authorising the distributor to resell the goods provided that he accounts for the proceeds—the typical Romalpa clause. The distributor has previously arranged a line of credit with its bank, secured by a charge on its book debts. When the goods are resold by the distributor on 28-day credit, the resulting receivable is claimed by the bank as original security and by the manufacturer as the traceable proceeds of goods to which it had reserved title. This type of problem constantly recurs in receivables financing, and I shall return to it in a later chapter when discussing some typical priority problems.

But first, some preliminary remarks about characteristics of security over receivables.

2. CHARACTERISATION AND FORMS OF SECURITY

Mortgage by assignment and mortgage by novation

3–03   It is necessary to draw a clear distinction between a mortgage by assignment and a mortgage by novation. A mortgage by assignment does not change the identity of the contracting parties; the mortgagor retains his contractual relationship with the account debtor,[6] and the account remains in the mortgagor's name. The assignment merely entitles the assignee to payment in place of the mortgagor upon giving notice of the assignment to the account debtor. Accordingly an assignment does not in principle require the consent

---

[5] See above, paras 1–58 *et seq.*; below, para.3–32.

[6] The account debtor is the debtor of the person assigning or charging the debt by way of security. The assignor is, of course, himself a debtor to the assignee. To avoid confusion the term "debtor" will be used to refer to the account debtor, his creditor as the mortgagor or intending mortgagor and the latter's creditor or intended creditor as the mortgagee or intended mortgagee.

of the account debtor. By contrast a mortgage by novation entails a change of parties through a transfer of funds which are to be held by the mortgagee as a segregated fund, separate from the mortgagee's own moneys, to which the mortgagee may resort in the event of default but must otherwise hold on trust for the mortgagor[7] and return to him if the debt for which the fund is security is discharged from other sources.[8] The provision of such cash collateral[9] is an everyday occurrence, for example, to provide margin deposits to a broker or cash cover to a bank by its customer for an anticipated liability to be incurred by the bank to a third party on the customer's behalf. So in contrast to an assignment, which preserves the original debt and results in the mortgagee taking over whatever claim the assignor had against the debtor, a novation replaces an existing debt in which the creditor was the mortgagor with a new debt which is owed not to the mortgagee in his own right, not as assignee.[10] Novation produces a change of parties and requires the consent of all parties involved.[11] In the straightforward case where mortgagor and mortgagee bank with same bank, all that is involved is an in-house transfer in the books of the bank, so that there is a novation solely by change of creditor. In the more complex case where the mortgagor and mortgagee hold their accounts with different banks the novation is not direct but takes place through the books of a higher-tier bank with whom the banks of both parties hold their accounts and transfer funds by an in-house transfer.[12] In this case there is a change of both creditor and debtor; the debtor's claim against its bank as paying bank is replaced *pro tanto* by the creditor's claim against its bank as the transferee bank. The same principles applies where the funds provided as cash collateral come not from the debtor directly but from a third party at the debtor's direction, including a third party buying goods from the debtor and paying them into the creditor's account.[13]

Both methods of mortgage, assignment and novation, allow of tracing.[14] The difference between them may, however, be significant in that as assignee the mortgagee takes subject to equities, including any rights of set-off the debtor may have against the mortgagor, whereas as recipient of a new right by way of novation the mortgagee is not concerned with equities available

---

[7] The mortgagee is not, of course, a trustee to the extent that he holds for an interest of his own, but he is a trustee to the extent of the mortgagor's equity of redemption.

[8] It is thus to be distinguished from an outright funds transfer by way of payment, which is by far the more common type of funds transfer, where the transferee becomes outright owner of the claim on its bank.

[9] "Cash" here refers not to physical notes or coin but, typically, to the chose in action represented by a claim on a bank.

[10] It follows that a mere charge, which creates no new debt, cannot be created by novation.

[11] The same novation technique is utilised in relation to shares, whether held directly from the issuer (in which case the mortgagee replaces the mortgagor on the share register) or indirectly through a securities account with a bank or other securities intermediary, in which case there will be a book-entry transfer in the books of the intermediary if common to the parties or, if not, in the books of a common higher-tier intermediary. See further below, para.6–02.

[12] If the parties' banks themselves hold their accounts with different higher-tier banks, it is necessary to go further up the chain until one reaches a common bank, which in the case of the clearing banks is the Bank of England.

[13] For an example of such a fact situation, see *Palmer v Carey* [1926] AC 703. See above, para.1–26.

[14] See above, para.1–60; below, para.3–37.

to the debtor against the assignor, only with those available against the mortgagee himself, *e.g.* a right of set-off against the mortgagee's credit balance, and then only if the debtor is not on notice that its creditor holds the credit balance as mortgagee.[15] The rest of this chapter is devoted to security transfers by assignment except where otherwise stated.

Security distinguished from purchase

3–04 It is necessary at the outset to distinguish a loan on the security of receivables from a purchase of receivables. A transaction described by the parties purchase and sale may be characterised as a secured loan either because the document evidencing the transaction is a sham in that it does not represent the true intention of the parties or because, though it is genuine, its provisions viewed as a whole show that, contrary to the description given by the parties, its legal effect is that of a mortgage or charge.[16] A loan on security postulates a repayment obligation and a right to redeem the security by repayment. A purchase involves an outright transfer, in which the transferor has no duty to repay and no right to redeem. In practice, the distinction is not always so clear cut. The following deserve particular mention:

(1) *Sale with recourse*

3–05 The transferor of receivables (whom I shall refer to hereafter as the assignor, to distinguish him from the account debtor) may dispose of them by way of sale but guarantee payment by the debtors and, by way of convenient implementation of his guarantee, furnish an instalment note, or series of bills of exchange, covering the amount of his recourse liability. In this type of transaction, there is an exchange of money for money, so that in terms of cash flow and economic effect it is virtually indistinguishable from a mortgage of receivables. Yet in law the character of the transaction as a sale is not altered by the giving of the guarantee, for the assignor's liability is not to *repay* an advance but to *pay* a sum in discharge of a recourse obligation.[17] Provided

---

[15] Thus where the mortgage is effected by transfer of funds from the mortgagor's bank account to an account in the name of the mortgagee the bank may exercise a right of set-off in respect of moneys due from the mortgagee on another account so long as it is not on notice that the mortgagee is a mortgagee and not the beneficial owner of the account. But if it is on notice the bank cannot, it is thought, exercise a right of set-off even for the amount of the mortgagor's indebtedness in respect of which the mortgagee has a right of recourse to the credit balance, for this would erode the mortgagor's equity of redemption if it were to discharge its indebtedness from other sources. See further above, para.1–69; below, para.7–82.

[16] *Re Curtain Dream plc* [1990] B.C.L.C. 925; *Re Welsh Development Agency v Export Finance Co. Ltd.* [1992] B.C.L.C. 148 (where the transaction was upheld as producing its intended legal effect). See also *Agnew v Inland Revenue Commissioners* [2001] 2 A.C. 710, *per* Lord Millett at 725–726, cited above, para.1–39, and generally W.J. Gough, *Company Charges* (2nd ed.), Ch.21.

[17] *Olds Discount Co. Ltd. v John Playfair Ltd.* [1938] 1 All E.R. 275; *Chow Yoong Hong v Choong Fah Rubber Manufactory* [1962] A.C. 209; *Lloyds & Scottish Finance Ltd. v Cyril Lord Carpet Sales Ltd.* (1979) 129 N.L.J. 366, discussed by A. D. G. Giddins in *Block Discounting—Sale or Charge* (1980) 130 N.L.J. 207.

that the transaction is genuine and not a sham,[18] the courts will uphold it as a sale, even if the parties use commercial language which to the legal mind would suggest a loan on security.[19]

(2) *Outright transfer of debt with creditor's personal obligation to repay excess of proceeds over amount of debt*

Again, an agreement by which a debtor assigns to his creditor a debt exceeding the amount he owes the creditor, the latter agreeing to repay any excess he receives, is not a security agreement, for the debtor has parted with the debt due to him unconditionally and with no right of redemption.[20] **3–06**

(3) *Non-recourse loan*

A non-recourse loan on the security of receivables, in which the assignor **3–07** undertakes no personal repayment obligation and the financier agrees to look exclusively to the receivables to secure recoupment, looks very much like a sale disguised as a mortgage. But the concept of non-recourse lending is well established in English law. The transaction remains a loan transaction even though the parties have agreed that the assignor is to make repayment only from an identified fund, not from his own resources.[21] The transaction is in fact distinguishable from sale in that once the financier has recouped his advance with stipulated interest, any remaining value in the receivables belongs to the assignor.

(4) *Sale and repurchase; sale and lease-back*

A provision by which the seller of a debt is given a right of repurchase may **3–08** be an indication that the transaction as a whole is a mortgage and the right of repurchase a right to redeem, particularly when it is accompanied by language suggestive of a loan, such as a line of credit and a rate of interest.[22]

But it should not be too readily assumed that a right of repurchase indicates an intention to create a mortgage. Sale and repurchase transactions in securities ("repos"), where the seller is required to buy back the securities at the original sale price plus a finance charge calculated by reference to a

---

[18] There appears to be no reported case in which a purported sale of receivables has been struck down as a disguised loan on security, but the cases on chattel mortgages disguised as outright sales would be equally in point here. See, for example, *Polsky v S. & A. Services* [1951] 1 All E.R. 185, affirmed [1951] 1 All E.R. 1062; *North Central Wagon Finance Co. Ltd. v Brailsford* [1962] 1 All E.R. 502. For an analysis of the authorities, see R. M. Goode, *Hire-Purchase Law and Practice* (2nd ed.), Chs 4 and 5.

[19] *Lloyds & Scottish Finance Ltd. v Cyril Lord Carpet Sales Ltd.*, above.

[20] See above, para.3.

[21] *Mathew v Blackmore* (1857) 1 H. & N. 762; *De Vigier v Inland Revenue Commissioners* [1964] 2 All E.R. 907.

[22] *Re Curtain Dream plc* [1990] B.C.L.C. 925.

notional interest rate occur daily, and there is no reason to suppose that such transactions are other than genuine sales with provision for repurchase, entered into for perfectly good commercial reasons, including but not limited to the raising of funds.[23] The same considerations apply to the repo's close relation, the sell/buy-back.[24] Similarly, sales and lease-backs of land and goods are common transactions, and while they are frequently utilised as a means of raising capital they are not on that account to be characterised as other than what they purport to be.

Significance of the distinction between purchase and secured loan

3–09   Quite apart from the presence or absence of repayment obligations and rights of redemption, the distinction between a purchase of receivables and loan on the security of receivables is legally significant in a number of respects. The sale of receivables is usually not registrable, the mortgage of receivables usually is.[25] A sale attracts *ad valorem* stamp duty, a mortgage does not.[26] The treatment of the transaction for tax and accounting purposes will vary according to whether it is done by way of sale or security.[27]

Forms of security

3–10   There are two types of security over receivables, namely mortgage and charge. As stated previously, a mortgage involves a security transfer of ownership, whereas a charge is a mere incumbrance, ownership being left in the chargor. The distinction is in practice of limited significance. In both cases the giving of notice of the secured creditor's interest to the account debtor protects the secured creditor both against the risk of payment to the mortgagor/chargor and against loss of priority to a subsequent incumbrancer.[28] It

---

[23] This is well described in the Law Commission's Consultation Paper *Registration of Security Interests: Company Charges and Property other than Land*, para.6.39. Moreover, there are international standard-term master agreements for repos, such as the Master Agreement of TBMA and ISMA. See further below, paras 6–17 and 6–18.

[24] The sell/buy-back produces effects similar to the classic repo but differs from it in instead of a sale back at the original purchase price plus a charge or interest the resale is at a forward price which is higher in order to cover what would otherwise have been interest. There are also other differences which need not be discussed here. See generally Moorad Choudhry, *The Repo Handbook*, pp. 99 *et seq*. See further below, para.6–17.

[25] Under s.395 of the Companies Act 1985. But a general assignment of book debts by an unincorporated trader is registrable as if it were a bill of sale (Insolvency Act 1986, s.344), whether the assignment is by way of security or outright sale.

[26] Stamp duty on mortgages was abolished by the Finance Act 1971, ss.64, 69.

[27] On sale of an asset, it disappears from the balance sheet and is replaced by the proceeds of sale. Where the asset is mortgaged, it continues to be shown as an asset of the mortgagor, the repayment obligation being recorded as a liability. However, for the purpose of value added tax there is no distinction between a sale of receivables and a mortgage of receivables; both are exempt supplies within item 1 of Group 5 of the 9th Schedule to the Value Added Tax Act 1994.

[28] There are, however, exceptions. For example, a company cannot be affected by notice of a trust or mortgage of its shares, so that to perfect his title the secured creditor needs to be

is true that in the absence of agreement a chargee, lacking legal ownership, does not have certain remedies available to a mortgagee, such as a right to sue in his own name or to sell or appoint a receiver without leave of the court. But a well-drawn charge will in practice provide for all the remedies the chargee may require, including a provision for the execution of a legal mortgage and a power of attorney to do so in the name of the chargor.

Existing and future debts

Security may be given over existing debts, future debts or both. The difference between existing and future debts is legally material in that a mortgage of the latter can take effect only in equity, whereas a present debt can be assigned under s.136 of the Law of Property Act 1925 so as to take effect at law. However, the distinction between a legal and an equitable assignment has no practical impact, beyond the fact that a statutory assignee can sue in his own name[29] whereas an equitable assignee may be required to join the assignor.[30] A sum growing due under an existing contract is regarded in law as a present debt, even though the right to payment has not yet matured, *e.g.* because this is dependent on performance of the work which is to generate the payment obligation.[31]

3–11

Charge-backs

In the first two editions of this book the writer argued that the giving of security over receivables necessarily involved three parties, the debtor, the creditor and the creditor's assignee or other encumbrancer and that it was conceptually impossible for the debtor to be given a security interest over his own obligation to his creditor, *e.g.* for a bank to take security over its own customer's credit balance. The reason was that as between creditor and debtor a debt is not a species of property, merely an obligation, and since the creditor purporting to take the security interest cannot sue himself, appoint a receiver to collect from himself or sell his own obligation the so-called security interest is in reality a contractual set-off. That view, which divided the legal profession, was adopted by Millett J. in *Re Charge Card Services Ltd.*,[32] and by the Court of Appeal in *Re Bank of Credit and Commerce International SA (No. 8)*,[33] but when the latter decision was

3–12

---

registered as the holder of the shares. Since this requires a transfer, an equitable chargee who becomes the registered holder is necessarily converted into a legal mortgagee.

[29] Law of Property Act 1925, s.136(1).

[30] A requirement which was frequently ignored in practice. Non-joinder of the assignor was not a ground for dismissing the action (R.S.C. Ord. 15, r. 6(1)). The effect of the Civil Procedure Rules 1998 is that the assignee may bring proceedings in his own name and the assignor may be added as a party if this is desirable to resolve the issues in dispute (CPR, Pt 19, r. 2).

[31] *G. & T. Earle Ltd. v Hemsworth R.D.C.* (1928) 140 L.T. 69.

[32] [1987] Ch. 150.

[33] [1996] Ch. 245.

appealed to the House of Lords, Lord Hoffmann opined that there was no conceptual reason why a bank should not be able to take a charge over its own customer's credit balance, which a charge like any other except that it was enforceable only by book-entry.[34] Lord Hoffmann's statement, though obviously of great persuasive value, was *obiter*, so that the point remains open.

I have addressed elsewhere[35] both the conceptual problems of charge-backs and the policy issues which deserved consideration but appear never to have been argued.[36] But the force of business practice cannot be denied. Lord Hoffmann himself drew attention to legislation in Hong Kong and Singapore giving statutory effect to charge-backs. There was in fact a good example at home in the shape of s.215(2)(a) of the Insolvency Act 1986, which empowers the court, when making a declaration of wrongful trading under s.214 of the Act, to direct that the defendant's liability be charged on any debt or obligation due to him from the company. Art.9 of the American Uniform Commercial Code provides for perfection of a security interest in a deposit account by control,[37] and states that a secured party has control of a deposit account if *(inter alia)* it is the bank with which the deposit account is maintained.[38] Finally, Art.4 of the EC Directive on financial collateral arrangements[39] requires Member States to ensure that on the occurrence of an enforcement event cash collateral may be realised by setting off the amount against or applying it in discharge of the relevant financial obligations.[40] The provision of cash collateral to banks and brokers is commonplace. Accordingly conceptual problems such as the blurring of the distinction between property and obligation, and policy problems such as the fact that the only method of distinguishing a charge-back from a contractual set-off is by the label given to the transaction by the parties, must yield to business practice and legislative developments designed to accommodate it.

---

[34] [1998] A.C. 214 at 226–228.

[35] *Commercial Law in the Next Millennium* (the 1997 Hamlyn Lectures), pp. 69–71.

[36] Indeed, Lord Hoffmann expressly stated (at 228) that there was no objection of public policy.

[37] §9–312(b)(1).

[38] §9–104(a)(1).

[39] Directive 2002/47 dated June 6, 2002.

[40] Similarly, UCC § 8–106 provides for a securities entitlement to be given in security to the securities intermediary with whom the securities account is maintained and Art.1(2)(b) of the 2002 Hague Convention on the Law Applicable to Certain Rights in respect of Securities held with an Intermediary expressly covers a disposition in favour of the account holder's intermediary. Under existing English law set-off is not available against cash collateral or against any surplus remaining after the mortgagee has taken what is due to him in respect of the secured debt, since the debtor's equity of redemption is a property right and a money claim cannot be set off against a property right (see above, para.1–69). So the prudent creditor takes not only a charge-back but a general right of set-off as well.

3. ATTACHMENT OF SECURITY INTEREST IN RECEIVABLES

Mortgage

As stated above a mortgage of receivables is effected either by assignment or **3–13** by novation. An assignment may be a statutory assignment taking effect at law or an equitable assignment. The difference between the two is of little practical significance, since the normal rule giving priority to a subsequent purchaser of a legal title in good faith and without notice of a prior equitable does not apply to successive dealings in receivables, which are governed by the rule in *Dearle v Hall*.[41] Of more importance is the fact that where the receivable is a book debt it is registrable and registration displaces the rule in *Dearle v Hall* as regards a competing post-registration assignment, whereas dealings in a receivable which is not a book debt are governed by the rule.

(1) *Statutory assignment*

To constitute a statutory assignment, so as to vest the receivable in the **3–14** assignee at law and enable him to sue solely in his own name, the assignment must be effected in accordance with the requirements of s.136 of the Law of Property Act 1925. The assignment itself must be in writing under the hand of the assignor, it must be absolute and not by way of charge,[42] it must relate to the whole of the debt[43] and it must be notified to the debtor in writing.[44] An assignment which fails to meet any of these conditions takes effect in equity only. A statutory assignment is not possible where the account debtor or other counterparty is not obliged, and may not even be entitled, to receive notice of the assignment—for example, (a) on a transfer of shares,[45] which to take effect in law must be done by novation, *i.e.* substitution of the transferee for the transferor in the books of the issuer; or (b) where the claim is embodied in a negotiable instrument, in which case the acceptor's duty is to pay the holder on presentation, regardless of notice

---

[41] See below, paras 3–32, 5–28.

[42] But an assignment by way of mortgage is within the section (*Tancred v Delagoa Bay & East Africa Ry.* (1889) 23 Q.B.D. 239).

[43] *Forster v Baker* [1910] 2 K.B. 636; *Re Steel Wing Co. Ltd.* [1921] 1 Ch. 349.

[44] The notice of the assignment is not required to contain any direction to the debtor to pay the assignee. He is expected to infer this from the fact that the debt has become vested in the assignee. There is much to be said for a rule along the lines of ss.9–318(3) of the Uniform Commercial Code authorising the debtor to make payment to the assignor unless the notice to him requires payment to the assignee. Art.8(1)(b) of the 1988 UNIDROIT Convention on International Factoring is to the same effect. It is by no means uncommon for the purchaser of a receivable, *e.g.* a factor, to agree with his assignor that despite notice of the assignment to the debtor the assignor will continue to collect, as agent of the assignee, until otherwise directed. It is important that the debtor should be left in no doubt as to whom payment is to be made, and notice of the assignment, though sufficient under s.136 of the Law of Property Act, is not necessarily informative enough to achieve its commercial purpose.

[45] See below, para.5–08.

of assignment from someone else[46]; or (c) where the contract to which the assignment relates prohibits assignment.

(2) Equitable assignment

3–15   The rules for an equitable assignment by way of mortgage are very much more relaxed. All that is necessary is that the intending mortgagor shall manifest a clear intention to make an irrevocable transfer of the receivable. The assignment will be effective as between mortgagor and mortgagee even if no notice is given to the debtor,[47] though the debtor will not, of course, be affected by the assignment himself unless and until he has notice of it. There are four methods by which a receivable may become vested in equity in the intended mortgagee:

3–16   (a) *Transfer or agreement for transfer* The most common is for the intending mortgagor either to sign a written transfer and send this to the intended mortgagee or to make a binding agreement for assignment to which equity will give effect, either immediately, in the case of a present receivable, or upon its coming into existence, in the case of a future receivable.[48] But neither writing nor signature is necessary. An assignment is equally effective in equity if made by word of mouth or by conduct; all that is necessary is an intention, manifested to the intended mortgagee, to make a present assignment by way of mortgage.[49]

3–17   (b) *Declaration of trust* The second method of creating an equitable assignment by way of mortgage is for the intending mortgagor to declare himself a trustee of the receivable for the intended mortgagee. Such a trust may be express or implied from the agreement between the parties, as where the intending mortgagor undertakes to account to the intended mortgagee for sums paid by the debtor to the intending mortgagor.[50] Such an undertaking is common in a master invoice discounting agreement, where a trade supplier discounts its debts to a factoring company or invoice discounter on terms that the supplier's customers will not be given notice of the assignment in the absence of special circumstances and the supplier will continue to collect the receivables, account for the collections to the factor or invoice discounter and meanwhile hold them on trust.

3–18   (c) *Transfer to trustees* A third method, which is a variant of the second, is for the debt to be transferred to a trustee or nominee to hold on behalf

---

[46] See above, para.2–20.

[47] If the assignor becomes bankrupt, his trustee in bankruptcy stands in his shoes. It follows that the trustee cannot secure priority over the assignee by being the first to give notice to the debtor (*Re Wallis* [1902] 1 K.B. 719; *Re Anderson* [1911] 1 K.B. 896).

[48] See above, paras 2–12 *et seq.*

[49] *William Brandt's Son & Co. v Dunlop Rubber Co.* [1905] A.C. 454.

[50] *G.E. Crane Sales Pty. Ltd. v Commissioner of Taxation* (1971) 46 A.L.J.R. 15; *International Factors Ltd. v Rodriguez* [1979] 1 All E.R. 17.

of the mortgagee. This is a basic technique in the securitisation of secured receivables, where the originator, *i.e.* the creditor, transfers the receivables and the mortgages or charges securing them to a special-purpose vehicle which issues loan notes against them and grants a sub-mortgage or sub-charge to trustees on behalf of the note holders, assigning to the trustees by way of additional security all relevant contracts, including rights under the sale agreement, insurances and credit enhancement contracts.

(d) *Direction to make payment to the intended mortgagee* The fourth method is for the intending mortgagor to communicate with the debtor directing him to make payment to the intended mortgagee. But this by itself is not enough.[51] In order for the direction to be effective it must either be given pursuant to prior agreement between the intending mortgagor and the intended mortgagee[52] or be communicated to the latter afterwards.[53] A direction to the debtor which has neither been previously arranged with the intended mortgagee nor subsequently communicated to him is merely a revocable authority to pay, even if it is expressed to be irrevocable.[54] Moreover, the direction itself must be couched in such language as to convey to the debtor that he is required to pay the intended mortgagee not merely as a matter of convenience to the intending mortgagor but because the right to receive payment has become vested in the mortgagee. If the direction does not make this clear, the debtor will be entitled to assume that the intending mortgagor is still entitled to receive payment.[55] **3–19**

(3) *Novation*

As stated earlier,[56] a mortgage by novation is effected by a transfer in which the mortgagee replaces the mortgagor as creditor. The question of notice to the debtor therefore does not arise. **3–20**

Charge

Whereas a mortgage of receivables transfers ownership to the secured creditor, either at law or in equity, a charge is a mere encumbrance. Nevertheless, **3–21**

---

[51] *Bell v London & North Western Ry. Co.* (1852) 15 Beav. 248; *Curran v Newpark Cinemas Ltd.* [1951] 1 All E.R. 295.
[52] As in *Re Kent & Sussex Sawmills Ltd.* [1947] Ch. 177; and *Winn v Burgess, The Times,* July 8, 1986. In the former case all parties and the court appear to have proceeded on the assumption that the assignment was by way of security, but as Dr. Oditah has appointed it may equally have been the case that the moneys assigned were to go in reduction of an indebtedness to the assignee (Fidelis Oditah, *Legal Aspects of Receivables Financing*, p. 80), and this does not constitute the giving of security. See *Siebe Gorman & Co. Ltd. v Barclays Bank Ltd.* [1979] 2 Lloyd's Rep 142, and above, para.1–34.
[53] *Curran v Newpark Cinemas Ltd.*, above; *Alexander v Steinhardt, Walker & Co.* [1903] 2 K.B. 208.
[54] *ibid.*
[55] *James Talcott Ltd. v John Lewis & Co. Ltd.* [1940] 3 All E.R. 592.
[56] See above, para.3–03.

most of the effects of a mortgage apply to a charge. Notice of the charge to the debtor precludes him from making payment to the chargor, preserves the chargee's priority against subsequent incumbrancers and cuts off the debtor's right of set-off in respect of cross-claims arising from future dealings with the chargor.[57] The one major difference, in theory at least, relates to enforcement. A charge (otherwise than on land) is purely the creation of equity; it does not exist at common law, nor does it come within s.136 of the Law of Property Act 1925 so as to be capable of conferring on the chargee a right of action solely in his own name against the debtor. Accordingly the chargor may need to be joined as a party to any proceedings by the chargee for recovery of the debt, and a chargee has no power of sale otherwise than under an order of the court.[58] In practice a well-drawn charge over receivables will confer on the chargee all the powers it needs, including power to convert the charge into a mortgage, for which purpose the charge should incorporate a power of attorney to the chargee to execute an assignment in the name of the chargor.

Since a charge leaves ownership of the debt with the chargor it cannot be effected by novation. All that is required for attachment is an agreement for a charge.

4. PERFECTION OF SECURITY INTEREST IN RECEIVABLES

3–22 Hitherto we have been concerned with *attachment* of a security interest in receivables, that is, its efficacy as between assignor and assignee. It is now necessary to see what steps have to be taken to make the security assignment enforceable against third parties. Of the six methods of perfection discussed earlier,[59] only possession is not available for receivables. We consider each of the remaining five in turn. The perfection requirements are the same for charges as for mortgages except that it is not possible to perfect a charge by novation.

Perfection by attachment only

3–23 No separate act is necessary to perfect a mortgage or charge of a receivables that is not a book debt.[60]

---

[57] See *Business Computers Ltd. v Anglo-African Leasing Ltd.* [1977] 2 All E.R. 741 and below, paras 7–62, 7–66.
[58] See above, para.1–51, n.70.
[59] See above, para.2–17.
[60] See above, para.2–21; below, para.3–27.

Perfection by registration under the Companies Act 1985

A charge on receivables is registrable under s.395 of the Companies Act 1985 **3–24** if the receivables constitute book debts. Several points arise.

(1) *The registration requirement*

S.395 applies only to charges created by the company, not to charges arising **3–25** by operation of law.[61] Accordingly, a security interest in book debts which arises not by agreement but by virtue of an equitable tracing right—*e.g.* as the proceeds of a disposition of stock or equipment—is not registrable. The same applies where the agreement, though specifying a duty to account for receivables as proceeds, is merely spelling out rights which would in any event vest in the chargee in equity.[62] The position is otherwise where it is apparent from the security instrument that the receivables resulting as proceeds of other security are to be regarded as the property of the chargor, but subject to a charge created by the instrument.

(2) *What is a charge?*

The term "charge" includes a mortgage.[63] The registration requirement **3–26** applies whether the mortgage is effected by assignment or by novation.

(3) *What is a book debt?*

A book debt is a debt arising in the course of a trader's business which is of **3–27** such of a kind that it would ordinarily be entered in a trader's books (or the modern equivalent of books[64]), whether in fact so entered or not.[65] It is generally considered that money deposited by a trader with his bank does not give rise to a book debt, since although the banker is the trader's debtor the debt does not arise in the way of trade but is merely a consequence of the deposit of surplus funds. Certainly the general accounting view is that such deposits do not fall to be treated as book debts, and this view was adopted by

---

[61] *Capital Finance Co. Ltd. v Stokes* [1969] Ch. 261.
[62] *Aluminium Industrie Vaassen BV v Romalpa Aluminium Ltd.* [1976] 1 Lloyd's Rep. 443. Hence a trust receipt by which pledged documents of title to goods are released by the pledgee to the pledgor to enable him to sell them as the pledgee's trustee-agent upon terms that the proceeds are to be held in trust for the pledgee does not constitute a charge over those proceeds as book debts, since these are vested in the pledgee in equity from the beginning as the proceeds of his original security (*Re David Allester Ltd.* [1922] 2 Ch. 211).
[63] Companies Act 1985, s.396(4). But it would seem that for the purposes of s.150 of the Companies Act 1985 "charge" bears its narrower meaning. See below, para.6–23.
[64] *e.g.* computer records.
[65] *Shipley v Marshall* (1863) 14 C.B.(N.S.) 566; *Dawson v Isle* [1906] 1 Ch. 633; *Independent Automatic Sales Ltd. v Knowles & Foster Ltd.* [1962] 3 All E.R. 27. See generally W.J. Gough, *Company Charges* (2nd ed.), Ch.26.

Hoffmann J. in *Re Brightlife Ltd.*,[66] though in a subsequent case he added the caveat that this would necessarily be true in every case.[67] Sums deposited as part of a company's trading activity, for example, as a dealer in the money market, might well be considered book debts. Debts embodied in securities issued on a market, do not, it is thought, constitute book debts, whether the securities are registered securities or bearer securities,[68] but the position as regards declared dividends is unclear. For that reason it is common to register charges on shares even though these are not in themselves a registrable category. In the case of indirect holdings of securities by book-entry in the records of a securities intermediary, the securities entitlement is not a book debt as regards the securities themselves, nor does a declaration of dividend by the issuer give rise to a charge on book debt, because the company's indebtedness is owed to the registered shareholders, not to lower-tier intermediaries of their customers. But the position may be otherwise as regards dividends or other cash received by the securities intermediary, who thus becomes a debtor to his customer, so that if cash is included in a charge of the customer's securities entitlement the charge could perhaps constitute a charge on a book debt.[69] Interests in a money fund are not book debts, since these are proprietary in character and therefore not debts at all.[70]

A liquidation creditor's entitlement to dividend, charged to a senior creditor under a turnover subordination,[71] is not a book debt. In the first place, the book debt is that which produced the dividend, not the dividend itself. Secondly, a dividend entitlement is not a debt at all, for while the liquidator who declares a dividend has statutory duties to perform he is not a debtor in respect of a dividend declared by him and no action lies against him for payment of the dividend.[72]

(4) *Negotiable instruments*

3–28 The monetary obligation embodied in a negotiable instrument is a book debt, at any rate if the instrument is held by way of conditional payment of the underlying obligation.[73] However, the deposit of negotiable instruments given to secure payment of a book debt[74] is exempt from

---

[66] [1987] Ch. 200. See to the same effect *Waters v Widdows* [1984] V.R. 503.
[67] *Re Permanent Houses (Holdings) Ltd.* [1988] B.C.L.C. 563.
[68] For the position in relation to negotiable instruments, see below.
[69] But as to the prospective effect of the 2002 EC Directive on financial collateral arrangements, see below, para.6–39.
[70] See above, para.1–55.
[71] See above, para.1–81.
[72] *Spence v Coleman* [1901] 2 K.B. 199, applying to winding up a similar rule enunciated in bankruptcy in *Prout v Gregory* (1889) 24 Q.B.D. 281 and now enshrined in s.325(2) of the Insolvency Act 1986.
[73] *Dawson v Isle*, above.
[74] In this context security means personal security in the shape of the payment obligations of the parties to the negotiable instrument.

registration,[75] in order to avoid interfering with the concept of negotiability. Thus negotiable instruments taken from a debtor in respect of a book debt may be pledged by the creditor without attracting any registration requirement. As stated above, money obligations embodied in a negotiable bond issue, though debts, would not appear to constitute book debts.

(5) *The effect of registration*

Registration perfects the security and constitutes notice to those who could reasonably be expected to search, but not otherwise.[76]   **3–29**

(6) *The effect of failure to register*

Failure to register a charge on book debts renders the charge void against a   **3–30**
liquidator or administrator and creditors,[77] by which is meant creditors in a winding up or administration and secured creditors,[78] as opposed to unsecured creditors where no winding up or administration has occurred. Non-registration does not avoid the charge as against a next line purchaser of the debt, but if he acquires the legal title without notice of the unregistered charge he has priority under the normal priority rules.

The effect of non-registration is exhausted if the debts are collected before anyone has acquired a *locus standi* to complain of non-registration, *i.e.* before winding up or administration or the grant of specific security.[79]

Registration of assignment of book debts by unincorporated trader

The Bills of Sale Acts, which require the registration of written chattel   **3–31**
mortgages granted by individuals, do not apply to choses in action.[80] However, s.344 of the Insolvency Act 1986 provides that a general assignment by a trader of his existing or future book debts, or any class thereof, shall be void against his trustee in bankruptcy as regards book debts not paid before the presentation of the bankruptcy petition unless registered as if it were an absolute bill of sale. But the section does not apply to an assignment of book debts due at the date of assignment from specified debtors, or debts growing due under specified contracts, or any assignment of book debts included in a transfer of a business made bona fide and for

---

[75] Companies Act 1985, s.396(2).
[76] See above, para.2–29.
[77] Companies Act 1986, s.395(1).
[78] *i.e.* secured creditors whose interests are created after that of the non-registering chargee. See further above, para.2–22; below, para.5–25.
[79] *Re Row Dal Constructions Pty. Ltd.* [1966] V.R. 249. cf. the position under the Bills of Sales Acts, described in Halsbury's Laws of England (4th ed.), Vol.4(1), para.837.
[80] Which are excluded from the definition of "personal chattels" in s.4 of the Bills of Sale Act 1878.

value or in any assignment of assets for the benefit of creditors generally.[81] For the purpose of the section, "assignment" includes an assignment by way of security and other charges on book debts.[82] The meaning of "book debts" has been considered above. Registration merely perfects the assignment so as to prevent it from being impeached by the assignor's trustee. It does not constitute notice to the outside world or guarantee the priority of the assignment over subsequent interests.[83]

Perfection by notice to the account debtor

3-32   Where the security is created by assignment or charge (as opposed to transfer by novation), notice to the account debtor[84] may be important for at least five different reasons:

(1)   To prevent him from making payment to the assignor. If he does so despite the notice of assignment, he can be made to pay again, to the assignee[85];

(2)   To stop new equities arising in favour of the debtor[86];

(3)   To prevent modification of the agreement between assignor and debtor under which the debt arose[87];

(4)   To secure priority over another encumbrancer. Under the rule in *Dearle v Hall*,[88] a later encumbrancer taking without notice of the earlier assignment and giving notice to the debtor first would obtain priority;

(5)   To obtain the benefit of a statutory assignment, and thus the right to sue for the debt in the assignee's own name without joining the assignor.[89]

---

[81] Insolvency Act 1986, s.344(3)(b).

[82] *ibid.* s.344(3)(a).

[83] See cases cited n.90, below.

[84] That is, the debtor's debtor.

[85] *Brice v Bannister* (1878) 3 Q.B.D. 569.

[86] *Roxburghe v Cox* (1881) 17 Ch.D. 520. By contrast, defences arising out of the transaction giving rise to the debt (*e.g.* where the debt is for goods sold, that they are defective) are available regardless of the date of receipt of the notice of assignment, for the assignee cannot acquire greater contractual rights than those possessed by his assignor.

[87] *Brice v Bannister*, above. In practice, an assignee usually finds it necessary to allow some leeway to the assignor in regard to modifications, particularly in the case of a contract involving continuing performance, such as a construction contract. Art.11:308 of the Principles of European Contract Law provides that a modification made without the consent of the assignee after notice of assignment does not bind the assignee "unless the modification is provided for in the assignment agreement or is one which is made in good faith and is of a nature to which the assignee could not reasonably object." A construction contract is given as an illustration in Comment E to Art.11:204 of the Principles.

[88] (1828) 3 Russ. 1. See above, para.3-13; below, para.5-28.

[89] Law of Property Act 1925, s.136(1).

It should be observed that registration of the assignment, assuming it to be registrable, does not dispense with the need to give notice to the debtor, for he is not required to search a register for encumbrances before settling the debt.[90] Perfection by notice is unavailable where the debtor or other obligor is not obliged to have regard to the notice, for example, where it relates to a non-assignable debt or to registered shares or negotiable instruments.[91]

Perfection by novation

As an alternative to assignment, a receivable may be mortgaged by transfer of the receivable into an account in the name of the mortgagee. This gives to rise to a novation.[92]　　**3–33**

Perfection by attornment

A third party receiving a fund as trustee of the debtor acknowledges the creditor's interest and agrees that until that interest has been discharged the third party will act in accordance with the instructions of the creditor, not the debtor. The effect of this attornment is to give the creditor control of the account[93] and perfect a charge on the fund in favour of the creditor.[94] Since this can only properly be done by agreement of the debtor the charge is to be treated as created by the debtor,[95] and differs from an ordinary charge only in that the third party's attornment produces the same effect as receipt of a notice of assignment, the third party in both cases becoming bound to respect the creditor's interest in the fund. Attornment by the third party is therefore a form of perfection alternative to notice to him.　　**3–34**

　　Where the debtor holds a cash or securities account with a bank or securities intermediary, a common method of setting up the control is by transfer of the required amount of cash or securities to a "pledge" or escrow account in the name of the debtor but under the control of a third party, such as an escrow agent.[96]

---

[90] *Snyder's Ltd. v Furniture Finance Corp.* (1930) 66 D.L.R. 79; *Re Royal Bank of Canada* (1979) 94 D.L.R. (3d) 692.

[91] See further below, paras 3–40, 5–08 and 5–28.

[92] See above, para.3–03.

[93] The concept of control is an important feature of Arts 8 and 9 of the Uniform Commercial Code. See §§ 8–106, 9–104 to 9–107. The nearest English law equivalent is attornment.

[94] The attornment merely perfects the charge, it does not create it, for this stems from the prior agreement of the debtor.

[95] But it is probably not a registrable charge, since the third party is not merely a debtor but holds the fund as trust property.

[96] As to escrow balances in CREST accounts, see below, para.6–26.

5. RIGHTS ACQUIRED BY THE ASSIGNEE

Assignee takes subject to equities

3–35   The assignee of a receivable takes subject to equities, *i.e.* to all defences available by the debtor against the assignor and all rights of set-off open to the debtor against the assignor in respect of claims arising prior to the debtor's receipt of notice of assignment.[97]

Assignor is trustee of sums received by him

3–36   Where the debtor, despite notice of assignment, makes payment of a receivable to the assignor, the latter holds the sum received, whether in cash or in the form of a cheque or other instrument, on trust for the assignee.[98] In the latter case, wrongful appropriation of the instrument, *e.g.* by paying it into the assignor's bank account, constitutes a conversion,[99] with an alternative liability to account for the proceeds of the instrument in an action for money had and received.

Tracing receivables into proceeds

3–37   A security interest in receivables automatically attaches to any proceeds received in exchange for them, except where the assignor has been given freedom to deal with the receivables and to mingle the proceeds with his own moneys. So if receivables are disposed of by the assignor without the assignee's authority, or if it is evident that the assignor is in any event required to keep collections and other proceeds as a separate fund for the assignee, the latter's security interest will automatically attach to them, whether they result from collection or sale by the assignor and whether they take the form of cash, instruments, other receivables, goods, land, or indeed anything given in exchange. This tracing right is available against the assignor and the assignee's trustee in bankruptcy or liquidator. Whether it is equally available against a subsequent purchaser or incumbrancer is a priority question which I shall examine a little later.[1]

---

[97] *Roxburghe v Cox* (1881) 17 Ch.D 520; *Re Pinto Leite & Nephews* [1929] 1 Ch. 221; Law of Property Act 1925, s.136(1). See further below, para.7–66. However, if the receivable is embodied in a document which provides that it is to be transferrable free from equities the court will give effect to this *provision* (*Hilger Analytical Ltd. v Rank Precision Industries Ltd., The Times*, December 13, 1983).

[98] *G.E. Crane Sales Pty. Ltd. v Commissioner of Taxation* (1971) 46 A.L.J.R. 15; *Barclays Bank Ltd. v Willowbrock International Ltd.* [1987] 1 F.T.L.R. 386.

[99] The measure of damages is the face value of the cheque. (*Morison v London County & Westminster Bank* [1914] 3 K.B. 356; *International Factors Ltd. v Rodriguez* [19791 1 All E.R. 17).

[1] See below, para.5–36.

6. LEGAL IMPEDIMENTS TO THE CREATION OF SECURITY OVER A RECEIVABLE

In an earlier chapter we have listed the principal types of property which are **3–38** incapable of being given in security.[2] Two of these need to be examined in more detail, namely bare rights of action, on grounds of public policy, and debts made unassignable by contract.[3]

Bare right of action not assignable

The law views with disfavour those who seek to support another's litigation **3–39** without just cause (maintenance) or to exact as the price of such support a right to share in the *fruits* of the litigation (champerty). An agreement by which a party purports to assign a bare right of action, unconnected to any legitimate interest of the assignee, savours of maintenance and champerty and is unenforceable as being contrary to public policy,[4] for its effect would be to enable the assignee to intervene in an action in which he had no proper interest. On the other hand, the assignment of a debt carries with it the right to sue for its recovery, and an assignment is not open to attack as champertous merely because the debt is disputed or it is clear that it will be recovered only through proceedings by the assignee.[5] There is no objection to the assignment of the fruits of an action under an agreement which does not involve either financial support for the litigation or the assignment of a right to intervene in the proceedings.[6] Again, the assignment of a right of action itself is unobjectionable where, looking at the totality of the transaction, the assignment is one in which the assignee had a genuine commercial interest, as where the action concerns property held by the assignee as principal or agent[7] or where the assignor will be able to reduce his indebtedness to the assignee from the fruits of the action[8] or to assign the claim in satisfaction of the debt.[9]

A good illustration of what is and is not permitted is furnished by the decision of the House of Lords in *Trendtex Trading Corp. v Crédit Suisse*[10]:

> The plaintiff owed money to its bankers, the defendants. The plaintiff had a substantial claim against the Central Bank of Nigeria for dishonour of a

---

[2] See above, para.1–35.

[3] An impediment to assignment contained in a negative pledge clause is not discussed here, for it is not inherent in the obligation itself; the question is simply one of priorities. See below, para.5–40.

[4] *Trendtex Trading Corp. v Crédit Suisse* [1981] 3 All E.R. 520, the facts of which are given below.

[5] *Camdex International Ltd. v Bank of Zambia* [1998] Q.B. 22.

[6] *ibid.*

[7] *Kaukomarkkinat O/Y v Elbe Transport Union GmbH: The Kelo* [1985] 2 Lloyd's Rep. 85.

[8] *Trendtex Trading Corp. v Credit Suisse*, above.

[9] *Re Timothy's Pty. Ltd. and the Companies Act* [1981] 2 N.S.W.L.R. 706.

[10] See above.

letter of credit, and the action was financially supported by the defendants, whose only hope of recouping their advances lay in the successful outcome of the proceedings. Subsequently the plaintiff assigned its right of action to the defendants, who almost immediately resold it to an unidentified third party for a substantially higher figure.

In an action by the plaintiff for a declaration that the assignment to the defendants was void as constituting an assignment of a bare right of action, the House of Lords, affirming the decision of the Court of Appeal, held that the assignment in itself was unobjectionable, in that the defendants had a legitimate interest in the success of the action; that the arrangements for sub-sale of the right of action to the third party, who had no legitimate interest in the proceedings, were champertous; but that by virtue of an exclusive jurisdiction clause in the agreement the dispute fell within the jurisdiction of the Swiss courts and was governed by Swiss law.

Contractual prohibition against assignment or charge

3-40 A more serious threat is posed by the common practice on the part of large customers of inserting in their purchase orders a clause prohibiting the supplier from assigning his right to payment under the supply contract. The reasons for such a clause are, first, to avoid the risk of the debtor having to pay twice by inadvertently overlooking notice of assignment and paying the assignor, secondly, to preserve its right to set up new equities notwithstanding receipt of notice of assignment, and thirdly, to avoid exposure to an assignee whom it does not know and who may have a more severe approach to delay in payment or a less amenable attitude to the handling of complaints about the performance for which the payment is exacted.[11]

It is clear that the debtor is not obliged to recognise the title of an assignee under an assignment in breach of a no-assignment clause. It is equally clear that a contractual provision against assignment entitles the debtor to refuse to deal with the assignee and to continue making payment to the assignor, so that the assignment is not capable of taking effect as a statutory assignment. The debtor can therefore safely disregard any notice of assignment by the assignee or any person to whom the assignee itself assigns the debt, and, contrary to the usual rule,[12] he can continue to assert against the assignor rights of set-off arising from mutual dealings concluded after receipt of the notice of assignment.

---

[11] Nevertheless, such a prohibition is inimical to receivables financing, where it is simply not practicable for the assignee (such as factoring company) to examine individual contracts to check for assignment clauses. The issue is scarcely one of protection of the weaker party, since a debtor is unlikely to be able to impose the prohibition unless it holds the stronger bargaining position. In § 9–406(d) of the American Uniform Commercial Code, recognising the impediment to receivables financing that could be created by non-assignment clauses, it is roundly declared that they shall be of no effect. A similar provision appears, with qualifications, in Art.6(1) of the UNIDROIT Convention on International Factoring and in Art.9 of the 2001 United Nations Convention on the Assignment of Receivables in International Trade.

[12] See below, para.7–68.

Further a purported assignment by the original creditor would place him in breach of contract and entitle the debtor to exercise any remedies for breach of contract given him by the agreement or by law. In short, the prohibition is effective as between debtor and assignee, and if the assignee brings proceedings his claim will be dismissed. Such was the outcome of *Helstan Securites Ltd. v Hertfordshire County Council.*[13]

Assignments in breach of a no-assignment are commonly described as void, invalid or ineffective.[14] Such statements, however, do not refer to the proprietary effects of such an assignment as between assignor and assignee but rather to the ineffectiveness of the assignment against the debtor, who is not bound to recognise it. This is made clear in the speech of Lord Browne-Wilkinson in *Linden Gardens Securities Ltd. v Lenesta Sludge Disposals Ltd.*, in which the assignee sought to recover from the debtor despite a prohibition against assignment in the contract. Rejecting the argument that such a prohibition was of no effect even against the debtor Lord Browne-Wilkinson said:

"Therefore the existing authorities establish that an attempted assignment of contractual rights in breach of a contractual prohibition is ineffective to transfer such contractual rights. I regard the law as being satisfactorily settled in that sense. If the law were otherwise, it would defeat the legitimate commercial reason for inserting the contractual prohibition, viz., to ensure that the original parties to the contract are not brought into direct contractual relations with third parties."[15]

However, the debtor is not concerned with the proprietary effects of an assignment as between the parties themselves, whether in relation to the application of the collected proceeds of the debt or in relation to the contract under which it arises. I shall take the former first because in most cases the interest of the assignee lies in the proceeds rather than in the assigned contract as such, under which he is precluded from collecting from the debtor.

(1) *Assignment of right to proceeds*

I have suggested elsewhere,[16] the debtor can have no legitimate interest in controlling the application of his payment after it has reached the hands of the assignor, and reason rebels against the proposition that the assignor, having received from the assignee the price of sale of the debt, is then entitled to keep the debtor's payment for himself. A purported prohibition on the assignment **3–41**

---

[13] [1978] 3 All E.R. 262. See also *Re Turcan* (1889) 40 Ch.D 5; *Shaw & Co. v Moss Empires & Bastow* (1908) 25 T.L.R. 190; and *Spellman v Spellman* [1961] 2 All E.R. 498.

[14] See, for example, *Helstan Securities Ltd. v Hertfordshire County Council*, above, *per* Croom-Johnson J. at 265; *Linden Gardens Trust Ltd. v Lenesta Sludge Disposals Ltd.* [1994] 1 A.C. 85, *per* Lord Browne-Wilkinson at 109.

[15] *ibid.*, at 108.

[16] "Inalienable Rights? "(1979) 42 M.L.R. 553, to which extensive references will be found in Lord Browne-Wilkinson's speech in the *Lenesta Sludge* case, above.

of the collected proceeds would, it is thought, be contrary to public policy as an unacceptable restraint on alienation. This proposition[17] receives support from the judgment of Darling J. in *Tom Shaw & Co. v Moss Empires Ltd.*[18] and a measure of encouragement from the speech of Lord Browne-Wilkinson in the *Lenesta Sludge* case. In the former case Darling J. observed that a prohibition against assignment "could no more operate to invalidate the assignment than it could interfere with the laws of gravitation. It would not prevent that being an equitable assignment which would be one apart from it."[19] Lord Browne-Wilkinson did not dissent from this statement insofar as it was directed to receipts in the hands of the assignor rather than recoverability from the debtor, and while expressing no view on the public policy point he was prepared to recognise that it might well be correct:

> "The case [*Tom Shaw & Co. v Moss Empires Ltd.*] is inadequately reported and it is hard to discover exactly what it decides. Given that both B. and Moss Empires were parties and Moss Empires was in effect interpleading, it may be that the words I have quoted merely indicate that as between the assignor, B., and the assignee Tom Shaw, the prohibition contained in the contract between B. and Moss Empires could not invalidate B.'s liability to account to Tom Shaw for the moneys when received and that, since B. was a party, payment direct to Tom Shaw was ordered. This view is supported by the fact that no order for costs was made against Moss Empires. If this is the right view of the case, it is unexceptionable: a prohibition on assignment normally only invalidates the assignment as against the other party to the contract so as to prevent a transfer of the chose in action: in the absence of the clearest words it cannot operate to invalidate the contract as between the assignor and the assignee and even then it may be ineffective on the grounds of public policy. If on the other hand Darling J. purported to hold that the contractual prohibition was ineffective to prevent B.'s contractual rights against Moss Empires being transferred to Tom Shaw, it is inconsistent with authority and was wrongly decided.
>
> In the *Helstan Securities* case [1978] 3 All E.R. 262 Croom-Johnson J. did not follow the *Tom Shaw* case and held that the purported assignment in breach of the contractual provision was ineffective to vest the cause of action in the assignee. That decision was followed and applied by the Court of Appeal in the *Reed Publishing Holdings* case, May 25, 1983: see also *In re Turcan* . . ."[20]

(2) Assignment of benefit of contract

3–42 While the assignee of a non-assignable debt or other contract right looks primarily to the proceeds, he may also have a legitimate interest as beneficiary of

---

[17] See "Inalienable Rights?", above, n.16 at 555–556.
[18] (1908) 25 T.L.R. 190.
[19] *ibid*. at 191.
[20] [1994] 1 A.C. 85 at 108.

the contract right before any proceeds have been received, and the court will give effect to this so long as it does not affect the right of the debtor to continue to deal exclusively with the assignor. Thus in *Re Turcan*[21] it was held that provisions in a life policy rendering it unassignable did not preclude them from coming within the terms of a covenant to settle after-acquired property. In that case the settlor had already died before the matter came before the court, so that the issue was whether the proceeds of the life policies should be handed over to the trustees of the settlement. An order to that effect was upheld by the Court of Appeal, which did, however, go on to hold that the covenant to settle the policies would have been enforceable in the settlor's lifetime despite the prohibition against assignment. This makes good sense, for even if a beneficiary has no right to enforce a contract itself or to interfere in its management, he has an interest in ensuring that trust assets are held in accordance with the trust. The point was thrown into sharper focus in *Don King Productions Inc. v Warren & Co.*,[22] where the facts were as follows:

> The plaintiff and the defendant entered into a partnership agreement for the management and promotion of registered boxers. The agreement provided for the assignment of earlier management and promotion contracts despite the fact that these contained prohibitions against assignment. Subsequently a new partnership agreement was entered into providing for all such existing and future contracts to be held on trust for the partnership. The parties undertook not to be engaged in any business carried on by the partnership otherwise than through the partnership. Nevertheless one of the partners later entered into another agreement for his own benefit, whereupon the remaining partners instituted proceedings for breach of the partnership agreement and subsequently dissolved the partnership. The defendant contended, among other things, that the effect of the prohibition against assignment was to limit the interest of the partnership to a trust of the receipts coming into the hands of the would-be assignor prior to dissolution of the partnership.
>
> The Court of Appeal, affirming the decision of Lightman J., rejected this argument and held that the contract rights themselves, though assigned to a partnership in breach of a no-assignment clause, could nevertheless form part of the partnership property. Morritt L.J. quoted with approval a passage from the judgment Lightman J. in which he had said:

> > "I can see no objection to a party to contracts involving skill and confidence or containing non-assignment provisions from becoming trustee of the benefit of being the contracting party as well as the benefit of the rights conferred. I can see no reason why the law should limit the parties' freedom of contract to creating trusts of the fruits of such contracts received by the assignor or to creating an accounting relationship between the parties in respect of the fruits."[23]

---

[21] (1888) 40 Ch.D 5.
[22] [1999] 2 All E.R. 218, criticises Andrew Tettenborn [1999] L.M.C.L.Q. 353.
[23] *ibid.*, at 634.

3–43   The last case to be considered on this topic is the decision of the Court of Appeal in *Foamcrete (UK) Ltd. v Thrust Engineering Ltd.*[24]

> PTE, a company, granted its bank a debenture containing (*inter alia*) a floating charge over its undertaking and property, present and future. Later it entered into two agreements with Thrust Engineering, a joint venture agreement ("the principal agreement") and a supplementary "purchase of stock agreement" under which Thrust became liable to make payments for stock and work in progress. The principal agreement provided that rights and obligations under it could not be assigned by either party without the consent of the other. Subsequently PTE went into liquidation, and thereafter the bank transferred the debenture to Foamcrete, who gave notice of assignment to Thrust and, payment not having been made, instituted proceedings. Thrust contended that the assignment of the debenture was ineffective, being in breach of the no-assigment clause.
>
> The Court of Appeal rejected the defence, holding, first, that the no-assignment clause was contained not in the principal agreement but in the purchase of stock agreement, but, secondly, if it was contained in the principal agreement then the bank's rights derived not from the assignment but from the floating charge, by which it "acquired an immediate beneficial interest in all the property, present and future, subject to the equitable charge prior to the creation of the debt due to PTE from Thrust Engineering"[25] and that the grant of the debenture could not possibly infringe the prohibition against assignment, which did not then exist.

The decision is puzzling. Quite apart from the fact that a floating charge confers no interest in any specific asset prior to crystallisation,[26] it is well established that even in the case of a fixed charge of after-acquired property the chargee takes the property as he finds it, warts and all, so that if, for example, the property is acquired with the aid of an advance secured by a mortgage or charge agreed prior to the purchase the after-acquired property clause catches the property in its incumbered form, and therefore attaches only to the chargor's equity of redemption.[27] By the same token, where the after-acquired property clause picks up the benefit of a future contract, it can do so only on the contract terms, including any prohibition against assignment. Accordingly the debtor, Thrust, was not obliged to recognise either the fixed security interest produced by crystallisation of the floating charge or the title of the bank's assignee, and its defence should, it is submitted, have succeeded.

---

[24] [2002] B.C.C. 221.
[25] *ibid., per* Mummery L.J. at 225.
[26] See below, paras 4–03 *et seq.*
[27] See below, para.5–62.

IV

The Floating Charge

The floating charge is one of the most subtle creations of equity, and despite **4–01** the volume of case law and literature devoted to its analysis it remains conceptually elusive.[1] This is because a floating charge is an interest not in specific assets but in a constantly changing fund of assets and English law has always found it difficult to grapple with the concept of a fund. To Maitland, one of the most brilliant legal minds in the history of English law, all equitable rights, including the rights of a beneficiary under an active trust, were rights *in personam*[2]; to the modern equity lawyer the beneficiary has something more, a proprietary interest in a trust fund which, though not attaching to specific assets while the trust continues in force nevertheless attracts proprietary remedies for the preservation of the fund, including the equitable right to claim traced assets improperly disposed of by the trustees. It can now be taken as settled that the floating charge creates an immediate interest *in rem*; what continue to be the subject of debate are the nature and incidents of that interest. It is these that I propose to explore in the present chapter. The general characteristics of a floating charge are described in section 1 below. A detailed analysis of the distinction between fixed and floating charges and the degree of control necessary to ensure that a charge is characterised as a fixed charge is provided in section 4. Priority issues, including the priority effect of a negative pledge clause in a floating charge, will be examined in Chapter V.

The present chapter focuses on floating charges by companies. In general, it is not possible for an unincorporated trader to grant a floating charge over goods, for under the Bills of Sale Act (1878) Amendment Act 1882 a security bill of sale is void, except as against the grantor, in respect of any personal chattels not specifically described in the schedule to the bill[3] or in respect of personal chattels so described of which the grantor was not the true owner at the time of execution of the bill.[4] Other classes of asset are outside the Bills of Sale Acts, but a general assignment of book debts by an unincorporated trader must be registered as if it were a bill of sale.[5] Moreover, there are

---

[1] The most comprehensive and penetrating treatment is to be found in W.J. Gough, *Company Charges* (2nd ed.), Chs 5–16.
[2] Equity (2nd.), Lecture IX.
[3] s.4.
[4] s.5.
[5] Insolvency Act 1986, s.344(1). See also above, para.3–31.

various exemptions from the Bills of Sale Acts. In particular, they do not apply to agricultural charges by a farmer, whether fixed or floating.[6]

1. THE CONCEPTION OF THE FLOATING CHARGE

The genesis of the floating charge[7]

4–02   In *Holroyd v Marshall*[8] the House of Lords settled once and for all the efficacy of a fixed charge over future property. The concept was not new; indeed, in *Holroyd v Marshall* itself it was considered established. Such a device was most beneficial to the creditor, for it gave him a hold over all after-acquired property of the debtor falling within the classes of asset specified in the charge and precluded the debtor from disposing of such property free from the charge without the debtor's consent. From the debtor's viewpoint, the arrangement was quite acceptable as regards fixed assets but it was another matter in the case of stock in trade. To require a trading company borrowing money on the security of its stock to obtain the consent of the creditor every time it wished to dispose of an item of stock would create an intolerable administrative burden for both parties; and since the debtor could repay the advance only from the proceeds of sales, it was necessary to allow the company freedom to dispose of its trading stock in the ordinary course of business free from the charge. Could a charge instrument allow this to be done without vitiating the security effect of the agreement?

It is interesting to contrast the answers to this question in American and English jurisprudence. Courts in the United States roundly declared that to allow such freedom to the debtor was incompatible with the creation of a genuine security interest and was a fraud on creditors. If the creditor did not exercise reasonable dominium over the asset covered by the security agreement, his security was illusory and void.[9] At best, the security agreement conferred contractual rights on the creditor.

The approach of the English courts was more accommodating to the needs of the inventory financier. The effect of the provision allowing the debtor company freedom to deal with the charged assets in the ordinary course of business was not to negate the security interest but merely to postpone its

---

[6]   Agricultural Credits Act 1928, s.8(1). s.7 of the Act has special provisions as to crystallisation of agricultural floating charges. See below, paras 4–30, 4–52.

[7]   See R.R. Pennington, "The Genesis of the Floating Charge" (1960) 23 M.L.R. 630; and the historical account given by Lord Millett in *Agnew v Commissioners of Inland Revenue* (also known as *Re Brumark*) [2001] 2 A.C. 710 at 717, giving the decision of the Privy Council on appeal from the New Zealand Court of Appeal.

[8]   (1862) 10 H.L. Cas. 191.

[9]   *Geilfuss v Corrigan*, 95 Wis. 651; 70 N.W. 306 (1897); *Benedict v Ratner*, 268 U.S. 354; 45 S.Ct. 566; 69 L.Ed. 991 (1925). For a detailed description of the American position prior to the Uniform Commercial Code, see Grant Gilmore, *Security Interests in Personal Property*, Chs 6 and 8.

attachment so long as the debtor's powers of management continued.[10] In conformity with the principle previously stated, that a security interest does not attach until fulfilment of the conditions for attachment specified in the agreement, the charge floated over all assets of the company, present and future, within the description in the charge instrument, until the debtor company's power to manage the assets was brought to an end by the creditor's intervention in accordance with the terms of the charge instrument or by the debtor going into receivership or liquidation or upon the occurrence of some other event specified in the charge instrument. The charge then crystallised, fastening *in specie* on property within the description in the charge instrument in which the debtor company then had or subsequently acquired an interest. Thus in contrast to American law, English law permitted a form of security in which attachment was contractually postponed. It was not a specific security with a licence to the debtor company to deal with the assets in the ordinary course of business, but an ambulatory security dependent for its attachment on the fulfilment of a condition precedent, namely the occurrence of a crystallising event. The new device was first ruled effective by the Court of Appeal in *Re Panama, New Zealand and Australia Royal Mail Co.*,[11] a decision upheld and applied in *Re Yorkshire Woolcombers Association Ltd.*[12]

The nature and characteristics of a floating charge

Despite *Re Panama*, some judges found it difficult to see how any security interest could be said to exist prior to crystallisation. Surely until this time there was merely a contract between creditor and debtor for the provision of security? Certainly a floating charge does not do much for the creditor prior to crystallisation. He cannot exercise proprietary or possessory rights over the assets either as against the company or as against third parties, nor does he have a *locus standi* to obtain an injunction against the company to restrain dealings with its assets in the ordinary course of business where the dealings are not in breach of the debenture or subject to the creditor's veto and his security is not in jeopardy.[13] Nevertheless, it is now established that a floating charge creates an immediate, albeit unattached, security interest. This idea is most clearly expressed by Buckley L.J. in *Evans v Rival Granite Quarries Ltd*[14]:

4–03

---

[10] Indeed, for several centuries equity appears to have recognised the concept of a *fixed* mortgage by individual traders and partnerships covering both present and future property, the mortgagor being left in possession with power to deal with the mortgaged assets in the course of carrying on business, a process brought to an abrupt halt by the controversial decision of Jarvis C.J. in *Graham v Chapman* (1852) 12 C.B. 85. See the illuminating historical analysis by Roger Gregory and Peter Walton, "Fixed and floating charges—a revelation" [2001] L.M.C.L.Q. 123, which notes the influence of bankruptcy law in the development of constraints on non-possessory charges over future property.

[11] (1870) 5 Ch.App. 318.

[12] [1903] 2 Ch. 284, affirmed sub nom. *Illingworth v Houldsworth* [1904] A.C. 355.

[13] *Re Borax Co.* [1901] 1 Ch. 326; *Lawrence v West Somerset Mineral Ry Co.* [1918] 2 Ch. 250.

[14] [1910] 2 K.B. 979.

"A floating charge is not a future security; it is a present security which presently affects all the assets of the company expressed to be included in it ... A floating security is not a specific mortgage of the assets, plus a licence to the mortgagor to dispose of them in the course of his business, but is a floating mortgage applying to every item comprised in the security, but not specifically affecting any item until some act or event occurs or some act on the part of the mortgagee is done which causes it to crystallise into a fixed security."[15]

How, then, do we identify a floating charge? What are the hallmarks of such a security? Valuable guidance is offered by the much-quoted judgment of Romer L.J. in *Re Yorkshire Woolcombers Association Ltd*[16]:

"I certainly do not intend to attempt to given an exact definition of the term 'floating charge,' nor am I prepared to say that there will not be a floating charge within the meaning of the Act, which does not contain all the three characteristics that I am about to mention, but I certainly think that if a charge has the three characteristics that I am about to mention it is a floating charge. (1.) If it is a charge on a class of assets of a company present and future. (2.) If that class is one which in the ordinary course of the business of the company would be changing from time to time; and (3.) If you find that by the charge it is contemplated that, until some future step is taken by or on behalf of those interested in the charge, the company may carry on its business in the ordinary way so far as concerns the particular class of assets I am dealing with."

When read with the extract from the judgment of Buckley L.J., previously quoted, this passage (if modified to take account of automatic crystallisation) shows the two essential ingredients of a floating charge, namely that it is a *present* security in a *fund* of assets which the debtor company is left free to manage in the ordinary course of its business,[17] though not necessarily completely free.[18] Though on a literal reading of the judgment by Romer L.J. the type of charge he is describing is a charge on a changing fund of assets, it seems clear that what he was actually referring to was not a change in the nature of the fund (*i.e.* a shift from one class of asset to another) but rather a change from time to time in the composition of the fund, as where the fund consists of stock in trade where items of stock will move out of the fund on sale while others will move into the fund on production or acquisition. The status of the floating charge as a present security distinguishes it from a mere contract to give security at a future date on the occurrence of a desig-

---

[15] [1910] 2 K.B. at 999.

[16] [1903] 2 Ch. 284, at 295. See also [1904] A.C. 355, *per* Lord Macnaghten at 358.

[17] The concept of a floating charge as an interest in a fund has recently been endorsed in the decision by the Privy Council in *Agnew v Commissioners of Inland Revenue* [2001] 2 A.C. 710, *per* Lord Millett at 719. For the meaning of "ordinary course of business" in the context of priorities see below, para.5–39.

[18] See below, para.4–21.

nated uncertain event. Its characteristic of an interest in a changeable fund of assets distinguishes it from an agreement for the provision of security over a particular asset where attachment is postponed.

In English law, a fund is considered to have an existence distinct from that of **4–04** its components. The contents of the fund are constantly changing as assets are removed from the fund and new assets come into it, but the identity of the fund itself remains unchanged, in much the same way as the river Thames remains the river Thames despite the fact that the water in it is never the same from one minute to the next. Indeed, an open-ended fund (*i.e.* one which by the terms of its establishment is capable of increase with the addition of new assets) has a notional existence even at times when there are no assets comprised in it. To carry the river simile a stage further, we should continue to speak of the river Thames even if, through a drought, it had temporarily dried up.[19]

An analogy is not hard to find. The interest of a beneficiary in a trust fund is exactly in point. So long as the trustee's power of management continue, the beneficiary has no rights in any specific asset within the fund. His interest is a floating interest of the same kind as that of the chargee under a floating charge.

Hence the peculiarity of the floating charge is that, like an interest in a trust fund, it has immediate existence even prior to attachment. But is it of the essence of a floating charge that the fund should be open-ended? In *Re Bond Worth Ltd.*[20] Slade, J., in the course of a superb analysis of the nature of security, answered this question in the negative. He pointed out that whilst Romer L.J., in the passage quoted earlier, had referred to a floating charge as covering future as well as present assets, he had also made it clear that it was not necessarily the case that a floating charge should possess all the three characteristics he had mentioned. Similarly, in *Re Agnew*[21] Lord Millett, in referring to the three characteristics of a floating charge described by Romer L.J. in *Re Yorkshire Woolcombers Association Ltd.*,[22] observed that Romer L.J.'s judgment offered a description, not a definition, and that while the first two characteristics (charge on a class of present and future assets, the class changing[23] from time to time in the ordinary course of business) are typical of a floating charge they are not distinctive of it, and it was the third characteristic (freedom to deal) which was the hallmark of a floating charge. Hence a closed fund, which is restricted to existing assets and cannot increase but can only reduce, because the debtor is obliged to pay over to the chargee the proceeds of assets sold instead of being able to use these to acquire new assets, nevertheless suffices for a floating charge.[24] So long as the debtor's

---

[19] As with the river Todd in Alice Springs, Australia, which is dry for most of the year. The annual boat race, designated Henley on Todd, is run by the two teams carrying their respective boats on their shoulders.

[20] [1979] 3 All E.R. 919.

[21] [2001] 2 A.C. 710.

[22] [1903] 2 Ch. 284.

[23] More accurately, the individual components of the class changing.

[24] This was the point overlooked in *Re Atlantic Computers Systems plc* [1992] Ch. 505. See below, para.4–15.

powers of management continue, the fund remains in being until the last unit comprised in it is disposed of. In short, while a fund usually consists of a class or collection of present and future assets the test of a fund is not whether it encompasses future assets or even the number of present assets comprised in it but the power given to the manager to deal with them free from interference by the beneficial owner or chargee so long as the power continues.

The relevance of intention to characterisation

4-05 It is necessary to distinguish the intention of the parties from the legal effect of what they have intended. Their intention is to be gathered from the terms of their agreement; whether what they have agreed produces the intended effect is a matter of law.[25] So the parties may intend to create a fixed charge rather than a floating charge, but this is not enough, as if it was, all the parties would have to do would be to label the charge a fixed charge.[26]

Significance of the floating charge as a present security

4-06 At this point, you might well ask why the courts have found it necessary to describe the floating charge as a present security. This has led some commentators to advance the theory that a floating charge is a defeasible security interest which confers on the chargee the same quality of proprietary interest as that of a fixed chargee except that it is defeasible.[27] However, there are fundamental objections to this approach. In the first place, it is impossible to distinguish such a floating charge from a fixed charge with a licence to deal, a characterisation which the authorities have rejected.[28] Secondly, it is clear from the cases referred to above and many others in which they have been cited[29] that until crystallisation the charge does not attach to any asset *in specie*, so that it is quite different in nature from a fixed charge; if that were not the case, there would be no need for a concept of crystallisation. Thirdly, it is equally clear that crystallisation is not retrospective.

What, then, does this presently existing security interest give the floating chargee which he would not have under a mere contract to assign assets in the future? First, the occurrence of the crystallising event causes the charge to

---

[25] *Agnew v Commissioners of Inland Revenue* [2001] 2 A.C. 710; *Re Keenan Bros. Ltd.* [1986] B.C.L.C. 242, *per* McCarthy J. at 247.

[26] *Agnew v Commissioners of Inland Revenue* [2001] 2 A.C. 710, *per* Lord Millett at 725–726.

[27] See, for example, Sarah Worthington, *Proprietary Interests in Commercial Transactions*, pp.79–86.

[28] The difference is said to be that the fixed charge with a licence to deal is not defeasible (Worthington, *op. cit.*, at 81), but the licence to deal plainly has the effect that it *is* defeasible.

[29] See, for example, *Re Benjamin Cope & Sons Ltd.* [1914] 1 Ch. 800, *per* Sargant J. at 806; *Agnew v Inland Revenue Commissioners* [2001] 2 A.C. 710; *Re Cosslett Contractors) Ltd.* [1998] Ch. 495, *per* Millett L.J. at 509–510.

attach without the need for any new act on the part of the debtor. Secondly, the debenture holder has the right, on crystallisation, to follow the assets into the hands of a purchaser or incumbrancer who prior to crystallisation took them from the company otherwise than in the ordinary course of the company's business.[30] Thirdly, restrictions in the floating charge on dealings in the assets by the company bind a subsequent party taking with notice of such restrictions, so that upon the floating charge crystallising it will have priority[31] Fourthly, the procedural security which an execution creditor obtains by delivery of a writ of execution to the sheriff[32] takes effect subject to the prior equity of the debenture holder under the floating charge, so that if the charge crystallises before the execution is completed, the debenture holder obtains priority over the execution creditor, even though crystallisation does not occur until after the goods have become bound by the writ or even, indeed, until after their seizure by the sheriff.[33] Finally, by virtue of the fact that he has an existing security interest, albeit floating in character, the debenture holder has the right to apply to the court for the appointment of a receiver where his security is in jeopardy, even if the charge has not crystallised[34] and even if there has been no default.[35] Though the holding of a property interest by the applicant is not an essential condition of the appointment of a receiver by the court[36] it greatly strengthens the case for such appointment, which has the effect of crystallising the charge.[37] Similar considerations apply to the grant of an injunction at the behest of the holder of a floating charge to restrain the company from disposing of its assets otherwise than as permitted by the charge.[38]

Attachment of the floating charge

When the debtor company's powers of management come to an end, the charge is said to crystallise, that is, it ceases to be an interest in a fund of assets and becomes attached to the specific assets then comprised in the fund and any further assets acquired by the company. Like a fixed charge, a

4–07

---

[30] See below, para.5–44.
[31] See below, para.5–40, and as to the notice paras 2–24, 2–26 above.
[32] Supreme Court Act 1981, s.138.
[33] *Re Standard Manufacturing Co.* [1891] 1 Ch. 627; *Re Opera Ltd.* [1891] 3 Ch. 260; *Evans v Rival Granite Quarries Ltd.* [1910] 2 K.B. 979, *per* Fletcher Moulton L.J. at 996; *Taunton v Sheriff of Warwickshire* [1895] 2 Ch. 319.
[34] *Hubbuck v Helms* (1887) 56 L.T. 232; *Edwards v Standard Rollins Stock Syndicate* [1893] 1 Ch. 574; *Re London Pressed Hinge Co. Ltd.* [1905] 1 Ch. 576; *Re Victoria Steamboats Ltd.* [1897] 1 Ch. 158, where Kekewich J. held that the court could also appoint a manager.
[35] *Re London Pressed Hinge Co. Ltd.*, above.
[36] See Lightman and Moss, *The Law of Receivers and Administrators of Companies* (3rd ed.), paras 22–006 *et seq.*
[37] See below, para.4–43.
[38] See below, para.4–48. Whether the court would grant a mandatory injunction to undo a disposition which to the knowledge of the disponee was in breach of the restriction in the floating charge is another matter. The court might well take the view that such an injunction is unnecessary, since on crystallisation the floating charge would anyway have priority, so that there is nothing to undo.

floating charge takes effect as a security from the date of the security agreement. It is often said that once a floating charge has crystallised so as to become fixed it is treated in the same way as if it had been fixed from the outset. This, however, is not the case. In the first place, crystallisation is not retrospective. Secondly, the fact that the charge started life as a floating charge means that even after crystallisation the company may have ostensible authority to deal with the charged assets, and this may affect priorities in the event of subsequent dealings.[39] Thirdly, for the purpose of certain provisions of the Insolvency Act 1986 the rule is: once a floating charge, always a floating charge. More accurately, a floating charge is defined as a charge which, as created, was a floating charge.[40] It follows that crystallisation of a charge before a winding-up or other event attracting the rights of preferential creditors does not prevent the charge from being subordinated to preferential debts.[41] Conversely, a charge created as a fixed charge retains its status as such for the purposes of the Insolvency Act even though it has subsequently been converted into a floating charge pursuant to an agreement to that effect.[42] The result is that the chargee is not postponed to preferential creditors; on the other hand, he cannot appoint an administrative receiver.[43]

2. FIXED CHARGE VERSUS FLOATING CHARGE

4–08 I have taken some time to examine the nature of a floating charge and the characteristics which distinguish it from a fixed (or specific) charge. Though the distinction is relatively easy to state, it has been found much harder to apply in practice. Particular difficulty has been occasioned by charges over book debts and the relationship between book debts and their proceeds. Everything turns on the extent to which the chargee has contractual control, an issue we shall examine in detail a little later.[44] At this stage it is just worth emphasising that the distinction is not, as is frequently supposed, between a charge over existing assets and a charge over future assets, because *Holroyd v Marshall*[45] reaffirmed the efficacy of a fixed charge over after-acquired property, nor between a charge over fixed assets and a charge over current assets, but between a charge which leaves control with the chargee and one which does not.

---

[39] See below, paras 4–29, 5–50.
[40] Insolvency Act 1986, s.251; and see *ibid.*, s.40(1); Companies Act 1985, s.196(1) and below, para.5–65.
[41] See below, para.5–65.
[42] See below, para.4–57.
[43] As to the prospective abolition of administrative receivership except in specified cases, see above, para.1–01, below, paras 4–09, 4–61.
[44] See below, paras 4–21 *et seq.*
[45] (1862) 10 H.L. Cas. 191.

Significance of the distinction

Meanwhile we must address a preliminary question: what is the significance **4–09** of the distinction between a fixed and a floating charge? Is one preferable to the other? Here it is necessary to distinguish legal from commercial considerations. Assuming that the debtor company has a sound business, it is not in the interests of either party unduly to fetter the company's ability to run its business, for it is from the income generated by the company's trading activities that the creditor will ultimately be paid. For the creditor to tie up the debtor with covenants so stringent that the creditor will have to turn a blind eye to breaches in order to avoid paralysing the business or impairing its efficiency is not good sense. This is a point which lawyers are all too inclined to overlook. Just as the old-style wills draftsman used to provide a life interest for the testator's widow, rather than an absolute interest, in order to defer estate duty, with the result that duty was deferred but the widow was left destitute, so also the modern draftsman of debentures is inclined to go for overkill, forgetting that a sound business is best run by the directors, not by the debenture holder. I shall revert to this later.[46]

A further advantage of the floating charge is that if this, with other security, covers the whole or substantially the whole of the debtor company's property, the chargee can take power to appoint an administrative receiver to manage the entire business of the company, continue trading and hive down or sell off the business as a whole in the event of default instead of merely having to sell specific assets. Only the holder of a charge which as created was a floating charge can do this.[47] However, with certain exceptions administrative receivership is to be abolished,[48] reflecting a concern that it undermined the prospects of reorganisation of a company through administration.[49]

Despite the virtues of a floating charge there is no question that a fixed **4–10** charge has several advantages over a floating charge when it comes to protection of the creditor. In the first place, the creditor acquires immediate real rights over the asset which can only be cut off by a disposition to a bona fide purchaser of the legal estate or title for value without notice. Since most charges are registrable, most categories of third party will be fixed with notice of the charge,[50] and will accordingly be bound by it. By contrast, the disposition of an asset which is the subject of a floating charge will as a general

---

[46] See below, para.4–54.
[47] See Insolvency Act 1986, s.29(2). So long as there is a floating charge it is irrelevant that most of the company's property is subject to fixed charges.
[48] Insolvency Act 1986, s.72A(1), inserted by the Enterprise Act 2002, s.250(1). See para.4–61.
[49] This is because s.9(3) of the Insolvency Act 1986 generally requires the court to dismiss an application for an administration order where there is an administrative receiver unless he consents. One would have thought that the perceived mischief to which the insolvency provisions of the Enterprise Act are directed could have been dealt with by simply repealing s.9(3), so that an administration order could be made despite the appointment of an administrative receiver, who upon the making of the order would have to vacate office (Insolvency Act 1986, s.11(2)). It is not clear why this short and elegant way of dealing with the problem was not utilised.
[50] Companies Act 1985, s.395.

rule take effect free from the charge, whether the disposition be outright or by way of charge or mortgage and whether or not the charge has been registered or the disponee knows of it.[51] Secondly, a floating charge is postponed to the rights of preferential creditors if the debenture holder takes possession of any of the charged assets[52] or if the company goes into receivership[53] or liquidation,[54] whereas a fixed charge[55] has priority over all unsecured claims, preferential or otherwise. Thirdly, a floating charge given by an insolvent company within the twelve months[56] prior to the onset of insolvency[57] is void except as to new value.[58] Fourthly, all floating charges given by a company require to be registered, whereas a fixed charge is registrable only if taken over a class of asset listed in s.396 of the Companies Act 1985 or if it would have been registrable as a bill of sale if granted by an individual.[59] So fixed charges by a company which would, if given by an individual, be outside the Bills of Sale Acts[60] or exempt from them[61] are not within s.395 unless registrable under some other head within that section, for example as a charge on book debts. Finally, the recommendation made by the Insolvency Law Review Committee two decades ago that a fund equal to 10 per cent of the net realisations of assets subject to a floating charge should be made available for distribution among unsecured creditors[62]—a recommendation rejected by the government of the day—has now resurfaced in the form of a new s.176A of the Insolvency Act 1986.[63] If this provision is enacted, prospective lenders on the security of a floating charge will need to be aware that the value of the crystallised security, already potentially reduced by subordination to preferential debts, will be further reduced by the contribution to the fund.

---

[51] See below, paras 5–38 et seq.

[52] Companies Act 1985, s.196.

[53] Insolvency Act 1986, s.40.

[54] ibid., s.175. See further below, para.5–65, as to the effect of this provision and those referred to above, nn.52 and 53. Crown preference, already restricted to collected taxes, is now to be abolished altogether. See below, para.5–65.

[55] i.e. a charge which starts life as a fixed charge. See above, para.4–07.

[56] Or two years in the case of a charge in favour of a person connected with the company.

[57] As defined by the Insolvency Act 1986, s.245(5).

[58] ibid., s.245(2). See further para.5–69.

[59] See Bills of Sale Acts 1878–1891, and Halsbury's Laws of England (4th ed.), Vol.4, 235.

[60] e.g. charges (1) created orally or by conduct; (2) over goods to be imported (Bills of Sale Acts 1890–1891); (3) over choses in action (Bills of Sale Act 1878, s.4; but a charge over book debts is specifically registrable under s.395 and a general assignment of book debts under the Insolvency Act 1986, s.344(3)(6)).

[61] See Halsbury's Laws (4th ed.), Vol.4(1), paras 665 et seq.

[62] Insolvency Law and Practice (Cmnd. 8558, 1982), paras 1538 et seq. The origin of the idea for the 10 per cent fund is not generally known—even to members of the Insolvency Law Review Committee! It was the present writer who, while serving on the Legal Panel set up by the Committee, suggested it to a member of the Committee, as a means of taking the heat off the floating charge, while passing the time in conversation on the train home after cerebral stimulation in the shape of a couple of pints of beer at St. Pancras Station. Somewhat to the writer's astonishment it featured in the Committee's report six months later!

[63] Inserted by the Enterprise Act 2002, s.252, which leaves the percentage to be prescribed by statutory instrument.

Over what classes of asset may a fixed charge be taken?

Until 1978 it was widely assumed that, because a floating charge is custom-   **4–11**
arily taken over assets of a shifting character, any charge is a floating charge
as regards such assets. In other words, it was thought that a fixed charge
could not be taken over current (or circulating) assets, only over fixed assets.
The latter have been statutorily defined for the purposes of a company's
accounts as assets which are intended for use on a continuing basis in the
company's activities, all other assets being current assets.[64] Thus fixed assets
will normally include land and buildings,[65] fixtures, plant, equipment used for
office purposes or in the manufacture of goods for sale or rental, and intellectual property rights, while the most common current assets are cash, trade
and other debts, and inventory, including raw material and finished stock in
trade held for sale or lease.

The reason why it had been assumed that current assets were not susceptible to a fixed charge was that by their nature they are either spent (*e.g.* cash)
or consumed in the course of manufacture (*e.g.* raw materials) or held only
temporarily as stock in trade prior to being sold or let on lease in the ordinary course of business, for which purpose it was essential for them to be
transferred free from any security interest. But the decision in *Siebe Gorman
& Co. Ltd. v Barclays Bank Ltd.*[66] exposed the fallacy of this approach and
showed that the material factor was not whether the charged assets were fixed
or current but whether the debtor company was left with the right to deal
with the assets in the ordinary course of business free from the security interest, a freedom incompatible with the concept of a fixed security but perfectly
consistent with a floating charge, from which assets escape when disposed of
in the ordinary course of business and which thus provides the creditor with
security without paralysing the business. This led to the realisation that it is
possible, if in most cases very inconvenient, to have a fixed charge over current assets, and conversely (but with less inconvenience) to have a floating
charge over fixed assets, such as land.

Again, the mere fact that assets subject to a charge are fixed assets and   **4–12**
therefore likely to be held on a more permanent basis and not disposed of
until they need replacement does not conclusively establish that the charge
itself is a fixed charge, particularly where the assets are items of plant, furniture or equipment which are likely to need replacement from time to time.
When read as a whole the charge instrument may be open to the construction
that such assets were intended to be left outside the control of the chargee in
the same way as current assets covered by the charge, as where the charge
instrument is expressed to cover not only stock in trade and book debts but
also plant, equipment and furniture of a kind likely to need replacement from

---

[64] Companies Act 1985, s.262(1).
[65] But land held by a developer may well constitute the developer's trading stock. See, for example, the decision of the New South Wales Court of Appeal in *Boambee Bay Resort Pty. Ltd. v
Equus Financial Services Ltd.* (1991) 26 N.S.W.L.R. 284.
[66] [1979] 2 Lloyd's Rep. 142. See below, paras 4–13 *et seq.*

time to time, and these assets are grouped with the stock in trade and book debts without differentiation.[67] The moral for the draftsman, in expressing a charge over such fixed assets as a fixed charge, is to make it very clear that the fixed assets are not to be disposed of free from the charge except on terms that they are replaced on a unit-by-unit basis, replacements then becoming subject to the charge. In other words, a contrast should be drawn between a general power of disposition and a power to make item-by-item substitutions as and when needed.[68]

But subject to any contrary inferences to be drawn from the charge instrument itself it is generally true to say that there is a presumption that a charge over current assets is a floating charge and one over fixed assets is a fixed charge. Thus a charge on land will usually be considered a fixed charge even if it does not contain any express provision restricting disposition of the land by the chargor free from the charge. Such a restriction is taken for granted as inherent in the nature of the charge. The position might be otherwise where the chargor is a developer holding the charged land as part of its stock.

With these preliminary observations I turn to consider the application of the principles stated above to different classes of current asset.

Book debts

4-13   The principal area of dispute in relation to the characterisation of a charge as fixed or floating concerns charges over book debts. Banks in particular have been concerned to show that restrictions in their debentures have established their charges as fixed, while liquidators have been equally astute to seek to strike such charges down as unregistered floating charges. The result has been a substantial volume of litigation, in which we may distinguish four phases. In the first it was established in *Siebe Gorman*[69] that it is possible to take a fixed charge over book debts. In the second it was decided in *Re Brightlife*[70] that this required not only restrictions on the sale of book debts but control over their proceeds, whether these resulted from sale of the book debts or (the most common in the reported cases) their collection by the chargor. This control could be exercised either by the chargee collecting the debts itself or by the chargor collecting them for the account of the chargee

---

[67] See, for example, *National Provincial Bank of England Ltd. v United Electric Theatres Ltd.* [1916] 1 Ch. 132; *Re G.E. Tunbridge Ltd.* [1995] 1 B.C.L.C. 34; *Re ASRS Establishment Ltd.* [2000] 2 B.C.L.C. 631.

[68] See *Holroyd v Marshall* (1862) 10 H.L. Cas. 191, in which a charge over existing machinery and all machinery subsequently placed in the chargor's mill in addition to or in substitution for the original machinery was upheld as a fixed charge; and *Cimex Tissues Ltd.* [1995] 1 B.C.L.C. 409, in which Mr. Stanley Burnton Q.C. pointed out in his judgment (para.32) that, by way of exception to the general rule that a person can only grant a security bill of sale over goods of which he is the true owner at the time of granting the bill (Bills of Sale Act 1878 (Amendment) Act 1882, s.5), s.6 of the Act permits the inclusion of fixtures, plant and trade machinery brought on to land or premises in substitution for fixtures, plant and machinery specifically described in the Bill.

[69] [1979] 2 Lloyd's Rep. 142.

[70] [1987] Ch. 200.

and without liberty to use them for its own purposes except with the post-collection consent of the chargee. The third phase showed a weakening of this approach and a trend towards accepting the label attached to the transaction by the parties, as well as some unorthodoxy in delineating the characteristics of a floating charge. Cases illustrative of this phase are *Re Atlantic Computer Systems plc*,[71] *Re Atlantic Medical Ltd.*,[72] and *Re New Bullas Trading Ltd.*[73] The fourth and final phase has seen a return to orthodoxy with the decision of the Privy Council in *Agnew v Commissioners of Inland Revenue*,[74] emphasising that while the court looks to the agreement of the parties to determine their intention, the effect of what they have agreed is a matter of law.

In the analysis which follows it is assumed that the debts are collected by the chargor, not by the chargee, so that the crucial issue is whether the chargor collected for its own account or for that of the chargee.

(1) *From Siebe Gorman to Brightlife*

In the early 1970s, Barclays Bank began to use a form of fixed charge over book debts. There was much discussion in legal circles as to whether such a charge was possible, and in *Siebe Gorman & Co. Ltd. v Barclays Bank Ltd.*[75] the plaintiffs threw down the gauntlet. The challenge was successfully resisted by Barclays Bank. The facts were as follows: **4–14**

> A company gave a debenture to the defendant bank which provided *(inter alia)* that to secure its present and future indebtedness the company as beneficial owner charged to the bank by way of first fixed charge all book debts and other debts then and from time to time due or owing to the company, and undertook to pay all monies received in respect of such debts into the company's account with the bank and not to charge or assign the same to any other person without the written consent of the bank.
>
> Among the debts charged by the debenture were certain bills of exchange.[76] The same bills were subsequently assigned outright by the debtor company to the plaintiffs in reduction of the company's indebtedness to them.[77] Later, the defendant bank collected in the bills and declined

---

[71] [1992] Ch. 505.

[72] [1992] B.C.C. 653.

[73] [1994] B.C.C. 36.

[74] [2001] 2 A.C. 710.

[75] See above.

[76] Held to be book debts for the purpose of the provisions of the debenture relating to book debts (*cf. Re Stevens* [1888] W.N. 110; *Dawson v Isle* [1906] 1 Ch. 633). Note that the deposit by way of security of a negotiable instrument given to secure the payment of a book debt is exempt from registration (Companies Act 1985, s.396(2)), in order to preserve the negotiable character of such instruments.

[77] This was held by the judge not to be a mortgage, as no equity was retained by the assignor. This useful method of obtaining reduction or discharge of an indebtedness without taking a security is typically employed in situations where the value of the assigned debt does not exceed the amount owing to the assignee. Where the former is greater the assignor will need an undertaking by the assignee to refund the excess. As to this see above, para.1–35.

to account to the plaintiffs for the proceeds. The plaintiffs pleaded *(inter alia)* that the purported fixed charge was in reality a floating charge and was thus overridden by the assignment to the plaintiffs.

Slade, J., applying the Canadian decision in *Evans Coleman & Evans Ltd. v R. A. Nelson Construction Ltd.*[78] held that there was no reason why book debts could not be the subject of a fixed charge. The vital element distinguishing a mere floating charge from a fixed charge, namely the debtor's freedom to manage its assets in the ordinary course of business,[79] was lacking. The restrictions imposed by the debenture, and the requirement that proceeds of bills should be paid into the company's bank account with the defendants, showed that the bank was intended to have a fixed security from the outset.

In *Siebe German* the debenture not only prohibited the debtor company from disposing of the charged debts without the plaintiffs' consent, it also imposed controls on receipts by requiring these to be paid into an account from which they could not be withdrawn without the bank's consent.

A similar decision was reached by the Irish Supreme Court in *Re Keenan Bros. Ltd.*,[80] where the chargee's control was even more explicit in that the proceeds had to be paid into a special blocked account, not into the company's ordinary account. The vital element of control of the proceeds was omitted from the debenture given in *Re Brightlife Ltd.*,[81] where the debtor company, though prohibited from selling, factoring or discounting the charged debts without the consent of the debenture holder, was left free to collect in the debts, pay the proceeds into the bank account and use them or its own moneys. It was held by Hoffmann J. that the charge, though described as a fixed charge, was in truth a floating charge,[82] for the company's ability to deal with receipts as its own was inconsistent with a fixed security. This was plainly correct.[83]

(2) *From Brightlife to Re New Bullas*

4–15   There followed a curious interlude in which two lines of authority appeared to develop in opposite directions, each evolving independently of and with-

---

[78] (1958) 16 D.L.R. (2d) 123.

[79] A freedom which may be given at the outset or at a later date after execution of the charge, in which event the latter is converted from a fixed charge to a floating charge. This situation is most likely to arise through the use of excessively wide automatic crystallisation clauses. See below, para.4–55.

[80] [1985] I.R. 401; [1986] B.C.L.C. 242.

[81] [1987] Ch.200.

[82] See also the decision of the High Court of Northern Ireland in *Re Armagh Shoes Ltd.* [1982] N.I. 59; [1984] B.C.L.C. 405, in which the Court held that the mere designation of a charge on book debts as a fixed charge did not make it so, and that if the charge contemplated that the debtor would have freedom to manage the assets comprising the security it was a floating charge, even though that freedom was not expressly stated in the charge instrument.

[83] See above, para.4–13.

out reference to the other.[84] On one side were *Re Brightlife,*[85] *Re Keenan Bros.*[86] and *William Gaskell Group Ltd. v Highley*[87]; on the other, *Re Atlantic Computers,*[88] *Re Atlantic Medical*[89] and *Re New Bullas.*[90] In the first of these trilogies of cases the Court of Appeal held that a charge on sub-leases and rentals was a fixed charge because it was not ambulatory in character but related to rights under specifically identified sub-leases in existence at the time of he charge, and was thus to be contrasted with the type of charge described by Romer L.J. and covering a class of present and future assets. This reasoning appears to have reflected two distinct ideas. The first was that the distinction between a fixed and a floating charge is largely correlated with the distinction between security over existing property[91] and security over future property. But *Holroyd v Marshall*[92] and *Tailby v Official Receiver,*[93] both decisions of the House of Lords, clearly establish the efficacy of a fixed charge over after-acquired property. Conversely, it is not a prerequisite of a floating charge that it extends to future assets as well as existing assets.

The second idea underlying *Re Atlantic Computers* was that as the charge related to rentals due and to become due under existing and identified sub-leases it was not over a changing fund of assets. However, we have seen that the fund may be a closed fund, and its character as such is determined not by whether the assets are described as a class or are specifically identified (though the latter may be an indication that the charge is intended to be fixed) but whether the chargor is given continued power of management in the ordinary course of business free from interference by the chargee so long as that power continues. It is not necessary that the fund be a changing fund in the sense of picking up new assets.[94] Under the terms of the charge in that case the debtor was to be free to receive and utilise the sub-rentals it received until the chargee chose to intervene. Accordingly it could not be said that the sub-rentals had been unconditionally appropriated to the secured obligation. *Re Atlantic Computers* also drew a false analogy between the income from an asset and the proceeds of that asset.[95]

Next came *Re Atlantic Medical,*[96] where, however, the charge covered both present and future hire-purchase agreements, sub-leases and rentals. Vinelott J., having rather surprisingly concluded that the fact that the security covered

---

[84] See Roy Goode, "Charges over Book Debts: A Missed Opportunity" (1994) 110 L.Q.R. 592.
[85] [1987] Ch. 200.
[86] [1986] B.C.L.C. 242.
[87] [1993] B.C.C. 200.
[88] [1992] Ch. 505.
[89] [1993] B.C.L.C. 386.
[90] [1991] 1 B.C.L.C. 485.
[91] The court quite correctly classified sums payable in the future under existing contracts as present property.
[92] (1862) 10 H.L. Cas. 191.
[93] (1888) 13 App. Cas. 523.
[94] This follows both from the decision in *Siebe Gorman* and from the observation of Lord Millett in *Re Agnew* that of the three characteristics of a floating charge described by Romer L.J. in *Re Yorkshire Woolcombers Association Ltd.* only the last one was truly determinative.
[95] See Goode, *loc. cit.,* above, n.84 at 599.
[96] [1993] B.C.L.C. 386.

future assets was not a ground for distinguishing *Re Atlantic Computers*, left unclear what exactly turned on the characterisation. Finally, in *Re New Bullas Trading*,[97] involving an agreement by which the debenture was expressed to provide two distinct charges, a fixed charge over the book debts and a floating charge over the proceeds, the Court of Appeal succumbed to the beguiling argument that since the two assets were different the fact that the charge over the proceeds was expressed to be floating could not affect the fixed nature of the charge over the book debts themselves, and it was entirely open to the parties themselves to agree that the charge on the book debts should be fixed and on the proceeds, floating.

In *Commissioners of Inland Revenue v Agnew*,[98] the New Zealand Court of Appeal concluded that *Re Atlantic Computers Ltd.* was not in accordance with established authority. In upholding the substantive decision[99] the Privy Council made no comment on *Re Atlantic Computers*. It is, however, submitted that neither that decision nor the decision in *Re Atlantic Medical* can stand.

(3) From Re New Bullas to Agnew

4–16   Though the decision in *Re New Bullas* had its supporters,[1] it was not viewed with enthusiasm by lower courts and it was the views of its critics[2] that finally prevailed in the decision of the Privy Council in *Agnew v Commissioners of Inland Revenue*.[3] That case concerned a debenture which was expressed to confer a fixed charge on the company's book debts and their proceeds, excluding those proceeds which the bank might require to be paid into an account with itself. Such a requirement was never imposed. The effect of the debenture, therefore, was that while the bank reserved the power to intervene and take control of the proceeds, that power was never exercised. The Privy Council had no hesitation in concluding, in agreement with the Court of Appeal of New Zealand, that the charge was a floating charge and that *Re New Bullas* had been wrongly decided.[4] The proposition that a charge over book

---

[97] [1991] 1 B.C.L.C. 485.

[98] [2000] 1 N.Z.L.R. 223.

[99] See below.

[1] See, for example, Alan Berg, "Charges over Book Debts: A Reply" [1995] J.B.L. 433; D.W. McLauchlan, "Fixed Charges over Book Debts—*New Bullas* in New Zealand" (1999) 115 L.Q.R. 365; and "*New Bullas* in New Zealand: Round Two" (2000) 116 L.Q.R. 211; and Peter Watts, "Fixed Charges over Book Debts" [1999] N.Z.L.R 46; and Varen and Rubenstein, "Separation of Book Debts and their Proceeds" [1994] C.L.J. 225.

[2] See, for example, Goode, *loc. cit.*, above, n.84; Gavin Lightman and Gabriel Moss, *The Law of Receivers of Companies* (3rd ed.) paras 3–030 *et seq.*; Sarah Worthington, "Fixed Charges over Book Debts and other Receivables" (1997) 113 L.Q.R. 562; and, *sub silentio*, Millett L.J. in *Royal Trust Bank v National Westminster Bank plc* [1996] 2 B.C.L.C. 682.

[3] [2001] 2 A.C. 710.

[4] It is ironic that just over a year after the decision in *Agnew* the floating charge in New Zealand, though not abolished, ceased to exist as a distinct form of security upon the coming into force of the Personal Property Securities Act 1999, which converted it into a fixed security interest. See Linda Widdup and Laurie Mayne, *Personal Property Securities Act: a conceptual approach* (2nd ed.) Ch.22, entitled "The Demise of the Floating Charge."

debts could be characterised independently of the contractual provisions governing the application of the proceeds was robustly rejected:

"While a debt and its proceeds are two separate assets, however, the latter are merely the traceable proceeds of the former and represent its entire value. A debt is a receivable; it is merely a right to receive payment from the debtor. Such a right cannot be enjoyed in specie; its value can be exploited only by exercising the right or by assigning it for value to a third party. An assignment or charge of a receivable which does not carry with it the right to the receipt has no value. It is worthless as a security. Any attempt in the present context to separate the ownership of the debts from the ownership of their proceeds (even if conceptually possible) makes no commercial sense."[5]

The decision is to be welcomed as restoring the clear position established in *Re Brightlife*. It also effects a symmetry with cases going back to the nineteenth century which established that the mere existence of a power of intervention is not sufficient to give a floating charge priority over the claims of execution creditors; it is necessary that the debenture holder shall actually have intervened to crystallise the charge by taking control of the charged assets.[6]

While it is not possible to have a fixed charge on book debts if the chargor is left free to collect the debts for its own account, the converse is not true. There is nothing to preclude the grant of a floating charge on book debts, giving the chargor freedom to dispose of them in the ordinary course of business, and a fixed charge on the collected proceeds through a requirement that these are to be under the control of or held for the account of the chargee.

Stock in trade

The success of Barclays Bank in establishing the validity of a fixed charge over book debts leads to the question whether a fixed charge is also possible over stock in trade. Plainly the theoretical answer is, yes. Now that the issue is seen to be the presence or absence of the debtor's freedom to manage its assets in the ordinary course of business, there is no reason to distinguish one class of changing asset from another. Where the instrument of charge over stock in trade precludes the debtor from disposing of its stock without the prior consent of the creditor then if the parties operate the agreement on the basis of this restriction a valid fixed charge is created.

That is the theory. In practice, there is a significant difference between receivables and stock in trade. There is in general no commercial necessity for a company to be given liberty to dispose of its receivables or collections in the course of business. The company need not sell or charge its receivables; it can

4–17

---

[5] *per* Lord Millett at 729.
[6] See below, paras 4–59 *et seq.*

simply collect them in. Equally, it need not sell the collections; the most natural thing to do with them is to pay them into its bank account. It is quite another matter with stock in trade. Stock is held for sale, not for use in the business, and a company cannot operate at all unless it can dispose of its stock in such a way as to give purchasers unencumbered title. So while the imposition of restrictions on disposal of book debts does not suffice to make the charge a fixed charge if the chargor is left free to collect them for its own account, restrictions on the sale of stock in trade would usually be commercially impracticable anyway.

It would be open to the creditor to stipulate that no item of stock was to be disposed of without the creditor's prior written consent, but in most cases the debtor company would find it impossible to live with such a restriction. A blanket consent in advance would not do, for this would be incompatible with the existence of a fixed security interest and would make the charge a floating charge.[7] So whilst the imposition of appropriate restrictions on dealings in stock in trade would preserve the efficacy of the charge as a fixed charge, in practice it is rare that the parties will find such an arrangement workable.

An alternative is to utilise some form of pledge through constructive delivery to the creditor. One way of doing this is by field warehousing.[8] Another, less elaborate, method requires the debtor to acknowledge that any stock in trade of which it is in possession is held to the order of the chargee and that while the chargor is permitted to sell the goods in the ordinary course of business it does so as agent of the chargee and is to hold the proceeds of sale on trust for the chargee. This is not different in principle from the trust receipt mechanism.[9]

As with book debts, there is nothing to prevent the chargor from granting a floating charge over the stock in trade and a fixed charge over the proceeds.[10]

Raw materials and goods in process

4–18   Similar considerations apply to security over raw materials and goods in process of manufacture. It is theoretically possible to have a fixed charge over these classes of asset, but generally impracticable to require the debtor company to obtain the creditor's consent to the processing of each batch of raw materials or to the making up of each item of goods in process.

---

[7] See W.J. Gough, *Company Charges*, (2nd ed.) pp.630–631.
[8] See below, para.4–23.
[9] See above, para.2–10; below, paras 4–19, 4–23.
[10] *Re CCG International Enterprises Ltd.* [1993] B.C.L.C. 1428.

Documents of title to stock in trade

What applies to stock in trade must at first sight be equally applicable to doc-   **4–19**
uments of title to trading stock. There is, however, the important difference
that documents, unlike goods, can conveniently be possessed by the creditor.
This allows a pledge of the goods by deposit of the documents, a common
procedure for banks advancing the price of imported goods. The business
purpose of the transaction can be achieved without significant loss of security by releasing the documents to the pledgor against a trust receipt, thus preserving the pledge.[11] For further security the bank may require the goods to
be stored in an independent warehouse, the bank's consent being required
before any goods are released from the warehouse.

3. SHIFTING ASSETS: CONTROL TECHNIQUES

Current assets distinguished from fixed assets

In considering what controls need to be imposed on the debtor company to   **4–20**
ensure that the courts will recognise a charge as fixed rather than floating, the
distinction between fixed and current assets becomes of some importance. If
I take a charge over the defendant company's factory or its business equipment it is not necessary in law for me to stipulate that the company shall not
dispose of or incumber the asset without my consent, for assets of this kind
are held by the company for use in its business, not for resale, and it is therefore presumed that any disposal, whether absolute or by way of security,
requires my consent.[12] Of course, if I habitually stand by and allow the company to sell or charge its fixed assets free from my security without my prior
consent the court will consider this inconsistent with my holding a fixed security, for I cannot on the one hand assert a fixed charge and on the other allow
the company to deal with the charged assets as its own.[13] By contrast it is
in the nature of circulating assets that they are turned over by manufacture
(in the case of raw materials), sale (in the case of stock in trade) and collection (in the case of receivables), and the continuance of the debtor company's
management powers over such assets is thus assumed unless negated by the
agreement of the parties. Hence the need for legal and practical control techniques to prevent the debtor company from dealing with the charged assets
as its own. Again, in relation to a charge on book debts, where it is necessary
for the chargee to have control over the proceeds,[14] it is not sufficient to provide for such control in the charge instrument if in practice the chargee does

---

[11] *Re David Allester Ltd.* [1922] 2 Ch. 211.
[12] But this presumption gives way to any contrary inference to be drawn from the language of
the charge instrument itself. See above, para.4–12.
[13] *Re Bond Worth Ltd.* [1980] Ch. 228, *per* Slade J. at 261.
[14] See above, paras 4–13 *et seq.*

not enforce the provision. So a stipulation that the account into which the proceeds are to be paid is to be a blocked account will not establish the charge as a fixed charge if the account is not operated as a blocked account in fact.[15] But where the chargee does have control over an account, the fact that this is limited to a specified amount is not inconsistent with the fixed nature of the charge. So in a Hong Kong decision, *ABN Amro Bank NV v Chiyu Banking Corp. Ltd.*,[16] Deputy Judge Susan Kwan held that where the chargor was obliged to maintain an amount of not less than HK$3,000,000 or its equivalent in a specified deposit account with the plaintiff bank which was charged back to the bank, the fact that the chargee was free to draw on any excess above that amount did not render the charge a floating charge.

Degree of control necessary

4–21   How much freedom can the debtor company be given to deal with charged assets if the charge is to retain its status as a fixed charge? Or to put the question another way, how far must the debtor's power to manage the charged assets be restricted? It is not possible to give an exhaustive reply to this question. At one end of the spectrum is total freedom of management. This is plainly incompatible with a fixed security interest. A creditor cannot claim a fixed security in an asset in one breath and then in the next allow the debtor to dispose of the asset as if it were the debtor's own. At the other end of the spectrum is a total prohibition on dealings of any kind in the asset or its proceeds. Clearly in this case the charge is a fixed charge. Between the two ends of the spectrum lies an infinite range of possibilities. All one can say is that the greater the control exercised by the creditor through the charge instrument and its enforcement, the greater the chance of his establishing the fixed nature of the security. Merely to label the charge "fixed" is not enough.[17] The instrument must restrict the debtor's dealing powers; and the restrictions must be meaningful, not a mere sham. A creditor who, having imposed restrictions on dealings on the debtor company, persistently stands by and allows the debtor to ignore those restrictions will have difficulty in persuading the court that they are to be taken seriously.[18]

Let us now consider some of the more important control techniques. These divide into two groups; control through the charge instrument; and active policing of the control provisions.

---

[15] *Agnew v Commissioners of Inland Revenue* [2001] 2 A.C. 710, *per* Lord Millett at 730.
[16] [2000] 3 H.K.C. 381.
[17] *Re Armagh Shoes Ltd.* [1982] N.I. 59; [1984] B.C.L.C. 405; *Re Brightlife Ltd.* [1986] 3 All E.R. 673.
[18] See above, para.4–20; below, para.4–54.

Control through the charge instrument

Controlling provisions in the charge instrument will vary according to the   **4–22**
type of property given as security, and in particular, whether it is tangible
(goods or documents) or intangible (debts, contract rights).

(1) *Provision for direct control of goods*

In the case of goods, the creditor may stipulate for direct control by himself   **4–23**
or his agents. There are various ways of achieving this, most of them being
equally applicable to a pledge, which is the more common security device
where the auditor assumes direct control of the goods. The fullest control is
exercised by a requirement that the goods be stored in the creditor's own
warehouse and released only with the approval of the creditor's warehouseman. This is a costly procedure and one which most debtors would view with
the utmost disfavour. An alternative is to stipulate that the goods shall be
stored in the creditor's name in an independent warehouse, the debtor being
responsible for warehousing charges, or that, if stored by the debtor itself, the
debtor will on each occasion procure the warehouse to attorn to the creditor,
so that legal possession passes to the creditor. Warehousing in an independent warehouse is not uncommon and gives the chargee a considerable measure of security, but again involves the debtor in warehousing charges which it
may find burdensome. Yet another variant is the "field warehousing" type of
security, where the goods are warehoused on the debtor's own premises, the
charge instrument providing that they are to be segregated from the debtor's
other goods and kept in a distinct room or fenced off area under the super-
vision of an employee of the debtor who is for this purpose to be the agent
of the creditor and to act in accordance with the creditor's instructions. Such
a provision can sometimes be reinforced by a requirement that the segregated
part of the premises in question be leased to the creditor at a nominal rent.

These different forms of warehousing arrangement provide a relatively high
measure of control. But English law, in contrast to American law, also recognises a pledge or charge in which the debtor simply acknowledges that he
holds the goods to the order of the creditor until sale and holds the proceeds
of sale on trust for the creditor.[19]

In the case of goods covered by documents of title—*e.g.* imported goods
shipped under a bill of lading—the security agreement could provide for the
shipping documents to be deposited with the creditor. Usually, this would be
by way of pledge, rather than charge. The goods should not be consigned to
the creditor—who might incur liability for unpaid freight—but the agreement
should provide for them to be consigned to the debtor and indorsed to the
creditor in blank. The shipping documents can later be released to the debtor
under a trust receipt.

---

[19] See above, paras 2–10, 4–19.

(2) *Provisions for segregation and preservation of charged property*

4–24   To emphasise the point that the creditor regards himself as having an interest *in specie* in the charged assets, the instrument of charge should contain provisions requiring the assets to be segregated from the debtor's other property, even if it is not possible to impose a requirement that the premises shall be under the actual control of a third party. This should be reinforced by undertakings as to insurance, safe custody and repair.

(3) *Restrictions on dealings*

4–25   Typically, these take the form of a prohibition against a dealing with or transfer of possession of any of the charged assets without the creditor's prior written consent, "dealing" here covering both outright transfer and the grant of a mortgage, charge or lease. Such a prohibition is effective to establish the charge as a fixed charge on goods even though there is no duty to account for the proceeds. This is because, in contrast to book debts, which can be realised either by sale or by collection, goods have to be sold to produce proceeds, and if the chargor of goods cannot dispose of the goods themselves without the chargee's consent it is not in a position to collect the proceeds. As an alternative, the debenture can empower the debtor company to deal with the charged assets as the debenture holder's fiduciary agent, holding the proceeds separately for the debenture holder's account.[20] The debenture should make it clear that the agency is confined to the relations between the debenture holder and the company and that the latter is to deal as principal in the third parties and is not to commit the debenture holder to any contractual relationship with or liability to any third party.[21] It is also desirable to require dealings to be on commercially reasonable terms.

(4) *Accounting for proceeds*

4–26   Where the debtor company is left free to dispose of the charged assets or, in the case of debts, to collect them in, it is essential that the company be required to account for proceeds, meanwhile holding these on trust for the creditor and keeping them separate from the debtor's own moneys and property. Leaving the debtor free to commingle the proceeds with his own moneys is incompatible with the existence of a trust, which presupposes a duty on the trustee to keep trust moneys separate from his own.[22] There are various ways in which the required control can be effected: by providing for the chargee

---

[20] See (4) below.

[21] This is the so-called "commission agency" which English law tends not to regard as an agency at all. See R. M. Goode, *Proprietary Rights and Insolvency in Sales Transactions*, pp.36–39 and, in relation to a comparable problem with reservation of title, pp.93–94.

[22] *Henry v Hammond* [1913] 2 K.B. 515, *per* Channell J. at 521; *Royal Trust Bank v National Westminster Bank plc* [1996] 2 B.C.L.C. 682.

rather than the chargor to collect the proceeds; by requiring the chargor to collect as agent for the chargee and pay the proceeds into a separate account opened by the chargor with its own bank but capable of being drawn on only with the chargee's consent; or, where the chargee is itself a bank, by requiring the chargor to pay the proceeds into a blocked account opened with the chargee.[23] But frequently debtor companies are reluctant to submit to such a restriction on their ability to handle incoming moneys representing trading income, and without it the court is likely to rule that the charge is not fixed but floating.[24] There is usually less difficulty in stipulating for control of proceeds of a fixed asset, such as an insurance policy.[25]

Policing of the control provisions

As stated earlier, it is not sufficient to specify controls in the charge instrument. These must be shown to be more than a mere paper exercise. In particular, if the debtor is regularly allowed to dispose of the charged assets without regard to the restrictions imposed on it, the court is likely to take the view either that the contractual provisions were mere camouflage or that they have been waived by the creditor, in either case resulting in the security becoming characterised as a floating charge.[26] If substantial amounts are at stake, regular inspections of physical assets comprising the security, and of the debtor company's accounts, are advisable. A final cautionary word—though control is important, there is a line beyond which the activity of the secured creditor will cease to be mere control over the disposition of specific classes of asset and will constitute an exercise of management of the company's business with the concomitant statutory duties and liabilities imposed on officers, directors, and shadow directors.[27]

4–27

4. CRYSTALLISATION OF A FLOATING CHARGE[28]

As we have seen, the essence of a floating charge is the liberty given to the debtor company to manage and deal with the assets comprising the security in the ordinary course of business. In taking a floating charge, the creditor binds himself not to intervene in the handling of the assets so long as the

4–28

---

[23] See Andrew McKnight, "Brumark: The Difference between Fixed and Floating Charges" [2001] J.I.B.L. 157 at 159–160.

[24] *Re Brightlife Ltd.* [1987] Ch. 200.

[25] *Re CCG International Enterprises Ltd.* [1993] B.C.L.C. 1428, where the chargee bank took a charge over (*inter alia*) policies of fire insurance and could elect to apply any proceeds either to reinstatement of the property damaged by fire or to reduction of the chargor's indebtedness.

[26] *Re Bond Worth Ltd.* [1922] 2 Ch. 211; *Waters v Widdows* [1984] V.R. 503.

[27] See Insolvency Act 1986, ss.206–219 and 251 (definition of "shadow directors"); Company Directors Disqualification Act 1986.

[28] Priority issues in relation to the crystallisation of a floating charge, including the effect of negative pledge clauses, are discussed in the next chapter.

company runs under its own steam as a going concern. When the company goes into liquidation or receivership or its management powers are brought to an end under the provisions of the charge instrument. When this occurs, the charge is said to crystallise; and it is with crystallisation and its effects that much of the present chapter is concerned.

The general effect of crystallisation

4–29   Crystallisation puts an end to the authority conferred on the debtor company to manage the assets comprising the security. In consequence, the charge becomes converted into a fixed charge, fastening on all assets in which the company then has or subsequently acquires[29] an interest. Though crystallisation does not *per se* put an end to the company's ability to continue its business,[30] it ceases to be able to dispose of the charged assets free from the charge without the consent of the chargee, who cannot give a blanket permission without refloating the charge.[31]

Crystallisation does not involve re-registration in the Companies Registry or avoid the effects of non-registration, for no new security interest is created. All that happens is that the security interest brought into being by the floating charge ceases to float over a fund of assets and attaches *in specie*.

The effect of crystallisation is customarily analysed in purely property terms. In my view, this is unfortunate, for it conceals the fact that by authorising the company to trade in its circulating assets free from the charge the debenture holder has held the company out as having wide powers of disposition, so that we are concerned as much with principles of agency law as those of property law.

If, then, we look at the effect of crystallisation in agency terms, it immediately becomes clear that we must distinguish the relationship between the chargee and the company from the relationships between the chargee and rival claimants to the security. Termination of the company's *actual* authority to manage its assets is purely a matter between the company and the debenture holder. No outsider is entitled to dictate the terms on which the company's management powers are to be brought to an end, or to complain if the company has accepted as a crystallising event acts or omissions which

---

[29] *N. W. Robbie & Co. Ltd. v Witney Warehouse Ltd.* [1963] 3 All E.R. 613; *Ferrier v Bottomer* (1972) 126 C.L.R. 597. In other words, crystallisation of the floating charge does not affect the continued operation of the after-acquired property clause. The scope of that clause is, of course, a matter of construction of the charge instrument. In *Re Rex Developments Pty. Ltd.* (1994) 13 A.C.S.R. 485, the Supreme Court of the Australian Capital Territory held by a majority (Higgins J. dissenting) that the security was confined to after-acquired property covered by a floating charge, so that once the charge crystallised no future property could fall within it. This construction is rather surprising, for a natural reading of the instrument, and the only one making commercial sense, would seem to indicate that all after-acquired property was intended to be covered, whether acquired before or after crystallisation of the charge.

[30] Assuming, of course, that the crystallising event is not an act which itself denotes cessation of trading. See below, para.4–31.

[31] See below, para.4–57.

to the outsider may seem entirely trivial or capricious. But whether the ending of the company's actual authority binds third parties dealing with assets is an entirely separate question. In answering this, it is not necessarily sufficient to say that the company is no longer authorised to sell or charge its assets, for it may still have *apparent* authority to do so. This is a matter to which I shall return in the following chapter.

Categories of crystallising event

Crystallising events fall broadly into four groups. First, there are events **4–30** denoting the cessation of trading by the company as a going concern. Secondly, there is intervention by the debenture holder to enforce his security which deprives the company of *de jure* control of the charged assets and thus terminates its authority to deal with them free from the security interest. Thirdly, there are other acts or events specified in the debenture as causing the charge to crystallise. Fourthly, in the case of agricultural charges granted by a farmer the Agricultural Credits Act 1928 contains specific provisions for crystallisation. Crystallisation cannot occur during a moratorium under s.1 of the IA 2000.[32]

Group 1: events denoting cessation of trading as a going concern

A floating charge crystallises on the occurrence of an event which is incom- **4–31** patible with the continuance of trading by the company as a going concern. Crystallisation is, in such cases, said to occur as a matter of law,[33] but this does not mean that there is any mandatory rule of law which precludes a charge from continuing to float where the company ceases trading, merely that the intention by the debenture holder to allow this to happen is so unlikely, and the result in most cases would be so nonsensical, that an express provision for crystallisation on cessation of trading or the ability to trade is unnecessary since the law will imply a term to that effect.[34] On the other hand, an event would not appear to be a crystallising event within this first category merely because its effect is to remove the management of the company's assets from its directors and transfer them to an administrative receiver[35] or an administrator.[36] Such an event may constitute a crystallising event within the second category but it is not inconsistent with continued

---

[32] IA 2000, Sch.1, para.13. Crystallisation occurs simultaneously with the relevant event; the law does not treat this as a conceptual impossibility by predicating that the crystallising event and crystallisation itself occur in sequence and not at the same time. *Fire Nymph Products Ltd v The Heating Centre Pty Ltd* (1992) 10 A.C.L.C. 629, *per* Gleeson C.J. at 636; adopted by Chadwick J. in *Re Real Meat Co. Ltd.* [1996] B.C.C. 254.

[33] *Re Crompton & Co. Ltd.* [1914] Ch. 954 at 964, 965.

[34] *Re Brightlife Ltd.* [1986] 3 All E.R. 673, *per* Hoffmann J. at 679; referring to the judgment of Warrington J. in *Re Crompton & Co. Ltd.* above, at 964–965.

[35] See below.

[36] See below.

trading by the company or even with the ultimate return of the company's management to the directors.[37]

There are at least two types of event falling within the first category, namely liquidation of the company and *de facto* cessation of trading.

(1) *Liquidation*

4–32 The winding up of a company, whether by resolution of the members or by order of the court, causes a floating charge to crystallise,[38] for upon liquidation a company must cease to carry on its business, except so far as may be required for its beneficial winding up.[39] This is so whether or not the liquidation is an insolvent liquidation. Hence the fact that the company is prosperous and goes into winding up purely for the purpose of reconstruction does not prevent the charge from crystallising.[40] In the case of a compulsory winding up, crystallisation occurs on the date of the winding up order and is not retrospective to the commencement of the winding up,[41] namely the date of presentation of the winding up petition.[42] The mere presentation of a winding up petition does not of itself crystallise a floating charge,[43] for the company is not thereby disabled from continuing trading and the petition may in any event be dismissed. For the same reason the appointment of a provisional liquidator does not crystallise the charge.[44] *A fortiori* the mere fact that the company has become insolvent is not a crystallising event unless so designated by the charge instrument,[45] in which event the case falls within Group 3 below.[46]

(2) *Cessation of trading*

4–33 Where a company ceases trading, the law implies a term in the debenture that the floating charge will thereupon crystallise, whether or not the company is in winding up.[47] The practical problem is to determine at what point trad-

---

[37] See below, para.4–57.

[38] *Re Panama, New Zealand and Australian Royal Mail Co.* (1870) 5 Ch.App. 318; *Re Colonial Trusts Corp.* (1879) 15 Ch.D. 465; *Wallace v Universal Automatic Machines Co.* [1894] 2 Ch. 547; *Re Crompton & Co. Ltd.*, above; *Evans v Rival Granite Quarries Ltd.* [1910] 2 K.B. 979.

[39] Insolvency Act 1986, ss.87(1), 167(1) and Sch.4, para.5.

[40] *Re Crompton & Co. Ltd.*, above.

[41] *Stein v Saywell* (1969) 121 C.L.R. 529.

[42] Insolvency Act 1985, s.129(2). However, if the company has previously gone into voluntary winding up, the date of commencement of winding up is the date of passing of the resolution (*ibid.*, s.1 29(1)).

[43] *Re Victoria Steamboats Co.* [1897] 1 Ch. 158.

[44] *Re Obie Pty. Ltd.* (No. 2) (1983) 8 A.C.L.R. 574.

[45] *Covacich v Riordan* [1994] 2 N.Z.L.R. 502.

[46] See below, paras 4–49 *et seq.*

[47] *Re Woodroffes (Musical Instruments) Ltd.* [1986] 2 All E.R. 908, *per* Nourse J. at 913–914; *Re Real Meat Co. Ltd.* [1996] B.C.C. 254, *per* Chadwick J. at 261; *Re Sperrin Textiles Ltd.* [1992] N.I. 323.

ing has ceased. Until the enactment of the Insolvency Act 1985 this could have been important, since as the law then stood a floating charge which crystallised otherwise than by appointment of a receiver, winding up or the taking of possession of the charged property had priority over subsequent preferential debts, for it had ceased to be a floating charge at the time such debts came into existence.[48] The possibility of such priority was, however, extinguished by a change in the definition of a floating charge so as to cover a charge which, as created, was a floating charge.[49]

Events not denoting cessation of trading

It is inherent in a floating charge that the debtor company retains the ability **4–34** to function as a going concern. Once it ceases trading or is disabled from continuing to trade as a going concern the rationale for the freedom given to the company by the floating charge to dispose of its assets in the ordinary course of business disappears. But trading as a going concern does not necessarily require that the powers of management of the charged assets remain with the directors of the company. Those powers may have passed to an administrative receiver or an administrator or may have ceased to be exercisable through some other crystallising event but this does not of itself indicate that the company is no longer able to continue trading. Indeed, it is one of the functions of receivers and administrators to carry on the business of the company. I shall examine in turn the effect of the appointment of a receiver by the debenture holder himself or by the court on his application, the impact of crystallisation of a prior or subsequent floating charge, and the effect of an administration order and the appointment of an administrator.

(1) *Appointment by or at the instance of the debenture holder*

The appointment of an administrative receiver by the debenture holder does **4–35** not by itself result in a cessation of trading. On the contrary, the administrative receiver will usually carry on the business for a significant period in order to get it into shape before a "hive down" by transfer of the assets to a new company which can then be sold off to a purchaser with assets but no liabilities. The same applies to a receiver appointed by the court on the application of the debenture holder and authorised by the court to carry on the company's business.[50] The fact that a company can continue as a going concern

---

[48] *ibid.*, where, however, the debenture holder was unable to show that the company had in fact ceased trading prior to the appointment of the receiver.

[49] See now Insolvency Act 1986, ss.251 and 40(1).

[50] Of course, the appointment of a receiver, whether by the debenture holder or by the court, may lead to the cessation of trading, where the receiver, pursuant to a power conferred on him by the debenture deed or the court, decides to close the business. This will have no crystallising effect in relation to the debenture under which he was appointed (since this will

even though under receivership is of little significance to the question of crystallisation where the receiver is appointed by the debenture holder himself, for it is settled that this falls within a distinct category of crystallising event, namely withdrawal of the company's authority from the debenture holder to deal with its assets in the ordinary course of business.[51] But the point becomes of considerable importance where the receiver is appointed by a prior or subsequent debenture holder.

(2) Crystallisation of a prior floating charge

4–36 In *Re Woodroffes (Musical Instruments) Ltd.*,[52] a bank holding a floating charge contended that this crystallised automatically as the result of the crystallisation of an earlier floating charge through service of a crystallisation notice. The argument advanced on behalf of the bank was that crystallisation of the earlier charge paralysed the business, rendering any further use of the charged assets unlawful and impracticable, so that the company must be taken to have ceased trading at that time. This contention was rejected by Nourse J. as running contrary to fundamental principles of the law of contract. The events causing crystallisation of the bank's debenture were those contained, expressly or by implication, in that debenture. There was no good reason to imply a term that the charge would crystallise automatically on crystallisation of an earlier charge. That might or might not prove to be in the bank's interests, but equally the bank might have concluded that it was in its interest that the business should continue. As against the bank the company remained free to deal with its assets in the ordinary course of business, and whilst this would necessarily have involved a breach of the company's contract with the earlier debenture holder the bank might have been willing to give the company an indemnity or even pay off the earlier debenture.[53] The decision of the High Court of Australia in *Stein v Saywell*,[54] which had been thought to be authority for the proposition advanced by the bank, was found on closer examination to have involved a debenture which expressly provided that it should crystallise if a receiver were appointed under the earlier charge. The decision was therefore of no assistance to the bank.

---

previously have crystallised by virtue of his appointment—see below), but will have the effect of crystallising floating charges created under other debentures.

[51] See below, para.4–42.
[52] [1985] 2 All E.R. 908.
[53] For a contrary view see Sir Gavin Lightman and Gabriel Moss, *The Law of Receivers and Administrators of Companies* (3rd ed.) para.3–076.
[54] (1969) 121 C.L.R. 529.

(3) *Crystallisation of a subsequent floating charge*

If a debenture is not crystallised by crystallisation of a prior charge, then *a*   **4–37**
fortiori it will not be crystallised by crystallisation of a subsequent charge,
which leaves the priority of the earlier charge undisturbed.[55]

(4) *Making of an administration order*

The Insolvency Act 1986 contains provisions empowering the court to make   **4–38**
an administration order in relation to a company where it is satisfied that
the company is or is likely to become unable to pay its debts and considers
that an administration order would be likely to achieve the rescue of the
company as a going concern, the achievement of a better result for the company's creditors than would be likely if the company were wound up, or a
realisation of property in order to make a distribution to one or more secured
or preferential creditors.[56] Pending the hearing of a petition for an administration order the company cannot be put into winding up, nor can security
be enforced against the company (except for the appointment of an administrative receiver and the carrying out of his functions) or proceedings be
commenced or continued against it without leave of the court.[57] Once an
administration order is made these restrictions continue during the currency
of the order unless the administrator otherwise agrees and in addition a
debenture holder cannot appoint an administrative receiver. An administrator appointed by the court may do anything necessary or expedient for the
management of the affairs, business and property of the company and may
in particular exercise all the powers conferred by the 1st Schedule to the
Act.[58] That Schedule, which applies equally to administrative receivers,
empowers the administrator *(inter alia)* to carry on the business of the
company.[59] Hence the making of an administration order is in no way
incompatible with the continuance of the company's business as a going
concern and does not, it is thought, result in crystallisation of a floating
charge in the absence of any express term to that effect in the debenture.[60]

---

[55] See Hubert Picarda, *The Law Relating to Receivers and Managers*, (3rd ed.), pp.42–44, which
contains an excellent discussion of the point.
[56] Insolvency Act 1986, s.8 and Sch.B1, paras 3, 11. The Schedule, inserted by Sch.16 to the
Enterprise Act 2002, replaces Pt II of the Insolvency Act. As to impending changes in relation
to administrative receivership, see below, para.4–61.
[57] *ibid.*, paras 43, 44.
[58] *ibid.*, paras 59(1), 60.
[59] Para.14.
[60] This view is supported by Lightman and Moss, *The Law of Receivers and Administrators of
Companies* (3rd ed.) para.3–067. The position is otherwise as regards the appointment of an
administrator on the petition of the debenture holder himself. See below, para.4–42.

Group 2: intervention by debenture holder to take control of the assets

4-39 By taking a floating charge the debenture holder binds himself to allow the debtor company freedom to manage and deal with the charged assets in the ordinary course of business until such time as its authority from him to do so is withdrawn pursuant to the express or implied terms of the debenture. We have seen that there is an implied withdrawal of authority when the company goes into liquidation or ceases trading. The debenture holder can also signify the termination of the company's management powers by intervening to take control of the charged assets. But what types of intervention are to be considered sufficient for this purpose? An analysis of the authorities indicates that to be effective in crystallising a floating charge the debenture holder's act of intervention must satisfy a threefold test. First, it must be done with the intention of converting the charge into a fixed charge.[61] Secondly, it must be authorised by the express or implied terms of the debenture. Thirdly, it must divest the company of *de jure* control of the assets. With the application of these tests it becomes relatively easy to determine whether the debenture holder's intervention has been effective to crystallise the charge.

(1) *Intervention which is effective to crystallise the charge*

4-40   (a) *Taking of possession* If the debenture holder lawfully takes possession of the charged assets this crystallises the charge,[62] for it ends the company's control. It is not necessary that he should seize all the assets at once, which in most cases would be impracticable. The debenture holder may take possession of part in the name of the whole,[63] whether the assets consist of land or of goods.[64]

4-41   (b) *Order for possession or sale* Though there appears no decision directly on the point, it seems clear that an order requiring the company to deliver up to the debenture holder possession of land or goods crystallises the charge, for the effect of such an order is to terminate the company's right to hold and deal with the land or goods in question. The same applies to an order for sale. But the mere institution of proceedings would not appear to suffice, for this does not divest the company of *de jure* control.[65]

---

[61] *Evans v Rival Granite Quarries Ltd.* [1910] 2 K.B. 979, *per* Fletcher Moulton L.J. at 9 97.

[62] *Mercantile Bank of India Ltd. v Chartered Bank of India, Australia and China* [1937] 1 All E.R. 231.

[63] *i.e.* with the intention of asserting rights over the whole. The position is otherwise where the debenture holder seizes a particular asset with a view to leaving the company free to continue business with the remaining assets. Such a seizure, unless authorised by the debenture, is a breach of its terms and as such is ineffective to crystallise the charge. See below, para.4-56.

[64] See Pollock & Wright, *Possession in the Common Law*, pp.60–61, 70, 78–79.

[65] Moreover, the application might not succeed.

(c) *Appointment of receiver out of court* The appointment of a receiver **4–42**
by the debenture holder out of court has long been the most common
method of crystallising a floating charge and is well established as effective for that purpose.[66] The receiver here referred to is not, of course, the
old-style receiver appointed under a fixed charge to collect income from a
specific asset but one who under a floating charge is appointed receiver
and manager of the whole or substantially the whole of the company's
assets and undertaking, and who is now termed an "administrative
receiver."[67] Crystallisation does not depend on the receiver taking possession of the assets; the commencement of the receiver's appointment is all
that is required,[68] for by executing a debenture which authorises the
debenture holder to appoint a receiver in stated events the company
implicitly recognises that its right to continue managing its business is terminated upon such appointment. The appointment is of no effect unless
accepted by the appointee before the end of the business day next following that on which the instrument is received by him or on his behalf,
but subject to this, is deemed to be made at the time the instrument of
appointment is so received.[69] Notice of the receiver's appointment is not
necessary to crystallise the charge.[70] The appointment of an administrator on the petition of the debenture holder under Sch.31, para.14 to the
Insolvency Act 1986 also crystallises the charge.

(d) *Appointment of receiver by the court* Where at the instance of the deben- **4–43**
ture holder a receiver is appointed by the court,[71] the floating charge
crystallises when such appointment takes effect.[72] Again, crystallisation

---

[66] *Evans v Rival Granite Quarries Ltd.*, above, and cases there cited.

[67] Insolvency Act 1986, s.29(2). But the post is about to disappear. See above, para.1–01.

[68] Dr Gough (*Company Charges* (2nd ed.) pp.165–166) considers it at least arguable that the
mere appointment of a receiver does not by itself cause the charge to crystallise and that it is
necessary for the receiver to take possession, for it is that that deprives the company of management powers and constitutes an appropriation to the security on behalf of the debenture
holder. But the requirement of possession is not only unsupported by any authority, apart
from a few fleeting and speculative judicial utterances, it runs counter to numerous cases in
which the courts have held it to be settled law that appointment of a receiver by the debenture
holder suffices to crystallise the charge. The fact that possession is unnecessary is put beyond
doubt by cases which establish that an execution creditor on whose behalf the sheriff levies
execution against goods the subject of a floating charge is postponed to the debenture holder
if the latter appoints a receiver before sale by the sheriff (*Re Standard Manufacturing Co. Ltd.*
[1891] 1 Ch. 627; *Re Opera Ltd.* [1891] 3 Ch. 260). The reason why possession is unnecessary
is that in conferring on the debenture holder the power to appoint a receiver the company
accepts that the appointment brings its own powers of management to an end.

[69] Insolvency Act 1986, s.33(1).

[70] *Alberta Paper Co. Ltd. v Metropolitan Graphics Ltd.* (1983) 49 C.B.R. (2d) 63, in which it was
also held that the rule in *Dearle v Hall* (1828) 3 Russ. 1 does not apply in relation to a dispute
between the holder of a floating charge and a judgment creditor garnisheeing a debt. See further, as to the inapplicability of the rule in *Dearle v Hall* to floating charges, below, para.5–39.

[71] This is unusual, since from the viewpoint of the debenture holder an appointment by the court
has many disadvantages—delay, expense, restrictions on the receiver's freedom of action,
etc.—which are avoided by an appointment out of court. One of the few advantages of having
a court-appointed receiver is that foreign courts are more likely to recognise his status.

[72] This will be at the time the order is made unless the receiver is ordered to give security and is
not given liberty to act until such security is given, in which case his appointment takes effect

---

does not depend on the receiver taking possession, for the effect of the order is to place the charged assets in the custody of the receiver as an officer of the court and thus to divest the company of control of them. The institution of a debenture holder's action for the appointment of a receiver would not appear sufficient in English law to crystallise the charge,[73] despite dicta in *Evans v Rival Granite Quarries Ltd.*[74] suggesting that the time of application for the appointment is the relevant time and decisions of Canadian courts[75] that where the debenture holder's right to enforce his security is not in issue the commencement of proceedings for the appointment of a receiver crystallises the charge. No doubt the application for the appointment of a receiver indicates the debenture holder's intention to intervene to bring a halt to the company's dealing powers, but neither a right to intervene nor an intention to do so suffices. If it did, the presentation of a winding-up petition would cause the charge to crystallise, and it is well established that this is not the case.[76]

(2) *Intervention which is ineffective to crystallise the charge*

4-44   (a) *Default by the company* It is well established that unless otherwise provided by the debenture[77] the mere fact that the company has defaulted and the debenture holder has become entitled to enforce his security does not by itself crystallise the charge; the debenture must actively intervene to terminate the company's right to continue trading with the charged assets.[78]

4-45   (b) *Demand for payment* Similarly, a demand for payment does not by itself crystallise the charge,[79] for it does not indicate an intention to make the security a fixed security.

4-46   (c) *Assertion of rights over part of security* In the absence of a provision in the debenture empowering him to do so, the debenture holder is not enti-

---

when he furnishes the security. If the receiver, though ordered to furnish security, is given liberty to act immediately, his appointment takes effect at once but lapses if the security is not duly furnished. This presumably results in a refloating of the charge.

[73] *Re Hubbard & Co. Ltd.* (1898) 68 L.J. Ch. 54; *Re Roundwood Colliery Co.* [1897] 1 Ch. 373 (where the company's lessor levied distress not only after the commencement of the debenture holder's action but after a subsequent order for the appointment of a receiver which was never drawn up and never became effective, and the distress was held valid against the debenture holder); *Norton v Yates* [1906] 1 K.B. 112. Until the order the company retains *de jure* control, and the order may never be made.

[74] [1910] 2 K.B. 979, *per* Vaughan Williams L.J. at 986.

[75] See, for example, *Industrial Development Bank v Valley Dairy Ltd.* [1953] O.R. 70; *Gatsby Enterprises (Kelowna) Ltd. v Gatsby Kelowna (1976) Ltd.* (1978) 30 C.B.R. (N.S.) 1; *Mercantile Bank of Canada v Nelco Corp.* (1982) 47 C.B.R. (N.S.) 165.

[76] See below.

[77] See below, paras 4-49 *et seq.*

[78] *Evans v Rival Granite Quarries Ltd.* [1910] 2 K.B. 979, *per* Fletcher Moulton L.J. at 993.

[79] *Re Hubbard & Co. Ltd.*, above.

tled to crystallise his security as to part only of the assets while leaving the charge to float as to the remaining assets.[80] The assets comprised in the floating charge constitute an indivisible fund and the debenture holder must assert his security interest in relation to the fund as a whole or not at all. If he purports to pounce down on a particular asset only, leaving the debtor company free to continue trading with the remaining assets, this constitutes a breach of his contract with the company and is accordingly ineffective as an act of intervention, so that the charge will continue to float as to all the charged assets.[81] So a debenture holder whose security covered the entire undertaking and assets of the company was held not to be entitled to give notice to the company's bank contesting the attachment of the company's credit balance by a judgment creditor in garnishee proceedings while leaving the company free to continue dealing with the rest of its assets. A purported partial crystallisation of the debenture in this way was inconsistent with the nature of a floating security, and unless the charge was crystallised as to all the assets it continued to float on all of them including the bank balance, so that the judgment creditor was entitled to have the garnishee order made absolute.[82] Similarly, a notice to the company purporting to terminate its dealing powers as to part only of the assets and the purported appointment of a receiver of that part alone were held ineffective to crystallise the charge even as to such part.[83] The position is otherwise where partial crystallisation is permitted by the terms of the debenture.[84]

(d) *Institution of proceedings to enforce security* As stated earlier, the institution of proceedings by a debenture holder to enforce his security by an order for possession, sale or the appointment of a receiver appears insufficient to crystallise the charge, as it does not itself put an end to the company's management powers. **4-47**

(e) *The grant of injunctive relief* It has been suggested that the grant of an injunction to restrain the debtor company from dealing with the assets in breach of a restriction in the floating charge necessarily causes the charge to crystallise, on the ground that until crystallisation the chargee cannot treat the charged assets as specifically appropriated so as to ground an injunction.[85] This would not, however, seem to be correct. In the first place, it is predicated on the assumption that an injunction lies only where the subject-matter of the application is specific or ascertained property, that is, where the charge has crystallised. But as we have noted earlier,[86] an injunction can be granted to restrain any threatened breach of **4-48**

---

[80] *Evans v Rival Granite Quarries Ltd.*, above.
[81] *ibid.*, *R. v Consolidated Churchill Corp.* [1978] 5 W.W.R. 625.
[82] *ibid.*
[83] *R. v Consolidated Churchill Corp.*, above.
[84] See below, para.4–56.
[85] Gough, *Company Charges* (2nd ed.) p.231.
[86] See above, para.4–06.

contract, even if it involves no property rights at all. Moreover, the proposition confronts the logical difficulty that if it is only the injunction itself which produces crystallisation the holder of a floating charge has no *locus standi* to obtain it, for the charge has not yet attached to any specific assets. Secondly, an injunction to restrain a threatened dealing in breach of the terms of the charge instrument is not in itself inconsistent with the debtor company's continuing authority to manage its business using the charged assets; all it does is to prohibit the company from dealings in excess of its authority. If an injunction to restrain the trustee of an active trust from dealing with the trust fund in breach of trust does not of itself convert the active trust into a bare trust,[87] it is hard to see why an injunction which seeks to do no more than keep the chargor to the terms of the floating charge should be treated as ending its dealing powers altogether. The position is, of course, otherwise where the breach complained of denotes the cessation of the company's business, as in *Hubbuck v Helms*,[88] where the debtor company decided to discontinue its business and implemented that decision by contracting to sell all its major assets. The cessation of business is itself a crystallising event preceding, and independent of, the grant of injunctive relief.

Group 3: other acts or events specified in the debenture as causing crystallisation

4-49 As we have seen, the mere fact that the debenture holder has become entitled to enforce his security under the terms of the debenture does not by itself crystallise the charge; he must actually exercise the right of enforcement. However, since the acts or events which terminate the company's authority from the debenture holder to manage its assets are a matter of contract between them, it is open to the debenture holder to specify any method of crystallisation he chooses.[89] Two distinct types of provision for crystallisation have been used. In the first, the debenture holder is empowered to crystallise the charge by notice; in the second, crystallisation is made to occur automatically on the occurrence of a designated event.

(1) *Crystallisation by notice*

4-50 This mode of crystallisation is sometimes termed "semi-automatic."[90] The debenture holder is given the right to make the floating charge specific by

---

[87] Which would normally be incompatible with the terms of the settlement or trust instrument. The trustee might be replaced but that would not affect its continuance as an active trust.

[88] (1887) 56 L.J. Ch. 536.

[89] *Re Brightlife Ltd.* [1987] Ch. 200; *Governments Stock and Other Securities Investment Co. Ltd. v Manila Ry. Co. Ltd.* [1897] A.C. 81, where the speeches in the House of Lords showed that they regarded the matter as one of construction of the debenture.

[90] Lightman and Moss, *The Law of Receivers and Administrators of Companies* (3rd ed.) para.3–068.

notice, either at will or after the occurrence of a specified event. In *Re Woodroffes (Musical Instruments) Ltd.*[91] it was conceded that this method of crystallisation was effective. In *Re Brightlife Ltd.*[92] it was contended that the events of crystallisation were fixed by law and were three in number, namely winding up, the appointment of a receiver and cessation of the company's business, and that both as a matter of authority and in terms of public policy it was not open to the parties to stipulate other events as crystallising events. This contention was rejected by Hoffmann J., who held that the question was purely one of contract, and that Parliament having intervened on various occasions to regulate floating charges—as by requiring their registration and by subordinating them to preferential debts—it was not for the courts to impose additional restrictions on the parties' freedom of contract on grounds of public policy.[93] The Agricultural Credits Act 1928 provides expressly for crystallisation of a floating charge by notice, where so authorised by the charge instrument, where it is an agricultural charge given to a bank by a farmer.[94]

(2) *Automatic (express) crystallisation*

Under an automatic crystallisation clause, no action on the part of the debenture holder is needed to crystallise the charge; crystallisation occurs automatically on the occurrence of a specified event. The use of automatic crystallisation clauses became fashionable in the 1970s, during which period there was a tendency to expand the range of crystallising events. Winding up and receivership were also invariably specified, though as mentioned earlier this was not strictly necessary, for it is a term implied by law that these events cause a charge to crystallise. Other events sometimes specified as crystallising events were the grant of security to another creditor; the levy of distress or execution against the debtor's assets; default by the debtor in its obligations to other creditors; the failure to maintain a given ratio of assets to liabilities or to keep the debtor's external borrowings to a given level. In recent years there has been a growing awareness of the disadvantages of automatic crystallisation, as described below, and insofar as automatic crystallisation clauses are used at all, their scope tends to be narrowly confined.

4–51

Group 4: agricultural charges

S.7 of the Agricultural Credits Act 1928 lists four categories of event causing a floating charge which is an agricultural charge given by a farmer to become fixed, though only as regards property comprised in the charge as existing at the time of crystallisation. These are (i) the making of a bankruptcy order

4–52

---

[91] [1985] 2 All E.R. 908.
[92] See above.
[93] *ibid.* at 680–681.
[94] s.7. See below, para.4–52.

against the farmer; (ii) the death of the farmer; (iii) the dissolution of the partnership where the property charged is partnership property; and (iv) notice in writing to that effect by the bank on the happening of any event which by virtue of the charge confers on the bank a right to give such a notice.

The "validity" of automatic crystallisation clauses[95]

4–53 A question much canvassed is whether an automatic crystallisation clause is "valid." I have put the word "valid" in quotation marks because it seems to me that it conceals the real issue, which is not whether chargor and charge are free to agree upon the circumstances in which the charger's management powers are to come to an end (clearly they can reach any agreement they like on this point) but what is the effect of crystallisation on third parties who are not aware of its having occurred. In other words, it is for the parties to the charge, and for them alone, to decide in what circumstances the security interest created by the charge is to attach so as to be enforceable against the debtor company in regard to specific assets; but whether the attached security interest prevails over a third party is a question not of validity but of priority, a point forcefully made by Dr W. J. Gough in his excellent book on company charges.[96] Unfortunately much of the argument directed against the validity of the automatic crystallisation clause fails to separate the issues of attachment and priority. It is assumed that to give effect to the wishes of the parties as to the events that are to cause the security interest to attach will as a necessary consequence result in the crystallised charge having priority over a subsequent fixed charge. But this is to confuse relations between chargor and chargee with relations between the chargee and third parties. More specifically, it confuses the debtor company's *actual* authority to dispose of its assets, which may be terminated at any time in accordance with the agreement between the parties, with the debtor's *apparent* authority to deal with its assets, which may continue notwithstanding that its actual authority has come to an end and the charge has thus crystallised. Once this point is appreciated, much of the ground for criticism of the automatic crystallisation clause falls away.

My central proposition, then, is that *in the relations between chargor and chargee it is open to them to agree on any event they choose, however trivial, capricious or invisible to the outside world, as an event which will cause the charge to crystallise automatically.* The only qualification is that the occurrence of the designated event must be designated with sufficient certainty to be capable of being given legal effect.[97] Since the effect of crystallisation is simply to cause the security interest to attach to the assets, and since attach-

---

[95] See Tan Cheng Han, "Automatic Crystallisation, De-Crystallisation and Convertibility of Charges" [1998] C.F.I.L.R. 41; Gough, *Company Charges* (2nd ed.) Ch.11.

[96] *Op. cit.*, pp.409 *et seq.*

[97] *Covacich v Riordan* [1994] 2 N.Z.L.R. 502.

ment concerns only creditor and debtor,[98] there is nothing in this proposition which has any impact on third party rights. I can state without fear of contradiction that there is no reported case, here or overseas, which denies to the parties to a floating charge the freedom to determine at what point and on the occurrence of what events the debtor's authority to dispose of its assets free from the charge is to come to an end. It is true that according to some writers the judgments of Vaughan Williams and Fletcher Moulton L.J.J. in *Evans v Rival Granite Quarries Ltd.*[99] point in the other direction and suggest the need for active intervention by the debenture holder; but this is because the clause there under consideration was not an automatic crystallisation clause at all but one which merely *empowered* the debenture holder to intervene in stated events. Mere default by the debtor which entitled the debenture holder to intervene did not crystallise the charge in the absence of actual intervention. The same observation applies to the Canadian decision in *R. v Churchill Copper Corp. Ltd.*,[1] where Berger J. inveighed against the concept of "self-generating crystallisation". But again, that case did not concern the occurrence of a contractually designated crystallising event; the debenture holders sought to assert that mere default—which would have entitled them to intervene by appointing a receiver if they had so wished—sufficed to crystallise the floating charge. Since the debenture contained no provision for automatic crystallisation on default, Berger J. quite rightly rejected the contention and held that in the absence of intervention the charge remained a floating charge.

The efficacy of a provision for automatic crystallisation on the occurrence of a contractually designed crystallising event, which had been supported by dicta in a number of English cases, was tested in *Re Brightlife Ltd.*,[2] where Hoffmann J. had no difficulty in holding that the events upon which a floating charge is to crystallise are purely a matter of contract. Though that case involved crystallisation by notice rather than automatic crystallisation, the reasoning is equally applicable to automatic crystallisation clauses; indeed, Hoffmann J. several times referred to, and rejected, the submission by counsel that automatic crystallisation could occur only by reason of winding up, the appointment of a receiver or the cessation of business by the debtor company.[3] Automatic crystallisation upon the occurrence of a contractually designated event has also been endorsed by courts in Australia[4] and New Zealand.[5]

Hence termination of the debtor company's actual authority to manage the charged assets by reason of such an event can be taken as established. The

---

[98] See above.
[99] [1910] 2 K.B. 979.
[1] (1978) 90 D.L.R. (3d) 357.
[2] See above.
[3] [1987] Ch. 200 at 212 *et seq.*
[4] *Fire Nymph Products Ltd. v Heating Centre Pty. Ltd.* (1992) 7 A.C.S.R. 365; *Deputy Commissioner of Taxation v Horsburgh* [1984] V.R. 773.
[5] *Re Manurewa Transport Ltd.* [1971] N.Z.L.R. 909; *Covacich v Riordan* [1994] N.Z.L.R. 502, where the designated triggering event was insolvency, *i.e.* the advent of a state of insolvency as opposed to a subsequent formal insolvency proceeding such as liquidation.

impact of crystallisation on priorities is a separate question discussed in the next chapter.[6]

The problem of overkill in automatic crystallisation clauses

4-54 The temptation to use the automatic crystallisation clause as a device to protect the charge from subordination to preferential creditors on a receivership or winding up has now been removed so far as English law is concerned.[7] There remains, however, the inducement of protecting the assets from execution creditors.[8]

Nevertheless, the draftsman of the debenture should discipline himself against the adoption of a long catalogue of crystallising events. I have cautioned elsewhere[9] about the danger of overkill in the use of automatic crystallisation clauses. The draftsman has always to keep in mind the commercial objectives of the parties. It is all too easy, when acting for a lender, to set up safeguards which, if fully operated, would prevent the debtor from doing any business at all. Crystallisation is not something to be brought about lightly. Its effect is to paralyse the business, an event likely to cause as much damage to the debenture holder as to the debtor if it is made to occur needlessly. Suppose, for example, that the debenture were to provide for the charge to attach if the debtor committed a breach of any of its covenants to the debenture holder or to any other secured creditor. The length and detail of present-day covenants are such that it is quite easy for the debtor to commit a purely technical breach without either party being aware of the fact. Some trivial default, such as the delay of a day in furnishing information or documents required to be furnished by a given date, may bring down the pack of cards by causing the charge to crystallise, despite the fact that the company is a profitable, soundly managed enterprise. The debenture holder, having discovered the occurrence of the crystallising event, then has the choice of actively reversing the crystallisation or of tacitly ignoring it by allowing normal trading to continue. In either event, the charge would become de-crystallised, by agreement or estoppel.[10]

4-55 If this were all, the debenture holder's advisers might still feel that no harm had been done. On the contrary, their client is surely getting the best of both worlds. He relies on the crystallisation clause where it suits him and ignores it where it does not. If only life were so simple! But the legal battlefield is strewn with the corpses of those who wanted the facility of saying one thing and doing another, of blowing hot one minute and cold the next. One of the most important concerns of the legal draftsman should be to see that his

---

[6] Below, paras 5–50 *et seq.* See also above, para.4–29.
[7] See below, para.5–65.
[8] Below, paras 4–56, 5–43.
[9] [1981] J.B.L. 473, 474.
[10] See further below, para.4–57.

documents correspond to what the parties intend to do. It is bad drafting and dangerous practice to provide for automatic crystallisation on the assumption that if it proves inconvenient it can be ignored on the day. The tacit waiver of an automatic crystallisation clause may well have a much more profound effect than to de-crystallise the charge; it may lead the court to conclude that the whole clause should be ignored as not truly reflecting the intention of the parties. Put another way, no amount of legal language to the effect that waiver on one occasion is not to constitute waiver on other occasions will prevent the court from ruling, in a proper case, that if one crystallising event is simply disregarded the parties ought not to be taken too seriously in their specification of other crystallising events.

How, then, should the crystallisation provisions be drafted? The answer is to restrict automatic crystallisation to those events which are of such significance that, if one of them occurs, the creditor will almost inevitably want the company's powers of management to end, and to specify other less important events as entitling the debenture holder to intervene—by taking possession or by appointing a receiver—if he so chooses. Further flexibility can be achieved by a suitably drafted clause providing for partial crystallisation of the charge.

Partial crystallisation

It is open to the parties to a debenture to stipulate that the charge shall attach only to part of the assets comprising the security. There is no case bearing on the efficacy of automatic partial crystallisation, but in principle there can be no objection to it, for as previously stated, attachment of the security interest is purely the concern of chargor and chargee. Dr Gough has ingeniously suggested the use of partial crystallisation as a method of avoiding undesirable overkill. The charge would provide that if any particular asset was placed in jeopardy, *e.g.* through attempted mortgage or execution, the charge would crystallise as regards that asset but continue to float over the other assets of the debtor company.[11] Alternatively, though less effectively, the debenture could simple empower the debenture holder to intervene in relation to the asset in question, *i.e.* the partial crystallisation would not be automatic but would require some active step by the debenture such as the taking of possession, or the appointment of a receiver of the asset.

If the debenture makes no provision for partial crystallisation, the debenture holder is not entitled to appoint a receiver of part only of the assets comprised in the floating charge.[12]

4–56

---

[11] Gough, *op. cit.*, pp.168 *et seq.*, 401 *et seq.*
[12] See above, para.4–46.

5. DE-CRYSTALLISATION AND RE-CRYSTALLISATION

De-crystallisation (reflotation)

4–57 Can crystallisation be reversed so as to cause the charge to float again over the assets? There is no authority on the point, but in principle there can be no objection to the debenture holder restoring the company's management powers, provided that the debenture holder is still in control of the business. So if the charge has crystallised but no receiver has been appointed and the company is not in liquidation, it is open to the debenture holder to agree that the charge shall refloat. But the charge is not de-crystallised merely because the debenture holder releases specific assets from the charge at the chargor's request.

Even in the absence of agreement, if the debenture holder stands by and allows the debtor company to continue to dispose of the charged assets in the ordinary course of business it will be treated as waiving the effect of crystallisation and refloating the charge. However, this presupposes that the chargee is aware of the crystallising event. A party cannot be held to have waived the effect of an event of which it had no knowledge. It is possible for crystallisation to occur without the knowledge of the chargee or, indeed, of either party, as where the relevant crystallising event is the advent of insolvency, the chargee is unaware of this and the chargor honestly believes that it is still solvent. In such a case the crystallisation remains effective as between the parties but the chargee may be estopped from asserting its rights against third parties acquiring an interest in the charged assets in good faith and without notice of the crystallisation.[13] Again, de-crystallisation, like crystallisation, does not necessitate any fresh registration under s.395 of the Companies Act 1985, for it is the same security interest that was originally created, became attached and is now being detached once more from the specific assets.

The position is otherwise if the company is in receivership or liquidation. Where an administrative receiver has been appointed, it is he, not the debenture holder, who is in control of the assets, and except as otherwise provided by the debenture deed, it is not open to the debenture holder to instruct the receiver to hand back the management of the assets to the company. Indeed, the receiver has a statutory duty to pay preferential debts out of the proceeds of assets comprised in the floating charge.[14] Moreover, the debenture holder no longer has power to remove the receiver, which under s.45(4) of the Insolvency Act 1986 can only be done by the court. If the receiver pays the preferential debts and the company is not in winding up, the debenture holder can presumably waive his right to payment out of the proceeds and instruct the receiver to return control to the directors. Where the company is

---

[13] See below, para.5–50.
[14] Insolvency Act 1986, s.40(2).

in liquidation, this is not possible, and there is no way in which the charge can then be reconverted into a floating charge.

Just as a well-drawn debenture will allow for partial crystallisation,[15] so also it will provide for partial de-crystallisation,[16] thereby giving the parties maximum flexibility.

Re-crystallisation

A de-crystallised charge can, of course, be crystallised again as the result of **4–58** a fresh withdrawal of the company's authority to manage the charged assets.[17] As with the original crystallisation, re-crystallisation does not give rise to a new charge, merely the termination once again of the company's dealing powers.

6. CONVERSION OF FIXED CHARGE TO FLOATING CHARGE

Just as a charge instrument may provide for conversion of a floating charge **4–59** to a fixed charge by a crystallisation notice or some other designated crystallising event, so also it may provide for the conversion of a fixed charge into a floating charge. The principle is the same as for de-crystallisation except that the charge is fixed from the outset rather than having to be crystallised.

7. ENFORCEMENT OF THE SECURITY

On the debtor company's default, the holder of a floating charge has all the **4–60** remedies conferred by the terms of the debenture creating the floating charge. These will typically include the power to take possession of the charged assets, to sell them and to appoint a receiver,[18] the latter in turn being empowered to collect in and realise the assets and manage the business.[19] Where the debenture is under seal and the charge has crystallised the chargee has a statutory power to sell or to appoint a receiver,[20] and even in the case of a debenture not under seal he can apply to the court for an order for sale or for the appointment of a receiver. But unless the debenture entitles the chargee

---

[15] See above, para.4–56.

[16] Gough, *op. cit.*, p.406.

[17] For some of the possible complications resulting from this see Lightman & Moss, *The Law of Receivers and Administrators of Companies* (3rd ed.) paras 3–087 *et seq.*

[18] Now termed an administrative receiver. But see below, para.4–61.

[19] It is no longer necessary to set out the powers of the administrative receiver *in extenso* since these are listed in the Insolvency Act 1986, Sch.1.

[20] Law of Property Act 1925, ss.101(1), 205(1)(xvi). But a statutory receiver has limited powers, which do not include the management of the company.

to reinforce his charge by calling for a mortgage he has no power, even after crystallisation, to take possession unless so provided by the debenture, nor may he apply for foreclosure, this being a remedy limited to mortgagees, by virtue of their security ownership.[21] There have, it is true, been a few cases in which the debenture holder under a debenture creating a floating charge has been held entitled to a foreclosure order but in none of these was there any discussion of the inherent distinction between a charge and a mortgage. In the first case, *Sadler v Worley*[22] Kekewich J., in granting foreclosure, admitted that he was making an order "the like of which has never been made before",[23] and the true issue, namely whether there was an express or implied agreement to give a mortgage, was never discussed, the whole argument focusing on the difficulties thought to be created by the subject-matter of the debenture, in particular the uncalled capital of the borrower company; whilst in the second case, *Re Continental Oxygen Co.*,[24] decided by the same judge, he merely followed his earlier decision, having been unable to ascertain how far it had been criticised or approved by other judges or by the profession.[25] It is significant that there appears to be no subsequent reported English decision in which the real point at issue has been argued and foreclosure ordered.[26] Given that a crystallised floating charge is still a charge, not a mortgage, it is submitted that foreclosure is not available as a remedy in the absence of an express or implied agreement for a mortgage. The moral for the legal draftsman is obvious: always include in the debenture a power to convert the charge into a mortgage if you envisage that your client may wish to apply for foreclosure.

8. THE FUTURE OF THE FLOATING CHARGE

4–61 From its early days the floating charge has generated intense hostility because of its potentially all-embracing scope and its perceived unfairness to ordinary trade creditors.[27] Legislation has sought to address this in various ways, for example, by making the floating charge a distinct registrable category under

---

[21] See above para.1–51, n.70.

[22] [1894] 2 Ch. 170.

[23] *ibid.*, at 176.

[24] [1897] 1 Ch. 511.

[25] *ibid.* at 514.

[26] There have been later decisions in which crystallisation of a floating charge has been held to create an assignment (*e.g. George Baker (Transport) Ltd. v Eynon* [1974] 1 All E.R. 462, *per* Edmund Davies L.J. at 745; *Business Computers Ltd. v Anglo-African Leasing Ltd.* [1977] 2 All E.R. 741, *per* Templeman J. at 745) but nothing turned on the distinction between an assignment and a charge in those cases, where the essential question was whether notice of crystallisation of a floating charge cut off the debtor's continuing right of set-off and for this purpose reference was made to decisions on the effect of assignment. Since a crystallised charge, being a specific security, operates *in rem* and thus has the same effect on set-off as an assignment, it is not surprising to find the courts using the language of assignment in this context.

[27] See, for example, *Re London Pressed Jinge Co. Ltd.* [1905] 1 Ch 576, *per* Buckley J. at 583.

the Companies Act 1985[28] by defining a floating charge as one which as created is a floating charge,[29] and by providing a special ground of avoidance of
floating charges in winding-up which is stricter than for fixed charges.[30]
Recently there has been a further assault in that one of the advantages of a
floating charge, namely the ability of the holder to appoint an administrative
receiver,[31] is about to be substantially reduced.[32]

Hand-in-hand with the policy objections to some aspects of the floating
charge has come the growing realisation that, however brilliant the conception and however useful the floating charge as a financing tool, it has become
so overladen with case law and doctrine that it is now a subject of excessive
complexity—as will have become apparent even from the relatively brief
treatment in the present chapter—and that the desired results can be achieved
much more simply by treating all charges, even if expressed as floating
charges, as fixed security interests and laying down a priority rule to protect
those to whom the company sells or charges assets in the ordinary course of
business.[33] The floating charge owes nothing to statute; it is the pure creation
of equity judges of the nineteenth century. Its success has been remarkable,
but judge-made law, which is necessarily a patchwork of large numbers of
individual cases each influenced by its own particular facts, can no longer
serve as a substitute for structured personal property security legislation of
the kind enacted throughout the United States and Canada, and more
recently in New Zealand, and under active consideration in Australia.[34]
Moreover, the utility of the floating charge will be much reduced by the
impending abolition of the debenture holder's power to appoint an administrative receiver under a "qualifying charge"[35] and its replacement by the
power to appoint an administrator.[36] It is to be hoped that the Law Commission's project on registration of company charges will provide a springboard
for more general and all-embracing legislation of this kind, which was advo-
cated long ago by the Crowther Committee on Consumer Credit, endorsed
by the Cork Committee on Insolvency Law and Practice and reaffirmed in
the detailed report by Professor Aubrey Diamond on security in property.[37]

---

[28] Companies Act 1985, ss.395. 396(1)(f).
[29] Thereby negating the priority of a crystallised floating charge over post-crystallisation preferential debts.
[30] Insolvency Act 1986, s.245. See R.M. Goode, *Principles of Corporate Insolvency Law* (2nd ed.)
pp.409 *et seq.*
[31] See above, para.4–42.
[32] See above, para.1–01.
[33] See Roy Goode, "The Exodus of the Floating Charge" in *Corporate and Commercial Law:
Modern Developments* (Feldman and Meisel eds), Ch.10.
[34] See above, para.1–04.
[35] Insolvency Act 1986, s.72A.
[36] *ibid.*, Sch.B1, para.14.
[37] For references, see above, para.1–04, n.17.

V

Fixed and Floating Charges: Some Problems of Priority

1. INTRODUCTION

The holder of a security interest may well find himself in competition with **5–01** others claiming rights in the collateral. The competitor may be an outright buyer, another secured creditor, an execution creditor, a landlord or other person claiming a right to distrain on the collateral, a liquidator seeking to invalidate the security interest and thereby claim the collateral for the benefit of the general body of creditors, or some other contender for superior rights. The considerations which lead to the taking of security in the first place[1] also apply to the priority of the interest taken. The primary concern, as before, is to provide the secured creditor with safeguards against the debtor's insolvency. If it were not for insolvency, the creditor would, sooner or later, recover his money with or without security and regardless of the ranking of any security taken. It is the risk of the debtor's insolvency that is the prime factor in the decision to take security, but the value of the security interest depends upon its priority. This does not, of course, mean that second, or even third, mortgages or charges have no value, merely that each successive mortgagee or chargee must be satisfied that after giving the prior security interests the debtor retains sufficient equity in the asset to provide the assurance each junior incumbrancer requires. However, a first mortgage is obviously superior to a second, not only because the first mortgagee has the primary claim on the asset but also because priority gives him control in the event that the debtor gets into financial difficulties. This control is at its most visible when a creditor holding a floating charge covering, with any fixed charges, the whole or substantially the whole of a debtor company's property appoints an administrative receiver to run the business, where possible sell it as a going concern either directly or through a hive-down,[2] and pay off his debenture

---

[1] See above, para.1–01.

[2] A procedure by which some or all of the assets of the company are sold, without transfer of the liabilities, to a specially formed subsidiary which is controlled by the receiver and which as a clean company free of debt may be able to trade profitably with a view to its sale, the proceeds flowing back to the company in payment of the price for the transferred assets. See generally Lightman and Moss, *The Law of Receivers and Administrators of Companies* (3rd ed.) paras 9–058 *et seq.*

holders.[3] It is in the priority stakes that perfection of a security interest[4] acquires significance. Perfection does not guarantee priority, but an unperfected security interest will almost always be subordinated to or displaced by competing interests and by unsecured creditors in the debtor's bankruptcy or winding up.

The subject of priorities is of great complexity because English law has never developed a coherent legal structure for the ordering of competing interests. The common law adopted a straightforward first-in-time principle. The development of equitable ownership and security interests brought in its train a number of refinements, such as the relationship between an equitable interest and a subsequent legal title, priority as between competing equitable interests, including interests in debts and other intangibles, and the concepts of inferred and constructive notice of an interest. The introduction of a variety of statutory registration systems, each with its own priority rules and its own sanctions for failure to register, added to the complexity, and this has been exacerbated by the dual perfection requirements imposed by s.395 of the Companies Act 1985, as regards categories of charge listed in s.396, and statutory provisions regulating the various specialist registers.[5] The courts have also had to consider the extent to which registration of a charge constitutes constructive notice of the existence of the charge and of its provisions. The result is an amalgam of common law rules and statutory provisions many of which lack any rational policy or responsiveness to modern commercial and financial requirements and by their complexity add significantly to transaction costs.

5–02   That this state of affairs continues to be tolerated in the 21st century, when the United States and Canada have for many years had highly developed, market-responsive legislation which has worked and when successive government reports have recommended the adoption of similar legislation in this country,[6] is a shocking indictment of the indifference of successive governments to the modernisation of our commercial law. However, with the publication of the Law Commission's excellent consultation paper on registration of company charges,[7] which the Law Commission rightly concludes cannot be considered in isolation from general issues of perfection and priorities and from security by non-corporate debtors, the groundwork is being laid for a modern personal property security law which responds to the needs of the market rather than being rooted in outdated concepts and doctrine.

At the outset we need to be aware of the fundamental difference between a fixed mortgage or charge and a floating charge. In relation to the subject of a fixed charge, the priority of the charge as against competing interests is

---

[3] The receiver also has a duty to discharge preferential debts from the proceeds of assets subject to a floating charge to the extent that the company's free assets are not sufficient for the purpose. See below, para.5–65. For the impending near-demise of administrative receivership, see above, para.4–61.

[4] See above, paras 2–16 et seq.

[5] See above, paras 2–19 et seq.

[6] See above, para.1–04, n.17.

[7] Registration of Security Interests: Company Charges and Property other than Land (Law Commission Consultation No. 164, 2002).

governed primarily by rules of property law and equity.[8] But in the case of assets the subject of a floating charge, the power of disposition given to the company attracts rules of commercial law as well, for the company is trading in the assets comprising the security with the consent of the debenture holder, so that under the principle of authority akin to that which underlies agency law the debenture holder's security interest may be overreached by a disposition which is within the company's actual or ostensible powers of management. This does not mean that the company is the agent of the debenture holder; on the contrary, the company deals with the charged assets on its own behalf. But in so doing it is held out by the debenture holder as authorised to deal with the assets in the ordinary course of business free from the floating charge, and a third party taking without notice of any restriction of such authority is thus entitled to the act in reliance on the company's apparent powers of disposition even if the transfer to the third party is in breach of the terms of the debenture.[9] In general, those apparent powers are limited only by the requirement that the dealing be in the ordinary course of the company's business, a requirement liberally interpreted by the courts.[10] Accordingly priority issues arising in relation to floating charges will be examined separately.

2. PRINCIPLES OF PRIORITY AT COMMON LAW[11]

The following are the principal priority rules established at common law to **5–03** regulate the priority of competing fixed interests generally.[12] Competition between fixed security interests is discussed in section 3 and between a fixed security interest and other types of interest in section 4, while the ranking of the floating charge is examined in section 5.

Rule 1: *nemo dat quod non habet*

A person cannot in general transfer a better title than he himself possesses. **5–04** Another formulation of the rule is that as between competing interests the first-in-time prevails. The first formulation is usually used in relation to competing legal interest in goods, the second to competing equitable interests and interests in land. The rule applies where the competing interests are both legal interests and also where they are both equitable interest. However, in a competition between an equitable interest and a subsequent legal interest, this

---

[8] See below.
[9] The doctrine of apparent authority is conventionally treated as part of the law of agency even though it is not confined to agency situations. See *Bowstead & Reynolds on Agency* (17th ed.) para.8–027.
[10] See below, para.5–39.
[11] "Common law" is here used in its broad sense of judge-made law, including equity.
[12] For a very clear description of the principal rules, see the judgment of Millett J. in *Macmillan Inc. v Bishopsgate Investment Trust plc (No. 2)* [1995] 1 W.L.R. 978 at 999 *et seq.*

rule may be overridden by Rule 2, below. It follows that as between competing equitable interests, the conversion of one of these into a legal interest may move the case from Rule 1 to Rule 2.

Rule 1 is subject to a number of exceptions at common law.[13]

Common law exceptions to the *nemo dat* rule

(1) *Actual or apparent (ostensible) authority*

5–05   A non-owner can sell or charge an asset if he has either actual or apparent (ostensible) authority from the owner to do so. Even if not in fact authorised to make the disposition, he will have apparent authority to do so if he has been held out by the owner as authorised to dispose; and where there is such a holding out, an innocent third party will not be bound by limitations on the power of disposal which were not known to him.[14] This principle is of particular importance in the case of the floating charge. The chargee confers on the chargor power to deal with its assets in the ordinary course of business free from the charge, but may seek to impose restrictions on the exercise of such power. The question then is what steps are necessary and sufficient to give notice of those restrictions to third parties, a matter discussed earlier.[15]

(2) *Apparent ownership*

5–06   Distinct from apparent authority is the concept of apparent ownership, where the owner of an asset holds out another as being the owner. This is significantly wider in its effect in that while an unauthorised disposition by an agent binds his principal only if the agent acts within the scope of his apparent authority, no such limitation applies to a disposition by a person invested with apparent ownership, for an owner needs no authority, so that the fact that the disposition is on unusual terms or not in the ordinary course of business is irrelevant except so far as it bears on the transferee's good faith and the reasonableness of his belief that the transferor was the owner.[16]

(3) *Postponement of equitable interest to subsequent legal interest*

5–07   An equitable interest is in certain circumstances postponed to a subsequent legal interest. See Rule 2, below.

---

[13] For the statutory exceptions, see below, paras 5–13 *et seq.*
[14] For a detailed treatment, see *Bowstead & Reynolds on Agency* (17th ed.) paras 8–013 *et seq.*
[15] See above, paras 2–24 *et seq.*
[16] *Lloyds and Scottish Finance Ltd. v Williamson* [1965] 1 W.L.R. 404.

(4) *Successive assignments of choses in action*

The priority of successive assignments of a debt or other chose in action is **5–08** governed by the rule in *Dearle v Hall*[17] under which an assignee who takes without notice of an earlier assignment and is the first to give notice of assignment to the debtor obtains priority over the earlier assignee.[18] The rule applies also to a contest between the holder of an equitable right to claim a debt as proceeds of his property and a subsequent purchaser or mortgagee of the same debt.[19] The statutory provisions for registration of security interest considerably reduce the impact of the rule in *Dearle v Hall* in receivables financing, for the second assignee will usually have notice of a prior security interest by virtue of its registration.[20] The rule does not apply at all in relation to the assignment of registered shares in a company, since the company can neither enter a notice of assignment in its register of members[21] nor validly accept such a notice,[22] and the same applies to an assignment of dematerialised ("uncertificated") securities registered electronically in the CREST system[23]; nor does the rule apply to a negotiable instrument[24] or to a contest between the holder of a floating charge and a subsequent fixed chargee or assignee[25] or to the assignment of debt which by the terms of the contract creating it is non-assignable, for the debtor is then under no obligation to recognise a notice of assignment.[26] So if the holder of a bill of

---

[17] (1828) 3 Russ. 1.

[18] The requirement that the later assignee be without notice of the earlier assignment, which is the so-called second limb of the rule in *Dearle v Hall*, was not in fact part of the decision in that case and was a refinement added by later cases. For a good historical account of the development of the rule see John de Lacy, "Reflections on the Ambit of the Rule in *Dearle v Hall* and the Priority of Personal Property Assignments," (1999) 28 Anglo-American Law Review 87, 197. The rule is wholly unsuited to modern receivables financing. Over a century ago Lord Macnaghten commented: "I am inclined to think that the rule in *Dearle v Hall* has on the whole produced at least as much injustice as it has prevented" (*Ward v Duncombe* [1893] A.C. 369 at 393). For a more sustained assault, see Fidelis Oditah, *Legal Aspects of Receivables Financing*, pp.140 *et seq.*

[19] See below, para.5–36.

[20] However, the duty to register a security interest is fulfilled by lodging the application for registration containing the prescribed particulars and the instrument of charge in accordance with s.395(1) of the Companies Act 1985. Where for any reason the charge is not entered on the register—*e.g.* through inadvertence or because the Companies Registrar takes the view that it is not of registrable category—a subsequent chargee or assignee may well take without notice and thus be able to invoke the rule in *Dearle v Hall*.

[21] Companies Act 1985, s.360, which provides that no notice of any trust, express, implied or constructive, shall be entered on the register. The assignment of shares constitutes the assignor a trustee for the assignee (*Hardoon v Belilios* [1901] 1 A.C. 118. Hence the method by which a mortgagee perfects his title is by entry on the register in place of the mortgagor, a process which is a novation, not an assignment. See above, para.3–14; below, para.6–26.

[22] *Société Générale de Paris v Walker* (1885) 11 App. Cas. 20, *per* Earl of Selbourne at 30–31.

[23] Uncertificated Securities Regulations 2001, reg.23(3), which prohibits an Operator of a system from entering on its register notice of any trust, express, implied or constructive. Before he has been entered on the register a mortgagee or other transferee has a mere equitable interest, and this continues to be the case during the period between the time the transferor has been removed from the register and the time the transferee is entered on it, during which time the transferor is a trustee for the transferee (*ibid.*, regs 31(2)(b), 31(4)).

[24] See below, para.5–28.

[25] See above, para.4–42, n.70; below, para.5–39.

[26] See above, para.3–40.

exchange assigns the underlying debt to A and then negotiates the bill to B, B has priority notwithstanding that A has given notice of assignment to the acceptor, for the latter is required to pay the current holder who presents the bill for payment, and no one else.[27]

Rule 2: a legal interest acquired for value and without notice overrides prior equitable interest

5–09   An equitable interest is overreached by a disposition of the legal title to a bona fide purchaser for value without notice. The principle remains unaffected by the 1925 property legislation, but the registrability of most categories of security interest in one register or another makes it difficult for a subsequent legal purchaser to claim that he took without notice. However, the concept of notice continues to give rise to difficulties, as explained earlier.

The time when the subsequent purchaser is required to be without notice is not when he takes the legal title but when he makes his advance. This rule enables the holder of a later equitable interest who makes his advance without notice of the prior equitable interest to effect a *tabula in naufragio* by getting in the legal title,[28] thereby securing priority even if by the time he takes the legal title he has acquired notice of the prior equitable right.[29] But it would seem that only a fixed equitable interest can be promoted in this way, and that the interest of the holder of a floating charge is too nebulous to enable him to jump ahead of a prior fixed charge by getting in the legal title after notice of the fixed charge. The *tabula in naufragio* is not available in the case of competing assignments of a debt. A statutory assignee, despite having the legal title, is postponed to a prior equitable assignee who gave notice first, for s.136 of the Law of Property Act 1925 expressly provides that the statutory assignee is to take subject to equities, and this includes a prior equitable interest of which the debtor has been given notice.[30] However, a statutory assignee who collects payment without notice can rely on his legal title.[31]

---

[27] Indeed, even if the holder of the bill assigns it while retaining the instrument, the debtor can ignore the notice of assignment, for his duty remains to the holder who presents the bill, whether the holder is the assignor or anyone else (*Bence v Shearman* [1898] 2 Ch. 582).

[28] Or having the best right to the legal title, as where he procures the mortgaged property to be conveyed to trustees on his behalf.

[29] *Taylor v Russell* [1892] A.C. 244; *Bailey v Barnes* [1894] 1 Ch. 25. The rule applies also to a mortgage of shares, where a creditor who takes a share certificate and executed transfer by way of equitable mortgage and makes his advance without notice of a prior equitable interest can obtain priority by registering the transfer (*Dodds v Hills* (1865) 2 H. & M. 424; which Millett J. in *Macmillan Inc. v Bishopsgate Investment Trust plc (No. 2)* [1995] 1 W.L.R. 978 considered (at 1004) to be still good law despite attacks made upon it).

[30] *Harding Corp. Ltd. v Royal Bank of Canada* [1980] W.W.R. 149.

[31] A point left open by Phillips J. in *E. Pfeiffer Weinkellerei-Weineinkauf GmbH & Co. v Arbuthnot Factors Ltd.* [1988] 1 W.L.R. 150 at 163 but conceded in *Compaq Computers Ltd. v Abercorn Group Ltd.* [1991] B.C.C. 484 at 500.

Rule 3: a mortgagee may in certain conditions tack further advances for which he will rank in priority to a subsequent mortgagee

The common law attached great importance to the legal estate, so much so **5–10** that it provided two situations in which a legal mortgagee or a person having the best right to under a mortgage could tack such advances to his initial advance and rank in priority to a subsequent mortgagee even if the mortgage was not expressed to cover further advances and even if these were not made until after the execution of the second mortgage. The first situation was where the further advances were made without notice of the second mortgage. Under the rule in *Hopkinson v Rolt*,[32] notice of the second mortgage terminated the right to tack further advances, a rule considered necessary to avoid the first mortgagee having a monopoly over the debtor's financing. The rule was applied even if the prior legal mortgagee was under an obligation to make the further advances. The second situation was the *tabula in naufragio*, where if a legal mortgage was granted to A followed by a mortgage to B and then a third mortgage to C, who made his advance without notice of B's mortgage, C could purchase A's interest and use the legal estate he had thereby acquired to tack his own advance in priority to B, who was thus squeezed out. In addition to these cases, any mortgagee, legal or equitable, could tack further advances if the mortgage expressly covered such advances and the mortgagee, at the time of making them, had no notice of the subsequent mortgage. As will be seen, the *tabula in naufragio* has been abolished by statute but the other form of tacking remains, albeit modified by statute.

Rule 4: priority rules may be varied by agreement

The rights of a secured creditor may be subordinated or waived altogether by **5–11** agreement with the party in whose favour the subordination or waiver is to be given. The priority effect of waivers and subordinations is discussed later in the present chapter.[33]

3. THE IMPACT OF LEGISLATION

The priority rules laid down at common law have been significantly affected **5–12** by legislation, which either changed the rules or, through the operation of registration systems, provided a new system of perfection and greatly reduced the number of cases in which a person could claim to be without notice of a competing interest, as well as making notice irrelevant in some cases.

---

[32] (1861) 9 Cas. 514.
[33] See below, paras 5–53 *et seq.* As to whether a subordination agreement creates a security interest, see above, paras 1–79 *et seq.*

Statutory exceptions to the *nemo dat* rule

5–13   The principle *nemo dat quod non habet*, to which, as we have seen, there were several exceptions at common law, has been further qualified by legislation designed to protect innocent transferees for value and thereby facilitate the free movement of goods in the stream of trade. Principal among these are dispositions by a mercantile agent,[34] a seller or buyer in possession[35] and a hirer or buyer holding a motor vehicle under a hire-purchase or conditional sale agreement.[36]

The effect of registration provisions on priority rules

5–14   As has been previously described, registration systems fall into two broad groups: registration of company charges under s.395 of the Companies Act 1985 and registration in specialist registers provided by special statutes, *e.g.* in relation to land, ships, aircraft, and intellectual property.

(1) *Registration as notice*

5–15   The effect of registration of a charge as notice of its existence varies from one statutory system to another. Registration under s.395 of the Companies Act 1985 constitutes notice to all those who could reasonably be expected to search the register,[37] and thus reduces the ability of a subsequent incumbrancer to plead want of notice and thereby take advantage of the legal purchaser principle or the rule in *Dearle v Hall*, though it probably has little, if any, impact on the doctrine of tacking.[38] Registration of a charge of unregistered land under the Land Charges Act 1925 is deemed to constitute actual notice to all persons and for all purposes connected with the land affected.[39] The question of notice does not arise in relation to competing legal charges over registered land, where priority is determined by the order of registration irrespective of notice.[40] Equitable charges are protected by notice in the register under the Land Registration Act 2002.[41]

---

[34] Factors Act 1889, s.2.
[35] *ibid.*, ss.8, 9; Sale of Goods Act 1979, ss.24, 25. A disposition by a buyer holding under a conditional sale agreement falling within the Consumer Credit Act 1974 is excluded from the operation of s.8 of the Factors Act and s.25 of the Sale of Goods Act.
[36] Hire-Purchase Act 1964, s.27–30. For detailed analyses of the common law and statutory exceptions to the *nemo dat* rule, particularly in the context of sale transactions, see Roy Goode, *Commercial Law* (2nd ed.), Ch.16; *Benjamin's Sale of Goods* (6th ed.), Ch.7.
[37] See above, para.2–29.
[38] See below, para.5–22.
[39] Law of Property Act 1925, s.198.
[40] Land Registration Act 2002, s.48(1).
[41] s.32. This gives protection under s.29(2)(a)(i).

(2) *When registration is a priority point*

Registration under the Companies Act is merely a perfection requirement, not a priority point, so that the order of registration is irrelevant, and the primary, first-in-time common law rule prevails so long as the registration is effected within the statutory 21-day period. The same would seem to be true of successive charges over unregistered land, though the position remains unclear. Under s.97 of the Law of Property Act 1925 the priority of puisne mortgages[42] is determined by the order of registration, whereas s.4(5) of the Land Charges Act 1972 renders such a puisne mortgage void against a subsequent purchaser (including a subsequent mortgagee) unless this is registered before completion of the purchase. The better view is that s.97 takes effect subject to s.4(5),[43] so that registration is a perfection requirement, not a priority point. To this extent registration under the Land Charges Act possesses the same characteristic as registration under the Companies Act. However, the requirements of the two systems for the preservation of priority are different. Under s.395 of the Companies Act all that the first chargee has to do is to register within the 21 days allowed[44]; under s.4(5) of the Land Charges Act he has to register before completion of the subsequent mortgage. Registration of mortgage of a patent is also merely a perfection requirement in that a mortgagee of a patent who takes without notice of an earlier unregistered mortgage has priority.[45]

By contrast the priority of interests registrable in other specialist registers is usually determined by the order of registration,[46] not by the order of creation. This is true, for example, of mortgages of registered land,[47] ship mortgages,[48] aircraft mortgages,[49] and bills of sale.[50]

5–16

Statutory changes to the rules on tacking

The *tabula in naufragio* was abolished by s.94(3) of the Law of Property Act 1925, which modified the existing rules for tacking of further advances. S.94(3) does not apply to registered land; it covers mortgages of unregistered

5–17

---

[42] *i.e.* mortgages not protected by deposit of the title deeds.

[43] Megarry and Wade, *Law of Real Property* (6th ed.) paras 19–225 *et seq.*

[44] The effect is that the subsequent mortgagee who makes a search before expiry of the 21 days allowed to the first mortgagee for registration and who finds nothing on the register will be postponed to the first mortgagee if he registers within the 21-day period, even if by then the second mortgagee has registered.

[45] Patents Act 1977, s.33(1).

[46] Subject to certain rules designed to give protection for a limited period to a party who registers a priority notice or makes a pre-completion search prior to registration of the security interest. See below, paras 5–30, 5–31.

[47] Land Registration Act 2002, s.48. This is subject to the qualification that an equitable charge may be protected by notice in the register (s.32(3)).

[48] Merchant Shipping Act 1995, s.16(1) and Sch.1, para.8(1).

[49] Mortgaging of Aircraft Order 1972, SI 1972/1268. Art. 5 allows for the registration of a priority notice, but the intended mortgage must be completed and registered within the ensuing 14 days. In all these cases notice of the prior interest is irrelevant.

[50] Bills of Sale Act 1878, s.10.

land and also, it would seem, mortgages of personalty. Tacking in relation to mortgages of registered land is currently governed by s.30 of the Land Registration Act 1925, but this is prospectively repealed by s.49 of the Land Registration Act 2002, which introduces significant changes. It is also necessary to consider the impact of registration of a company charge under s.395 of the Companies Act 1985.

(1) Mortgages of unregistered land

5–18　Where a mortgage[51] of unregistered land is taken to secure further advances—the typical case is a mortgage to secure a bank current account—s.94 of the Law of Property Act 1925 gives the mortgagee the right to make further advances ranking in priority to subsequent mortgages, legal or equitable, in three cases:

(a) Where an arrangement has been made to that effect with the subsequent mortgagees;

(b) Where the prior mortgagee had no notice of such subsequent mortgage at the time he made the further advance;

(c) Where the mortgage imposes on him an obligation to make such further advances.

Hence a mortgagee who makes a further advance without notice of the subsequent mortgage is now given priority even if he is only an equitable mortgagee and the mortgage is not expressed to secure further advances. But unless the prior mortgagee makes the further advance pursuant to an arrangement with the subsequent mortgagee or alternatively is committed by the terms of the prior mortgage to make the further advance, the prior mortgagee will be postponed to the subsequent mortgagee if he makes the further advance after notice of the second mortgage. If the legislation had stopped at this point, banks operating current accounts would have been in considerable difficulty, for registration of the second mortgage constitutes actual notice,[52] and it is obviously impracticable for the bank to make a search every time the mortgagor draws on his account and before honouring such drawing. To deal with this, s.94(2) of the Law of Property Act provides that a mortgagee is not deemed to have notice of a mortgage merely by reason that it was registered as a land charge if it was not so registered at the time when the original mortgage was created or when the last search (if any) by the prior mortgagee was made, whichever last happened. The correct sequence for the prior mortgagee to adopt is: take mortgage, search, make initial advance. To make a search and *then* take the mortgage and make the initial advance is not

---

[51] This includes a charge (Law of Property Act 1925, s.205(1)(xvi)).

[52] Law of Property Act 1925, s.198. For the effect of registration under s.395 of the Companies Act 1985, see below, para.5–22.

safe, for the second mortgagee might register between the time of the search and the time of the first mortgage.

It should be borne in mind that s.94 only gives protection in relation to *further* advances. Thus if the mortgagor grants a mortgage to M1 to secure a current account and before drawing on the account mortgages the same property to M2, who registers his mortgage, and M1 then makes his initial advance, then under the rule in *Hopkinson v Rolt*[53] he will be postponed to M2 as regards that advance even if not having actual notice of the second mortgage and even if committed to make the advance,[54] though as to any further advances he would enjoy the protection of s.94. The moral for M1 is to search before making his initial advance.

5–19

The first mortgagee should be careful to ensure that he reserves in his mortgage instrument the right to exclude the rule in *Clayton's Case*,[55] *e.g.* by ruling off the debtor's account upon receiving notice of a subsequent mortgage and crediting later payments to a new account. If the creditor fails to do this, such payments will, under the rule in *Clayton's Case,* be applied in reduction of the earlier indebtedness first, thus reducing that part of the debt as regards which the mortgagee has priority over the later mortgage. For example, M1 takes a charge to secure a current account and has advanced £1,000 when he receives notice of a second charge in favour of M2. Subsequently the debtor pays £800 into his account, and later draws £800 out of it. The debit balance is £1,000, the figure at which it stood when M1 received notice of M2's charge, but the effect of *Clayton's Case* is to reduce the pre-notice indebtedness to M1 to £200, leaving the post-notice advance of £800 postponed to M2's charge. A line across the account is all that is necessary to prevent this unfortunate occurrence. It was the failure of Barclays Bank to draw that line which led to their having to meet almost the whole of the plaintiff's claim in the *Siebe Gorman Case*,[56] despite having won the argument on the legal issues raised in that case.

(2) *Mortgages of registered land*

S.94 of the Law of Property Act 1925 does not apply to mortgages of registered land,[57] so that in principle the position of a lender who takes a mortgage of registered land to secure further advances is governed by the common law rule in *Hopkinson v Rolt*[58] under which notice of the second mortgage, whether actual or constructive, puts an end to the right to tack.[59] Presumably protection of the second mortgage by entry on the register (whether as a registered charge or by way of notice or caution) constitutes notice for this purpose. However, s.30 of the Land Registration Act 1925 protects the first

5–20

---

[53] (1861) 9 H.L.C. 514. See above, para.5–10.
[54] On which point the rule surely deserves reconsideration by the House of Lords.
[55] *Devaynes v Noble, Clayton's Case* (1816) 1 Mer. 572.
[56] *Siebe Gorman & Co. Ltd. v Barclays Bank Ltd.* [1979] 2 Lloyd's Rep. 142.
[57] Law of Property Act 1925, s.94(4).
[58] (1861) 9 H.L.C. 514.
[59] For the effect of registration under s.395 of the Companies Act 1985 see below.

mortgagee by providing that where a registered charge is made for securing further advances the registrar, before making any entry which would prejudicially affect the priority of any further advance, must give notice to the proprietor of the charge, who is not, in respect of any further advance, to be affected by such entry unless the advance is made after the date when the notice ought to have been received in due course of post.[60] Where the registered proprietor receives such a notice he should take the same steps to exclude the rule in *Clayton's Case* as a first mortgagee of unregistered land.[61]

The Land Registration Act 1925 is prospectively repealed by the Land Registration Act 2002.[62] s.49 of the Act provides that the proprietor of a registered charge may make a further advance ranking in priority to a subsequent charge if:

(a) he has not received from the subsequent chargee notice of the creation of the subsequent charge; or

(b) the further advance is made pursuant to an obligation which was entered in the register at the time of creation of the subsequent charge; or

(c) the parties to the prior charge have agreed a maximum amount for which the charge is security and such agreement was entered in the register at the time of creation of the subsequent charge.

Limb (c) represents a marked departure from the rule in *Hopkinson v Rolt* in that it applies even if the further advance is made after notice of the subsequent charge and is entirely voluntary. Effectively this enables the first chargee to obtain a monopoly of the debtor's non-purchase-money financing[63] by the simple device of specifying a maximum sum well beyond any amount that the chargee is likely to lend or the asset given in security is likely to be worth. This seems a retrograde step.[64]

(3) *Mortgages of personalty*

5–21 Where the mortgage relates to pure personalty, such as goods or receivables, the mortgagee's right to tack further advances is governed by s.94 of the Law of Property Act 1925, but the provisions of s.94(2) as to the effect of registration as a land charge do not, of course, apply, and notice of the subsequent mortgage, whether actual of constructive,[65] puts an end to the right to

---

[60] If the registered proprietor suffers loss through any failure on the part of the registrar or the below office, he is entitled to be indemnified by the registrar (Land Registration Act 1925, s.83(1), re-enacted by the Land Registration Act 2002, s.103 and Sch.8).

[61] See above.

[62] Sch.13.

[63] A purchase-money security interest will usually enjoy favoured treatment. See below, para.5–62.

[64] It has received criticism from other quarters. See, for example, *Emmet and Farrand on Title*, Bulletin No. 21, July 2002, p.6.

[65] For the effect of registration under s.395 of the Companies Act 1985, see below.

tack except where the further advance is made by arrangement with the subsequent mortgagee or the first mortgagee is obliged to make it by the terms of the mortgage.

(4) *Registration under the Companies Act 1985*

Whilst s.94 of the Law of Property Act 1925 prevents registration of a land **5–22** charge from constituting notice for the purpose of tacking, no such provision has been enacted in relation to the effect of registration in the Companies Registry of a charge (whether on land or on other assets) of a charge given by a company, pursuant to s.395 of the Companies Act 1985. If such registration were to constitute notice to a prior mortgagee under a mortgage securing a current account it would destroy the efficacy of s.94, a conclusion any court would be reluctant to reach. There is in fact nothing in the Companies Act itself which makes registration equivalent to notice; such an effect, where it occurs at all, results from the equitable doctrine of constructive notice which (*inter alia*) fixes a party with notice of facts which he would have discovered if he had made usual and proper enquiries. Registration in a public register may constitute constructive notice of matters recorded in the register,[66] but as has been submitted earlier[67] this is the case only where the circumstances are such that the party in question could reasonably have been expected to search. Having regard to the impracticability of searches by banks prior to each drawing by the mortgagor, and to the express provisions of s.94 of the Law of Property Act designed specifically to deal with the problem, it seems clear that registration under s.395 of the Companies Act does not constitute notice sufficient to put an end to the prior mortgagee's right to tack.

4. PRIORITY OF COMPETING SECURITY INTERESTS

I now turn to examine the particular case of competition among fixed secur- **5–23** ity interests. This would be much easier if, as under Art.9 of the Uniform Commercial Code, it was possible to take the requisite steps for perfection in any order, with priority going back to the time of filing of a financing statement covering an existing or intended security interest, and filing was always a priority point, not merely a perfection requirement. Unhappily the lack of a coherent system of perfection and priority means that the outcome of a priority dispute concerning registrable interests depends very largely on the particular type of registration system that is applicable, coupled with the overriding effect of s.395 of the Companies Act 1985 where the charge is given by a company and falls within the list set out in s.396 and the company later goes into liquidation or administration. The number of variables thus

---

[66] See, for example, *Re De Leeuw* [1922] 3 Ch. 540.
[67] See above, para.2–29.

involved makes it difficult to set out a simple set of rules. The right to tack further advances ranking in priority has already been discussed[68] and we do not need to return to it.

We should note as a preliminary that s.395 trumps all other perfection requirements in the sense that where a security interest registrable under s.395 is also registrable in a specialist register, any priority given by registration in the latter will be displaced if the security interest is not also registered under s.395 within the time allowed. A charge registrable under that section and not registered within 21 days or such later time as is permitted by the court is void against a liquidator or administrator and creditors. For this purpose "creditors" means subsequent secured creditors, execution creditors and lienees and creditors in the winding-up or administration; it does not include unsecured creditors of a company that is not in winding-up or administration. A charge not registered within the 21-day period may be registered later with leave of the court,[69] which is almost invariably given unless the company is already in liquidation or administration or the process for putting it into liquidation or administration has been initiated. But the order granting leave is invariably expressed to be subject to a proviso that it is without prejudice to the rights of intervening secured creditors, so that the penalty for late registration is subordination to a security interest created after the expiry of the 21 days allowed for registration of the earlier interest.[70] The proviso does not, however, protect intervening unsecured creditors.[71]

There are seven main priority rules.

First rule: where there are no additional perfection requirements, priority is determined by the order of creation

5–24   There are various cases in which attachment alone suffices to perfect a security interest without more.[72] In such case priority is determined by the order of creation of the security interest.

Second rule: in certain cases an unperfected security interest has priority over an earlier unperfected security interest

5–25   The first rule is displaced where there are statutory provisions which render an security interest void if not perfected prior to the *creation* of a subsequent

---

[68] See above, paras 5–10, 5–17.
[69] Companies Act 1985, s.404. The order does not itself perfect the unregistered security interest, which must be registered in conformity with the order.
[70] If the later interest is created within the 21-day period it is not protected by the proviso (*Watson v Duff, Morgan & Vermont (Holdings) Ltd.* [1974] 1 W.L.R. 450). This makes sense in policy terms because the later chargee, by taking his security in reliance on a clear search before expiry of the time allowed for registration of the earlier charge, is taking a chance and cannot claim to have been misled by the absence of a registration which had not become due.
[71] *Re MIG Trust Ltd.* [1933] Ch. 542, *per* Romer L.J. at 570.
[72] See above, para.2–18.

security interest, *i.e.* regardless whether the later interest has been perfected or not. So a charge not registered in conformity with s.395 of the Companies Act 1985 is void against a subsequent chargee,[73] whether or not the latter perfects his interest by registration. Again, a charge not registered under the Land Charges Act 1972 is void against a mortgagee, regardless whether he later registers. In both cases want of perfection of the first security interest results in its subordination to the second security interest.

Third rule: in cases outside the first and second rules, unperfected security interests rank in order of creation

For example, if there are successive assignments of a debt but neither assignee gives notice to the debtor and the equities are otherwise equal, the assignments rank in order of creation.[74] Similarly, two unregistered mortgages of registered land rank in order of creation, even if protected by a notice or caution.[75] However, the priority thus given to the first in time is provisional in that the second assignee can always jump ahead by giving notice if the first assignee has not done so and the second mortgagee can secure priority by registering his mortgage before the first has been registered.

5–26

Fourth rule: a perfected security interest normally has priority over an unperfected security interest

This rule, in contrast with the preceding three rules, deals with a contest between a perfected security interest and an unperfected security interest. In general, the perfected security interest wins. There are two qualifications. First, the perfection requirement embodied in s.395 of the Companies Act 1985 allows a 21-day period of protection for the unregistered charge.[76] Secondly, in a registration system which allows for the registration of priority notices an unperfected interest registered before expiry of the priority notice has priority as from the time of registration of the notice or, under the rules of some registration systems, before the time of creation.[77]

5–27

---

[73] Professor Robert Pennington takes a different approach, arguing that if neither of the competing charges is registered each is void against the other (*Company Law* (8th ed.), p.625. But, with respect, this cannot be right. In the first place it is not in conformity with s.395, which renders an unregistered charge void against creditors (including secured creditors even before a winding-up) but does not state that their charges must have been registered. Secondly, the purpose of registration is to give notice to *subsequent* chargees; prior chargees are obviously not affected by the failure to register. See above, para.2–22, text and n.8.

[74] See *Rice v Rice* (1854) 2 Drew 73, *per* Sir R.T. Kindersley V.C. at 77–78.

[75] *Mortgage Corp. Ltd. v Nationwide Credit Corp. Ltd.* [1994] Ch. 49.

[76] However, this will not help the unregistered chargee if the charge is of a kind which is also registrable in a specialist register the rules of which give a registered charge priority over an unregistered charge and the subsequent chargee effects registration first.

[77] See below, paras 5–29 *et seq.*

Fifth rule: perfected security interests usually rank in order of perfection

5–28   Thus under the rule in *Dearle v Hall* the priority of successive assignments of a chose in action is governed by the order in which notice of assignment is given to the debtor.[78] Accordingly priority is determined by the order of perfection.[79] The same is true of successive bills of sale and mortgages of registered land, ships and aircraft, which in each case rank in order of registration in the relevant register.[80] The rule also holds good where one of the competing interests is perfected by possession and the other by registration. So in a contest between a pledgee of goods under a pledge by a company and a chargee of a registered charge on the goods priority goes to the first to perfect. The principal exception relates to successive charges by companies for which the sole perfection requirement is registration in the Companies Registry. Where all of such charges are registered within the 21 days allowed priority is determined by the order of creation. A further exception relates to negotiable instruments where a person to whom the instrument is negotiated by delivery has priority over an assignee of the underlying obligation even if notice of assignment was given before the negotiation.[81] The rule is also inapplicable to dealings in investment securities.[82]

Sixth rule: where perfection is by registration in a specialist register, pre-completion protection may be given by a priority notice or a pre-completion search

5–29   Some specialist register systems give an intending secured creditor temporary protection for his prospective security interest by one or both of two protective devices, the priority notice and the pre-completion search.

(1) *Priority notice*

5–30   The priority notice procedure allows the intending secured creditor to obtain priority for his prospective security interest by registering a priority notice and then taking and perfecting his security interest within a specified period

---

[78] Subject to the qualification that the second assignee had no notice of the prior assignment. See above, para.5–08.

[79] This does not depend on the question whether it is legally possible for both assignments to take effect as statutory assignments. Dr Oditah considers that this is not possible on the ground that a legal assignment exhausts the assignor's interest in the receivables, leaving nothing for him to assign (Fidelis Oditah, *Legal Aspects of Receivables Financing*) and cites in support a dictum of Goff J. in *Ellerman Lines Ltd. v Lancaster Maritime Co. Ltd.* [1980] 2 Lloyd's Rep. 497 at 503. However, English law has always taken the position that title is relative and that the effect of a double assignment or transfer is an issue of priority, not of validity. Hence the numerous exceptions to the *nemo dat* rule.

[80] See above, para.5–16, text and n.50.

[81] See *Chalmers & Guest on Bills of Exchange* (14th ed.), pp.334–335.

[82] See above, para.5–08.

(renewable for successive periods before each period has expired), priority then dating back, under some rules, to the time of registration of the (latest) priority notice[83] and, under others, to the time of creation of the security interest.[84]

(2) Pre-completion search

An intending mortgagee of unregistered land who makes a search for regis-   **5–31**
trable charges is not affected by any entry in the register before the expiration of the 15th day after the date of the search certificate and before
completion of his mortgage if such entry is not made pursuant to a priority notice and the mortgage is completed before the expiration of 30 days
from the date of the certificate.[85] Similarly, an intending mortgagee of registered land can, by making a search with priority, secure protection against
a subsequent incumbrancer if he completes and registers his mortgage
within 30 days.[86]

Seventh rule: priorities may be varied by agreement

Nothing in either the common law or the statutory priority rules precludes   **5–32**
competing secured creditors from making an agreement to vary the priority
that would otherwise apply, and most of the statutory registration rules make
express provision for this. As has previously been pointed out,[87] a subordination agreement does not result in an exchange of security interests between
the two secured creditors, it merely gives the beneficiary of the subordination
priority over the grantor of the subordination, not over an intermediate
secured creditor. Subordination agreements are extremely common in domestic and international finance and do not require the consent of the debtor.[88]
Subordination agreements, which can give rise to difficult circularity problems, are discussed later in this chapter.[89] They remain effective in the debtor's
winding up as they do not affect the position of other creditors so as to
contravene the principle of *pari passu* distribution.[90]

---

[83] As in the case of shipping mortgages (Merchant Shipping Act 1995, Sch.1, para.8 and
Merchant Shipping (Registration of Ships) Regulations 1993, SI 1993/3138, reg.59 and aircraft mortgages (Mortgaging of Aircraft Order 1972, SI 1972/971, art.14(2). For aircraft mortgages the priority is lost unless the mortgage is made and registered within 14 days. There is
no time limit for ship mortgages.
[84] As in the case of land charge over unregistered land (Land Charges Act 1972, s.11). But the
charge must be taken and registered within 30 days.
[85] Land Charges Act 1972, s.11(5),(6).
[86] Land Registration (Official Searches) Rules 1993, SI 1993/3276 regs 2(1),(6).
[87] See above, para.1–80.
[88] *Cheah Theam Swee v Equiticorp. Finance Group Ltd.* [1992] 1 A.C. 472.
[89] See below, paras 5–58 *et seq.*
[90] See below, para.5–59, and, for a discussion of the nature of subordination, above, para.1–80.

Marshalling of securities

5–33   It may happen that the junior secured creditor, SC2, has security in one item of property, asset A, while the senior secured creditor, SC1, has security both over asset A and over asset B. Without the doctrine of marshalling, SC2 could be adversely affected by SC1's decision to look to asset A in the first instance to obtain payment of the amount due to him, which would reduce S2's security or even extinguish it altogether. The doctrine of marshalling does not affect SC1's right to look to asset A,[91] either on its own or at the same time as resorting to asset B, but it protects SC2 by allowing him to resort to asset B to the extent to which he has been deprived of his own security by reason of SC1's recourse to asset A.

Effect of priorities on enforcement by a secured creditor

5–34   If mortgages are granted in succession to SP1 and SP2 and there are no factors to displace SP1's priority, he may realise his security, take what is due to him and then account for any surplus to SP2, who will in turn deduct what is due to him and hand over any remaining surplus to the mortgagor. Where there are three or more incumbrancers it would seem that SP1's duty is to hand over the whole of any surplus to SP2, leaving it to him to take what is due to him and pass any balance to SP3, rather than SP1 being responsible for distribution among all interested parties in order of priority.[92]

However, it is not only the senior mortgagee who can enforce. SP2 may realise his security, but if he is selling free from SP1's mortgage he must obtain SP1's consent and must apply the proceeds in discharge of that mortgage before taking what is due to him. If, however, SP2 is selling subject to SP1's mortgage SP1 is not affected by the sale and his consent is not required. His mortgage continues to attach to the property and SP2 is not accountable to him for any part of the proceeds, but must take what is due to him and then pass any surplus to the next mortgagee, if any, or, if none, to the debtor. Where SP1 has himself become entitled to enforce his mortgage and chooses to do so after SP2 has initiated steps to enforce his own mortgage, SP1 is entitled to take control in priority to SP2.

---

[91] *Manks v Whiteley* [1911] 2 Ch. 448, *per* Parker J. at 466; *Chase Corporation (Australia) Pty. Ltd. v North Sydney Brick and Tile Co. Ltd.* (1994) A.C.S.R. 586, *per* Cohen J. at 1008–1009. For a detailed discussion of the topic see the monograph by Paul A.U. Ali, *Marshalling of Securities*.

[92] *Re Thomson's Mortgage Trusts* [1920] 1 Ch. 508; *Fisher & Lightwood's Law of Mortgage* (11th ed.) para.20.47.

5. COMPETITION BETWEEN A FIXED CONSENSUAL SECURITY INTEREST AND OTHER TYPES OF INTEREST

Secured creditor versus outright buyer

A legal mortgagee has priority over a subsequent buyer to whom the mort-   **5–35**
gagor wrongfully sells the charged asset.[93] An equitable mortgagee or chargee
is postponed to a subsequent buyer who acquires the legal title in good faith
and without notice of the prior equitable mortgage or charge. The extent to
which registration constitutes notice has been discussed earlier.[94]

There is one oddity. While a charge not duly registered under s.395 of the
Companies Act is void as against a subsequent chargee, the section says
nothing about a subsequent buyer. Accordingly failure to register does not
invalidate the unregistered charge against the buyer, and priorities will be
determined by the common law rules. A legal mortgagee will retain its priority under the first-in-time rule; an equitable mortgagee or chargee will be
postponed to a buyer who takes the legal title for value and without notice
but prevails against any other kind of buyer.

Secured creditor versus holder of non-consensual right or interest

A consensual security interest may come into conflict with a right or interest   **5–36**
created by law. If the non-consensual right is purely personal or is *ad rem*
rather than *in rem*,[95] the security interest usually prevails. There are, however,
exceptions both at common law and by statute. A landlord is entitled to distrain for rent on any goods on the demised premises, whether or not the property of the tenant, though if distress is levied on goods the subject of a fixed
charge the chargee may perhaps be able to procure their release by service of a
notice under s.1 of the Law of Distress Amendment Act 1908.[96] A contractual
right to arrest an aircraft for non-payment of airport dues has priority over a
security interest in the aircraft.[97]

Where the consensual security interest comes into conflict with a non-
consensual right *in rem*, such an equitable tracing right, the principles governing priority between competing consensual interests apply. Suppose, for
example, that B, in the possession of O's goods, wrongfully sells them on
credit, and assigns the proceeds, in the shape of the debt due from the purchaser for the price, to M by way of mortgage under a statutory assignment
in conformity with s.136 of the Law of Property Act 1925. O asserts an equitable tracing claim to the debt as proceeds of its asset,[98] while M claims as

---

[93] There are certain exceptions, such as estoppel, which are not discussed here.
[94] See above, para.2–23.
[95] See above, para.1–17.
[96] See below, para.5–52.
[97] See *Channel Airways Ltd. v City of Manchester* [1974] 2 Lloyd's Rep. 456, *per* Forbes J. at 461.
[98] See above, para.1–60.

mortgagee. In this situation M cannot simply rely on his legal title, even if he took without notice of O's equitable interest, because even a statutory assignee takes subject to equities, which for this purpose includes O's equitable interest in the proceeds,[99] and this overrides the general rule giving priority to a bona fide purchaser of the legal title for value and without notice.[1] So that the starting position is that O has the superior interest by virtue of being first-in-time. But this will be displaced in favour of M if he is the first to give notice to the debtor[2] and thereby obtain priority under the rule in *Dearle v Hall*.[3]

Various kinds of lien have priority even over a consensual security interest created before the events giving rise to the lien. These include the possessory lien of carriers and the various kinds of maritime lien. Whether a consensual security interest has priority over statutory charges depends on the particular statute.[4]

6. RANKING OF THE FLOATING CHARGE

5–37   So far, the discussion has been confined to priority issues relating to fixed security interests. The floating charge attracts entirely different principles because of the right given to the debtor, and much depends on whether the competing interest arose before or after crystallisation. The position of the holder of a floating charge in relation to preferential creditors raises distinct considerations and will be dealt with separately later in the present chapter.[5]

As against interests arising prior to crystallisation

5–38   The ranking of a floating charge in relation to subsequent interests arising prior to the crystallisation of the charge depends partly on the type of interest in question and partly on whether the floating charge contains restrictions on dealings of which the subsequent claimant has notice. The peculiar nature of the floating charge creates difficulties of analysis in the context of priorities,

---

[99] *Compaq Computers Ltd. v Abercorn Group Ltd.* [1992] B.C.C. 484. So far, this and other cases have arisen in the context of a conflict between a title-retention seller claiming the proceeds of resale under the title reservation clause and a subsequent factor or invoice discounter buying the receivable resulting from the resale, an issue generating much academic debate (see the 2nd edition of this book at pp.120–122, and Roy Goode, *Commercial Law* (2nd ed.) pp.818–819). Usually the issue has been rendered moot by a finding that the contractual proceeds provision created a charge void for want of registration. But where this is not so the same priority principles established in those cases apply to a contest between the holder of an equitable tracing right and a mortgagee of the proceeds.

[1] *ibid.*, following the decision of Phillips J. in E. *Pfeiffer Weinkellerei-Weineinkauf GmbH v Arbuthnot Factors Ltd.* (1987) 3 B.C.C. 608.

[2] As he almost always will, since it is likely to be some time before O discovers the wrongful resale and the identity of the purchaser.

[3] *Compaq Computers Ltd. v Abercorn Group Ltd.*, above.

[4] An example of a statutory charge having priority over a mortgage is provided by s.87(6) of the Agricultural Holdings Act 1986 in relation to tenants' charges created under s.85(2) of the Act.

[5] See below, para.5–65.

for whilst the charge is a present security it is non-specific and in principle does not affect third parties at all while it continues to float. Since crystallisation of the charge, which converts it from a floating security to a fixed security, is not retrospective, the subordination of intervening interests which occurs in certain conditions described below is not always easy to explain and, indeed, has never been fully analysed by the courts.[6] It is clear that there are certain situations in which a floating charge retains its priority over subsequent interests, but it would seem that such priority is inchoate so long as the charge continues to float and can only be asserted upon crystallisation.

(1) *Buyer or incumbrancer in ordinary course of business*

It is the essence of a floating charge that the company has an implied authority to dispose of its assets in the ordinary course of business. For this purpose "ordinary course of business" is widely interpreted, embracing dispositions by way of sale,[7] hire-purchase,[8] specific mortgage or charge,[9] and, indeed, any other form of bona fide disposition which is *intra vires* the company and is designed to promote rather than to terminate or destroy its business.[10] Even a sale of its goodwill, assets and undertaking will be considered in the ordinary course of business if intended in furtherance of the business,[11] and not with a view to ceasing trading.[12] In *Countrywide Banking Corp. Ltd. v Dean*[13] the Privy Council, in the context of a New Zealand statutory provision protecting payments in the ordinary course of business from attack as a preference, cited with approval the following passage from the judgment of Fisher J. in *Re Modern Terrazzo Ltd*[14]:

5–39

> "Whether a payment should be regarded as commercially routine at a day to day trading and operating level will turn at least in part upon a comparison with the practices of the commercial community in general. But equally, the way in which the particular company has acted in the past, and its dealings with the particular creditor, would seem pertinent. That the payment was simply a repetition of past patterns of behaviour would make it more difficult to argue that it represented special assistance

---

[6] A point well made by Mahoney J.A. in *Reynolds Bros. (Motors) Pty. Ltd. v Esanda Ltd.* (1983) 8 A.C.L.R. 422, 427.

[7] *Hamer v London, City & Midland Bank Ltd.* (1918) 87 L.J.K.B. 973; *Reynolds Bros. (Motor) Pty. Ltd. v Esanda Ltd.* (1983) 8 A.C.L.R. 422.

[8] *Dempsey and National Bank of New Zealand v Traders' Finance Corp. Ltd.* [1933] N.Z.L.R. 1258.

[9] *Cox Moore v Peruvian Corp. Ltd.* [1908] 1 Ch. 604; *Re Hamilton's Windsor Ironworks* (1879) 12 Ch.D. 707.

[10] See W.J. Gough, *Company Charges* (2nd ed.) p.198.

[11] *e.g.* by way of amalgamation (*Re Borax Co.* [1901] 1 Ch. 326) or disposal of a loss-making part of the business to enable the remainder of the business to be continued profitably (*Re H.H. Vivian & Co. Ltd.* [1900] 2 Ch. 654).

[12] *Hubbuck v Helms* (1887) 56 L.J. Ch. 536; *Hamilton v Hunter* (1982) 7 A.C.L.R. 295; *Torzillu Pty. Ltd. v Brynac Pty. Ltd.* (1983) 8 A.C.L.R. 52.

[13] [1998] A.C. 338.

[14] Subsequently reported in [1998] 1 N.Z.L.R. 160.

to an insider or the result of special enforcement measures or a situation in which the subject creditor ought to have investigated before extending credit. So at a policy level there is something to be said for the view that relevant considerations should extend to the prior practices of the particular company."[15]

It is thought that similar considerations apply to the question whether a dealing by a floating chargor is in the ordinary course of business.

Given the implied authority of the debtor company to continue to deal with its assets in the ordinary course of business, it follows that the buyer, incumbrancer or other party acquiring an interest in the charged assets in the ordinary course of business has priority over the holder of the floating charge, even if he takes with knowledge of its existence.[16] Where, in this situation, the charge covers book debts or other receivables, the rule in *Dearle v Hall* does not apply, for the floating chargee, having impliedly authorised the subsequent fixed charge, cannot jump ahead by being the first to give notice to the debtor after the charge has crystallised.[17]

5–40   If the debenture imposes restrictions on sales or subsequent incumbrances and the particular sale or charge, though in the ordinary course of business, is in breach of such restrictions, the floating charge will, on crystallisation,[18] retain its priority if the buyer or incumbrancer took with notice of the restrictions, whether his interest is legal or equitable.[19] This stems from the fact that the floating charge, though ambulatory, is a present security,[20] not a mere contract right, so that restrictions contained in it will constitute an equity binding those who have notice of them. It is true that in *Griffiths v Yorkshire Bank plc*[21] Morritt J., disapproving of a dictum by Chadwick J. in *Re Portbase Clothing Ltd.*,[22] expressed the view that a restriction on the grant of subsequent charges is purely contractual and has no proprietary or priority effects.[23] But the learned judge's attention does not appear to have been drawn to the earlier authorities clearly supporting the position taken by Chadwick J. to the effect that a negative pledge clause creates an equity in favour of the holder of the floating charge[24] or to the authorities stating that

---

[15] Subsequently reported in [1998] 1 N.Z.L.R. at 175.

[16] *Re Castell & Brown Ltd.* [1898] 1 Ch. 315; *English & Scottish Mercantile Investment Co. v Brunton* [1892] 2 Q.B. 700.

[17] *Ward v Royal Exchange Shipping Co. Ltd.* (1887) 58 L.T. 174; *Re Ind Coope & Co. Ltd.* [1911] 3 Ch. 223.

[18] See below.

[19] *English & Scottish Mercantile Investment Co. Ltd. v Brunton* [1892] 2 Q.B. 700, *per* Lord Esher M.R. at 707; *Cox v Dublin City Distillery Co.* [1906] I.R. 446; *Wilson v Kelland* [1910] 2 Ch. 306. The subordination of the later equitable interest does not in this case derive from the maxim *qui prior est tempore, portior est jure*, for without the restriction that interest would have priority by virtue of the dealing power accorded to the debtor company under the floating charge. As to whether registration constitutes notice, see above, paras 2–24, 2–26.

[20] See above, para.48.

[21] [1994] 1 W.L.R. 1427.

[22] [1993] Ch. 388 at 401.

[23] *ibid.* at 1435–1436.

[24] See n.19, above.

the grant of a subsequent floating charge ranking in priority to the first float-ing charge is *prima facie* outside the chargor's dealing powers.[25] The position is otherwise, however, where the subsequent purchaser or incumbrancer takes without notice of the restrictions contained in the floating charge,[26] for the third party is entitled to assume that the company retains the power to deal with its assets in the ordinary course of business and in the absence of notice of the restriction he will obtain priority.[27]

Where the subsequent purchaser or incumbrancer takes with notice of the fact that the disposition to him is in breach of the debenture creating the float-ing charge, the debenture holder's right to assert his security interest would appear to be exercisable only on crystallisation and until then would, it is thought, be merely inchoate. Unless otherwise provided by the debenture, the wrongful dealing by the company does not of itself cause the charge to crys-tallise,[28] and until crystallisation the debenture holder has no right to any spe-cific asset capable of being asserted against the third party. Moreover, a mandatory injunction requiring the third party to restore the assets to the company, even if theoretically available, would not normally be appropriate, for *ex hypothesi* the debenture holder will have priority on crystallisation of the charge, so that the improper dealing causes him no loss and the only relief he could expect is a declaration that his charge enjoys priority. If he discovers the debtor company's intentions in time he can no doubt obtain a *quia timet* injunction to restrain a threatened disposition in breach of the debenture, but it seems unlikely that the court would go further than ordering that any dispo-sition should be on terms preserving the priority of the floating charge, for in most cases such a disposition would be permitted by the debenture.

(2) *Buyer or incumbrancer outside ordinary course of business*

A buyer or incumbrancer whose interest derives from a transaction entered **5–41** into by the debtor company outside the ordinary course of business remains postponed to the floating charge, for the transaction is *ex hypothesi* outside both the actual and the apparent authority of the company.[29] The effect of such a disposition is similar to that of a disposition in breach of a restriction contained in the debenture. Thus the priority of the debenture holder as floating chargee is inchoate and can only be asserted once the charge has crystallised.[30] The mere fact that the disposition is outside the ordinary

---

[25] *Re Benjamin Cope & Sons Ltd.* [1914] 1 Ch. 800; *Re Household Products Co. Ltd.* (1981) 124 D.L.R. (3d) 325.

[26] As to when registration constitutes notice, see above, para.2–23.

[27] *English & Scottish Mercantile Investment Co. v Brunton* [1892] 2 Q.B. 700; *Welch v Bowmaker (Ireland) Ltd.* [1980] I.R. 251.

[28] *Reynolds Bros. (Motors) Pty. Ltd. v Esanda Ltd.* (1983) 8 A.C.L.R. 422, *per* Mahoney J.A. at 427.

[29] *Taylor v M'Keand* (1880) 5 C.P.D. 358; *Payne v Fern* (1881) 6 QBD 620.

[30] See, for example, *Hamilton v Hunter* (1982) 7 A.C.L.R. 295 (receivers and managers under crystallised floating charge held entitled to a declaration that they were entitled to the charged assets as against an assignee who acquired the assets outside the ordinary course of business

course of business does not in itself cause crystallisation, though it may entitle the debenture holder to intervene to assert his security interest and thereby crystallise the charge, either pursuant to the terms of the debenture or by obtaining an order for appointment of a receiver on the ground of jeopardy to the security.

(3) Later floating charge

5–42 The courts have held that the dealing power implied in a floating charge does not extend to the grant of a subsequent floating charge over the same assets,[31] but that it remains permissible for the company to grant a subsequent floating charge over part of those assets ranking in priority to or *pari passu* with the earlier floating charge.[32] However, despite some rather loose dicta by Warrington L.J. in *Re Automatic Bottle Makers Ltd.*,[33] the true ratio of these cases is based not on a distinction between a floating charge over all the assets and a subsequent floating charge over part of them but on a proper construction of the charge instrument. *Prima facie* a company which has given a floating charge over all its assets is not at liberty to give a subsequent floating charge over all or any of such assets displacing the priority of the earlier floating charge. It would, however, be open to the parties to the debenture, or to the issuer in case of an issue of debentures, to provide otherwise. So where the first floating charge conferred a power to grant subsequent charges, ranking in priority to the floating charge, over assets which included those not normally appropriate to a fixed charge, such as raw materials and stock in trade, the Court of Appeal held that by necessary implication this included the power to grant a floating charge over such assets, for if they were charged by a fixed charge the business would be paralysed.[34] Where the first floating charge is only over part of the assets there is, of course, no objection to the grant of a subsequent floating charge over different assets ranking in priority to the first floating charge unless this otherwise provides.

---

before crystallisation of the charge); *Torzillu Pty. Ltd. v Brynac Pty. Ltd.* (1983) A.C.L.R. 52 (receivers appointed after disposition outside ordinary course of business held entitled to retain possession as against purchaser).
[31] *Benjamin Cope & Sons Ltd.* [1914] 1 Ch. 800. Hence the first floating charge has priority even though the later charge is the first to crystallise (*Re Household Products Co. Ltd.* (1981) 124 D.L.R. (3d) 325).
[32] *Re Automatic Bottle Makers Ltd.* [1926] Ch. 412.
[33] *ibid.* at 423.
[34] *ibid., per* Sargant L.J. at 425.

(4) *Execution creditor*

An execution creditor takes free from a floating charge if, but only if, the **5-43** execution is completed,[35] or payment is made to avoid execution,[36] prior to crystallisation of the charge. There remain some unresolved questions as to when execution is to be considered completed for this purpose:

(a) *Execution against goods* Mere seizure by the sheriff does not suffice; **5-44** there must at least have been a sale.[37] The question is whether sale alone defeats the debenture holder if the floating charge crystallises after sale and before receipt of the proceeds by the sheriff or their transfer to the execution creditor. For the purpose of insolvency law, seizure and sale are all that are necessary to complete the execution,[38] subject to the execution creditor being divested of his rights if within 14 days of receipt of the proceeds by the sheriff the judgment creditor becomes bankrupt or goes into liquidation or the sheriff receives notice of a pending bankruptcy or winding up petition or of a meeting having been called to pass a resolution for voluntary winding up.[39] There seems no reason why seizure and sale should not equally perfect the execution creditor's right to the proceeds *vis-à-vis* the holder of a floating charge even before these have been paid to the sheriff,[40] subject to divestment as stated above. If the execution creditor is divested of his rights under the above statutory provisions and the floating charge has crystallised after sale but before divestment, do the statutory provisions ensure for the benefit of the debenture holder or the general body of creditors? Under such provisions the title of the trustee or liquidator is expressed to be good only as against the execution creditor, not against third parties such as a chargee under a crystallised charge. However, we have predicated that the execution creditor obtains priority over the debenture holder as a result of a sale prior to crystallisation of the charge. Accordingly, since the trustee or liquidator displaces the execution creditor he necessarily displaces the debenture holder and is thus to be entitled to

---

[35] *Re Opera Ltd.* [1891] 3 Ch. 260; *Robson v Smith* [1895] 2 Ch. 118; *Evans v Rival Granite Quarries Ltd.* [1910] 2 K.B. 979. The rule is well established but has attracted much critical discussion. See, for example R.J. Calnan, *Priorities Between Execution Creditors and Floating Charges* [1982] 10 N.Z.U.L.R. 111; Diana M. Hare and David Milman, "Debenture holders and creditors—problems of priority" [1982] L.M.C.L.Q. 57; W.J. Gough, *Company Charges* (2nd ed.) pp.319 *et seq.*

[36] *Robinson v Burnell's Vienna Bakery Co.* [1904] 2 K.B. 624; *Heaton & Dugard Ltd. v Cutting Bros. Ltd.* [1925] 1 K.B. 655.

[37] See cases cited n.35, above. There is a curious provision in s.346(5)(a) of the Insolvency Act 1986 to the effect that for the purposes of s.346 an execution against goods is completed by seizure and sale "or by the making of a charging order under section 1 of the Charging Orders Act 1979". The quoted words are clearly a drafting error since the 1979 Act makes no provision for a charging order against goods.

[38] Insolvency Act 1986, ss.346(5)(a), 183(3)(a); *Roberts Petroleum Ltd. v Bernard Kenny Ltd.* [1983] 2 A.C. 192, *per* Lord Brightman at 213.

[39] *ibid.*, ss.346(3), (4), 184(3), (4); *Re Greer* [1895] 2 Ch. 217, *per* Chitty J. at 221.

[40] A view supported by a dictum in the judgment of Kneller J.A. in *Lochab Bros. v Kenya Furfural* [1985] L.R.C. (Comm.) 737, 747.

the proceeds of the execution up to the amount covered by the writ of *fi. fa.*, any surplus being caught by the crystallised charge.

5–45   (b) *Execution against debts* An attachment of debts by garnishee proceedings does not result in completed execution until their receipt by the execution creditor.[41] Even a payment into court by the garnishee pursuant to the garnishee order is insufficient, for this does not of itself vest title to the moneys in the execution creditor.[42]

5–46   (c) *Execution against land, securities and funds in court* By virtue of statute a special rule applies to attachment of land, securities and funds in court by way of a charging order. Under s.3(4) of the Charging Orders Act 1979 a charge imposed by a charging order has the like effect and is enforceable in the same courts and in the same manner as an equitable charge created by the debtor under his hand. This applies even to a charging order nisi,[43] which will thus have priority over an uncrystallised floating charge unless the effect of the order is negated by the court exercising its discretion to refuse to make it absolute.[44] Execution against land may be completed not only by a charging order but by seizure or the appointment of a receiver.[45]

(5) *Landlord or local authority levying distress*

5–47   A landlord levying distress for rent on the goods of the company on the demised premises is not subject to the floating charge. In this particular case, as will be seen,[46] it is irrelevant whether the distress is levied before or after crystallisation. A local authority may distrain for unpaid business rates before crystallisation of the floating charge but not after.[47]

(6) *Debtor asserting right of set-off*

5–48   The trading power implicit in a floating charge encompasses the ability of the company to engage in mutual dealings with a customer as the result of which

---

[41] *Cairney v Back* [1906] 2 K.B. 746. The case is distinguishable from the earlier decision in *Robson v Smith* [1895] 2 Ch. 118 in that the charge had not crystallised in that case, the debenture holder's attempt to collect in the garnisheed debt being held ineffective in the absence of the appointment of a receiver or other crystallising event. In *Cairney v Back* Walton J. expressed the view that the absence of the appointment of a receiver in *Robson v Smith* was irrelevant to the decision in that case, but this dictum is plainly incorrect. It may be noted that for the purpose of insolvency law also it is the time of receipt of the garnisheed debt which constitutes completion of the execution (Insolvency Act 1986, ss.346(5)(c), 183(3)(b); *Roberts Petroleum Ltd. v Bernard Kenny Ltd.* [1983] 2 A.C. 192, *per* Lord Brightman at 213. See to the same effect the Insolvency Act 1986, s.346(5)(c).
[42] *Coopers & Lybrand Ltd. v National Caterers Ltd.* (1982) 47 C.B.R.(N.S.) 57.
[43] *Roberts Petroleum Ltd. v Bernard Kenny Ltd.*, above, *per* Lord Brightman at 205.
[44] *ibid.*
[45] Insolvency Act 1986, s.346(5)(b).
[46] See below, para.5–62.
[47] *Re ELS Ltd.* [1995] Ch.11, rightly declining to follow *Re Marriage, Neave & Co.* [1896] 2 Ch. 663.

the customer acquires a right of set-off. Since on crystallisation the debenture holder cannot acquire rights over the company's assets greater than those the company has itself, it follows that the debenture holder's rights over book debts and other contract sums due to the company are subject to the debtor's rights of set-off in respect of cross-claims arising prior to notice of crystallisation.[48] The fact that the debtor was aware of the existence of the floating charge at the time he concluded the transaction generating the right of set-off is irrelevant, for *ex hypothesi* the company had authority to enter into such a transaction free from the ambit of the floating charge. A good illustration is *Biggerstaff v Rowatt's Wharf Ltd.*[49]:

> The defendant company, having executed a debenture creating a floating charge over its assets, contracted to sell 7,000 barrels of oil to a firm of oil merchants, who paid the price in advance. The company failed to deliver the majority of the barrels. The oil merchants themselves owed the company a substantial sum for wharfage rent, but when, on the appointment of a receiver for the debenture holders, he sought to recover the rent, the oil merchants claimed a right to set off their cross-claim for recovery of the price of the undelivered barrels.

The Court of Appeal held that they were entitled to exercise the right of set-off against the receiver, despite the fact that at all relevant times they were aware of the floating charge.

As against interests arising subsequent to crystallisation

Once a floating charge crystallises, so as to become fixed, the general rule is that except for preferential insolvency creditors it has priority over subsequent interests,[50] including rights of set-off,[51] in just the same way as if it had been fixed at the outset. To this principle there are at least three exceptions: **5–49**

(1) *Subsequent purchaser or chargee without notice of crystallisation*

Though there appears to be no authority directly on the point, it is my submission that, in accordance with the principle of apparent authority referred to earlier,[52] a purchaser or incumbrancer under a transaction concluded after crystallisation but before the purchaser or incumbrancer had notice of crystallisation, takes free from the floating charge (in the case of purchase) or has priority over it (where he is an incumbrancer) if he had had dealings with the **5–50**

---

[48] *Biggerstaff v Rowatt's Wharf Ltd.* [1896] 2 Ch. 93. See below.
[49] See above.
[50] See *Re Real Meat Co. Ltd.* [1996] B.C.C. 254. For insolvency, see para.5–65.
[51] But only rights of set-off arising after the account debtor (the debtor company's debtor) received notice that the charge had crystallised. See below, para.7–66.
[52] See above, paras 4–29, 5–02.

company prior to crystallisation or was aware of the existence of the floating charge at the time he paid out his money. In such a case, the subsequent party is entitled to say that he was unaware of the termination of the company's authority to manage its assets and is thus not bound by the termination of that authority. This, of course, is on the assumption that the transaction was in the apparent course of the company's business. As I have said, there is no reported case on the point, but the result suggested is in accordance with principle, and I am happy to see that this view is shared by Dr Gough in his monograph on company charges.[53]

This situation does not apply to unsecured creditors, for they have no interest in the assets of the company and are therefore not concerned with the company's actual or ostensible dealing powers. So an execution creditor who fails to complete his execution before crystallisation of the floating charge is postponed to the charge even if he proceeds to complete the execution without notice of the fact that there is a charge which has crystallised.[54]

(2) *Subsequent purchaser or chargee of debts and the rule in Dearle v Hall*

5–51 In a contest between the holder of a crystallised charge over debts and a subsequent purchaser or fixed chargee, the fact that crystallisation comes first is not by itself enough to guarantee priority, for if the purchaser or later chargee took without notice of the crystallisation then even if it does not qualify for priority on the principle described in (1) he will still gain priority under the rule in *Dearle v Hall* if he is the first to give notice to the debtor.[55]

(3) *Landlord levying distress*

5–52 Crystallisation does not put an end to a landlord's right to distrain on the goods of the company for rent. This is because at common law the landlord is entitled to distrain on any goods on the demised premises, whether or not belonging to the tenant.[56] An unresolved question is whether the debenture holder or his receiver is entitled, after crystallisation of the charge, to invoke s.4 of the Law of Distress Amendment Act 1908 in the way that the outright owner of the distrained goods can do. I have drawn attention elsewhere to the difficulty confronting a receiver who seeks to rely on s.4.[57]

---

[53] *Company Charges* (2nd ed.) p.255 when dealing with the effect of express crystallisation clauses.
[54] *Robson v Smith* [1891] 3 Ch. 260.
[55] *ABN Amro Bank v Chiyu Banking Corp. Ltd.* [2000] H.K.C. 381.
[56] See *Woodfall's Law of Landlord and Tenant* para.9–040.
[57] [1981] J.B.L. 396, 398.

7. WAIVER OF A SECURITY INTEREST

It is not uncommon for the holder of a security interest to agree to waive or **5–53** subordinate it in favour of a third party proposing to finance the debtor by purchase of or loan against assets comprising the security. It does not usually pay the first financier to try to preserve a monopoly of the debtor company's financing. The debtor's access to other funding will expand his business base and thus enhance the value of the first financier's security. It may therefore be of advantage to the secured creditor, or at least of no disadvantage to him, to grant a waiver to a subsequent financier or to subordinate his security interest to that of the later financier. I shall deal with subordination a little later. For the moment I want to discuss waiver of a security interest, or of covenants contained in the security agreement, by a promise not to invoke them against the later financier. Waiver is to be distinguished from contractual subordination in that it is voluntary rather than contractual[58] and it may deal with matters other than subordination, for example, waiver in favour of a purchaser (which operates as a release and not merely subordinates but destroys the security) and waiver of a negative pledge clause in a floating charge.

Waivers take a variety of forms.[59] They may be formal or informal; often no more than an exchange of letters is involved. They may be given without reference to any limit of indebtedness or they may be a waiver as to a given slice of the obligations owed to the first financier, on the basis that as regards indebtedness above the stated figure, the security will continue to bind the assets. It is not usually necessary to get a waiver from a creditor who holds a floating charge imposing no restrictions on the debtor's dealing powers; but even in such a case, now unusual, a waiver may be desirable in certain situations to avoid a possible argument that the later transaction was not within the company's ordinary course of business. Waiver of a negative pledge clause in a floating charge is designed to preclude the chargee from invoking the clause against the subsequent secured creditor in whose favour it was waived.

The effect of waiver

In what circumstances is a waiver enforceable by the party in whose favour it **5–54** is given? Though the question appears not to have been decided in this specific context, the general principle of promissory (or equitable) estoppel applies to preclude the secured creditor giving the waiver, either temporarily or permanently, from asserting his security interest or restrictive clause against the subsequent secured creditor[60] where the latter alters his position

---

[58] This is the legal characterisation (see *Chitty on Contracts* (28th ed.) para.23–039 *et seq.*), but in the world of commerce and finance the term "waiver" is not infrequently used to denote a contractual release or subordination.

[59] See Wilken and Villiers, *The Law of Waiver, Variation and Estoppel* (2nd ed.), Ch.4.

[60] A waiver may also be given to an unsecured creditor or to the debtor himself.

in reliance upon it (as by advancing the secured loan) so as to render it inequitable for the first creditor to resile from his promise.[61] Two questions arise in relation to waivers. First, is the effect of a waiver temporary or permanent? Secondly, does it bind the secured creditor's assignee if taking for value and without notice of it?

(1) *Temporary or permanent?*

5-55   An operative waiver cannot, of course, be withdrawn as to purchases already contracted or value already given by the beneficiary of the waiver in reliance on it, but it may be withdrawn, on reasonable notice, as to value given after expiry of the notice, except where there is a contractual commitment to provide such value.[62] For example, a bank holding a floating charge that contains registered restrictions on factoring of the company's debts waives that provision in favour of a factoring company which is considering entering into a factoring agreement with the debtor. If the agreement is a facultative agreement, under which the factor is not obliged to purchase receivables offered to it, the bank can give reasonable notice withdrawing its waiver as to purchases by the factor after expiry of the notice. By contrast a whole turnover agreement, under which all receivables not already in being are to be sold to and to vest in the factor upon their coming into existence, commits the factor to future purchases and creates a present assignment of future receivables taking effect as from the time of the agreement.[63]

(2) *Is a transferee bound?*

5-56   A lender takes a fixed charge over a company's assets and then agrees to waive his security over part of those assets in favour of a third party. The lender then assigns its charge to a new financier, but inadvertently omits to inform that financier of the waiver. Is the latter bound? There appears to be no authority on the point but in previous editions of this book[64] the view was expressed that the new financier is bound even if without notice of the waiver, an analogy being drawn with the disposition of goods by one having apparent authority or apparent ownership. However, further reflection has led me to conclude that this view is wrong and that the analogy is false. Waiver of a security interest in favour of a subsequent incumbrancer does not constitute a disposition; it is a mere equity, binding the subordinated creditor and a transferee from him

---

[61] See generally *Chitty on Contracts* (28th ed.) paras 3–080 *et seq.*

[62] The position is thus closely analogous to that arising on the termination of a continuing guarantee. See below, paras 8–05, 8–06.

[63] See above, para.2–13. For an instructive discussion, see F.R. Salinger, *Factoring Law and Practice* (3rd ed.) paras 8–68 *et seq.*, and, for a form of priority agreement, App.9 to that work.

[64] And in *Commercial Law* (2nd ed.) p.666.

taking with notice of the waiver or by way of gift but having no effect on a purchaser for value (whether at law or in equity) taking without notice. The beneficiary of the subordination can readily protect himself against this result by requiring the charge in favour of the subordinated creditor to be indorsed with a note of the subordination. Similarly, waiver in favour of a purchaser, though operating as a release of the security as between the parties, does not affect a bona fide transferee for value without notice.

A distinct rule applies to unregistered land. If the party to whom the waiver was given neglected to obtain the muniments of title or to have a release indorsed on the relevant deed, he may find himself estopped as against a transferee of the mortgage for value and without notice.[65]

Waiver of a floating charge compared with certificate of non-crystallisation

It is not uncommon for those advising the purchaser or mortgagee of prop- **5–57** erty comprised in a floating charge to ask the chargee for a certificate that the floating charge has not crystallised. The presumed object of this procedure is to estop the debenture holder from subsequently claiming that at the time of the sale or mortgage the debtor company's powers of management had already been brought to an end. Now it may well be that a debenture holder is unwilling to give a waiver but prepared to give a certificate of non-crystallisation. In such a case, that is the best the purchaser or mortgagee can get and he must take his chance. He ought, however, to be left in no doubt that compared with a waiver a certificate of non-crystallisation is very much second best. The reason is that the debenture holder himself will not necessarily be aware of events that have caused his charge to crystallise; he is therefore unlikely to be willing to give a certificate that goes beyond a statement that he is unaware of the occurrence of any crystallising event. This will not protect the party to whom it is given if it transpires that, unbeknown to the debenture holder, his charge had in fact crystallised. Certainly no one should accept a certificate of non-crystallisation unless he is satisfied that he is unable to get a waiver, for if he can get the latter, which solves his problems, why go for the oblique approach of a certificate of non-crystallisation, when what he really wants is an assurance that the debenture holder will not assert his security over the assets in question?

8. SUBORDINATION OF A SECURITY INTEREST

I have discussed earlier the nature of secured and unsecured subordination[66] **5–58** and have referred to the fact that it is open to two creditors holding security

---

[65] See *Fisher and Lightwood's Law of Mortgage* (11th ed.) paras 24.48 *et seq.*
[66] See above, paras 1–79 *et seq.*

over the same asset to reverse by agreement the order of priority that would otherwise apply.[67] The effect is the same as that of waiver; the subordination constitutes an equity binding the party giving it and an assignee from him who is a volunteer or takes with notice of the subordination but not affecting a bona fide purchaser for value (whether acquiring a legal or an equitable interest) without notice of the subordination.

There are two aspects of subordination which I should now like to develop in the context of the impact of the debtor's insolvency. The first is whether a subordination agreement relating to unsecured debt is likely to be held unenforceable in bankruptcy or winding up as contravening the statutory requirement of *pari passu* distribution. The second is the resolution of a circularity problem which arises where the debtor has granted a floating charge to one creditor and a fixed charge to another over the same asset and because of a subordination agreement between the two creditors the floating charge has priority over the fixed charge.

Does contractual subordination contravene the *pari passu* principle?

5–59   Secured creditors are not affected by the *pari passu* principle, so that an agreement for the subordination of secured debt is not open to objection on that ground where the debtor becomes insolvent. There is, however, a widespread concern that a liquidator or trustee is precluded by statute from giving effect to that form of subordination agreement by which the junior creditor whose debt is unsecured undertakes not to prove in the bankruptcy or winding up until the senior creditor has received 100 pence in the pound. The reason advanced is that under the Insolvency Act 1986 (re-enacting previous insolvency legislation) the company's property remaining after the satisfaction of preferential debts is required to be applied in discharge of its liabilities *pari passu*,[68] that this requirement forms part of a mandatory set of statutory rules governing the administration of estates in bankruptcy and liquidation which cannot be excluded by contract,[69] and that the exclusion of the subordinated creditor from proving in the bankruptcy or winding up before the senior creditor has been paid in full contravenes the rule of *pari passu* distribution.

The argument turns essentially on the question whether the statutory rules for administration of assets in insolvency embody private rights in favour of creditors which any creditor is free to waive or subordinate so long as he does not thereby prejudice the others,[70] or whether they are rules of public policy designed to ensure that in the public interest insolvent estates are to be administered in a proper and orderly way. In *National Westminster Bank Ltd.*

---

[67] See above, para.1–80.

[68] *ibid.*, ss.107, 328(3).

[69] *National Westminster Bank Ltd. v Halesown Presswork & Assemblies Ltd.* [1972] A.C. 785; *British Eagle International Airlines Ltd. v Compagnie Nationale Air France* [1975] 1 W.L.R. 758.

[70] A principle expressed in the Latin maxim *quilibet potest renunciare juri pro se introducto.*

v Halesowen Pros-work & Assemblies Ltd.,[71] which considered statutory set-off on insolvency, the House of Lords (Lord Cross dissenting) settled a long standing controversy by adopting the latter view. In his dissenting speech Lord Cross said that he saw no reason why a creditor should not be free to agree in advance to give up a statutory rule of administration made for his protection. The majority felt bound by what they regarded as the peremptory language of the statute, and noted in particular the change from the permissive "may" to the obligatory "shall" in the Act of 1869. This view was unanimously adopted by the House of Lords in *British Eagle International Airlines Ltd. v Compagnie Nationale Air France*[72] where two of their Lordships dissented from the actual decision on a different ground.

Despite these decisions, Southwell J. in the Australian case *Home v Chester & Fein Property Developments Pty. Ltd.*[73] felt able to conclude, after a detailed review of the authorities, that a priority agreement between creditors was effective in a winding up since the rules for the administration of assets were matters of private right, not of public policy, and could thus be excluded so long as other creditors were not thereby prejudiced. That decision has been followed in this country by Vinelott J. in *Re Maxwell Communications Corp. plc. (No. 2)*,[74] who held that there was nothing in a subordination agreement which undermined either the principle of *pari passu* distribution or the rule of mandatory set-off. This is plainly correct. All that subordination does it to change priorities as between two creditors in their relations with each other; it has no effect whatsoever on other creditors. Nevertheless, the form of subordination used in *Maxwell Communications*, though no doubt appropriate in the circumstances of the arrangement there under consideration, is not in general advantageous for the senior creditor, since its effect is potentially to benefit not only him but other creditors as well.[75] The better approach is to have a turnover subordination where the subordinated creditor is required to lodge a proof and then to turn over any dividends he receives to the senior creditor, who thus receives a double dividend.

The principle established in *British Eagle* is in any event excluded as regards netting arrangements put in place by a recognised investment exchange or a recognised clearing house to limit systemic risk.[76]

---

[71] See above.
[72] See above.
[73] (1987) 11 A.C.L.R. 485.
[74] [1994] 1 B.C.L.C. 1.
[75] This will be the case either where the event that discharges the subordination never occurs or where, though it does, the surplus remaining from earlier distributions is insufficient to meet the subordinated creditor's proof, which is admissible until completion of the liquidation but cannot attract a divided to the extent that this would reopen earlier distributions to other creditors.
[76] Financial Markets and Insolvency (Settlement Finality) Regulations 1999, SI 1999/2979, implementing the EC Directive on Settlement Finality in Payment and Securities Settlement Systems, 98/26 dated May 19, 1998.

Subordination of a fixed charge to a floating charge: a circularity problem

5–60 A fixed chargee, C, who would ordinarily have priority over an earlier floating chargee, F, in the absence of restrictions of which he has notice, may agree with F that his charge shall be subordinated to the floating charge. If the company then goes into liquidation having preferential creditors (P), a neat circularity problem arises. The liquidator indicates that as there are insufficient free assets for the purpose, he proposes to pay P out of the assets comprised in the floating charge, pursuant to s.175(2)(b) of the Insolvency Act 1986.[77] On the other hand, he must allow C first bite out of the assets comprised in the fixed charge (which are also within the floating charge), as a fixed charge has priority over preferential claims. F protests that this cannot be right, since he has priority over C by virtue of the agreement between them. We thus have a scenario which is not unfamiliar to property lawyers:

- P has priority over F under s.175(2)(b);

- C has priority over P as a matter of general law;

- F has priority over C by virtue of their agreement.

How should the liquidator distribute the estate? As it happens, this particular circularity problem is a lot easier to solve than those posed by our property textbooks and arising from conflicting statutory provisions. Indeed, Professor Gilmore, who devotes an entire chapter to the mysteries of circularity which makes one wonder how we ever managed before computers, dismisses the circularity through contractual subordination as not a true circularity at all.[78] At all events, the problem is readily soluble through the principle of subrogation. Since F has priority over C by virtue of their agreement, so that C would be accountable to F for moneys received in the liquidation to the extent of C's subordination, all the interests are satisfied by treating F as subrogated to C to the extent necessary to give effect to the subordination agreement. That is to say, F will collect from the liquidator *in right of C* the amount due to C, or such part of that amount as is necessary to satisfy F's claim. As regards any balance due to F, this is postponed to the claims of P under s.172(2) (A). That this is the correct solution was conceded in *Re Woodroffe's (Musical Instruments) Ltd.*[79] However, in *Re Portbase Clothing Ltd.*,[80] Chadwick J. felt unable to adopt this approach and preferred to follow the Victorian decision in *Waters v Widdows*,[81] where Nicholson J. held that the fixed chargee, in subordinating its claims to those of the floating chargee, also subordinated them to the preferential debts. In that case the result was

---

[77] See further below, para.5–65, as to the subordination of a floating charge to the claims of preferential creditors in various insolvency-related events.
[78] *Security Interests in Personal Property*, para.39.1.
[79] [1985] 2 All E.R. 908, *per* Nourse J. at 912. Similarly Gilmore, above, n.78.
[80] [1993] Ch. 388.
[81] [1984] VR 503. See also *Deputy Commissioner of Taxation v Horsburgh* [1984] V.R. 773.

said to be dictated by the statutory policy of protecting preferential creditors. It is hard to see why. The purpose of the legislation is to give preferential debts priority over those secured by a floating charge, not over debts secured by a fixed charge. The result is that the preferential creditors gain a windfall from an agreement to which they were not party, which was not intended to benefit them and which can do so only at the expense of the fixed chargee.

It is, however, necessary to address the technical arguments on which **5–61** Chadwick J. reached his conclusions in his carefully reasoned judgment. First, whereas in the ordinary way the property the subject of the floating charge, and thus available for preferential creditors, was only the equity of redemption remaining in the chargor after the grant of the fixed charge, the effect of the priority agreement was that the whole of the debtor's interest in the property, not merely the equity of redemption, fell within the floating charge. So by subordinating itself to the holder of the floating charge the fixed chargee was in effect swelling the assets that are subject to the floating charge and thereby increasing the amount available to preferential creditors. Secondly, recourse to the doctrine of subrogation would have put the floating chargee in the same position as if the fixed chargee had assigned his charge to the floating chargee or declared a trust of the proceeds in favour of the floating charge, when in fact there has been no such assignment or declaration of trust, merely a subordination. It would have been open to the two chargees to exchange their security interests but they had not done so.

The answer to the first point is that the statutory provisions are designed to provide for payment to preferential creditors from assets which would be free assets of the company but for the floating charge. However, the additional assets that become available to the floating chargee as the result of the subordination do not come from the company and would not form part of its free assets if there were no floating charge; they come from the fixed chargee and are released on the basis that it is the holder of the floating charge, and no one else, who will benefit from them. As to the second point, it is in the nature of subrogation to a security interest that it places the subrogee in much the same position as if the security interest had been assigned to him. Thus a surety who pays off the debt is subrogated to the rights of the secured creditor, including any security interest, and it has never been an objection that the surety could have taken an assignment instead of paying off the debt.

If the fixed chargee, despite the subordination agreement, had collected the debt due to it when there was still an amount due to the holder of the floating charge, it is clear that the sum collected would have been held on trust for the floating chargee. Applying the principle of subrogation does no more than short-circuit this procedure and allow the floating chargee to enforce the chargee's priority directly and for its own benefit, so achieving the result intended by the subordination agreement but without disturbing the position of the preferential creditors, who are neither prejudiced nor enriched by a purely inter-creditor agreement.

9. THE AFTER-ACQUIRED PROPERTY CLAUSE AND THE SUBSEQUENT PURCHASE-MONEY SECURITY INTEREST

5–62 I now turn to a priority question which has caused difficulty in a number of countries and which in my view has been answered in a highly unsatisfactory manner by English case law. I refer to the case where A makes an advance to the debtor on the security of its future property and the debtor subsequently acquires an asset with funds provided by B on the security of that asset. Whose interest has priority, A's or B's? In policy terms, A's case has little merit. He may be first in the field, but why should that give him a monopoly over the debtor's financing? And since it is B's money that has furnished the new asset, why should this accrue as a windfall to A's security? Unfortunately, English law has never recognised the priority of the purchase-money security interest[82] as such except where it attaches at the very moment of the debtor's acquisition of the asset by virtue of a pre-acquisition agreement for security. Indeed, the courts have examined the sequence of operations with meticulous detail to find out whether the debtor's interest in the asset was encumbered at the outset by the purchase-money mortgage (in which case A's after-acquired property clause can attach to the asset only in its encumbered form, so that B wins, even if taking with notice of A's security interest) or whether on the other hand there was a moment of time (*scintilla temporis*) in which B was the unincumbered owner of the asset before granting the purchase-money security interest, in which event A's after-acquired property clause flashes in to catch the asset seconds before the purchase-money security interest takes effect.

All the leading cases concern competing claims to an interest in land. In the great majority of cases, B, even if not taking a complete transfer by way of mortgage until after acquisition of the asset, has an equitable interest in it by virtue of agreement from the outset, so that there is no gap into which A's after-acquired property clause can insert itself. A good example is furnished by *Re Connolly Bros. Ltd. (No. 2)*[83]:

A company issued debentures to A creating a floating charge over all its property, present and future, and undertaking not to grant any other mortgage or charge ranking in priority to the debenture. Subsequently the company applied to B for a loan to enable it to acquire certain premises and agreed to give B a charge on the property when purchased. After completion, the title deeds were deposited with B by way of security and a memorandum of deposit was subsequently executed in favour of B.

---

[82] Where the purchase-money interest is not a security interest but reservation of title under a conditional sale or hire-purchase agreement the problem does not arise, because it is clear that the after-acquired property clause in a mortgage can only attach to goods in the form in which they are acquired by the debtor, so that if they are acquired under a conditional sale or hire-purchase agreement the conditional seller or owner has priority, the debtor's interest being limited to its rights under the agreement.

[83] [1912] 2 Ch. 25.

It was held that, since the company had bound itself before the purchase to give the purchase-money charge to B on acquiring the premises, this itself constituted an equitable charge, so that there was never a moment at which the company was the unincumbered owner of the premises. Accordingly, even on the assumption that B had notice of the restriction in the debenture and was bound by it, A's rights under the debenture covered the asset only in its incumbered state, so that B had priority.

Similar decisions were given in *Wilson v Kelland*[84] and, more recently, in *Security Trust Co. v The Royal Bank of Canada*.[85]

However, the absence of a *scintilla temporis* is not by itself a sufficient explanation for the priority of the purchase-money security interest, for the argument that the prior charge attaches to the after-acquired property only in its encumbered state would apply equally to a non-purchase-money security interest taken by the second chargee before the debtor acquired the asset. But it has never been suggested that such an interest qualifies for protection against an after-acquired property clause in a prior charge. What establishes the priority for the purchase-money security interest is not merely its attachment to the new asset *ab initio* but the inequity that would result in allowing the prior chargee a windfall increase in his security brought about not with the debtor's money or new funds injected by the prior chargee but with financing provided by the later incumbrancer. Conversely, the reason why a later non-purchase-money security interest is postponed even where there is no *scintilla temporis* is that to accord it priority would enable the debtor to commit a fraud on the first incumbrancer by whittling down the value of his security in future property acquired by the debtor with his own money. Such a consideration cannot apply where the debtor's acquisition of the asset results not from the use of his own money but from funds provided by the second financier, who would not have advanced them at all without the protection of a purchase-money security interest.

The rigid insistence on the absence of a *scintilla temporis* between the acquisition of the new asset by the debtor and the attachment of the later security interest can no doubt be attributed to a desire on the part of the courts to avoid factual disputes as to whether the second incumbrancer's advance was or was not a purchase-money advance, that is, an advance intended to be used and in fact used by the debtor to acquire the new asset.[86] It is the combination of the purchase-money character of the security interest and the absence of a *scintilla temporis* that confers the priority on the second incumbrancer. From this we may conclude that where only part of the advance is required or used for the purchase his priority is limited to that part.

5–63

---

[84] [1910] 2 Ch. 306.

[85] [1976] A.C. 503.

[86] *cf.* §1(1) of the Ontario Personal Property Security Act: "purchase-money security interest means . . . (b) a security interest taken by a person who gives value for the purpose of enabling the debtor to acquire rights in or to the collateral to the extent that the value is applied in acquiring the rights."

As the case law now stands, a *scintilla temporis*, however short, in the attachment of the later security interest after acquisition of the new asset by the debtor is fatal to the later incumbrancer's purchase-money priority. In *Church of England Building Society v Piskor*,[87] the competing interest was not a prior charge but sub-tenancies granted by the purchaser before completion with the consent of the vendor. The building society advanced the money on completion, without any prior binding agreement to do so. The court declined to accede to the argument that the purchase and mortgage should be treated as one transaction. Execution of the conveyance vested the title in the purchaser, and fed the titles of the sub-tenants, an instant before the purchase-money mortgage took effect. Therefore the sub-tenancies were binding on the mortgagee.

5–64   The decision in *Piskor* was overruled by the House of Lords in *Abbey National Building Society v Cann*,[88] but in terms falling well short of a full recognition of the priority of a purchase-money security interest. The reason why the ruling in *Piskor* was rejected was not that a conveyance and purchase-money charge executed simultaneously constituted a single, indivisible transaction without the need for any prior agreement for the charge but that the finding that there was no evidence in that case to support the existence of such a prior agreement flew in the face of reality, which was that in the vast majority of cases the two transactions are indissolubly bound together in that there will almost invariably be a pre-completion agreement for a charge.[89] Both Lord Jauncey and Lord Oliver seemed to be in no doubt that the priority of the purchase-money charge resulted from the pre-completion agreement for a charge, which fettered the property at the moment of its acquisition.[90]

On this view of the case *Cann* does not appear to have changed the law at all; it merely rejected the inference of fact drawn in *Piskor* as to the absence of a pre-completion agreement. If this is as far as the decision goes then this is indeed unfortunate, for though at the time of *Cann* it was possible to enter into a mortgage very informally, an agreement for a charge is now rendered wholly void by statute unless it is in writing signed by or on behalf of both borrower and lender.[91] It is submitted that *Cann* addressed one factual reality, the near-inevitability of a pre-completion agreement for a charge, but failed to focus on the much more significant reality, that even without such an agreement the conveyance and simultaneously executed charge constitute a single, indivisible transaction. Such an approach would give substance to the priority of the purchase-money security interest, reflecting what the House of Lords appears to have intended but failed to state.

An unresolved question is whether, for the purpose of securing his priority, it suffices if the purchase-money financier secures an agreement for a charge before completion of the purchase or whether he must go further and

---

[87] [1954] 1 Ch. 553.

[88] [1991] 1 A.C. 56.

[89] *ibid.*, *per* Lord Oliver at 92–93; *per* Lord Jauncey at 101.

[90] *ibid.*, *per* Lord Jauncey at 102; *per* Lord Oliver at 92.

[91] Law of Property (Miscellaneous Provisions) Act 1989, s.2(1). See above, para.2–04, n.2.

get it before exchange of contracts. It seems to me that the latter is the only safe course. On exchange of contracts, the prior charge, by virtue of the after-acquired property clause, fastens on the debtor's equitable interest arising on exchange of contracts. If the agreement for the purchase-money mortgage is not concluded before that exchange, the equitable mortgage created by that agreement will be second in time and therefore rank after the prior charge. It is true that B may be able to jump ahead by getting a legal mortgage or charge on completion, but this *tabula in naufragio* is available to him only if he was without notice of the prior charge (or in the case of the floating charge, of restrictions on subsequent charges) before making his advance.

I believe that the *scintilla temporis* doctrine is highly unsatisfactory, in this context at least,[92] and that it is high time English law got round to upholding the priority of the purchase-money security interest without insisting on the need for a binding agreement for security before exchange of contracts or completion. But that is *de lege ferenda*. For the moment, we have to live with the law as it is.

10. IMPACT OF INSOLVENCY ON A SECURITY INTEREST

The floating charge and preferential debts

(1) *The nature of the priority*

In an earlier chapter, I drew attention to one of the major weaknesses of a floating charge, namely that it is subordinated to the claims of preferential creditors if, when the company is not in course of being wound up, the debenture holder takes possession of any property comprised in the charge[93] or appoints a receiver[94] or if the debtor company goes into winding up.[95] Until the enactment of the Insolvency Act 1985 (later replaced by the Insolvency Act 1986) a floating charge which crystallised otherwise than by reason of one of the above events took priority over preferential debts arising subsequent to crystallisation, for in relation to these the charge had ceased to be a

5–65

---

[92] It finds no place in Art.9 of the Uniform Commercial Code or in the Canadian Personal Property Security Acts. See Jacob S. Ziegel and David S. Denomme, *The Ontario Personal Property Security Act: Comment and Analysis* (2nd ed.) §1.23.1.

[93] Companies Act 1985, s.196(1), (2), as amended by the Insolvency Act 1986, s.439(1) and Sch.13.

[94] Insolvency Act 1986, s.40. This section applies whether or not the receiver is an administrative receiver.

[95] *ibid.*, s.175(2)(b), which applies whether the company goes into compulsory or voluntary liquidation. s.175(2)(b) differs from s.40 and from s.196 of the Companies Act 1985 in the way that it gives effect to the priority, providing that the preferential debts are to be paid out of the floating charge assets only to the extent that the assets available to general creditors are insufficient for the purpose, whereas the latter statutory provisions provide for payment to preferential creditors in the first instance out of assets subject to the floating charge, the chargee having a right to recoupment from the assets available for payment to general creditors.

floating charge[96] and was thus outside the statutory provisions then in force.[97] An astute draftsman could thus pave the way for circumventing the priority of preferential creditors by use of automatic or semi-automatic crystallisation clauses triggered by events other than possession, winding up or the appointment of a receiver. That has now changed. Both under the Insolvency Act 1986 and the Companies Act 1985 a floating charge means a charge which *as created* was a floating charge.[98] So preferential debts now have priority over a floating charge[99] whether they arise before or after crystallisation, and the assets out of which the preferential claims are to be discharged include not only the free assets of the company but those which are subject to a crystallised floating charge. Moreover—and this was the law even before the legislation change referred to above—assets which come in under the charge after it has crystallised (*e.g.* through the receiver's trading activity) are within the preferential net even though there was never a moment when they were subject to a floating charge, for the statutory provisions catch all assets *potentially* within the scope of the floating charge, including those acquired by the company after crystallisation.[1] The only good news for debenture holders is that the range of preferential debts has been significantly reduced, as recommended by the Cork Committee,[2] in that Crown preference, which was removed as regards assessed taxes by what is now the Insolvency Act 1986,[3] is to be abolished altogether.[4]

The receiver appointed under a floating charge is under a statutory duty to pay preferential creditors out of the assets coming into his hands in priority to the claims of the debenture holder.[5] However, this duty applies only in relation to assets the subject of the floating charge, not those comprised in a fixed charge. Hence if a receiver is appointed under a debenture containing both a fixed and a floating charge, the mere fact that he is appointed under a floating charge does not attract the operation of the statutory provisions to the assets coming into his hands under the fixed charge.[6] Further, if the

---

[96] *Re Griffin Hotel Co. Ltd.* [1941] Ch. 129; *Stein v Saywell* [1969] A.L.R. 481; *Re Christonette International Ltd.* [1982] 3 All E.R. 225 (in which the same result was reached by a different route, Vinelott J. holding that assets subject to a crystallised charge were no longer assets of the company for the purpose of the statutory provisions).

[97] *i.e.* the Companies Act 1985, ss.196(1), (2), 614(2)(6), re-enacting the Companies Act 1948, ss.94(1), 319(5).

[98] Insolvency Act 1986, ss.40(1), 251; Companies Act 1985, s.196(1), as amended by Insolvency Act 1986, s.439(1) and Sch.13.

[99] Insolvency Act 1986, ss.40, 175(2). Since the expenses of the winding up are the pre-preferential debts ranking ahead of preferential debts (*ibid.*, s.175(2)(a)), it seems clear that they also rank ahead of sums secured by a floating charge. In view of the judicial exegesis needed to arrive at this result under the former legislation (see *Re Barleycorn Enterprises Ltd.* [1970] Ch. 465), it is surprising that the 1986 Act does not expressly so provide. See also para.5–67.

[1] *Inland Revenue Commissioners v Goldblatt* [1972] 1 Ch. 498.

[2] *Report of the Review Committee on Insolvency Law and Practice* (Cmnd. 8558, 1982), para.1450.

[3] Sch.6, para.1, which confines Crown preference to taxes collected by deduction.

[4] Enterprise Act 2002, s.251. As to the fund for unsecured creditors, see above, para.4–10.

[5] Insolvency Act 1986, s.40(2). See further Roy Goode, *Principles of Corporate Insolvency Law* (2nd ed.) pp.259–260; and [1981] J.B.L. 473; Totty and Moss, *Insolvency*, Vol.2, para.H2–11.

[6] *Re Lewis Merthyr Consolidated Collieries Ltd.* [1929] 1 Ch. 498; *Re G.L. Saunders Ltd.* [1986] 1 W.L.R. 215.

receiver, on selling the assets the subject of the fixed charge, realises a surplus, that surplus cannot be said to be caught by the floating charge, even if the proceeds are in a form covered by the charge, for *ex hypothesi* the sum realised has been sufficient to discharge the debt due to the debenture holder, so that there is no longer any obligation left to be secured. It follows that the receiver's duty is to hand the surplus back to the company if it is not in liquidation or to the liquidator if it is.[7]

(2) *Events triggering the priority*

As stated above, any one of three distinct events can trigger the priority of preferential debts over a floating charge and thus establish a priority point at which the preferential debts have to be determined, namely the taking of possession of the security by or on behalf of the chargee,[8] the appointment of a receiver[9] and the winding-up of the debtor company.[10] It is theoretically possible for all three events to occur, in which case it becomes necessary to determine the preferential debts in existence at three different points in time, though there will usually be an overlap, as where preferential debts existing on the appointment of a receiver are still preferential[11] and unpaid at the time of winding-up. The debenture holder or its receiver is thus well advised to collect the amounts due under a crystallised floating charge while there are still sufficient free assets left to cover the preferential debts.

    There is a division of judicial opinion as to whether the appointment of a receiver by the holder of a floating charge subordinates only the appointing chargee to the claims of preferential creditors or all other holders of floating charges. In *Griffiths v Yorkshire Bank plc,*[12] Morritt J. adopted the former construction of s.40 of the Insolvency Act 1986, pointing out that there were various ways in which the holder of a floating charge could enforce his security without taking possession or appointing a receiver, *e.g.*

5-66

---

[7] *Re G.L. Saunders Ltd.*, above.

[8] A question which never seems to have been discussed is what is meant by "possession". In particular, is the section confined to tangible property? It is thought that it should be construed broadly to cover any kind of asset over which the chargee acquires control equivalent to possession. If the section were confined to tangibles it would exclude the receipt of money credited to the chargee's bank account.

[9] A receiver acts independently of the debenture holder who appointed him and therefore in taking possession does not act "on behalf of" the debenture holder so as to bring s.196 of the Companies Act 1985 into play concurrently with s.40 of the Insolvency Act 1986 (*Re H. & K. Medway Ltd.* [1997] 1 W.L.R. 1422).

[10] Preferential creditors have no special status in an administration. However, the advent of administration may be relevant in determining the relevant date on a winding-up. See Roy Goode, *Principles of Corporate Insolvency Law*, p.321.

[11] This will not necessarily be the case. For example, preferential claims for unpaid wages are limited to (*inter alia*) wages for the four months preceding the relevant date (as defined by the Companies Act 1985, s.196(3) and the Insolvency Act 1986, s.387), so that a claim for unpaid wages which is preferential at the time of appointment of a receiver may no longer be preferential at the time of winding-up.

[12] [1994] 1 W.L.R. 1427.

by sale of the asset given in security,[13] while in *Re H. & K. Medway Ltd.*[14] Neuberger J. held that all floating charges became subordinated, not merely the charge held by the creditor appointing the receiver. There are arguments to support either position but on balance those in favour of the latter decision seem preferable.

(3) *Expenses of winding up*

5–67 It may now be taken as established that since the expenses of winding up rank ahead of preferential debts, they also rank ahead of sums secured by a floating charge.[15]

(4) *The effect of successive priority events*

5–68 The three possible priority events are not mutually exclusive as regards the obligations of the receiver towards the liquidator (for expenses of the liquidation) and preferential creditors, but each set of preferential creditors is entitled to look only to assets remaining within the floating charge. Suppose, for example, that a receiver is appointed, that from the assets in his hands he pays the preferential creditors and makes a partial payment to his debenture holder and that before he has completed his receivership the company goes into liquidation with a new set of preferential creditors. The payments already made to the receivership preferential creditors and the debenture holder cannot be disturbed. But if the receiver is still holding assets subject to the floating charge the liquidator is entitled to resort to these for the liquidation expenses and payment to the liquidation preferential creditors.[16] So assets originally within s.40 of the Insolvency Act 1986 but not resorted to under that section may later fall within s.175(2)(b) of the Act on a winding-up.

---

[13] However, the proceeds of sale would themselves fall within s.40. An argument that might be advanced against this is that at the moment of receipt the proceeds constitute *pro tanto* payment of the debt secured by the charge, so that there is never a time when they represent an asset comprised in the charge. But in *Inland Revenue Commissioners v Goldblatt* [1972] Ch. 498 just such an argument was robustly rejected by Goff J., who, in the context of what was then s.94(1) of the Companies Act 1948 (now s.194 of the Companies Act 1985), considered (at p.506) that it would be extraordinary if the statutory provisions were to protect the preferential creditors when the debenture holder took possession as mortgage and not protect them when the debenture holder took assets in satisfaction of his claim.

[14] See above.

[15] *Re Leyland Daf Ltd., Buchler v Talbot* [2002] 1 B.C.L.C. 571; *Re Barleycorn Enterprises Ltd.* [1970] Ch. 465.

[16] *Re Leyland Ltd., Buchler v Talbot*, above.

Avoidance of a security interest in insolvency proceedings

Apart from avoidance at common law or in equity (*e.g.* for misrepresentation   **5–69**
or undue influence), there are various statutory grounds on which a validly
created security interest may be rendered void or liable to be set aside. In
every case except one the grounds for avoidance are dependent upon the company being in an insolvency proceeding of some kind. Some of the statutory
provisions apply to all forms of security, others are confined to floating
charges. Avoidance of the security has no effect on the secured creditor to the
extent that he has realised his security or otherwise obtained payment before
the commencement of the insolvency proceeding which renders the security
vulnerable,[17] because to that extent the security has already been satisfied,
there is nothing for the secured creditor to enforce and the invalidation of the
security interest is not retrospective. There are eight statutory grounds on
which a security interest given by a company can be attacked, namely that it:

(1)   contravenes the principle of *pari passu* distribution,[18] as where it is
       expressed to come into existence only on the advent of winding-up;

(2)   was not registered as required by statute[19];

(3)   is a transaction at undervalue[20];

(4)   is a preference of a creditor or surety[21];

(5)   secures an extortionate credit bargain[22];

(6)   is a floating charge given by an insolvent company otherwise than for
       new value and the company goes into winding up or administration
       within the statutory period[23];

(7)   was given after the commencement of a winding up by the court and
       has not been sanctioned by the court[24];

(8)   is a transaction made to defraud creditors.[25]

Ground (1) applies only in winding-up, voluntary or compulsory; grounds
(2)–(6) apply only if the debtor company is in administration or winding up;
ground (7) is confined to companies in compulsory winding up; and ground
(8) may be invoked whether or not the company is the subject of an insolvency proceeding. Provisions similar to those applicable in relation to

---

[17] *Re Row Dal Construction Pty. Ltd.* [1966] V.R. 249; *Mace Builders (Glasgow) Ltd. v Lunn*
[1987] Ch. 191.
[18] Now embodied in the Insolvency Act 1986, s.107 (voluntary winding-up), and the Insolvency
Rules 1986, r.4.181(1) (compulsory winding-up).
[19] Companies Act 1985, ss.395, 396. See above, paras 2–22, 3–25 and 3–30.
[20] Insolvency Act 1986, ss.238, 240, 241.
[21] *ibid.*, ss.239–241.
[22] *ibid.*, s.244.
[23] *ibid.*, s.245.
[24] *ibid.*, s.127. But see below, para.6–44, as to the Financial Collateral Directive.
[25] *ibid.*, s.423.

grounds (2)–(5) and (7) apply to security given by an individual,[26] and there is an additional provision, not applicable to security given by a company, which renders a general assignment of trade debts void against the debtor's trustee in bankruptcy unless this has been registered as if it were a bill of sale.[27] I have dealt with these in detail elsewhere.[28]

Market charges

5–70 Pt VII of the Companies Act 1989 introduced special rules for market charges designed to immunise charges in favour of an investment exchange, the Stock Exchange, and clearing houses, from many of the effects of general insolvency law and the Insolvency Act 1986.[29] To these were added money market charges[30] and system charges in favour of settlement banks.[31] The statutory provisions relating to market charges have been buttressed by subordinate legislation[32] and by regulations[33] implementing the 1998 EC Settlement Finality Directive.[34] They are not considered further except in the context of the Directive and the more recent Directive on Financial Collateral Arrangements.[35]

11. SOME TYPICAL PRIORITY PROBLEMS OUTSIDE INSOLVENCY

5–71 It may be helpful to conclude with a series of twelve short but typical priority problems arising from competing consensual interests[36] outside insolvency and the manner in which each problem is resolved by the priority rules described earlier. In each case the security is given by a company, it is assumed that any registration requirements have been duly complied with, and unless otherwise stated there is no waiver or subordination agreement.

---

[26] Bills of Sale Act (1878) Amendment Act 1882, s.8; Insolvency Act 1986, ss.284, 339–343.

[27] Insolvency Act 1986, s.344.

[28] *Principles of Corporate Insolvency Law* (2nd ed.) pp.141–163 and Ch.11.

[29] Companies Act 1989, ss.173–181.

[30] Financial Markets and Insolvency (Money Markets) Regulations 1995, SI 1995/2049.

[31] Financial Markets and Insolvency Regulations 1996, SI 1996/1469.

[32] Financial Markets and Insolvency Regulations 1991, SI 1991/880; Financial Markets and Insolvency Regulations 1996, SI 1996/1469.

[33] Financial Markets and Insolvency (Settlement Finality) Regulations 1999, SI 1999/2979, as amended.

[34] Directive on settlement finality in payment and securities settlement systems, EC 98/26. See below, para.6–35.

[35] Directive 2002/47 dated June 6, 2002.

[36] For two priority problems arising in receivables financing where one of the interests is an equitable tracing right, see below, paras 5–75 *et seq.*

Problem 1:

Debtor gives a first fixed charge on an existing tangible asset to A, followed **5–72**
by a second fixed charge to B.
   Assuming that the charge to A is not securing further advances on land,[37] *A
wins provided that his charge is duly registered. Since registration is purely a perfection requirement, not a priority point,*[38] *it makes no difference that B is the first
to register or that A's charge was not registered at the time B made his search.*

Problem 2:

Debtor gives a fixed charge over future property to A, then acquires equipment **5–73**
from B under reservation of title.
   *B wins, since A cannot acquire greater rights than the debtor company, and
the latter becomes the owner only on payment of the purchase price to B.*

Problem 3:

Debtor gives a fixed charge over future property to A, then acquires a new **5–74**
asset with money advanced by B, to whom debtor gives a purchase-money
mortgage.
   *Assuming that the mortgage, or an agreement for the mortgage, was made
prior to the debtor's acquisition of the asset, so that there was no scintilla temporis during which the asset was held by the debtor unincumbered,*[39] *B wins, for
A's after-acquired property clause can attach to B's future property only in the
form in which it is acquired, that is, mortgaged to B, and thus bites only on B's
equity of redemption.*[40]

Problem 4:

Debtor gives a fixed charge over existing and future book debts to A, then **5–75**
factors its existing and future book debts to B.
   *If, when the debts became vested in B under the factoring agreement, B had
notice of A's charge (whether by reason of registration or otherwise), A wins;
in any other case (including purchase by B before registration of A's charge and
without other notice of it) A has an initial priority but this is displaced under*

---

[37] As to which see Problem 6.
[38] See above, paras 2–22, 5–16.
[39] See above, paras 5–62 *et seq.*
[40] See above, para.5–62.

the rule in Dearle v Hall[41] *if B is the first to give notice of his interest to the relevant debtor, unless A collects the debt when still without notice.*[42]

Problem 5:

5–76　Debtor factors its existing and future book debts to A, then gives a fixed charge over existing and future book debts to B.

A has an initial priority but this is displaced under the rule in Dearle v Hall if B makes his advance without notice of A's rights and is the first to give notice to the relevant debtor. In this case notice cannot be derived from registration since A's rights are acquired by purchase, not by way of security, and are therefore not registrable.

Problem 6:

5–77　Debtor charges an existing asset to A to secure present and future advances. After A has advanced £10,000, debtor charges the asset to B to secure a contemporaneous advance. Later, A advances a further £5,000.

A has priority as to his initial advance of £10,000, and also has priority as to the further advance of £5,000 if at the time he made this he had no notice of the charge to B. If the asset consists of unregistered land, registration of B's charge does not constitute notice for this purpose.[43]

Problem 7:

5–78　Debtor gives a floating charge over book debts to A, then sells or grants a fixed charge over the debts to B.

B wins, unless the charge in favour of A precludes the debtor from granting a subsequent fixed charge ranking in priority to or pari passu with A's floating charge and B takes his charge with notice of the restriction on subsequent charges. For this purpose, entry of the restriction on the register does not constitute notice unless B searches the register.[44]

Problem 8:

5–79　Debtor gives a fixed charge over its equipment to A, who fails to register the charge. Subsequently debtor sells the equipment to B.

---

[41] See above, paras 5–08, 5–09.
[42] See above, para.5–08.
[43] See above, para.5–18.
[44] See above, para.2–24.

A's failure to register does not of itself invalidate the charge against B,[45] but B obtains priority by virtue of his legal title if he bought without notice of A's charge.

Problem 9:

Debtor charges its receivables to A under an agreement which provides that the charge is to be by way of fixed charge and Debtor is not to dispose of the receivables but is to collect them in and pay them into a special account controlled by A. Debtor receives payment by cheque from various customers but pays the cheques into its overdrawn account with B.   **5–80**

B wins if collecting the cheques without negligence[46] and without notice of A's claim, since B's acquisition of the legal title to the proceeds of the cheques for value and without notice overrides A's equitable charge.

Problem 10:

Debtor charges its receivables to A under an agreement which provides that the charge is to be by way of fixed charge and debtor is not to dispose of the receivables. Debtor is left free to collect them in and use them as its own moneys. Debtor subsequently grants a fixed charge of the receivables to B, with a duty to pay collections into an account controlled by B.   **5–81**

B wins. A's charge, though expressed to be fixed, is no more than a floating charge,[47] and this is subordinate to a subsequent fixed charge, in the absence of restrictions on subsequent charges of which the later fixed chargee has notice.[48]

Problem 11:

Debtor gives a floating charge over its stock in trade to A. The charge provides that A may at any time convert it into a fixed charge by service of a crystallisation notice. Subsequently A gives notice crystallising the charge. A week later, debtor gives a fixed charge over the stock in trade to B.   **5–82**

---

[45] Since s.395(1) of the Companies Act 1985 renders an unregistered charge void only against the liquidator or a creditor, not against a purchaser.

[46] Since A's agreement with Debtor gives A not merely equitable ownership of the cheques but also a right to their immediate possession, A has a claim against B for conversion in collecting the cheque (this being a strict liability tort) unless B can rely on s.4 of the Cheques Act 1957, which requires that B collect the cheque in good faith and without negligence. But s.4 operates solely to protect B against a claim for conversion; it does not in itself give B an overriding title (see R. M. Goode, "The Right to Trace and Its Impact in Commercial Transactions" (1976) 92 L.Q.R. 360, 528, at 558); for this, B must rely on the common law priority in favour of the bona fide legal purchaser for value.

[47] See above, paras 413 *et seq.*

[48] See above, paras 5–39, 5–40.

B wins if he had dealings with the debtor prior to crystallisation or if he dealt with the debtor after crystallisation and with knowledge of the floating charge, provided that in either case he had no notice that the charge had crystallised.[49]

Problem 12:

5–83   Debtor gives a floating charge over all its present and future assets and undertaking to A, the charge providing that debtor is not to dispose of its book debts or other receivables. Subsequently A gives B a waiver of its charge over debtor's receivables in consideration of B entering into a factoring agreement with debtor for sale of debtor's existing and future receivables. B purchases receivables under the factoring agreement. A then assigns its loan portfolio and security for payment to C, who buys without notice of the waiver.

Since B is a purchaser, the waiver operates as a release, so that B acquires unincumbered title to the receivables, and displaces A and A's assignee C.[50]

---

[49] See above, para.5–50.
[50] See above, para.5–56.

VI

Security Interests in Corporate Investment Securities

1. INTRODUCTION

This chapter is concerned with security interests in corporate investment **6–01** securities, that is securities issued by a company and traded on a market.[1] These take one of two forms: debt issues (bonds, notes, debentures, loan stock) and equity issues (shares, stock, warrants[2]). In their traditional form securities were paper-based and held by the investor directly from the issuer, and the law relating to security interests in them was, and remains, tolerably well settled. But the modern move from direct to indirect holdings, from segregated (or non-fungible) securities accounts to pooled (or fungible) securities accounts and from paper-based to paperless (dematerialised) securities, though greatly increasing efficiency and reducing cost and risk, nevertheless presents new challenges for the legal community which the present chapter seeks to identify and resolve. But first it is necessary to give a brief description of these changes in practice and their implications.

---

[1] See generally Joanna Benjamin, *Interests in Securities*; Joanna Benjamin and Madeleine Yates, *The Law of Global Custody* (2nd ed.); A.O. Austen-Peters, *Custody of Investments: Law and Practice*; Philip R. Wood, *Comparative Law of Securities and Guarantees*, Ch.VI; and, for a comparative treatment of the conflict of laws issues, Richard Potok, *Cross-Border Collateral: Legal Risk and the Conflict of Laws*. Once again the reader is reminded that "securities" should not be confused with security interests but denote issues on the market, and debt issues may be either secured or unsecured. Similarly, the grant of a security interest, though forming an element in a typical securitisation, is to be distinguished from it. Securitisation denotes the total process by which non-tradable debt assets are converted into tradable debt assets by transferring them from the original creditor (the originator) to a special-purpose vehicle which raises money from the market by issuing bonds or notes, using the transferred assets as security. Where the transferred debts are secured, the grant of a security interest in them operates as a sub-charge. A particular form of securitisation is the collateralised bond obligation. See generally Joanna Benjamin, *Interests in Securities*, Chs 11 and 12.

Mortgages and charges of securities arising in the context of stock loans and repurchase agreements are frequently concluded on the terms of a standard-term master or global master agreement published by one of the professional associations, such as the International Securities Lenders Association (ISLA) and, jointly, The Bond Market Association (TBMA) and the International Securities Market Association (ISMA), as amended by the specific agreements concluded between the parties.

[2] Warrants are negotiable documents which entitle the holder to convert them into shares. They are rarely issued for UK securities.

The move from direct to indirect (book-entry) holdings

6–02   Over the past few decades there has been a strong move from direct holdings of securities to indirect (book-entry) holdings. In the case of a direct holding of registered securities the investor's legal entitlement is recorded in, and derived from, registration in the issuer's books and is evidenced by a certificate, and the securities are transferred by execution of a transfer instrument and registration of the transfer.[3] In the case of bearer securities title is not recorded on the issuer's register but is vested in the holder of the certificate for the time being and is transferred by delivery.

By contrast, in the case of an indirect holding of securities the investor's rights are derived from credit to its securities account with a nominee, custodian or other intermediary which itself holds direct from the issuer or from a higher-tier intermediary, and transfers are made through the account in much the same way as a bank funds transfer. The first-tier intermediary, whose nominee holds direct from the issuer, is usually a national central securities depositary (CSD) for domestic issues[4] or an international central securities depositary (ICSD) for international issues. The world's largest depository is The Depository Trust Company of New York (DTC). The two leading ICSDs are Euroclear Bank and Clearstream International.

To reduce administration and the cost of security printing of individual certificates for investors international securities are commonly issued in the form of a single global note representing the entire issue and deposited with a common depository for Euroclear and Clearstream. Participants of Euroclear and Clearstream are the first-tier beneficiaries and they will in turn hold for customers of their own, and so on, down the chain. Interests in the global note may be exchangeable for definitive certificates, so that an investor exercising the right to obtain definitive certificates acquires a direct relationship with the issuer, either through delivery in the case of bearer or securities or through registration, in the case of registered securities. But not infrequently the global note is intended to be permanently immobilised and not to be exchangeable for definitives except in extreme situations, such as the issuer's default and failure of the trustee of the issue to take the requisite default measures when requested to do so by a given percentage of investors and on being furnished an indemnity.

This tiering of relationships, illustrated in figures 1 and 2 has several advantages. It creates a pyramid structure in which the issuer can deal with a relatively small number of large players, who in turn will hold accounts for a greater number of smaller participants, and so on down through the pyramid to the ultimate investor. The effect is substantially to reduce both the volume and the movement of paper involved in the issue and transfer of

---

[3] Though registration is necessary to confer or transfer the legal title, it is only *prima facie* evidence of ownership, and a person with a superior right to the securities may apply to the court for an order directing that he be placed on the register in placing of the existing registrant.

[4] There is no CSD in the United Kingdom for UK securities. CREST (see below) is a settlement system but in relation to UK securities it does not act as a CSD since its members hold direct from the issuer, not from CREST. See further below, para.6–05.

Figure 1 Specimen chain where global note deposits with ICSD

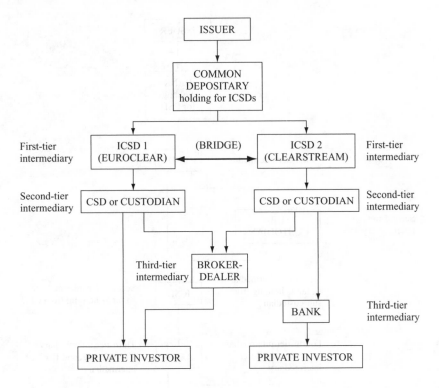

Notes

1. This diagram gives an example of a chain where a global note is issued to a (usually unnamed) common depository designated by the ICSDs, Euroclear and Clearstream. For registered securities the common depository's nominee is shown as the registered holder, and the note itself is held in the vaults of the common depository.
2. A global note is sometimes deposited with a single ICSD, in which case it is lodged with a specialised depository, usually a sub-custodian of the ICSD in the country of issue.
3. The issuer has to negotiate with the ICSD to secure eligibility of the issue for deposit with the ICSD.
4. Below the level of the ICSDs, chains can take a number of different forms, depending on the players involved and on whether a participant holds directly from another party or through an intermediary or has part of its holding direct and the rest through an intermediary. Participants in an ICSD may be custodians, broker-dealers, central banks, CSDs or corporates.
5. The diagram illustrates why a "look-through" legal regime may be difficult, if not impossible, to operate. The broker-dealer from whom the private investor on the left-hand side acquired its holding may have procured these by acquisition from the CSD or custodian participant of Euroclear, the CSD or custodian participant of Clearstream, transfer from its own house account or a mixture of the three. There may be no way of identifying the source of the private investor's entitlement, particularly when account is taken of netting through a clearing system.

Figure 2 Specimen chain where global note deposited with CSD

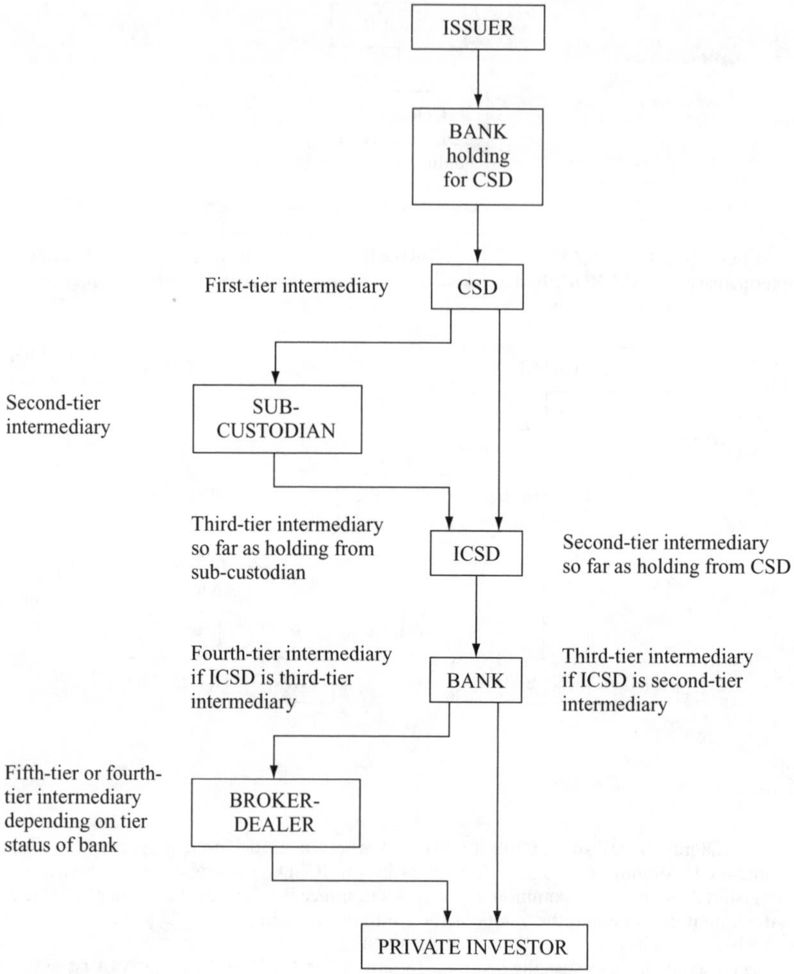

		ISSUER
		BANK holding for CSD
First-tier intermediary		**CSD**
Second-tier intermediary	**SUB-CUSTODIAN**	
Third-tier intermediary so far as holding from sub-custodian	**ICSD**	Second-tier intermediary so far as holding from CSD
Fourth-tier intermediary if ICSD is third-tier intermediary	**BANK**	Third-tier intermediary if ICSD is second-tier intermediary
Fifth-tier or fourth-tier intermediary depending on tier status of bank	**BROKER-DEALER**	
	PRIVATE INVESTOR	

Notes

1. This diagram gives an example of a chain where the global note is originally deposited not with an ICSD but with a national CSD, which may hold it either in its own vaults or with sub-custodians in its own country or abroad. In this case the ICSD acquires its interest at a lower level as a participant of the CSD or through its sub-custodian participant or partly the one and partly the other, as in the diagram. If the ICSD acquires its holding directly from the CSD it is a second-tier intermediary; if through its sub-custodian, which is the more usual practice, it is a third-tier intermediary.
2. The issuer has to negotiate with the CSD to secure eligibility of the issue for deposit with the CSD.
3. Fig.2, like fig.1, shows how the private investor's holding may be derived through different routes and different ICSDs.

securities and the risk of loss or theft of negotiable securities. Moreover, the aggregation of holdings in undesignated pools of intangibles held by a securities intermediary in an omnibus account[5] facilitates book-entry transfers of those securities from one customer of the intermediary to another, thus enabling a substantial volume of transfers to be effected in-house.[6] A transfer need be executed and registered only if and when a customer exercises his right to require delivery or redelivery of the securities credited to his account.

The movement of securities is not necessarily from issuer to first-tier intermediary and down the custody chain, but may start from the other end. Securities originally held by an investor direct may be deposited with its securities intermediary, who will either transfer them into its own name or deposit them with its intermediary into whose name they will be transferred. International securities may be localised by deposit with a sub-custodian or agent in the country of issue to facilitate receipt of dividends, voting, and the like, but much depends on relative costs, risks and efficiency.

Omnibus (pooled, fungible) accounts and segregated (non-fungible) accounts

The most common holding pattern for a securities intermediary is to hold **6–03** all securities of a particular issue in an omnibus account with the issuer or a higher-tier intermediary without designation of the individual customers for whom the securities are held. Such accounts are also known as pooled, or fungible, accounts.[7] The advantage of pooling is that it reduces administration and enables transfers of the securities from one customer to another to be effected solely through the books of the intermediary itself without the involvement of its own intermediary, who though aware that the omnibus account is held for the customers of its own customer, the lower-tier intermediary, and not for that intermediary for its own account, will have no knowledge of the interest of any particular customer of the lower-tier intermediary and thus no knowledge of transfers between its customers. A less common and convenient holding pattern is for the intermediary to hold a customer's securities entitlement in an account with the issuer or a higher-tier intermediary, the account being in the name of the customer's intermediary but carrying a designation showing that the account is held for a particular customer, segregated from the pooled securities held for other customers in an omnibus account. Such segregated accounts are also termed non-fungible accounts. Because each such account has to be separately recorded in the books of the higher-tier intermediary, transfers must be effected through that intermediary instead of being purely book-entry transfers within the

---

[5] See below.
[6] Where the transferee holds its account with a different intermediary, it is necessary to effect the transfer through the books of a higher-tier intermediary common to the intermediaries of transferor and transferee, if there is one, or if not, to go up the chain until a common intermediary is reached.
[7] The term "fungible" is in this context used in a somewhat different sense from its normal meaning. See below, para.6–09.

books of the customer's intermediary. Necessarily, therefore, the higher-tier intermediary is on notice of the particular customer's interest.[8]

Certificated (paper-based) and uncertificated (dematerialised) securities

(1) *The CREST system*

6–04   A further major step in the reduction of the issue and movement of paper has been the shift from certificated (*i.e.* paper-based) to uncertificated (*i.e.* dematerialised, or paperless) issues and transfers. Most of these are now effected through the CREST computer system operated by CRESTCo, which is given statutory underpinning by the Uncertificated Securities Regulations 2001,[9] supplemented by CREST rules and conditions. Participants in CREST, that is, those who have a business relationship with it, may communicate with CREST only through the gateway computer of a user, that is, a person who has a computer link to CREST and inputs instructions to CREST either for others on its own account. A participant may also be a user. Accounts are maintained only for CREST members. They may be full members, who have direct computer access to CREST as users, or sponsored members, who connect with CREST through the services of a user. Any individual or company may apply to become a CREST member. Dematerialisation does not by itself affect the direct relationship between investor and issuer; it simply reflects holdings and transfers in electronic form. It is for the investor himself to decide whether to hold his account directly or through an intermediary. Accounts are opened for members in their own name, whether they are full members or sponsored members. Issuers have dealings with CREST, usually through their registrars, for the purpose of dematerialising and rematerialising their securities, recording transfers, and the like.

(2) *Dematerialisation*

6–05   New securities may be issued in dematerialised form where permitted by the Operator and authorised by the issuer's articles of association or a directors' resolution.[10] Existing paper-based securities, including bearer securities, may be dematerialised, on a request to the issuer by or through a member, by lodgment with the issuer of the relevant certificates and an executed transfer in

---

[8] For the possible significance of this, see below, para.6–15.

[9] SI 2001/3755, made under s.207 of the Companies Act 1989 and replacing SI 1995/3272, as amended. Though the regulations do not refer specifically to CRESTCo., it is the organisation approved as Operator by the Treasury. It merged with Euroclear in September 2002. For a good general description of dematerialisation and the CREST system, see Joanna Benjamin and Madeleine Yates, *The Law of Global Custody* (2nd ed.) Ch.9; and Benjamin, *Interests in Securities*, paras 9.46 *et seq.* For fuller detail, see the CREST Reference Manual (January 2003).

[10] *ibid.*, regs 14–16.

favour of a member, followed by a dematerialisation notice from the issuer to the Operator.[11] The former bearer thereafter holds its securities entitlement through its account with CREST if it is a member or otherwise through its account with a securities intermediary. Both the Operator and the issuer of registered securities are required to maintain a share register, but it is the Operator register, not the issuer register, that now constitutes the primary and definitive record of entitlement to uncertificated shares.[12] Despite this, CRESTCo itself is neither the holder nor the custodian of UK securities[13] and is therefore not a securities intermediary standing between its members and the issuer but is more akin to a registrar who holds the primary records. It is therefore not a CSD, nor does it act as a nominee. CRESTCo is a recognised clearing house and provides an electronic transfer and settlement system.[14]

Each CREST member having a stock account with CREST for a particular issue of securities remains in a direct relationship with the issuer, though it can only effect registered transfers[15] through CREST. Each member will have a separate stock account for each class of securities he holds and a cash memorandum to record payments made and received in respect of securities. The accounts of securities intermediaries are required to distinguish between securities held for customers and those held for themselves. Securities held for customers are usually in an omnibus account which does not differentiate between one customer and another, though an account may be individually designated to show that the account in the name of the intermediary is held for a particular customer segregated from the holdings for other customers.[16] Securities belonging to the intermediary itself are held in a house account. Transfers can only be made on the instructions of a member and from one member's account to that of another.[17] A person other than a member wishing to initiate a transfer must do so through a member.[18] If the transferee

---

[11] *ibid.*, reg.33. Securities admitted to CREST are termed participating securities.

[12] See *ibid.*, reg.24(2),(3). The Operator maintains separate registers for each class of uncertificated securities, and the register for any one class consists of all the securities held by the system-members in their stock accounts.

[13] The position is otherwise as regards Irish, Isle of Man, and Jersey securities held through CREST, where it fulfils the normal function of a first-tier intermediary and custodian. Overseas securities issued in other foreign jurisdictions with whose settlement systems CREST has links may be held through a CRESTCo subsidiary, CREST International Nominees Ltd., which by virtue of its membership of the foreign settlement systems may acquire foreign securities, which it holds as bare trustee for another CRESTCo subsidiary, CREST Depository Ltd., which in turn holds them on trust for the acquiring CREST members under a deed poll pursuant to which a separate series of depository interests is issued to CREST members in dematerialised form in respect of each issue of underlying securities of a particular class. The depository interests are in effect a form of uncertificated depository receipt.

[14] The settlement function, involving delivery and payment, is now carried out on its behalf by the London Clearing House under arrangements with CRESTCo and the London Stock Exchange.

[15] Off-register dealings take effect in equity only.

[16] The CREST rules require that the description should not be such as to indicate the customer's identity.

[17] The system is thus closely analogous to the bank clearing systems, which are confined to the clearing banks, who make transfers to each other through their respective accounts with the Bank of England.

[18] Who is then termed the sponsoring system-participant.

holds an account with the same member the transfer is effected by in-house book entry, in other cases by transfer to the transferee's member for the account of the transferee. Legal title is *prima facie* conferred or transferred when the issue or transfer of securities to a member is recorded in the Operator register.[19]

(2) *Rematerialisation*

6-06 A person holding uncertificated securities may have them reconverted into certificated securities by arranging for its member to issue an instruction to the Operator to that effect, the Operator in turn issuing a rematerialisation notice to the issuer.[20] The Operator must thereupon delete the entry in its register recording the member as holder of the units in question and the issuer must enter the member as holder in the issuer register. Until that has been done the member retains title to the transferred units,[21] an important rule change which avoids conversion of a legal title into an equitable interest during the interval. The issuer must then issue a certificate to the relevant person where the terms of the issue of the security so require.[22]

Legal developments in relation to financial collateral

6-07 Investment securities, whether held directly or indirectly and whether in paper-based or dematerialised form, represent an immensely valuable form of collateral. It is therefore essential to the stability of financial systems and the avoidance of systemic risk that the legal regime in place should, wherever possible, remove grounds for uncertainty as to the validity of security interests in financial collateral and as to the law applicable to them. To that end the European Parliament and Council have issued two Directives,[23] while a conflict of laws Convention[24] was concluded at a Diplomatic Conference at the Hague in December 2002. Each of these instruments will be considered later. English law, though addressing the conversion of certificated to uncertificated securities, has not yet grappled with the implications of the move from direct to indirect holdings, a move which provided the motive power for the revision in 1994 of Art.8 of the Uniform Commercial Code and has particular implications for those taking an interest in investment securities as collateral. The Financial Markets Law Committee is examining the issue.

---

[19] Uncertificated Securities Regulations 2001, reg.24. Entry in the issuer register is also *prima facie* evidence of title but not if inconsistent with an entry in the Operator register (reg.24(2)).

[20] *ibid.*, reg.32(2)(b),(3)(b).

[21] *ibid.*, reg.32(6).

[22] *ibid.*, reg.32(7).

[23] Directive 98/26 on settlement finality in payment and securities settlement systems ([1998] O.J. L166/45) and Directive 2002/47 on financial collateral arrangements ([2002] O.J. L168/43).

[24] Convention on the law applicable to certain rights in respect of securities held with an intermediary.

2. THE NATURE OF THE SECURITIES ENTITLEMENT

In order to understand what rights are acquired by a creditor who takes a **6–08** security interest in investment securities we first have to examine the nature of the interest held by the debtor himself.

Shares directly held

In terms of property rights a share is no more and no less than a co- **6–09** ownership interest in a single asset, the company's issued share capital, carrying with it, among other things, entitlements to dividend and an ultimate right to participate in the company's surplus assets, if any, on a winding-up. Until then the shareholder has no interest in any specific item of property held by the company; his entitlement is rather like that of a beneficiary under a will, who receives his entitlement only when the estate has been wound up, creditors paid and the net realisations distributed.

Common wisdom has it that shares are fungible in that any one share is legally exchangeable for any other share and that on a repo transaction what the seller receives on the return leg of the repo is not the shares it transferred but their equivalent in number and kind. As stated earlier,[25] this is a misconception.[26] Fungibility requires the existence of at least two legally interchangeable units. But shares are not like bottles of wine or potatoes, where it is possible to segregate individual units from a bulk and dispose of them separately from the bulk. Individual shares in a company are no more segregable than shares in a racehorse. Just as it is impossible to own a share in a racehorse otherwise than as co-owner of the racehorse itself, so also it is impossible to own a share in a company otherwise than as co-owner of the company's issued share capital.[27] It follows that where in a repo transaction 50,000 shares in a company with an issued share capital of one million shares are sold and later bought back, what the original seller receives on the repurchase is not simply the equivalent of what he sold but the selfsame asset, namely co-ownership of the company's share capital in common with holders of the remaining 95 per cent. It follows also that a sale, mortgage or charge of shares of a particular issue cannot fail for want of ascertainment, for the subject-matter is not individual shares as distinct assets but the issued share capital itself. The decision of the Court of Appeal in *Hunter v Moss*[28] is therefore correct, even if the reasoning is perhaps not quite as apposite as that of Mr Colin Rimer Q.C. at first instance.[29]

---

[25] See above, para.2–06.
[26] And one which I myself long shared.
[27] See Roy Goode, "Are Intangible Assets Fungible?" in *Themes in Comparative Law in Honour of Bernard Rudden* (Peter Birks and Arianna Pretto, eds) 97, to be reproduced with revisions [2003] L.M.C.L.Q. August.
[28] [1994] 1 W.L.R. 452.
[29] [1993] 1 W.L.R. 934.

The principle that shares are not fungibles but simply co-ownership interests in a single asset is true of other corporate securities. This is so even if the securities are numbered[30] and even if they are bearer securities.[31] It is true that the certificates themselves, being in physical form, may be segregated and subject to separate ownership as pieces of paper, but they do no more than embody title to a co-ownership interest in the securities issue.

Shares indirectly held

6–10 English law is rather less clear on the nature of rights to book-entry securities, that is, shares or other securities held through a securities intermediary.[32] One thing is obvious, namely that where shares are acquired through an intermediary there is no relationship between the investor and the issuer, only between the investor and its intermediary,[33] and that where shares originally held directly are deposited with an intermediary not merely as bailee of the certificates but as transferee, the relationship previously existing between the investor and the issuer is broken and replaced by a relationship with the intermediary. The nature of that relationship is governed by the agreement between the parties. It would be possible for the investor to have no more than a personal right to the transfer of shares he has acquired or the retransfer of the shares he has deposited, and in the case of bearer securities a mere personal right to delivery or re-delivery. But with modern fund management such an arrangement would be highly unusual and would leave the investor exposed to the risk of his intermediary's insolvency. So under English law the normal agreement, express or implied, is that the intermediary's holding is as trustee for the investor to the extent of the latter's entitlement. Whether the intermediary at each level has a proprietary interest in the underlying securities will, of course, depend on the applicable law.

What, however, is the precise nature of that entitlement? It is here that things become a little fuzzy. I shall treat separately holdings through an omnibus account and holdings through a segregated account, though as we shall see the distinction is of limited legal significance.

---

[30] Which is no longer the case for UK shares.

[31] It is not the practice to issue bearer shares in the UK, but other forms of security, such as bonds and notes, are commonly in bearer form.

[32] See generally Roy Goode, "The Nature and Transfer of Rights in Dematerialised and Immobilised Securities" (1996) J.I.G.F.L. 167. The character of the investor's interest in indirectly held securities was potentially an issue in *Macmillan Inc. v Bishopsgate Investment Trust plc (No. 3)* [1996] 1 W.L.R. 387, where Robert Maxwell procured Macmillan shares in Berlitz to be transferred to England to be held on trust for Macmillan and then fraudulently transferred them to an account with the New York DTC held by his DTC agents, and arranged for them to be given in security to lenders to his private companies. However, as all the lenders held their interests through accounts with banks in New York, which was also the place of incorporation of Berlitz, New York law applied, whether as the law of the place of transfer into the accounts, as Millett J. held, or as the law of the place of incorporation, as the Court of Appeal held.

[33] See below, para.6–13.

(1) *Holdings through an omnibus account*

An investor who has either acquired securities through his intermediary or **6–11** acquired them direct and deposited them with his intermediary in an omnibus account typically has a combination of personal and proprietary rights: a personal right to the delivery or transfer[34] of the securities, with various ancillary personal rights,[35] and a proprietary right in the form of co-ownership of the pool of securities held by the intermediary from the issuer direct or through its account with a higher-tier intermediary.[36] The characteristic of an indirect holding is that the investor's title derives neither from registration in the issuer's register or in CREST nor from possession but from his account with his intermediary. It is therefore not inaccurate to describe the account as the root of title. The effect of the co-ownership is that if the intermediary becomes insolvent the securities held for its customers belong in equity to them and do not form part of the intermediary's estate available to its creditors. The intermediary is thus a trustee for its customers, who are beneficial co-owners of the pool of securities held on their behalf, and if the intermediary is a first-tier intermediary holding direct from the issuer it has legal title to the securities. A second-tier intermediary, however, will itself be merely an equitable co-owner of the pool of securities held by its own, first-tier intermediary for that intermediary's customers; and to the extent that the lower-tier intermediary is holding for its customers and not for itself it is a sub-trustee, while any such customer holding for customers of its own is a sub-sub-trustee, and so on.

An intermediary owes a duty to its customers to hold sufficient quantities of each issue of securities to meet their entitlements. If there is any shortfall, as where the intermediary misappropriates part of the pool, the co-ownership interests of its customers abate proportionately.

So far, the position is reasonably clear. But we still have to address the **6–12** question: what exactly is it that the customers co-own? Do they, as conventional trust law might suggest, have beneficial co-ownership of the underlying securities themselves? Or do they, as under Art.8 of the Uniform Commercial Code, have something based on a different concept, which is co-ownership not of a specific thing (the shares themselves) but of a package of rights *vis-à-vis* the intermediary which Art.8 describes as "a securities entitlement"? This package of rights has been well described by Professor James Rogers, reporter for the revised Art.8, in the following terms:

---

[34] Delivery in the case of bearer securities, transfer in the case of registered securities. Where these are dematerialised the investor has the option to have them rematerialised.

[35] *e.g.* to require the intermediary to collect and transfer to the investor dividends and other distributions it receives, and to vote in accordance with the investor's instructions.

[36] See to the same effect Austen-Peters, *op. cit.*, paras 2.35–2.36, 4.26; Benjamin, *Interests in Securities*, paras 1.86, 1.97, 2.33; Nicholas Papaspyrou, "Immobilisation of Securities" (1996) J.I.B.F.L. 430; Roy Goode, "Security Entitlements as Collateral and the Conflict of Laws" in *The Oxford Colloquium on Collateral and Conflict of Laws*, Special Supplement to the J.I.B.F.L. September 1998, p.22.

"The elements of this package are as follows:

the entitlement holder does not take credit risk of the intermediary's other business activities; that is, property held by the intermediary is not subject to the claims of the intermediary's creditors;

the intermediary will maintain a one-to-one match between the assets that it itself holds and all of the claims of its entitlement holders;

the intermediary will pass through to the entitlement holder payments or distribution made with respect to the securities;

the intermediary will exercise voting rights and other rights and privileges of ownership of the securities in the fashion directed by the entitlement holder;

the intermediary will transfer or otherwise dispose of the positions at the direction of the entitlement holder; and

the intermediary will act at the direction of the entitlement holder to convert the position into any other available form of securities holding, e.g., obtain and deliver a certificate."[37]

This description of the content of the securities entitlement under Art.8 precisely matches the entitlement of the holder of a securities account under English law, which consists of a combination of personal rights (including rights to delivery or transfer of the underlying security) and co-ownership of whatever is held by the intermediary for its customers, whether it holds direct from the issuer or from a higher-tier intermediary. There are several reasons why this right of co-ownership and other rights embodied in the securities entitlement should be treated as a separate bundle of rights exercisable only through and against the investor's own intermediary.

6–13 The first and most crucial point is that, to make the system of indirect holdings and pooled funds work, it is essential that each investor should be considered to have a relationship exclusively with its own intermediary and that neither he nor his secured or execution creditors should be able to assert rights against higher-tier intermediaries or the issuer. That is already the position in most cases under English trust law, where it is only in exceptional cases that the beneficiary under a sub-trust can have recourse to the head trustee; in general he must look exclusively to his own trustee.[38] If that is the

---

[37] James Steven Rogers, "Policy Perspectives on Revised U.C.C. Article 8", 43 U.C.L.A. L. Rev. 1431 (1996), an illuminating article which repays careful study. See also Steven L. Schwarcz, "Intermediary Risk in a Global Economy" 50 Duke L.J. 1541 (2001). The concept of the securities entitlement had its genesis in a pioneering article by Charles W. Mooney, "Beyond Negotiability: A New Model for Transfer and Pledge of Interests in Securities Controlled by Intermediaries," 12 Cardozo L. Rev. 305 (1990).

[38] For an example in relation to a house, see the decision of the Privy Council in *Hayim v Citibank NA* [1987] A.C. 730. Clauses in trust deeds usually restrict direct action against the issuer by investors and such no-action clauses are effective even in the issuer's winding-up (*Re Colt Telecom Group plc* [2002] EWHC 2815 (Ch.), December 20, 2002; *Feldbaum v McCrory Corp.* [1992] Del. Ch. Lexis 113).

rule even where the head trustee knows of the existence and ultimate entitlement of the beneficiary, it is even more necessary to adhere to it where, as in the case of tiered holdings of securities, the intermediary at each level knows only of, and deals only with, its own customers, not customers of lower-tier intermediaries. Indeed, even if an intermediary did know of a lower-tier customer it could not be expected either to reveal information about its own customer in breach of its duty of confidentiality or to concern itself with the lower-tier customer's rights so as to inhibit its obedience to transfer instructions given by its own customer. The concept of the securities entitlement identifies the securities intermediary as the exclusive source of the customer's rights and removes the temptation to think of him as having rights which are traceable up the chain of intermediaries. Professor Rogers has shown that in practice this would be difficult, if not impossible, not merely because an intermediary will not have knowledge of any customers other than its own but also because, with netting arrangements and sourcing of the same securities from different intermediaries, there is no reliable way of establishing the links in the chain.[39] Also the applicable law could differ from tier to tier.

Thus any interest the investor may ultimately have in the underlying security is derived only from his own intermediary, not from the issuer or a higher-tier intermediary. If, therefore, the investor's intermediary never acquired a valid title from its own intermediary or if, though it did, it has dissipated its security holdings, the investor is left with a purely personal remedy, while in the case of a shortfall the interests of all investors holding accounts with that intermediary abate proportionately. Again, the investor's entitlement against its own intermediary may become subject to contractual set-off. To allow the investor to by-pass his own intermediary by recourse direct to the issuer or to a higher-tier intermediary would be to risk treating him as having rights in the underlying security which he had never acquired and promoting him above those having a better right and would also interfere with the ability of the issuer and higher-tier intermediaries to honour their own contractual obligations. Moreover, it would be wholly impracticable, with a large and rapid turnover of transactions, for anyone other than the investor's own intermediary to be able to verify within the limited time available that the investor did indeed have an interest in the securities.

Detachment of the securities entitlement from the underlying security also enables us to see that the customer is the legal holder of the contractual rights conferred on him by the account agreement and that, in contrast to the position as regards any proprietary interest he may have, he may make a statutory assignment of his contractual rights.[40] Again, the priority of successive

6–14

---

[39] James Steven Rogers, "Of Normalcy and Anomaly: Thoughts on Choice of Law for the Indirect Holding System," *The Oxford Colloquium on the Conflict of Laws*, A Special Supplement to Butterworths Journal of International Banking and Financial Law, September 1998, p.47. "Policy Perspectives on Revised U.C.C. Article 8", 43 UCLA L. Rev. 1431 (1996). See also Steven L. Schwarcz, "Intermediary Risk in a Global Economy" 50 Duke L.J. 1541 (2001).

[40] It will be recalled that a transfer of legal title to registered shares themselves may be effected only by a novation through entry of the transfer on the register of the issuer or, in the case of dematerialised securities, and not by assignment. See above, para.3–14.

assignments of a securities account will be governed by the rule in *Dearle v Hall* if such assignments are not prohibited by the terms of the custody agreement.[41] Finally, the concept establishes the source and location of the entitlement for conflict of laws purposes, whereas if this is conceived as a direct entitlement to the securities themselves there is a danger that the entitlement will be treated as derived from the issuer and will therefore be governed by the issuer's law. The better view, and that which reflects the realities of the market place, is that embodied in the place of relevant intermediary approach (PRIMA), *i.e.* that the relevant law is that of the place of the relevant intermediary.[42] This is fully in accordance with general conflict of laws principles, which looks to the place of the root of title.[43] In the case of directly held registered shares, the root of title is the register maintained by the company,[44] so that the law of the company's place of incorporation applies; in the case of bearer securities, the root of title is the certificate and the applicable law is the *lex situs* of the securities at the time of the relevant dealing; in the case of indirectly held registered securities, the root of title is the securities account with the intermediary, hence the PRIMA law.

This principle that the securities account is the root of title was applied by Stein J. in the US District Court for the Southern District of New York in *Fidelity Partners Inc. v First Trust Company of New York*.[45] In that case a global bond issued by the Republic of the Philippines was payable in New York, a bank in Manila held an interest in the bond through an account with Morgan Guaranty as operator of Euroclear and the judgment debtor held a participation interest through an account with the Manila bank. It was held that in proceedings in the United States a judgment creditor could not levy execution against an account held by the judgment debtor outside the United States, nor could it require other intermediaries to deliver definitive certificates to the judgment creditor, since none of them carried on its books an account in the name of the judgment debtor. In short, the judgment debtor's entitlement was derived from its account with its own intermediary and not from any other source.

It is significant that PRIMA is now embodied in Art.9(2) of the 1998 EC Settlement Finality Directive[46] and Art.9 of the 2002 Directive on Financial Collateral Arrangements[47] as well as in the 2002 Hague Convention on the law applicable to certain rights in respect of securities held with an interme-

---

[41] In practice securities intermediaries usually prohibit assignment and decline to accept notice of assignment, so that the giving of a notice has no perfection effect and the rule in *Dearle v Hall* does not apply.

[42] See generally Richard Potok, *Cross Border Collateral: Legal Risk and the Conflict of Laws*; *The Oxford Colloquium on the Conflict of Laws, loc. cit.*; Dicey & Morris, *The Conflict of Laws* (13th ed.), paras 24–063 *et seq.* PRIMA is also the underlying approach adopted in the 2002 Hague Convention on the law applicable to certain rights in respect of securities held with an intermediary, but the parties can designate the applicable law. See below, para.6–46.

[43] *i.e.* the best evidence of title, though not necessarily conclusive.

[44] Or in the case of CREST securities, by CREST.

[45] 58 F.Supp 2d 52 (1997). See also above, para.6–13, n.38.

[46] Directive on settlement finality in payment and settlement systems, 98/26. See below, para.6–35.

[47] 2002/47. See below, para.6–36.

diary.[48] Moreover, the 2002 Directive, which refers to indirectly held securities as "book entry securities collateral", defines this as "financial collateral provided under a financial collateral arrangement which consists of financial instruments, title to which is evidenced by entries in a register or account maintained by or on behalf of an intermediary."[49] Nothing could make it clearer that for indirectly held securities it is the account, not the share register, that is the root of title.

Since English commercial law is anything if not practical, we can reasonably conclude that subject to the terms of the agreement between him and the securities intermediary, the credit of securities to a customer's securities account entitles him to a co-ownership interest in the bundle of rights held by the intermediary itself (from its own intermediary or, if none, from the issuer direct), coupled with a personal right to the delivery or transfer, or re-delivery or re-transfer, of the deposited securities, and consequent restoration of the customer's direct link with the issuer, but no rights against any other intermediaries. The nature of the investor's entitlement does not depend on whether the intermediary holds the interest as bare trustee or as trustee with dealing powers under a discretionary management agreement, though in the latter case a bona fide purchaser for value will take free of the beneficial interest, even if aware of it, unless he knows that the disposition to him was in breach of trust.

As previously mentioned,[50] a charge on a securities entitlement is not registrable under the Companies Act as regards the securities themselves but might be registrable as a charge on book debts in relation to any dividends or other cash distributions received by the intermediary. However, if there is such a requirement at present it will have to be dispensed with when the 2002 EC Directive is implemented, since this precludes Member States from imposing special perfection requirements such as registration in a public register as regards the provision of cash or financial instruments as collateral.[51]

(2) Holdings in a segregated (non-fungible) account

Suppose now that the customer's holding is in a segregated, or non-fungible, account, so that the holding does not form part of the pool of securities which its intermediary holds with its own intermediary but is reflected in a separate account showing that the lower-tier intermediary's holding is for the customer, not for itself or for customers generally. Does this affect the previous analysis? It is generally taken that it does, but for the wrong reason, and this is because of the misconception to which I have previously referred, that shares are individual, mutually exchangeable assets, so that a share in a

6–15

---

[48] Though in the interests of predictability Art.4(1) of the Convention applies to the various issues specified in Art.2(1) of the Convention the law selected by the parties to govern the account agreement. See below, para.6–46.

[49] Art.2(1)(g).

[50] See above, para.3–27.

[51] See below, para.6–39. But floating charges would still be registrable. See below, para.6–38.

common pool is a fungible whereas a share in a non-fungible account is held in individual ownership rather than co-ownership. Now that we have seen that a share is merely a co-ownership interest in the issuer's share capital, not a separate item of property, it will be apparent that what the investor holding a share entitlement in a non-fungible account possesses is the same as that held by participants in a common pool, namely a co-ownership interest in the issuer's share capital, not sole ownership of an interest in identified shares. Nevertheless the segregation in a non-fungible account may have legal consequences. Where, for example, the intermediary wrongfully disposes of part of the pooled funds, the disposition will not affect the holder of the non-fungible account.

Bearer securities held indirectly

6–16   Bearer bonds and other bearer securities originally in the investor's possession may be delivered to the investor's securities intermediary and replaced by a credit to the investor's securities account. The intermediary becomes the legal holder of the securities and thus occupies the direct relationship with the issuer previously enjoyed by the investor, except that its role is limited to arrangements for collection and distribution of payments and does not extend to the exercise of voting rights, which are exercised through a proxy to its account holders and sub-proxies given to the latter by lower-tier account holders.

    We are now in a position to examine the attachment, perfection and priority of security interests in investment securities, whether held directly or through a securities intermediary and in the former case whether held in certificated or uncertificated form. It will be assumed in what follows that the mortgage or charge is a not a floating mortgage or charge and that it is not given to secure the issue of a series of debentures. In either of these cases it would require registration under s.395 of the Companies Act 1985 in addition to any other mode of perfection.

3. CHARACTERISATION ISSUES RELATING TO TRANSFERS AND RE-TRANSFERS

6–17   In the securities industry it is common for securities to be transferred upon terms of re-transfer at a later date. The three principal types of arrangement are sale and repurchase ("repo"), sell/buy-back (also called buy/sell-back) and stock lending. The flow of dealings in international securities between parties regularly engaged in such transactions is usually governed by one of the forms of standard-term master agreement, with relevant annexes, issued by a global trade association. For repos and sell/buy-backs parties typically use one of the master agreements/annexes issued by the Bond Market Association (TBMA) in association with the International Securities Market

Association (ISMA),[52] while for stock lending the standard form is that issued by the International Securities Lenders Association (ISLA).[53]

Repos, sell/buy-backs and stock loans[54]

(1) Repos and sell/buy-backs

The classic repo is a sale of securities under an agreement by which the securities are to be repurchased at a later date at a repurchase price equal to the original sale price but with a separate additional payment equivalent to interest at a specified repo rate. The repo may be for a fixed term, which can range from overnight to a year or more, or it may be an open-term repo in which the buyer can renew its retain of the securities from day-to-day. The sell/buy-back is a form of repo in which the repurchase price, instead of being the same as the original sale price, is a forward price which consists of the aggregate of the original sale price and an interest equivalent. So the interest element is not a separate add-on, as in the case of the classic repo, but forms an element of the calculation of the repurchase price. However, the commercial objectives of the two types of transaction are broadly the same, namely, on the part of the seller to raise funds and, on the part of the buyer, to earn money through the finance charge.

6–18

(2) Stock lending

Stock lending differs from the repo both in its commercial purposes and in its legal characterisation. Whereas a repo is driven by a need for cash, the purpose of the stock loan is, from the perspective of the borrower, to cover a short position in the securities in question and, from the perspective of the lender, to put securities for which it has no immediate need to profitable use through a charge for the loan. A stock loan does not involve a sale for a money price and a repurchase for a money price. It is simply a transfer of ownership of securities[55] against an undertaking by the transferee to retransfer them at a later date and to pay a fixed fee for the loan.[56] Apart from the fee no money consideration is involved in either leg of the transaction.

6–19

---

[52] The current version is the TBMA/ISMA global master repurchase agreement 2000.

[53] The current version is the ISLA global master securities lending agreement 2000.

[54] See generally Moorad Choudry, *The Repo Handbook*, for a comprehensive treatment of repo, sell/buy-back and stock lending transactions.

[55] It is sometimes said that because of the transfer of ownership the label "stock lending" is a misnomer. This is a misconception. A loan is not the same as a bailment. It involves the transfer of ownership followed by retransfer at a later date (the typical case is the loan of money), whereas under a bailment the bailee acquires a purely possessory interest and ownership remains with the bailor.

[56] It is also usual for the borrower to provide collateral as security for its re-transfer obligation, typically either other securities or cash.

Title transfer and "pledge"

6–20   In the securities industry there are two principal forms of collateral, namely title transfer and "pledge". But we need to be aware of the difference between commercial and legal terminology. First, in the case of title transfer the word "collateral" is used to signify the commercial purpose of the transaction, namely the provision of security, whereas in law the transfer, being outright, does not constitute a security interest. Secondly, the word "pledge" is an industry term to cover the provision of security otherwise than by title transfer and is not limited to its legal meaning of possessory security.

(1) *Title transfer*

6–21   Although the securities industry treats repos and sell/buy-backs as secured transactions in terms of commercial purpose and economic effect, in law the outright transfer of ownership, if that is what is genuinely intended by the parties, is not converted into a security interest merely because the transfer agreement incorporates a repurchase obligation.[57] To reinforce this, the documentation usually includes an express provision that no security interest is intended. The reason why the repo and sell/buy-back are regarded commercially as secured transactions is that the parties safeguard themselves against the effect of a default—by the buyer in failing to resell or by the seller in failing to pay the repurchase price—by a close-out provision by which the resale/repurchase obligation is converted into a money obligation and the two money obligations set off against each other and reduced to a net balance payable by one party to the other.

From the viewpoint of the repo buyer title transfer has certain advantages over a pledge. First, as absolute owner the buyer can do what it likes with the purchased securities without having to stipulate for rights of sale or "use".[58] Secondly, possible registration requirements[59] are avoided.

While repos and sell/buy-backs involve an outright transfer of ownership, this is not true of all title transfers. Securities may be mortgaged by a security transfer of title, either off the register or by novation through entry of the mortgagee on the issuer's register.[60] Usually the mortgage will take the form

---

[57] See above, para.1–37. I have expressed the view earlier (above, para.6–09) that, contrary to the general understanding, what is retransferred on the reverse leg of the transaction is not simply the *equivalent* of the securities originally transferred but the identical securities, since the holding of securities is no more than co-ownership of a single asset, the issued share or loan capital relating to the issue in question. Accordingly the immunity of title transfer from attack as a security interest rests solely on the fact that it is intended as an outright transfer of ownership, not on any argument that the seller does not have a right to repurchase the same asset as that which it transferred.

[58] See further below, para.6–30, as to the right of use.

[59] See below.

[60] Or in the case of securities held indirectly through an account with an intermediary, by transfer from the mortgagor's account to an account in the name of the mortgagee. See below, para.6–28.

of a fixed security interest,[61] and will therefore not fall within any category of charge registrable under s.395 of the Companies Act 1985, except, perhaps, as regards dividend or interest entitlements, which might conceivably be regarded as book debts. However, under the EC Financial Collateral Directive Member States will be required to abolish all such registration requirements in relation to securities transactions covered by the Directive.[62]

(2) *"Pledge"*

In law, only bearer securities can be pledged, since a pledge requires the delivery of actual or constructive possession. But the term "pledge" is widely used to include what in English law would be considered a charge.   **6–22**

The comments made above concerning the non-registrability of mortgages of securities apply equally to pledges and charges.

4. SECURITY INTERESTS IN DIRECTLY HELD SECURITIES

Certificated registered securities

(1) *Attachment and perfection*

A security interest in certificated registered securities directly held by the debtor may be created either on or off the register. An equitable mortgage or charge may be effected by a transfer of ownership to the mortgage by way of security or by an agreement for transfer or for a charge. An off-register mortgage of registered securities takes effect in equity only, while a charge is necessarily equitable. Almost invariably the secured creditor will protect himself by taking a deposit of the share certificate and procuring the debtor's execution of a blank transfer form, which in case of need the creditor can complete by designating himself or a third party as transferee and lodge with the issuer for registration. Execution of the transfer is not an ingredient in the creation of the mortgage or charge, solely a means by which the creditor can get himself or a third party (*e.g.* the creditor's nominee or securities intermediary) on the register and thereby perfect his title. Registration converts the equitable mortgagee or chargee into a mortgagee by novation.[63] A mortgage by an   **6–23**

---

[61] For the possible effect of rights of substitution, see below, para.6–31.

[62] See below, para.6–39.

[63] Since what is registered is a transfer, the security interest is necessarily a legal mortgage, not a charge. A mortgagee is trustee of the mortgagor's equity of redemption and is therefore not entitled, in the absence of agreement, to look to any surplus resulting from realisation of the security to satisfy by way of set-off other, unsecured obligations of the debtor, since set-off is available only against money claims, not against property claims. See above, paras 1–40 and 1–69. The creditor should therefore obtain a general set-off agreement or alternatively, if there are mutual redelivery obligations, an agreement that for the purpose of settling

off-register assignment is also possible but is a vulnerable form of security in that the company is neither obliged nor entitled to register a notice of assignment, so that the rule in *Dearle v Hall* does not apply[64] and the mortgagee, as an equitable mortgagee, will be subordinate to a prior equitable mortgage or charge. Where the creditor has the transfer registered in the name of its nominee or intermediary, the latter will hold the legal title and the creditor will be the beneficial owner, in each case in common with others holding an interest in securities of the same issue.

Can certificated registered shares be mortgaged or charged back to the issuer to secure a loan by the issuer? As we have seen,[65] there is now considered to be no conceptual problem in doing this, but there are statutory restrictions. The general rule is that a company cannot acquire its own shares and any purported acquisition, whether by purchase, subscription or otherwise,[66] is void.[67] Moreover, the prohibition cannot be bypassed by taking the shares in the name of a nominee, for if this is done the shares are to be treated as held by the nominee on his own account and the company is to be regarded as having no beneficial interest in them.[68] However, a private company may provide in its articles for a lien or charge on shares to secure payments due to it, whether in respect of the shares or otherwise,[69] and while a lien or charge to a public company on its own shares is usually void,[70] a charge on the shares is permitted *(inter alia)* where the ordinary business of the company includes the lending of money or the provision of credit or hire-purchase if the charge arises in connection with a transaction entered into by the company in the ordinary course of its business.[71] In this context, "charge" would seem to bear its technical meaning of an incumbrance, as opposed to a mortgage, the grant of which would offend against the rule that a company cannot acquire its own shares. The charge may be enforced by sale of the shares.[72]

(2) *Priorities*

6–24 The normal priority rules apply. While the security interest is merely equitable it is subordinate to a prior equitable interest under the first-in-time

---

accounts these are to be converted into obligations to pay current market value, thus allowing of set-off. This position may change with the 2002 EC Directive on financial collateral arrangements. See below, paras 6–41, 6–44.

[64] See above, para.5–08.

[65] See above, paras 1–40, 3–12.

[66] These words would seem to preclude a mortgage of shares to the company, as opposed to a charge or lien. See below.

[67] Companies Act 1985, s.143(1),(2). Under s.143(3)(d) a company may forfeit or accept the surrender of shares, if so permitted by the articles, but only for failure to pay sums in respect of the shares.

[68] *ibid.*, s.144(1).

[69] See Boyle and Sykes (eds), *Gore-Browne on Companies*, para.14.11.

[70] Companies Act 1985, s.150(1).

[71] *ibid.*, s.150(3). It is necessary in addition for the charge to be authorised by the articles.

[72] In theory they may also be forfeited and cancelled, but this involves a reduction of capital and requires confirmation by the court.

rule[73] and is also liable to be displaced by a subsequent mortgage or sale to a third party who acquires them in good faith, for value and without notice and becomes registered as the holder. This could occur where the debtor fraudulently procures a fresh share certificate by misrepresenting that he has lost the original. A mortgagee with notice of prior equitable interests takes subject to them. However, if in the latter case the mortgagee grants a sub-mortgage and the sub-mortgagee is registered as transferee and takes without notice of the equitable interests he will have priority even though the mortgagee himself was subordinated.

Bearer securities

Bearer securities may be pledged or mortgaged by delivery, which simultaneously produces attachment and perfection of the security interest. The pledgee or mortgagee acquires in the case of pledge a limited legal interest and in the case of mortgage legal title by way of security. Alternatively bearer securities may be charged by an agreement for charge, with or without delivery, though delivery is necessary if the charge is to be perfected. It is also possible to assign bearer securities without delivery, but such an assignment takes effect only in equity and is displaced by a subsequent mortgage perfected by delivery.[74]   **6–25**

Bearer debt securities[75] may be pledged or mortgaged back to the issuer by delivery, which again perfects the security interest. On default they may be sold to a third party.

Uncertificated securities

(1) *Attachment and perfection*

Again, an equitable security interest in uncertificated securities directly held by the debtor may be created by an off-register mortgage or an equitable charge. An equitable mortgage is converted into a legal mortgage, and thereby perfected, by transfer from the mortgagor's stock account with CREST to the mortgagee's stock account or, if the mortgagee is not a CREST member or sponsored member, to the stock account of his nominee.[76] An equitable charge can be converted into a legal mortgage in the same way; alternatively it may retain its status as an equitable charge and be perfected by transfer of the   **6–26**

---

[73] See n.40, above. The rule in *Dearle v Hall* does not apply. See para.5–08.

[74] See above, para.5–28.

[75] Bearer shares are rarely issued in the UK because of their exposure to stamp duty, and in any event a purported mortgage of them would be void under s.143 of the Companies Act 1985. The prohibition does not apply to debt securities.

[76] Security agreements may provide for collateral transferred to the creditor or its nominee to be held in a segregated account, separate from the creditor's beneficially owned holdings, to avoid problems arising from commingling of the creditor's assets and the assets subject to the debtor's equity of redemption in the event of the creditor's insolvency.

charged securities to a sub-account as an escrow balance, the sub-account being in the name of the chargor but under the control of another member of CREST who is the chargee's escrow agent. CREST itself has no involvement in the escrow balance. On default the escrow agent can transfer the shares into the creditor's name if he is a CREST member. If the debt is discharged without recourse to the escrow balance this is transferred back to the chargor's main account. CREST does not accept notices of assignment, so although the debtor can effect a mortgage by assignment rather than by transfer to the account of the creditor or his nominee there is no way of perfecting the assignment, and the priority of successive assignments is governed not by the rule in *Dearle v Hall* but by the first-in-time rule.

The rules governing a charge-back of certificated securities to the issuer[77] apply equally to a charge-back of uncertificated securities.

(2) *Priority rules*

6–27 The priority rules are the same as for certificated securities.

5. SECURITY INTERESTS IN INDIRECTLY HELD SECURITIES

Certificated securities

6–28 Where securities are held indirectly by credit to a securities account they may be mortgaged by transfer to the mortgagee,[78] who thereby acquires a legal mortgage by novation, or charged by agreement, the charge being perfected by the agreement of the intermediary to allow the account to be operated only on the instructions of the chargee[79] or alternatively by transfer of part of the securities to a separate account in the name of the chargor but under the chargee's control. The securities could also be mortgaged by an assignment of the account, perfected by notice of assignment to the intermediary, but this has the disadvantage that the mortgagee takes subject to equities, including any rights of set-off the intermediary may have for cross-claims in respect of dealings prior to receipt of the notice of assignment. A security interest in indirectly held securities is perfected by notice of assignment to the securities intermediary or by transfer into the name of the creditor (novation). It is unlikely that a security interest given by a company will be considered registrable under s.395 of the Companies Act 1985.[80]

---

[77] See above, para.6–23.

[78] An in-house transfer if the mortgagee has an account with the same intermediary, or if not, a transfer to the mortgagee's intermediary through a common higher-tier intermediary. See above, para.6–02, n.6.

[79] *i.e.* an attornment. See above, para.3–34.

[80] Even assuming that a securities entitlement was held to be an interest in the underlying securities, charges on securities are not registrable as such. A security interest in the form of a

Priorities are governed by the normal rules. So a mortgagee by novation has priority over an earlier equitable interest of which he has no notice, while priority as between successive assignees is governed by the rule in *Dearle v Hall*.

Uncertificated securities

If the debtor holds uncertificated securities in CREST through an intermedi- **6–29**
ary and the creditor is a CREST member he may obtain a legal mortgage by having the securities transferred to his CREST stock account. All other modes of security—for example, transfer to the creditor's CREST nominee, transfer to a sub-account of the debtor as an escrow balance under the control of the creditor's escrow agent, or assignment of the debtor's security entitlement, perfected by notice of assignment to the debtor's intermediary—take effect in equity only, the first and third of these operating as an equitable mortgage, the second as an equitable charge. The priority rules are the same as for indirectly held certificates securities.

6. RIGHTS OF USE AND SUBSTITUTION

Right of use/re-hypothecation

The liquidity of the market is increased if a party taking an interest in secu- **6–30**
rities as collateral is given a right to "use" or "re-hypothecate" the collateral, which is generally understood in a broad sense to include outright sale or the grant of a sub-mortgage or sub-charge. Securities agreements commonly provide for such a right. In the absence of agreement, whether express or implied from a course of dealing or from market usage, a collateral taker is not allowed to make an outright disposal of the collateral unless the power of sale has become exercisable by statute.[81] However, it is open to the parties to agree that the mortgagee is to have a power of sale even without default, and such an agreement is not void as impairing the equity of redemption,[82]

---

floating charge is registrable but the documentation is usually effective to ensure that what is created is a fixed security. The only other possible category of registrable interest is a charge on book debts, but while security entitlements are assignable both at law and in equity they are not book debts, since they are entitlements to an interest in securities, not to money, except possibly as to dividends, interest and the like received as cash into the securities account.

[81] See Law of Property Act 1925, s.101, which is almost invariably displaced by an express power of sale. See further para.6–43 as to the right of use.

[82] *The Maule* [1977] 1 W.L.R. 528. See also *Langton v Waite* (1868) L.R. 6 Eq. 165, where the court held that until the time came for redelivery a broker had no right to sell stock mortgaged to secure a margin loan "in the absence of express contract," which plainly implies that the broker could have contracted for a right of sale. There seems no good reason why the right of sale should be express; it suffices that it is a term of the contract, express or implied.

which simply attaches to the proceeds of sale. The mortgagee ought normally to give notice before selling, though presumably even this can be dispensed with by agreement where it is not oppressive but part of normal market practice. The collateral taker is always free to sub-mortgage or sub-charge the securities without the debtor's consent, for this constitutes simply a dealing with his own security interest and takes effect subject to the debtor's equity of redemption.

Under Art.5 of the 2002 Directive on Financial Collateral Arrangements, Member States are required to ensure that the collateral taker is entitled to exercise a right of use (including sale) provided under the collateral arrangement.[83] Irrespective of implementation of the Directive the very existence of Art.5 should make it abundantly clear that conferment of a right of re-use is standard international practice and is not open to attack on public policy grounds.

Withdrawal and substitution

6–31 It is also common to have provisions in the security agreement permitting the debtor to withdraw securities to the extent that what is held by the creditor exceeds a given margin and also to substitute new securities for those comprised in the agreement. A question much discussed by English legal practitioners is whether the conferment of rights of withdrawal or substitution converts the charge into a floating charge, with potentially adverse consequences if the charge has not been registered.

(1) *Withdrawal of excess securities*

6–32 The debtor may wish to withdraw excess securities in order to take advantage of a rise in the market value of the securities or to avail itself of other market opportunities, such as additional income through stock lending. This does not, it is submitted, convert the charge into a floating charge. The debtor is not being given a general release in advance to deal with the securities in the ordinary course of business. These remain firmly in the creditor's control, and while the debtor has a contractual right to withdraw the excess securities this will only be allowed after checks (typically computerised) to ensure that the excess does indeed exist and other agreed criteria are met.

The 2002 EC Directive makes it clear that any right to withdraw excess financial collateral does not mean that the financial collateral has not been provided to the collateral taker as mentioned in the Directive.[84]

---

[83] See below, para.6–43.
[84] Directive on Financial Collateral Arrangements, 2002/47, Art.2(2).

(2) *Substitution*

For reasons similar to those relating to withdrawal of securities the debtor is **6–33** commonly provided with the right to substitute new securities for those subject to the security interest and to dispose of the latter as his own. A general advance authorisation to do this should be avoided as it risks converting the security interest into a floating charge. It is therefore very desirable to stipulate that the release of any securities by the creditor is dependent on the debtor having first furnished the substitute securities.[85] This not only gives the creditor a unit-by-unit control which preserves the fixed nature of the security, it also avoids exposure to the risk that the debtor, having disposed of the original securities, fails to provide substitutes.

The 2002 EC Directive makes it clear that the provision of a right of substitution does not prejudice the security given to the collateral taker as provided by the Directive.[86]

7. THE EC DIRECTIVES ON FINANCIAL COLLATERAL

The European Community has long been concerned to limit systemic risk[87] **6–34** to ensure both the efficiency and the stability of dealings among participants in recognised clearing and settlement systems. To that end two Directives have been issued, the 1998 Settlement Finality Directive[88] and the 2002 Directive on Financial Collateral Arrangements.[89] The latter in particular is designed to override rules of national law that impair the legal efficacy of financial collateral arrangements and provision within or outside insolvency.

The Settlement Finality Directive

The effect of the Directive and implementing regulations is largely to remove **6–35** from attack under general insolvency law the rules of a designated settlement system, and transactions (including the realisation of collateral security) effected in connection with participation in such a system. Thus system rules governing default arrangements, in particular, arrangements for netting and the closing out of open positions,[90] and the application or transfer of

---

[85] Or provided some other form of protection.

[86] Directive on Financial Collateral Arrangements, Art.2(2) (see below). The French text is clearer than the English on this point.

[87] The risk that the failure of one major participant will have a domino effect on the system as a whole.

[88] Directive on Settlement Finality in Payment and Securities Systems (98/26 dated May 19, 1998), implemented in the UK by the Financial Markets and Insolvency (Settlement Finality) Regulations 1999, SI 199/2979. The regulations were amended by SI 2001/997 but for technical reasons revoked immediately on the date of entry into force by SI 2001/1349.

[89] 2002/47. No regulations have yet been made implementing this Directive, which requires implementation within 18 months of its entry into force.

[90] See below, Ch.VII.

collateral security,[91] are to be respected notwithstanding any rules of insolvency law which might otherwise invalidate them. Thus the restrictions imposed by ss.10(1)(b) and 11(3)(c) of the Insolvency Act 1986 on the enforcement of security while a petition for an administration order is pending or the order is in force do not apply in relation to a collateral security charge,[92] and s.127 of the Act (which invalidates dispositions made after the commencement of a winding up unless approved by the court) does not apply to a disposition of property as the result of which it becomes subject to a collateral security charge.[93] Of some importance also is the conflict of laws rule embodied in Art.9(2) of the Directive[94] which provides that where securities are provided as collateral to a (system) participant and/or central bank of a Member State and their right with respect to the securities is legally recorded in a register, account or centralised deposit system located in a Member State the rights of holders of the collateral are to be determined by the law of that Member State. One effect of this is that concerning rights in relation to securities held through an account with a securities intermediary in a Member State, it is the PRIMA law[95] that applies.

The Settlement Finality Directive will require some revision in the light of Art.4 of the 2002 Hague Convention on indirectly held securities.[96]

The Directive on Financial Collateral Arrangements

6–36   The 2002 Directive on financial collateral arrangements is altogether broader and more ambitious in scope. Its purpose is to facilitate the provision of financial collateral under bilateral transactions, and thereby promote not only the stability of the market but also its efficiency, by requiring Member States to disapply rules of law and statutory provisions that would otherwise invalidate financial collateral arrangements and provision, whether before insolvency (as by rendering void transactions not carried out or perfected in conformity with prescribed formalities) or on insolvency. The Directive covers both directly held and indirectly held securities. Regrettably an understanding of the Directive is somewhat impeded by technical defects, linguistic problems in the English text and the practice of placing in the Preamble substantive rules of interpretation which should be in the text,[97] coupled with a measure of duplication of provisions[98] and inconsistency of terminology.[99]

---

[91] Including security provided under a charge or repurchase or similar agreement for the purpose of securing rights and obligations potentially arising in connection with the system.

[92] Financial Markets and Insolvency (Settlement Finality) Regulations 1999, SI 1999/2979, reg.19(1).

[93] *ibid.*, reg.19(3).

[94] Implemented in the UK by reg.23 of the Financial Markets and Insolvency (Settlement Finality) Regulations 1999. It is likely that Art.9(2) will be modified in the light of the Hague Convention on the law applicable to certain rights held with an intermediary.

[95] See above, para.6–13; below, para.6–46.

[96] See below, para.6–46.

[97] For example, Art.3(1) can be fully understood only by reference to paras (9) and (10) of the Preamble. See below, para.6–39.

[98] *e.g.* Art.3(2) repeats the substance of Art.1(5).

[99] *e.g.* in relation to the express of formal requirements. See below.

Nevertheless the Directive is to be warmly welcomed as a great step forward in ensuring the legal stability of financial collateral arrangements and provision.

(1) *Scope of the Directive*

The Directive covers financial collateral in the form of cash or financial **6–37** instruments.[1] It distinguishes between arrangements for the provision of collateral and its actual provision. The Directive applies only when the collateral has actually been provided and only where the provision is evidenced in writing[2] and the collateral arrangement (*i.e.* agreement) is evidenced in writing or in a legally equivalent manner.[3] Moreover, though this will be found only in the Preamble,[4] financial collateral is to be considered "provided" only where there is some form of dispossession, by which is meant that the collateral is delivered, transferred, held, registered or otherwise designated so as to be in the possession or under the control of the collateral taker or of a person acting on his behalf.[5] In short, the security interest must be not only created but perfected by possession or control. Until then, the Directive has no application and the efficacy of the security interest is left to national law. All the methods of possession or control referred to represent methods of perfection available under existing English law, as previously described.

(2) *Categories of financial collateral arrangement*

Financial collateral arrangements are divided into two categories, title trans- **6–38** fer financial collateral arrangements and security ("book-entry") financial collateral arrangements. The former are arrangements, including repurchase agreements, under which full ownership is transferred to the collateral taker.[6] This reflects the securities industry's usage in treating title transfer as a form of collateral even though in English law an outright transfer does not

---

[1] Art.1(4)(a). "Financial instruments" are defined in Art.2(1)(e) and cover virtually all forms of instrument issued on a market.

[2] This requires that the financial collateral be identifiable, which in the case of book-entry securities or cash is satisfied by crediting to an account.

[3] The Directive uses the phrase "can be evidenced in writing", which is a somewhat unusual way of saying that it *is* evidenced *in* writing. This does not mean the agreement must be in writing, merely that if it is made orally or inferred from conduct there must be written evidence of it. It is not clear why the phrase "or in a legally equivalent manner" appears in reference to arrangements for the provision of collateral but not in relation to the provision itself, nor what the phrase adds, given that by Art.2(3) "writing" includes recording by electronic means and any other durable medium.

[4] Para.(10).

[5] Para.(9). The same paragraph makes it clear that this requirement is not to exclude techniques for the substitution of collateral or withdrawal of excess collateral by the collateral provider. See further below.

[6] Some countries do not recognise the grant of security by title transfer. Art.6 requires Member States to ensure that a title transfer financial collateral arrangement can take effect in accordance with its terms.

constitute a security interest.[7] Security financial collateral arrangements ought logically to have been defined as arrangements for the provision of security not involving the transfer of full ownership. Unfortunately they are instead defined as arrangements for the provision of security where full ownership of the collateral remains with the collateral provider. Literally construed, this would exclude the transfer of ownership by way of security, *i.e.* in English law terms a mortgage, which would thus fall outside the Directive altogether. Plainly this is not intended.

In the case of direct holdings, outright title transfer is by entry on the share register; in the case of indirect, or book-entry, holdings title transfer presumably includes not only transfer by novation, that is, transfer to the collateral taker's account, but also assignment. As stated above, title transfer arrangements do not include mortgages, which transfer only security ownership, not full ownership, but do include outright sale and repurchase agreements which are intended to fulfil a security function even if not, under English law, constituting security agreements.[8] Security financial collateral arrangements are, in English law terms, arrangements which create charges or, in the case of bearer securities, pledges, and must also be taken to include mortgages even though on a literal construction these fall outside the definition. However, floating charges would appear to be outside the scope of the Directive, at least until crystallisation, since the requisite element of transfer of control to the creditor is lacking.[9]

(3) *Reduction of formalities*

6–39 One of the main purposes of the Directive is to reduce the requirements for attachment and perfection of a security interest in financial collateral to a minimum. Art.3, of which the first paragraph is expressed in very wide terms, provides as follows:

> "1. Member States shall not require that the creation, validity, perfection, enforceability or admissibility in evidence of a financial collateral arrangement or the provision of financial collateral under a financial collateral arrangement be dependent on the performance of any formal act."

> "2. Paragraph 1 is without prejudice to the application of this Directive to financial collateral only once it has been provided and if that provision can be evidenced in writing and where the financial collateral arrangement can be evidenced in writing or in a legally equivalent manner."

Art.9(1) states the basic principle that no formal act is necessary for the creation, validity, etc. of a financial collateral arrangement or the provision of financial collateral. This, however, is subject to Art.9(2), which would have

---

[7] See above, paras 1–37, 6–02.
[8] See above, para.1–37.
[9] Joanna Benjamin and Madeleine Yates, *The Law of Global Custody* (2nd ed.), para.4.45.

been clearer if it had said simply that Art.9(1) takes effect subject to the provisions of Art.1(5). These, as stated above, make the application of the Directive dependent on collateral having been provided the provision of collateral. What Art.9(2) fails to state is that in order for the collateral to be considered as "provided", the collateral taker's interest must be perfected by some form of "dispossession" of the debtor if the Directive is to apply. The effect would seem to be that notwithstanding Art.9(1) national law continues to apply to the creation and validity of security interests but that once perfected by possession or control by the collateral taker the provision of financial collateral must be recognised even if not created by some formal art.

Art.9(1) must also be read in conjunction with the Preamble, which in effect states[10] that Member States may continue to require the creation or transfer of a security interest in financial collateral to be effected by acts such as endorsement of instruments to order[11] and registration of transfers of directly held securities, which for the purposes of the Directive are not formal acts, but that there should be no formalities for the attachment or perfection of transfers of or security interests in indirectly held (book-entry) securities. As to these it will no longer be open to a Member State to require that a document be executed in any particular form or in a particular manner, that the date of its execution or the amount of the relevant financial obligations be evidenced in any manner or that perfection of a security interest be dependent on registration in a public register, filing with or notification to a public officer, or advertisement. In fact there are currently no formal requirements under English law for the *attachment* of a security interest in registered securities, and formal perfection requirements in the shape of registration in the Companies Registry apply only to floating charges, charges on book debts and charges to secure any issue of debentures. Except in relation to floating charges, which are thought to be outside the scope of the Directive,[12] these requirements will disappear when the UK implements the Directive, thereby eliminating, for registration purposes, the risk of recharacterisation of a purported fixed security as a floating charge or of a sale and repurchase as a registrable security transaction.

(4) *Enforcement*

Member States are required to ensure that on the occurrence of an enforcement event[13] the collateral taker has available to a range of enforcement measures, subject to the parties' agreement. These measures are:

6–40

---

[10] Paras (9) and (10).

[11] Instruments payable to bearer are transferred by delivery without the need for any endorsement.

[12] See above, para.6–39.

[13] Defined by Art.2(1)(l) as an event of default or any similar event agreed between the parties on the occurrence of which, under the terms of a collateral financial arrangement or by operation of law, the collateral taker is entitled to realise or appropriate financial collateral or a

6–41   (a) *Financial instruments* Sale or appropriation, the value[14] being set off in discharge of the relevant financial obligation. Subject to the terms of the financial collateral arrangement, there must be no requirement under the law of a Member State that prior notice of the intention to realise must have been given, the terms of realisation approved by any court, public officer or any other person, the realisation be conducted by public auction or in any other prescribed manner or any additional time period must have elapsed.[15] The effect of this provision is to override any otherwise applicable restrictions on enforcement, *e.g.* those imposed as the result of an administration order. Appropriation[16] is available only if the parties have agreed it in the security financial collateral arrangements[17] and have there agreed on the valuation.[18] Member States which do not recognise appropriation are not obliged to recognise it. English law does not currently recognise appropriation, which is in effect a sale by the mortgagee to himself and therefore not permitted even if at full value.[19]

6–42   (b) *Cash* Set-off against, or application in discharge of, the relevant financial obligations.

(5) *Right of use*

6–43   A right of use, which is defined so as to include disposal as owner,[20] is required to be recognised if conferred on the collateral taker by the arrangement.[21] The collateral taker is required to replace the original collateral or its equivalent or, if the financial arrangement so provides, set off the value against the or apply it in discharge of the relevant financial obligation.[22]

---

close-out netting comes into force. Again, the drafting is a little strange, for read literally it does not cover a right of realisation given by law unless the relevant event is one agreed between the parties! This comes from the misplacing of the phrase "or by operation of law", which should have been inserted after "parties." It is thought that Art.2(1)(l) is be interpreted as if drafted in this way.

[14] The reference to "value" rather than "proceeds" as regards the remedy of sale is no doubt designed to protect the collateral provider against the risk of a sale at undervalue.

[15] Art.4(4).

[16] By which the creditor takes the asset in or towards satisfaction of the debt to the extent of its value. It differs from foreclosure (which under English law requires a court order) in that if the asset is lower in value than the obligation the collateral taker remains entitled to recover the deficiency, while if the value exceeds the obligation the collateral taker is accountable to the collateral provider for the surplus.

[17] It is not clear why this provision does not also apply to title transfer arrangements, since although the collateral taker will be the legal owner title is vested in him solely by way of security, not as absolute owner. This is linked to the problem described above, para.6–38.

[18] This is probably intended to refer to the method of valuation rather than an actual figure, which may be correct at the time of the arrangement but bear no relation to the true value at the time of appropriation.

[19] *Hodson v Deans* [1903] 2 Ch. 647; *Farrar v Farrars Ltd.* (1888) 40 Ch. D 395.

[20] Art.2(1)(m).

[21] Art.5. Exercise of the right extinguishes the debtor's interest.

[22] *ibid.*

(6) *Protection from insolvency avoidance*

Arts 7 and 8 are designed to protect the provision of financial collateral **6–44** against avoidance for insolvency. Art.7 requires Member States to ensure that a close-out netting provision can take effect in accordance with its terms notwithstanding the commencement or continuation of winding-up proceedings or reorganisation measures and other specified events. One effect of this provision is to preserve the validity of close-out netting provisions expressed to be triggered by the commencement of a winding-up. Art.8 of the Directive requires Member States to ensure that financial collateral arrangements are protected from avoidance under various rules of insolvency law, *e.g.* that the financial collateral arrangement has come into existence, or the financial collateral has been provided, within a prescribed period prior to, and defined by reference to, the commencement of winding-up proceedings, or that top-up collateral was provided on the day of commencement of the winding-up proceedings or after the relevant financial obligations had been incurred. Art.8 will require the disapplication of s.127 of the Insolvency Act 1986 (avoidance of post-petition dispositions) to financial collateral.

8. *CROSS-BORDER SECURITIES AND THE CONFLICT OF LAWS*

Introduction

Where dealings in securities involve a foreign element, so that it is necessary **6–45** to make a choice between legal systems, the applicable law is to be determined by the conflict of laws rules of the forum State. In England the applicable law depends on whether the securities are registered or bearer securities and, it is submitted for the reasons already given, on whether the securities are held directly or indirectly.[23]

In all cases concerning certificated (as opposed to dematerialised) securities it is necessary to distinguish title to the certificate from title to the underlying securities. Where certificates relating to securities are transferred, it is for the *lex situs* of the certificates at the time of transfer to determine the effect of the transfer on title to the certificate, but it is for the law of the issuer's incorporation to determine the manner in which the underlying securities may be transferred and thus whether they are to be characterised as registered securities or bearer securities.[24] So if the holding of UK registered bonds is evidenced by a certificate which is later delivered to Creditor A by way of pledge in New York and the bonds are later mortgaged in London to Creditor B, who in good faith is told by the bondholder that the certificate has been lost, takes a transfer and registers it with the issuer of the bonds, then while the efficacy of the pledge will be determined by New York law,

---

[23] See generally Maisie Ooi, *Shares and Other Securities in the Conflict of Laws.*
[24] See *Macmillan Inc. v Bishopsgate Investment Trust (No. 3)* [1996] 1 W.L.R. 387; Dicey & Morris, *The Conflict of Laws* (13th ed.), paras 22–044 and 22–045.

priority between A and B will be determined by English law and normally be accorded to B as bona fide holder for value of the legal title through registration, A's interest in the bonds (as opposed to the certificate as a piece of paper) being purely equitable. Again, if the bonds are issued as bearer bonds in London and the certificates are taken to New York and there pledged, an English court, having characterised the bonds under English law as bearer bonds transferable by delivery, will apply New York law as the *lex situs* to determine the efficacy of the pledge. Neither the two EC Directives referred to above nor the Hague Convention discussed below deal with conflict of laws issues in relation to directly held securities.

As regards indirectly held securities the EC financial collateral Directive, like the settlement finality Directive, applies PRIMA in determining the law applicable to dealings in securities involving a foreign element.[25] However, under the Hague Convention this is adopted in modified form to give effect to party choice.

The Hague Convention on the law applicable to indirectly held securities

6–46   The 2002 Hague Convention on the law applicable to certain rights in respect of securities held with an intermediary embodies PRIMA as the underlying concept except that the focus is now on the law selected by the parties to govern the account agreement,[26] subject to satisfaction of a so-called "reality test" which in essence requires that the intermediary in question carries on the business of maintaining securities account (though not necessarily the particular account in question) in the State whose law is selected.[27] The Convention determines the law applicable to the legal nature and effects against the intermediary and third parties of (a) the credit of securities to a securities account with an intermediary; and (b) a disposition of securities held with an intermediary, including charge-backs to the intermediary and perfection requirements and priority rules, as well as requirements for realisation of an interest in securities and whether a disposition of securities held with an intermediary extends to entitlements to dividends, income and other distributions. It also preserves the application of the PRIMA law to these issues notwithstanding the opening of an insolvency proceeding.

The Convention is limited to securities held with an intermediary and has no application to securities held directly from the issuer. It is confined to proprietary rights and does not extend to contractual or other personal rights. However, the question whether the account holder's rights against its interme-

---

[25] Art.9. This is also thought to reflect the position at common law. See above, para.6–14.

[26] Art.4(1).

[27] *ibid.* Art.5(1) provides an intermediate fallback rule if the parties fail to select a law or the selection is ineffective for want of compliance with the reality test, while Art.5(2) provides the ultimate fallback rule (place of the intermediary's incorporation, etc.) if neither of the previous rules applies. It is recognised that this will in many cases have little or no connection with the parties or transaction; its one merit is certainty, and it is envisaged that it will be triggered only in a very small percentage of cases.

diary are proprietary or personal is determined by the PRIMA law. If under that law the rights are characterised as purely personal the Convention has no further application as regards relations between the account holder and the intermediary but it continues to govern the legal nature and effects of a disposition of those personal rights, since the disposition is a transfer of property.

The approach adopted in the Hague Convention, which was borrowed from Art.8 of the Uniform Commercial Code, seems at first sight strange and counter-intuitive, since it is axiomatic in most legal systems that parties to a contract cannot select a law to govern the rights of third parties. Nevertheless, the solution has a number of advantages. It subjects the determination of all proprietary rights to the same law and by focusing on the (deemed) place of the account it reflects the well-established *lex situs* principle in the conflict of laws. Third parties proposing to purchase a securities entitlement or to take such entitlement as collateral for a loan will certainly want to have sight of the account agreement and will thereby be able to see the full terms of the agreement, including designation of the deemed place of the account.

VII

Set-Off, Netting and Abatement

1. SET-OFF: NATURE, CLASSIFICATION AND DEVELOPMENT

(i) Nature of set-off and netting

Set-off

Set-off is the right of a debtor who is owed money by his creditor on another **7–01** account or dealing to secure payment for what is owed to him by setting this off in reduction of his own liability.[1] For example, A sells raw materials to B to be made up into finished products which B then sells to A. If A owes B £1,000 for products sold and delivered to him but is owed £400 by B for raw materials then in any claim against him A is not obliged to pay B the £1,000 he owes and then sue separately for recovery of the £400 (or if B is in liquidation, prove in the liquidation in competition with other creditors) he is owed but may set off the latter sum against his indebtedness and discharge the debt by paying B (or B's liquidator) the balance of £600.

Set-off is available both outside and within bankruptcy and liquidation. In both cases it provides a speedy remedy to secure payment but the policy reason for providing the remedy depends on the type of set-off involved. Contractual set-off is recognised as an incident of party autonomy in the conclusion of contracts. The banker's right of combination is similar except that it derives from implied rather than express agreement. In the case of independent (or statutory) set-off[2] the remedy is given primarily to avoid

---

[1] See Philip Wood, *English and International Set-Off*, and *Law and Practice of International Finance: Title Finance, Derivatives, Securitsations, Set-Off and Netting*, Pt III; Rory Derham, *Set-Off* (3rd ed.); Shelagh McCracken, *Banker's Remedy of Set-Off* (2nd ed.). The leading early works are Richard Babington, *A Treatise on the Law of Set-Off* (1827); Basil Montagu, *Summary of the Law of Set-Off* (2nd ed., 1828); and two American publications, Oliver Barbour, *Treatise on the Law of Set-Off* (1841); and T. W. Waterman, *Treatise on the Law of Set-Off* (2nd ed., 1872). For historical and comparative surveys, see William H. Loyd, "The Development of Set-Off" 64 U.Pa.L.Rev. 541 (1916); and Michael E. Tigar, "Automatic Extinction of Cross-Demands: Compensation from Rome to California" 53 Cal.L.R. 224 (1965).

[2] See below, paras 7–04, 7–36 *et seq.*

circuity of action. By contrast, the policy underlying transaction (or equitable) set-off is that it would be unjust to allow a party to enforce his money claim without giving credit for the cross-claim if so required. Similarly the provision of insolvency set-off reflects the view that where parties have been giving credit to each other in reliance on their ability to secure payment by withholding what is due from them it would be unjust, on the advent of liquidation, to deprive the solvent party of his security by compelling him to pay what he owes in full and be left to prove for his own claim. This has traditionally been the policy justification for what is a clear exception to the *pari passu* principle, in that it allows the solvent party to collect payment ahead of other creditors to the extent of the set-off and thus puts him in a position analogous to that of a secured creditor.[3]

Thus set-off is an essential tool in the hands of a debtor who has a cross-claim against his creditor and is particularly used in banking transactions and in mutual dealings in the financial markets. But in dealings on an organised market the legal protection of netting and set-off has in recent years been seen as fulfilling a much more fundamental need, namely the reduction of systemic risk, hence the issue of EC Directives and of implementing national legislation designed to ensure that rules of insolvency law do not imperil rights of set-off in market contracts.[4] This special treatment of market and related contracts should be constantly borne in mind as a major qualification of the general principles discussed in the present chapter.

Is set-off a substantive or procedural defence?

7–02   An important question is whether a right of set-off, either automatically or when asserted, operates as a substantive defence so as to reduce or extinguish the claim, or whether it is a mere procedural device which does not result in a merger of claim and cross-claim but keeps both alive until judgment is given for any balance. Another way of putting the question is to ask whether the set-off is a defence (*i.e.* a substantive defence) or a mere cross-claim which can be set up in proceedings to avoid circuity of action and when it enables the defendant to have any judgment against him reduced by the amount of the cross-claim. The distinction is significant in that set-off as a substantive defence, where at least equal to the claim, extinguishes it, so that the failure to meet the claim cannot be regarded as a default so as to trigger self-help default remedies such as acceleration of payment, termination of an agreement, repossession of goods, the appointment of a receiver, and the like. By contrast set-off as a procedural defence does not affect liability for the claim and can be asserted only in proceedings and for the purpose of reducing or extinguishing the amount for which the claimant is entitled to judgment or of

---

[3] Set-off does not in law constitute a form of security, for the debtor who asserts it is not acquiring any rights over an asset of the creditor but simply seeking to reduce or extinguish the claim against him. See below, para.7–14.

[4] See below, paras 6–35 *et seq.*

showing why non-monetary equitable relief based on default in payment should not be given. It follows that failure to meet the claim is a default entitling the holder of the claim to pursue self-help default remedies, though if he later sues for recovery of, say, an accelerated balance of liability, the set-off can be asserted in reduction of the accelerated sum.

We shall return to this question later. Suffice it to say at this point that the answer depends on the type of set-off. Independent set-off,[5] whether under the Statutes of Set-Off or as applied by analogy in equity, is procedural only and the claimant is entitled to treat the claim and cross-claim as entirely distinct and independent of each other, so that the latter does not operate to reduce or discharge the former or affect the remedies for its enforcement except in legal proceedings in which the set-off is asserted.[6] Other forms of set-off, including transaction (or equitable) set-off, are now recognised as substantive defences which have the effect that the party invoking them is considered never to have been liable for the full amount of the claim but only for that sum if any, remaining after application of the set-off.

Types of set-off

There are five main types of set-off. The labels traditionally used to describe these are decidedly uninformative, and I have adopted the terminology coined by Mr Wood[7] which is much more meaningful and is already gaining acceptance in the courts. Features common to all forms of set-off other than contractual set-off are that (a) they are confined to situations in which both claim and cross-claim are for money[8] or one party's claim is to money and the other's is to property which the first party is authorised to dispose of and thus convert into money, and (b) they require mutuality of parties, that is, the claim and cross-claim must be due from the same parties in the same right. The five types of set-off are the following: **7–03**

(1) *Independent set-off*

This embraces two distinct forms of set-off. The first is sometimes known as statutory set-off, by which is meant set-off under rules carried over from the   **7–04**

---

[5] See below.
[6] If the claim is for money, the set-off operates to reduce the amount for which the claimant is entitled to judgment. If it is for non-monetary equitable relief, such as specific performance, the existence of the set-off is a factor which the court can take into account in exercising its discretion whether to grant relief (*BICC plc* v *Burndy Corporation* [1985] 1 Ch. 232 . See below, para.7–52.
[7] In his superb and massive work *English and International Set-Off*.
[8] It is not clear what policy objection there can be to set-off in respect of non-money fungibles. If each party has a duty to deliver or transfer items of property that are mutually interchangeable, why should not the party with the larger obligation be entitled to deduct what is due to him and deliver or transfer the balance? This can be done by agreement but not, it seems, in the absence of agreement.

former Statutes of Set-Off, and sometimes as legal set-off, by way of contra-distinction with equitable transaction set-off. The second is that form of set-off which equity applied by analogy with the Statutes of Set-Off, where all the conditions for statutory set-off were present except that one of the liqui-dated cross-claims was equitable.[9] The particular characteristics of inde-pendent set-off are (a) that it is a purely procedural defence which does not operate to reduce or extinguish the creditor's claim except at the point where judgment is given for the balance; and (b) that, in contrast to transaction set-off, it is not necessary that the claim and cross-claim should be connected to each other. It is only in this latter feature that independent set-off has any utility in modern law; in all other respects it is overshadowed by the much broader transaction set-off.

(2) Transaction set-off

7–05   This form of set-off, traditionally labelled equitable set-off, arises where the claim and cross-claim, even if not arising from the same transaction, are so closely connected that it would be inequitable for one claim to be enforced without credit being given for the other. Though transaction set-off was his-torically seen as a purely procedural remedy,[10] in modern law it is now capable of operating as a substantive defence in those cases where this is not precluded by the nature or terms of a contract between the parties. It is thus different in character from set-off given by way of analogy to the Statutes of Set-Off.[11] There is, however, a divergence of judicial opinion as to the manner of its exercise, an issue to which we shall return later.[12]

(3) Contractual set-off

7–06   Contractual set-off is that for which provision is made by express agreement of the parties. Outside insolvency it is free of several of the limitations gov-erning other forms of set-off. It operates as a substantive defence, taking effect upon the occurrence of the act or event agreed between the parties.

(4) Current account set-off

7–07   By this is meant the implied contractual right given to bankers operating dif-ferent current accounts for the same customer to combine them and treat them as one, thus setting off a debit balance on one account against a credit balance

---

[9] See above, para.7–42.

[10] See below, para.7–48.

[11] See *BICC plc* v *Burndy Corp.* [1985] 1 All E.R. 417; *Pacific Rim Investments Pte Ltd.* v *Lam Seng Tiong* [1995] 3 S.L.R. 1, where the Singapore Court of Appeal rightly rejected the contrary view expressed in the second edition of this work at pp.138 *et seq.*

[12] See below, para.7–54.

on the other. Though current account set-off could be regarded as a form of contractual set-off,[13] the label "contractual set-off" is usually reserved for express contractual provisions by which mutual obligations may be netted out, *i.e.* set off against each other. Current account set-off is a substantive right which, when exercised, consolidates the different accounts and reduces the customer's monetary position to a single net debit or credit balance. It is not clear what type of act constitutes exercise of the right. The traditional view was that the accounts were to be treated as notionally a single account from the beginning unless otherwise agreed.[14] But it seems more realistic to treat the accounts as distinct until actually combined by notice, book-entry or the initiation of a computer process transferring balances to one account from the other or others, and until then to treat the right of set-off as an unexercised equity.

(5) *Insolvency set-off*

This is the right of set-off given by insolvency law, and as regards companies by r.4.90 of the Insolvency Rules 1986. It is now clear that this too operates as a substantive rule of law and is not dependent on the taking of any procedural steps. **7–08**

Netting

The terms "netting" and "set-off" are sometimes treated as interchangeable but in financial circles netting is used to denote contractual arrangements by which claims of different parties against each other are reduced to a single balance. The simple form of contractual set-off is a clause in a contract providing that one party is entitled to set-off against any sums it owes to the other all sums owed to it by the other. This basic form is typically used where it is known in advance that the mutual obligations will be monetary or the various contracts will be unilateral and thus executed from the beginning,[15] so that no special contractual arrangements are required to convert non-monetary obligations (*e.g.* to deliver commodities) into monetary obligations or to cancel executory contracts or close them out by offsetting or reverse transactions. But there are many contractual relationships which are not of this character and require a process that leads, automatically or by unilateral action by one party, to consolidation of the mutual claims into a single net balance. This contractually adopted process is what constitutes netting, now defined by statute as: **7–09**

---

[13] This predicates that the accounts are to be treated as separate rather than evidencing a single indebtedness. See below, para.7–11.

[14] See, for example, *Bailey v Finch* (1871) L.R. 7 Q.B. 34, *per* Blackburn J. at 40.

[15] Because a unilateral contract is by definition a contract in which only one party makes a promise and the other accepts by performance or commencement of performance.

"the conversion into one net claim or obligation of different claims or obligation between participants resulting from the issue and receipt of transfer orders between them, whether on a bilateral or multilateral basis and whether through the interposition of a clearing house, central counterparty or settlement agent or otherwise."[16]

Netting can thus be viewed as both the procedure for, and the outcome of, a contractually completed set-off. It includes such arrangements as bilateral contract consolidation,[17] settlement netting,[18] the conversion of non-monetary into monetary claims through the exercise of a right to cancel or close out transactions, and the adoption of institutional rules governing bilateral and multilateral clearing and settlement or providing for novation of all relevant contracts to a clearing house or central counterparty.[19] The main objectives of netting are to reduce the number of settlements, thus saving costs, and to minimise the risk of a party becoming insolvent. From a market and regulatory perspective netting, particularly multilateral netting, provides a measure of protection against systemic risk and, in so doing, influences capital adequacy requirements.

(ii) A brief history of set-off[20]

7–10 Both the common law courts and courts of equity recognised set-off by contract and in bankruptcy as far back as the seventeenth century. Set-off in other cases was not recognised at common law, though equity appears to have been more liberal even before the Statutes of Set-Off. Bankruptcy legislation on set-off was later extended to companies but subsequently separate rules were devised for companies.[21] Running in parallel with bankruptcy statutes from 1729 onwards were the Statutes of Set-Off, which were designed to mitigate the rigour of the common law and avoid circuity of action by allowing set-off of mutual debts where claim and cross-claim were both for liquidated debts which had become due. In considering whether the requirement of mutuality was satisfied the courts looked at the legal title only, whereas courts of equity, applying the Statutes by analogy, were willing to look behind the legal title to the beneficial ownership.

Though the Statutes of Set-Off were eventually repealed, the powers they conferred on courts were preserved and now exist by virtue of s. 49(2) of the Supreme Court Act 1981. However, in most cases this statutory, or independent or legal, set-off has become unnecessary, being subsumed by the

---

[16] Financial Markets and Insolvency (Settlement Finality) Regulations 1999, SI 1999/2979, reg.2(1).
[17] Otherwise known as netting by novation.
[18] Also termed payment netting.
[19] See below, paras 7–17 et seq.
[20] For a more extended account, see the second edition of this book at pp.133 et seq.
[21] See below, paras 7–75 et seq.

larger equitable doctrine which developed and which allows set-off both of liquidated and of unliquidated claims where claim and cross-claim were so inseparably connected that it would be inequitable to allow the claimant to enforce his claim without giving credit for the amount of the cross-claim.

Until modern times this transaction (or equitable) set-off was almost invariably raised by way of defence to a money claim in proceedings, rather than as an answer to a prayer for non-monetary relief or to the exercise of self-help default remedies, so that its significance as a substantive defence was slow to emerge. It is only relatively recently that the courts have given consideration to the position where the claimant, instead of suing for money, has resorted to self-help or has sought non-monetary relief such as specific performance, in either case based on the defendant's default in payment, and have concluded that the defence is substantive, so that where the cross-claim equals or exceeds the claim the defendant is entitled to assert that he was never in default, so that the claimant was not entitled to resort to self-help or to obtain non-monetary judicial relief.[22]

(iii) Set-off distinguished from cognate rights

Set-off distinguished from running-account balance

Set-off presupposes the existence of two distinct claims. It does not apply to individual debits and credits on a single current account, for these have no distinct identity but form part of a single blended fund under which only the balance is payable by or to a party.[23]   **7–11**

When set-off constitutes payment

Both statutory set-off and that form of equitable set-off applied by analogy to the statutes of set-off[24] are to be distinguished from payment in that they do not operate as a *pro tanto* satisfaction of the creditor's claim except at the point of judgment for the balance; payment discharges the obligation, whilst a plea of set-off admits the subsistence of the obligation but asserts the right to set a countervailing obligation against it.[25] However, the exercise of   **7–12**

---

[22] See below, para.7–55.

[23] *Halesowen Presswork and Assemblies Ltd. v Westminster Bank Ltd.* [1970] 1 Q.B. 1, *per* Buckley L.J. at 46; *Re Charge Card Services Ltd.* [1987] Ch. 150, *per* Millett J. at 174.

[24] See above, para.7–04.

[25] See above para.7–04. The distinction is well put in Halsbury's Laws of England (4th ed., reissue), Vol.42, para.410: "Set-off [*i.e.* independent set-off] is entirely distinct from payment. Payment is satisfaction of a claim made by or on behalf of a person against whom the claim is brought . . . Set-off exempts a person entitled to it from making any satisfaction of the claim brought against him, or of so much of the claim as equals the amount which he is entitled to set off . . . Where there has been payment, the party against whom the claim is brought pleads accord and satisfaction, which in effect alleges that the claim no longer exists. On the other

a contractual set-off in respect of an ascertained amount does constitute payment.[26] So also does the exercise of a right of transaction set-off as a substantive defence, though only, it is thought, by overt assertion of the right.[27] Where the debtor incurs expense in performing acts which should have been done by his creditor, such expenditure normally gives rise to a right of set-off rather than *ipso facto* constituting payment of his own indebtedness. However, there are exceptional cases in which such expenditure is itself deemed in law to represent a *pro tanto* payment of the debt. The most notable example is the right of the tenant who, after due notice to his landlord to carry out repairs for which the latter is responsible, executes the repairs at his own expense and is then entitled to treat that expenditure as *pro tanto* payment of rent under the lease.[28]

Set-off distinguished from condition of right to repayment

7–13   The claimant cannot, of course, claim payment under a contract unless the contractual conditions, if any, precedent to his right to payment have been fulfilled. This is not a matter of set-off but of contract. If I am to be paid £10,000 for performing acts A, B and C I am not entitled to payment until those acts have been performed. Moreover—and this is another factor which distinguishes a substantive defence from a set-off—it is not necessary that I shall have undertaken to perform the acts in question; it suffices that their performance is a condition[29] of my right to payment. By contrast set-off involves a cross-claim and thus an assertion that the claimant has broken a duty owed to the defendant.

Set-off distinguished from security over a credit balance

7–14   The right to set off one debt against another does not constitute an equitable security interest or, indeed, confer on the defendant any right *in rem* over the claim of the claimant; it is merely a right to set up one personal claim against another in reduction or discharge of the defendant's liability.[30] This distinction between a real right and a personal right is of particular significance in relation to contractual set-off, which I shall examine a little later. It has, however, been blurred by judicial recognition of the charge-back, by which a

---

hand, a plea of set-off in effect admits the existence of the claim, and sets up a cross-claim as being ground on which the person against whom the claim is brought is excused from payment and entitled to judgment on the plaintiff's claim. Until judgment in favour of the defendant on the ground of set-off has been given, the plaintiff's claim is not extinguished."

[26] See below, paras 7–17 *et seq.*

[27] See below, para.7–54.

[28] See below, para.7–59.

[29] The term "condition" is, of course, used here not as a contrast with warranty but as denoting any act or event, whether promissory or otherwise and whether constituting a major or a minor term, the performance or occurrence of which is necessary to earn payment.

[30] See above, para.1–19.

debtor takes a security interest over his own obligation.[31] Since the mechanism for enforcing this is by book-entry, which is also the means for effecting a contractual set-off, the question whether a particular transaction gives rise to a charge or a contractual set-off appears to depend upon the label given to it by the parties.

Set-off distinguished from abatement

The common law doctrine of abatement, though similar in its effect to substantive transaction set-off, is nevertheless an independent doctrine limited by its own rules. It is discussed later.[32]   **7–15**

Set-off distinguished from counterclaim

Whilst both set-off and counterclaim are cross-claims and as such are   **7–16** deemed to be separate actions for the purpose of the Limitation Act 1980,[33] they are different in character. Set-off is a defence to a money claim or a claim for relief based on the non-payment of money, it can only be asserted in respect of a cross-claim for money, and it is purely defensive, so that the defendant is not entitled to any judgment in his favour for any surplus of his cross-claim over the claim. A counterclaim is not as such a defence at all, merely a separate claim.[34] It is thus not confined to money but may encompass any cause of action which can conveniently be tried as part of the action. Accordingly any cross-claim capable of being asserted as a set-off can be pleaded as a counterclaim, either in lieu of set-off or as to any surplus over the sum covered by the plea of set-off, whereas a cross-claim capable of being asserted as a counterclaim can be pleaded as a set-off only if it is for a money sum and satisfies any other conditions for a valid set-off.[35]

2. CONTRACTUAL SET-OFF AND NETTING

(i) Types of netting arrangement

We have previously seen that netting includes a bilateral or multilateral   **7–17** arrangement for conversion of mutual claims into a single net claim. For this purpose a number of techniques are available which in normal circumstances can be expected to be effective. These include the following:

---

[31] See above, para.3–12.
[32] See below, para.7–71.
[33] Limitation Act 1980, s.35(1), by which the notional separate action is deemed to have been commenced on the same date as the original action.
[34] Under the Civil Procedure Rules it is designated as a type of Part 20 claim.
[35] See *Civil Procedure*, Vol.1, paras 16.6, 16.6.1.

Novation netting (contractual consolidation)

7–18 Novation netting, or contractual consolidation, involves the amalgamation of two or more executory contracts into a single new contract to be performed at a future time. The characteristic of this form of netting, which distinguishes it from settlement netting, is that the fusion of the claims on both sides into a new claim for a single balance or a single delivery obligation occurs immediately upon the occurrence of the event stipulated by the contract,[36] whereas in settlement netting the contracts remain separate until they have been netted out at maturity and the net balance paid or delivery obligation discharged.

Contractual consolidation may be effected by provision for bilateral consolidation of contractual obligations or by clearing house rules providing for novation of notified contracts to the clearing house. In the former case the contract may provide that in stated eventualities, which could include notice by one party to the other, all outstanding contracts between them shall be consolidated into and replaced by a single contract under which only the net balance is payable. Alternatively, each contract may provide for its automatic consolidation with subsequent contracts as and when these come into existence, so that no set-off situation ever arises. In contractual set-off through clearing house rules, the clearing house becomes substituted as a principal in relation to each of the parties.[37] For example, under the General Regulations of the London Clearing House (LCH), members who are parties to a sale transaction are required to register it with LCH, whereupon the transaction is automatically novated and replaced by two separate transactions in both of which LCH is substituted for one party as the principal, becoming seller to the original buyer and buyer from the original seller. The effect of this system of automatic novation is that payment and delivery obligations become owed by and to LCH. In this way payment rights and obligations arising from all dealings entered into by a particular trader are internalised and consolidated into a single credit or debit balance in the trader's current account with LCH.

Contractual netting does, of course, depend upon the obligations on both sides being of the same kind. It is not possible to net a payment obligation against a delivery obligation or *vice versa*. So where mutual dealings involve both delivery and payment obligations it is necessary to devise some contractual procedure, such as rescission or close-out, by which one type of obligation is converted to the other.[38] Similarly, while the fact that the claim and cross-claim are in different currencies is no bar to a right of set-off,[39] completion of the set-off requires either that one currency is converted to the other or that both currencies are converted to a third currency at a given rate of exchange.

---

[36] See below and Roy Goode, *Commercial Law* (2nd ed.), pp.514–517.
[37] See Wood, *English and International Set-Off*, paras 5–127 *et seq.*; Goode, *Commercial Law* (2nd ed.), p.158.
[38] See below, para.7–20.
[39] See below, para.7–24.

Settlement (or payment) netting

As mentioned above, whereas contractual consolidation involves the amalga- **7–19** mation of unmatured claims, settlement netting is the process by which matured claims are netted out and paid. It is only the act of payment of the net balance which extinguishes the claims on both sides. Again, settlement netting may be effected either by bilateral arrangements or by multilateral arrangements through a clearing house. In the former case the parties simply agree that when claims on both sides mature those on one side shall be set off against those on the other and the balance paid. In the case of netting through a clearing house the procedure is that at the end of each clearing (which may be daily or at such other intervals as the clearing house rules prescribe) the position of each clearing house member is netted out in relation to all other clearing house members to produce a "net net" series of balances in which members are either creditors or debtors in relation to the clearing as a whole. Payment is then made by in-house transfers from debtor members to creditor members in the books of the clearing house or of a bank (typically the central bank) where all the clearing house members hold an account. These multilateral netting arrangements have not always proved effective in the event of an insolvency of a clearing house member, but the problem has been considerably alleviated by European Community directives. The impact of insolvency on settlement netting is considered later.[40]

Close-outs

Insolvency set-off, like other forms of set-off, requires that claim and cross- **7–20** claim be monetary claims or involve relief based on the non-payment of money. Accordingly it is not possible to set off a money claim against an obligation to deliver or transfer property, tangible or intangible, except where the party invoking the set-off holds the property with instructions or authority to convert it into money and the instructions or authority have not been revoked at the time of liquidation.[41] So in a situation where the claims on one side or both are not to payment of money but to the delivery of assets, such as commodities or securities, it is important to have a close-out mechanism in place by which the delivery obligations are replaced by money obligations prior to the advent of liquidation. One way of doing this is by providing for acceleration or rescission of the two contracts, the replacement of delivery obligations with value-payment obligations and netting of the resultant money claims. Another is by providing for the conclusion of a reverse transaction, so that, for example, a contract to purchase securities is closed out by a countervailing contract to sell them, the parties then settling their mutual obligations by the payment of differences.[42]

---

[40] See below, para.7–29.
[41] See further above, paras 6–35, 6–44; below, para.7–31 in relation to close-outs.
[42] Despite Art.7 of the Financial Collateral Directive (see para.6–44) this form of close-out may still be vulnerable to cherry-picking by the liquidator.

(ii) Availability of contractual set-off

7–21 Barring the advent of insolvency, in which event contractual set-off is displaced by the rules governing insolvency set-off,[43] the limits on contractual set-off are for the most part practical rather than legal. The ordinary requirement of mutality may be overridden by the agreement of the parties, so that, for example, a parent company may agree to allow debts due from its subsidiaries to be set off against its own credit balance; the parties may agree to allow a claim that would not otherwise have become due to be accelerated for purposes of set-off; and set-off may be effected in any manner provided by the contract without need of legal proceedings. But since the object of set-off is to reduce a monetary liability to a net balance even a contractual set-off cannot be fully effected unless both claim and cross-claim have been reduced to money—in the case of an unliquidated claim, by having it crystallised into a liquidated claim[44]; in the case of property, by having it valued for set-off purposes; and in the case of a claim and cross-claim in different currencies, by converting one currency to the other, or both currencies to a third currency, at a specified or ascertainable rate of exchange. However, though it would not strictly be a case of set-off there is nothing to preclude the parties from agreeing to net out mutual claims relating to non-money fungibles, so that, for example, if A is due to deliver 100 tonnes of coffee to B under one contract and to receive 30 tonnes of coffee of the same description from B under another contract, A can perform his obligation by delivering 70 tonnes to B.

Contractual set-off in respect of unliquidated and contingent claims

7–22 It is not uncommon for a party to stipulate for a right to set off unliquidated, and even contingent, claims against moneys due to the other. Is such a stipulation valid? We cannot give a sensible answer to this question without first asking what the word "set-off" means in this context. It is important to bear in mind that exercise of contractual set-off results in the extinguishment *pro tanto* of the claim against which the right of set-off is exercised. Obviously it is not possible to do this unless and until the quantum of the two claims is ascertained. If, for example, a bank's customer has a credit balance of £10,000 and the bank seeks to exercise a contractual right to "set off" an unliquidated claim for damages for fraud, the two claims cannot at that stage be combined, because one of them is unquantified so that we are unable to say to what extent, if at all, the credit balance is reduced. On the other hand, we must seek to give some meaning to the term of the agreement which enables the bank to "set off" even an unliquidated claim. The answer seems clear enough; what the bank is really obtaining, when imposing such a stipulation, is a right to withhold payment of the credit balance pending quantifi-

---

[43] See below, paras 7–29, 7–75 *et seq.*
[44] See below, para.7–22.

cation of its claim (whether by agreement or by judicial decision or arbitral award), coupled with the right to set off that claim when it has been quantified. In other words, the so-called contractual set-off in relation to unliquidated claims is in effect two rights rolled up into one: in the first instance, a right to suspend payment, while leaving the customer's credit balance intact; and later, when the amount of the claim has become liquidated, a set-off which will result in *pro tanto* extinguishment of the credit balance.

The application of the set-off clause to a contingent claim is likely to produce a similar effect, though this depends on the circumstances and on the agreement between the parties. Where the contingent claim is of a known maximum amount—as in the case of a guarantee of a fixed indebtedness—it is a question of construction of the agreement whether the bank is intended to have a mere right to suspend payment until the liability matures and the actual amount becomes known, with an ensuing right of set-off, or whether on the other hand the bank is to have an immediate right to set off the maximum liability, upon terms of re-crediting the customer with the appropriate amount if the actual liability proves to be less. In most cases, the former construction is likely to prevail.

Cross-border set-off

Assuming that the right of set-off is governed by English law, the mere fact that the claim and cross-claim arise from accounts in different countries does not in itself affect a right of set-off given by contract. **7–23**

Cross-currency set-off

Similarly, the parties are entitled to contract for a claim in one currency to be set off against a claim in another,[45] though as stated above it is necessary to reduce the two claims to the same currency in order to give effect to the set-off. **7–24**

(iii) Legal limits of contractual set-off

In the relationship between them contracting parties are free to agree on almost any terms for contractual set-off they may choose and these will be effective so long as they are not cut off by insolvency.[46] It is, however, another matter where the rights of third parties may be affected. Three situations in particular require a brief comment, namely set-off against an assignee of the debt, set-off against a money claim in which a third party has an interest and the effect of a freezing injunction. **7–25**

---

[45] See further below, para.7–34, as to the banker's right of combination in respect of accounts maintained in different currencies.

[46] See below, paras 7–29 *et seq.* as to the impact of insolvency on contractual set-off.

Contractual set-off against an assignee

7–26   In general an assignee of a debt takes subject to equities, including the debtor's right of contractual set-off as regards cross-claims on another account for advances made to the creditor prior to the debtor's receipt of notice of assignment. Where the terms of the set-off extend to contingent liabilities of the creditor to the debtor it would seem that the assignee takes subject to those contingent liabilities. But the debtor cannot assert a contractual set-off in respect of claims arising from new dealings with the creditor after the debtor has received notice of assignment.[47] Moreover, where the payment undertaking is embodied in a negotiable instrument which comes into the hands of a holder in due course he takes free from all equities, so that a set-off available against the original creditor cannot be pleaded in answer to a claim on the instrument.[48] Finally, if the debtor has agreed not to assert rights of set-off against an assignee he is bound by that agreement.[49] Similarly, if a debenture is issued on terms that it is to be transferable free from equities the issuer is not entitled to assert a right of set-off against a transferee of the debenture.[50]

Set-off against a money claim belonging to a third party

7–27   Though other forms of set-off require mutuality of parties, so that, for example, A cannot set off against his indebtedness to B a debt due to B from C, it is usually open to a party to contract out of the requirement of mutuality and allow a claim vested in him to be made available as a set-off against another party's debt. A common example arises in relation to bank accounts maintained for a group of companies where each member of the group agrees that its credit balance may be the subject of set-off in respect of debit balances of other members of the group. But the requirement of mutuality can be abrogated only by consent of the party affected. So a money claim against a person in his personal capacity cannot be set off against money due to him as trustee unless the beneficiaries consent or the person asserting the money claim gave value and was without notice of the trust.[51]

---

[47] The cases establishing this principle relate to independent set-off and transaction set-off but the principle is equally applicable to contractual set-off.

[48] In relation to bills of exchange this is specifically provided by s.38(2) of the Bills of Exchange Act 1882.

[49] *Re Agra and Masterman's Bank, Ex p. AsiaticBanking Corp.* (1867) L.R. 2 Ch. 391; *John Dee Group Ltd. v WMH (21) Ltd.* [1998] B.C.C. 972; *Coca-Cola Finance Corp. v Finsat International Ltd.* [1996] 3 W.L.R. 849. In the latter case it was held that waiver of set-off against an assignee is not contrary to public policy. As to the exclusion of transaction and independent set-off by agreement, see below, para.7–69.

[50] *Hilger Amalgamated Ltd. v Rank Precision Industries Ltd.* [1989] B.C.L.C. 301.

[51] See Philip R. Wood, *English and International Set-Off*, pp.1050 *et seq.*; Rory Derham, *Set-Off* (3rd ed.), paras 17.90 *et seq.*

Contractual set-off and the freezing injunction

Where the claimant in an action obtains a freezing injunction[52] freezing the **7–28** defendant's bank account, then unless otherwise provided by the injunction a bank having notice of it may not exercise any right of set-off against the defendant's credit balance except by obtaining a variation of the injunction.[53] But to avoid the need for applications to vary, the injunction ought normally to permit the bank to exercise a right of set-off in respect of all advances made prior to its receipt of notice of the injunction.[54]

(iv) The impact of insolvency on contractual set-off and netting

Netting through a clearing house works perfectly well as regards transactions **7–29** settled before winding-up. The position is more complex if one of the members of the clearing house becomes insolvent. Once a company has gone into liquidation the rules of insolvency set-off, where relevant, come into play and are mandatory,[55] displacing all other forms of set-off not exercised prior to the winding-up. This is of no great significance in relation to independent set-off, transaction set-off and current-account, for in virtually every situation in which these forms of set-off are available there would be an automatic set-off under the rules of insolvency set-off. Indeed, the latter are broader, not only because they are self-executing but also because the principle of insolvency law under which future claims are accelerated and contingent claims are discounted and admitted to proof means that insolvency set-off extends to these claims, which would be outside the scope of the three other forms of set-off just mentioned. But contractual set-off is in a different category, for outside insolvency the parties are free to agree on almost any kind of netting and set-off arrangement they choose.

It thus becomes of importance to know whether a contractual set-off has come into effective operation before the winding-up of one of the parties to the mutual dealings. If it has not, two consequences follow. First, the right of set-off ceases to be exercisable. Secondly, if two or more contracts constituting the mutual dealing between the parties are executory the liquidator is free to cherry-pick, requiring performance of the profitable contract while disclaiming or declining to perform the unprofitable contract and leaving the

---

[52] Formerly known as a *Mareva* injunction, this restrains the defendant from dealing with its assets, or removing them from the jurisdiction, pending trial of the action. The injunction is granted where there is reason to believe that the defendant may dissipate his assets or withdraw them from the claimant's reach so as to defeat any judgment the claimant may obtain.

[53] *Oceanica Castelana Armadora S.A.of Panama v Mineralimportexport (The Theotokos)* [1983] 1 W.L.R. 1294. In Re K [1990] 2 Q.B. 298, which related to a restraining order in drug trafficking proceedings, Otton J. opined that in the case of the banker's right of combination (see below para.7–32) an application to the court, though prudent, might not be necessary, there being conceptually only one account.

[54] *ibid.*

[55] See below, para.7–78.

other party to prove in the winding-up without the benefit even of insolvency set-off.[56]

Netting arrangements are designed to ensure as far as possible either that all set-offs are completed before the relevant date,[57] so that there is no need to resort to insolvency set-off, or that the contractual rights on both sides will have undergone such conversion (if any) as may be necessary to satisfy the requirements of the Insolvency Rules as to mutuality of claims and parties.[58] For this purpose a number of techniques are available which in normal circumstances can be expected to be effective. These have been described earlier.[59]

We consider, first, the decidedly adverse impact of general insolvency law on uncompleted multilateral netting arrangements and, secondly, the ameliorating effect of provisions of the Companies Act 1989 relating to the settlement of market contracts and money market and related contracts under the rules of a recognised investment exchange or a recognised clearing house[60] and subsequent European Community Directives and implementing legislation.[61]

Effect under the general insolvency law

7–30   Once a clearing house member goes into liquidation then as a matter of general insolvency law its claim on other members can no longer be subjected to netting out through the clearing, for the effect of this is to reduce the member's claim against its counterparty by reference to sums due from that member to third parties, in contravention of the mutuality requirement, and to prefer other participants in the clearing to the member's creditors as a whole, contrary to the *pari passu* rule. In other words, an asset of the member, namely its claim against counterparty, is being removed from the general body of creditors and distributed exclusively among the clearing house members. This was the conclusion reached in the controversial decision of the House of Lords in *British Eagle International Air Lines Ltd. v Compagnie Nationale Air France*,[62] to which reference has previously been made and which now requires examination in a little more detail:

---

[56] This is because of the rule that sums earned by the company by post-liquidation activity are not part of its general assets and are thus not susceptible to set-off of pre-liquidation claims. See below, para.7–96.

[57] *i.e.* before the winding-up and before the creditor has notice of the creditors' meeting under s.98 or of the winding-up petition, as the case may be.

[58] See below, para.7–82. Netting is also an important technique for reducing the risk of failure of banks and other credit institutions and is now the subject of an EC Directive 96/10 ([1996] O.J. L58/17). See Dermot Turing, "Set-Off and Netting: Developments in 1996 Affecting Banks" [1997] 12 J.I.B.L. 155.

[59] See above, paras 7–17 *et seq.*

[60] See below, para.7–31.

[61] See above, para.6–44; below, para.7–31.

[62] [1975] 2 All E.R. 390.

The International Air Transport Association (IATA) set up a clearing house system by which sums due from member airlines to each other would be netted out each month, remittances being sent by IATA to airlines having a net credit balance and collected from airlines with a net debit balance. British Eagle went into liquidation owing money to a number of airlines but with a claim against Air France which the liquidator sought to recover. Air France pleaded that the liquidator was bound by the IATA system and could collect only from IATA and then only such sum (if any) as was due it after netting out the claims of airlines who were creditors of British Eagle. The liquidator's contention that this contravened the *pari passu* rule, in that it removed from British Eagle's estate for the benefit of other member airlines a sum due from Air France which would otherwise have been an asset available to the general body of creditors of British Eagle, was upheld by the House of Lords by a majority of three to two. It was not suggested that the arrangements were in themselves in any way improper, but in the view of the majority their effect was to give other members of IATA to whom British Eagle owed money a preference over its general creditors. Two of their Lordships[63] dissented on the ground that the arrangements were perfectly proper, were not intended to avoid rules of insolvency law, were to be applied no differently after liquidation than before and were as binding on the liquidator as they had been on British Eagle itself.

It is clear that the crucial question in *British Eagle* was whether its claim to payment was against Air France directly, with IATA acting simply as agent in providing a clearing mechanism, or whether on the other hand the claim was simply an item in the computation of British Eagle's net debit or credit balance with IATA, the latter acting as principal. If, as the majority held, British Eagle's contractual entitlement lay directly against Air France then clearly its subjection to the claims of other clearing house members was an infringement both of the *pari passu* principle and of the requirement of mutuality which precludes the set-off of claims of third parties against the amount due to the company in liquidation. But if, as was the view of the minority, the effect of the clearing house arrangements was that British Eagle's claim was only to such sum as after netting out in the clearing fell to be credited or debited to its account with IATA, then its counterparty for the purpose of computing its claim was IATA, which would clearly be entitled to set off cross-claims vested in it in respect of services supplied to British Eagle by other airlines.

It has to be said that the minority view is much more in keeping with commercial reality (to say nothing of commercial convenience) than that of the majority. Moreover, the decision of the majority is difficult to reconcile with the principle, emphasised by Lords Morris and Simon, that a liquidator stands in the shoes of the company in liquidation and takes each contract as he finds, so that he cannot procure the company to enforce those provisions

---

[63] Lord Morris of Borth-y-Guest and Lord Simon of Glaisdale.

which are for its benefit without at the same time being bound by the contractual conditions qualifying the company's entitlement.[64] In policy terms a multilateral netting arrangement should not be regarded as offensive to insolvency law if it is intended to operate in the same way outside and inside insolvency, so that it is not a device designed to improve the position of one party by reason of the insolvency of another.

The preservation of netting arrangements under market contracts and EC Directives

7–31   Fortunately, in relation to recognised markets and clearing houses, the effect of *British Eagle* has been largely negated by special statutory provisions relating to market contracts and money market and related contracts and by EC Directives and implementing legislation designed to preserve the validity of netting arrangements in insolvency in order to reduce systemic risk. In particular, the settlement rules of a recognised investment exchange or a recognised clearing house relating to the settlement of market contracts or money market and related contracts are not to be regarded as invalid at law on the ground of inconsistency with insolvency law.[65] The relevant provisions of the 1998 Settlement Finality Directive and the 2002 Directive on Financial Collateral Arrangements have been discussed in the previous chapter.[66]

3. CURRENT ACCOUNT SET-OFF

The nature of the right to combine accounts

7–32   Unless otherwise agreed between the parties, a banker has, by the custom of bankers, a right to combine two or more current accounts held for the same customer in his own right,[67] and this is so whether the accounts are held at the same branch[68] or at different branches.[69] So the bank can refuse to honour a cheque drawn on an account in credit if the credit balance[70] is insufficient to cover a debit balance on another current account with the customer of the

---

[64] See Roy Goode, *Principles of Corporate Insolvency Law* (2nd ed.) p.125.

[65] Companies Act 1989, ss.159, 171; Financial Markets and Insolvency Regulations 1991 (SI 1991/880); Financial Markets and Insolvency (Money Markets) Regulations 1995 (SI 1995/2049).

[66] See above, paras 6–34 *et seq.*

[67] *National Westminster Bank Ltd. v Halesowen Presswork & Assemblies Ltd.* [1972] A.C. 785; *Garnett v M'Kewan* (1872) L.R. 8 Ex. 10; *Cummins v Shand* (1860) 5 H. & N. 95.

[68] *National Westminster Bank Ltd. v Halesowen Presswork & Assemblies Ltd.*, above; *Direct Acceptance Corp. v Bank of New South Wales* (1968) 88 W.N. (N.S.W.) (Pt 1) 498; *Cummins v Shand*, above.

[69] *Garnett v M'Kewan*, above; *Prince v Oriental Bank* (1878) 3 App.Cas. 325.

[70] When added to any agreed overdraft facility.

bank.[71] Astonishingly it is still unclear whether the right of combination, which Mr Wood has conveniently termed "current account set-off," is a true set-off or merely an entitlement on the part of the bank to treat its relationship with its customer as a single relationship and the various accounts as a single account on which there is a single balance due from or to the bank. On the latter view, which enjoys considerable judicial support,[72] the accounting is automatic and, unlike set-off, requires no act on the part of the bank. Nevertheless there are strong arguments in favour of the view that the right of combination is not a matter of account but an implied contractual right to set off a debit balance on one account against a credit balance on another. In the first place, it is much more realistic. The notion that parties who establish and operate separate accounts are to be treated as dealing with each other only a single account is contrary not only to appearances but also to intentions. Secondly, if the combination were automatic this would enure for the benefit of the customer as well as the bank, so that the customer could overdraw on one account so long as he had a sufficient balance on another. But it is well established that he cannot do this. The bank is entitled to refuse to honour a cheque if there are insufficient funds in the account on which it is drawn even if there is a separate account, current or otherwise, with a credit balance sufficient to cover the cheque.[73] If the customer wishes the accounts to be combined he must give an instruction to the bank to transfer the balance on the account in credit to the account in debit. Thirdly, there are several judgments which make it clear that the combination of accounts, far from being automatic, is a matter of choice for the bank. Thus in *Halesowen* Lord Denning stated that "the banker has a right to combine accounts whenever he pleases,"[74] while in *Re EJ Morel Ltd.*[75] Buckley J. said that "where all the accounts are current the banker can combine these accounts in whatever way he chooses."[76] The fact that the banker has a right to combine accounts but not an obligation to do so indicates that combination is simply a form of contract consolidation, in which exercise of the contractual right of set-off and netting produces a single balance. The situation is thus quite different from that with which Millett J. had to deal in *Re Charge Card Services Ltd.*,[77] where there was in fact a single current account, so that the question of set-off could not arise.

As in the case of non-contractual set-off, there must be mutuality of parties, in the absence of agreement to the contrary. If the accounts are either held by or kept with two distinct legal entities there is no right of combination. So the account of a company at a particular bank cannot be combined with that of

---

[71] *Garnett v M'Kewan*, above.
[72] See, for example, *Garnet v M'Kewan* (1872) L.R. 8 Ex. 10; *Halesowen Presswork and Assemblies Ltd. v Westminster Bank Ltd.* [1971] 1 Q.B. 1, *per* Buckley L.J. at 46, applied by Millett J. in *Re Charge Card Services Ltd.* [1987] 1 Ch. 150 at 173–174.
[73] *Garnett v M'Kewan* (1872) L.R. 8 Ex. 10; *Barclays Bank Ltd. v Okenhare* [1966] 2 Lloyd's Rep. 87, *per* Mocatta J at 95.
[74] *Halesowen Presswork and Assemblies Ltd. v Westminster Bank Ltd.* [1971] 1 Q.B. 1 at 34.
[75] [1962] Ch. 21.
[76] *ibid.*, at 31.
[77] [1987] Ch. 150.

its parent or subsidiary at the same bank without an authorisation from both companies[78]; and the account of a company with one bank cannot, in the absence of agreement, be combined with that held by the company with a parent, subsidiary or associated company of the first bank.

Cross-border combination

7–33   Does the right to combine accounts apply where the accounts are not merely held in different branches of a bank in the same country but at branches in different countries? Assuming the right of set-off to be governed by English law, the answer in principle would seem to be yes, though it may be that in such a case the court would more readily infer an agreement to keep the accounts separate. Again, there must be mutuality of parties.

Cross-currency combination

7–34   The fact that the debit balance on one account is in a currency different from the credit balance on the other would not seem to preclude the bank from combining the two accounts, though again the difference in currencies will be a factor to take into account in determining whether there is an implied agreement to keep the accounts separate. There was at one time much debate as to whether claims arising in different currencies could be set off against each other, for on one view foreign currency was not money but a commodity. The obligation to furnish it was thus a delivery obligation for the breach of which the remedy was unliquidated damages, not a payment obligation, for which the remedy was a claim in debt, and it is well established that a delivery obligation may not in general be set off against a money claim.[79] In continental Europe there remains a diversity of views, the courts of some jurisdictions taking the view that obligations in different currencies are not of the same nature and are therefore not susceptible to set-off while others consider that set-off is available. In England it is now established that a claimant is entitled to judgment in a foreign currency,[80] that the judgment is for payment, not for delivery, and that the claim is thus for debt, not for damages. The commodity conception of foreign currency, so far as it ever existed, is now dead[81] and there seems no reason why a claim in one currency cannot be

---

[78] The assent of the company whose account is in credit is not sufficient, for the company whose account is in debit can object to an officious reduction or discharge of its liability. There is, of course, no problem where there is only one operating account, as where the account is in joint names or where one company in a group effectively acts as banker to the others, holds the operating account with the bank, receives payments for other companies in the group and makes payments on their behalf, these being recorded for information only by memorandum accounts designed to show the state of account between the account holder and the other members of the group.

[79] See above, paras 1–69, 7–18 and 7–20; below, para.7–82.

[80] See *Miliangos v George Frank (Textiles) Ltd.* [1976] A.C. 443; *The Halcyon The Great* [1975] 1 W.L.R. 515.

set off against a claim in another, though at the point of enforcement of any balance it is necessary to convert the foreign currency claim into sterling.

Exclusion of the right of combination

Current account set-off, or the right to combine accounts, may be excluded   **7–35**
by express or implied agreement. Where, for example, the customer has a fixed loan account and a current account, the court will usually infer an agreement that these accounts should be kept separate, as otherwise the customer could never safely draw cheques without having sufficient in the current account to cover the debit balance on the loan account, and this would frustrate the purpose of the arrangement.[82] But if the customer becomes bankrupt or goes into liquidation the agreement to keep the accounts separate comes to an end, not only as an implied term of the agreement but because the provisions of insolvency law as to set-off are mandatory.[83]

4. INDEPENDENT (STATUTORY) SET-OFF

Independent set-off as a procedural shield

Independent, or statutory, set-off is a procedural defence designed to avoid   **7–36**
circuity of action where both claim and cross-claim are liquidated and due. In contrast to transaction set-off, it is not necessary that the claim and cross-claim are closely connected; they may be wholly independent of each other. It will be recalled that there are two forms of this: set-off provided under the Statutes of Set-Off and set-off given in equity by analogy to the statute.

Both forms of independent set-off are procedural only. Though in modern practice pleaded as a defence,[84] the defendant's cross-claim does not constitute a denial of liability; on the contrary, it amounts to an admission that the defendant is liable on the claim and a contention that he is entitled to set off his cross-claim in reduction or extinction of the amount for which the plaintiff is entitled to judgment. Accordingly the cross-claim does not reduce the

---

[81] *Barclays Bank International Ltd v Levin Bros. (Bradford) Ltd.* [1977] 1 Lloyd's Rep. 51, *per* Mocatta J. at 59: "In my view, however, the decision in the *Miliangos* case has revolutionised the position and has disposed of the once common assumption that foreign currency must be treated by our Courts as if a commodity, e.g. a foreign cow . . ." See also *Camdex International Ltd v Bank of Zambia (No. 3)* [1997] 6 Bank. L.R. 43.

[82] *Bradford Old Bank v Sutcliffe* [1918] 2 K.B. 833. For an example of an express exclusion of set-off in a loan and guarantee transaction *see Continental Illinois National Bank & Trust Co. of Chicago v Papanicolaou* [1986] 2 Lloyd's Rep. 441.

[83] *National Westminster Bank Ltd. v Halesowen Pressork & Assemblies Ltd.*, above. See below para.177.

[84] C.P.R. r.16.6 (replacing R.S.C. Ord. 18, r.17), applicable also in the county court by virtue of s.38 of the County Courts Act 1984.

defendant's liability on the claim,[85] and the set-off takes effect only on and from the date of judgment.[86]

Significance of the procedural character of independent set-off

7–37   Several important consequences flow from the fact that independent set-off is a procedural defence, not a substantive defence. First, neither the existence of the cross-claim nor its assertion without or prior to proceedings provides justification for withholding payment to the other party. Secondly, since the remedy can be asserted only where the promisee has brought proceedings, it does not prevent him from exercising extra-judicial rights and remedies for default, such as forfeiture of a lease, distress,[87] contractual acceleration of the promisor's monetary liability, invocation of a cross-default clause,[88] termination of the contract and repossession of any goods of the promisee supplied, for example, under a leasing agreement. In all such cases the existence of the cross-claim does not in itself reduce the promisor's liability or affect the extra-judicial remedies available to the promisee, and the promisor's only resort is to such other forms of equitable relief as may be available, *e.g.* relief against forfeiture. Thirdly, since set-off is a cross-claim it can be answered with a plea that it is time-barred under the Limitation Act 1980.[89] Fourthly, the debtor is not permitted to set off against a claim by the creditor's assignee a cross-claim arising after the debtor received notice of the assignment,[90] whereas a substantive defence is an inherent qualification of the rights assigned and the fact that default by the assignor giving rise to the defence did not occur until after the debtor received the notice of assignment does not preclude him from pleading it against the assignee.[91]

The procedural character of set-off has no adverse effect on the defendant so long as the claimant does not exercise any self-help remedy but proceeds solely by action, for set-off then protects the defendant both as to the amount of the judgment and as to costs. But against self-help set-off gives no protection. Two simple illustrations will demonstrate the significance of the point.

---

[85] *Fuller v Happy Shopper Markets Ltd.* [2001] 2 Lloyd's Rep. 49.

[86] *Stein v Blake* [1996] A.C. 243, *per* Lord Hoffmann at 251; *Henriksens Rederi A/S v T.H.Z. Rolimpex (The Brede)* [1974 Q.B. 233, *per* Lord Denning M.R. at 245–246. The discussion here is concerned with independent set-off and transaction set-off. Contractual set-off provides a substantive defence (see above, paras 7–06, 7–17 *et seq.*), whilst set-off in bankruptcy is automatic (see below para.7–77).

[87] *Townrow v Benson* (1818) 3 Madd. 203.

[88] *i.e.* a clause in a contract entitling the promisee to exercise default remedies where the promisor defaults in his obligations under a separate contract, whether with the promisee under the first contract or with a third party. If proceedings are brought for the outstanding balance of the accelerated liability the defendant will be able to assert his cross-claim in diminution of that liability if the conditions for in dependent set-off are established, but that, of course, is quite different from the effect of the substantive defence provided by transaction set-off which would enable the defendant to say that, to the extent of his asserted cross-claim, he was never in default at all. See below, Example 1, and paras 7–48 *et seq.*

[89] See below para.7–68.

[90] See below para.7–66.

[91] See below paras 7–64, 7–66.

In each case it is assumed that the contract does not itself, either expressly or by implication, make the promise and the counter-promise mutually dependent or confer on the debtor a right to combine accounts.

Example 1 C agrees to lend D £12,000, repayable by 12 half-yearly instalments of £1,000 each. The loan agreement provides that on default in payment of any one instalment the full outstanding balance shall immediately become due. D, who under a totally unconnected transaction has previously sold goods to C at a price of £600 which C has not paid, pays the first instalment due under the loan agreement but deducts the £600 from the second instalment and remits the balance of £400 to C. In making this deduction D commits a breach of the loan agreement which entitles C to invoke the acceleration clause and call up the outstanding balance of £10,600. C invokes the clause and then sues D for the £10,600. In those proceedings D can set off his cross-claim for £600 by way of independent set-off. That cross-claim did not reduce D's liability under the loan agreement so as to entitle him to withhold payment of it; the cross-claim could be enforced only by set-off in C's action or by separate action, and was thus ineffective to prevent the triggering of the acceleration clause. **7–38**

Example 2 O supplies equipment to H under a hire-purchase agreement which empowers O Ltd. to terminate the agreement and repossess the goods if H fails to pay an instalment of the total price within 14 days of the due date. Shortly afterwards O enters into a separate hire-purchase agreement with H pursuant to which O delivers different equipment to which he has no title. Upon discovering this, H demands repayment of the instalments paid under the second agreement and, when repayment is not forthcoming, deducts the amount from an instalment due under the first agreement. This he is not entitled to do, and if the amount due under the first agreement remains unpaid for more than 14 days O can terminate the agreement and repossess the equipment. If O brings proceedings to recover the arrears H can set off his cross-claim as a *pro tanto* defence to the claim but cannot recover the equipment unless he obtains relief against forfeiture. **7–39**

In the above cases, the creditor exercised self-help remedies—acceleration of liability in the one case, termination and repossession in the other—against which the debtor's right of set-off was no protection. But where the creditor exercises no self-help remedies and institutes proceedings for both the amount due and non-monetary relief consequent on default in payment, a set-off sufficient to extinguish the amount due (whether or not claimed by the plaintiff in addition to the non-monetary relief) would seem to entitle the defendant to have the claim dismissed.[92]

---

[92] See below para.7–52.

Independent set-off may be pleaded in addition to or in lieu of a substantive defence

7–40   A defendant who has a substantive defence to a claim for payment may nevertheless decide not to invoke it and rely simply on a right of independent set-off; or he may plead the substantive defence with an alternative plea of set-off in case the first plea is unsuccessful. In order for set-off to be available under the rules established by the Statutes of Set-Off, five conditions must be satisfied:

Conditions of entitlement to independent set-off

(1) *Both claim and cross-claim must be for sums of money or for relief based on the non-payment of money*

7–41   It is, of course, inherent in all forms of set-off that they concern the setting of one money claim against another. However, it is not essential that the claim should itself be for money; it suffices that it is a claim for relief based on the non-payment of money, *e.g.* specific performance[93] or forfeiture of a lease.

(2) *Both claim and cross-claim must be for debts*

7–42   Independent set-off is confined to debts, so that both claim and cross-claim must be liquidated or ascertained with certainty at the time of pleading.[94] However, it has been held that if the claim is by nature a liquidated claim, *e.g.* is for agreed hire charges, the fact that the amount is in dispute does not prevent it from being asserted by way of independent set-off.[96]

Equity regards beneficial ownership of a liquidated claim as sufficient for independent set-off even if the bare legal title was in another, and applies the Statutes of Set-Off by analogy.[95]

(3) *Both debts must be due at the time of pleading and judgment*

7–43   In contrast to transaction set-off or insolvency set-off, independent set-off is available only where both claim and cross-claim are due at the commencement of the action.[97] Neither a future claim nor a contingent claim may be

---

[93] *BICC plc v Burndy Corp.* [1985] 1 All E.R. 417, Kerr L.J. dissenting.
[94] *Hanak v Green* [1958] 2 All E.R. 151, *per* Morris L.J. at 145; *Stooke v Taylor* (1880) 5 Q.B.D. 569, *per* Cockburn J. at 575; and see text and n.27, above.
[95] See above, paras 7–04, 7–10.
[96] *Aectra Refining and Manufacturing Inc. v Exmar NV* [1994] 1 W.L.R. 1634.
[97] *Richards v James* (1848) 2 Exch. 471. Semble, this is unaffected by the general principle that all matters may be considered, whether arising before or after the institution of proceedings (see

set off against a present debt. Accordingly an unmatured note may not be set off against a deposit that has become repayable to the maker of the note, still less may a contingent claim against the creditor as surety be set off against the debt due to the creditor, except in bankruptcy or by contract. Moreover, the cross-claim must not only be due at the time of pleading but must still be outstanding at the time of judgment.[98]

(4) *The claim and cross-claim must be mutual*

By this is meant that the two claims must be between the same parties in the same right. So a purely joint liability cannot be pleaded by way of set-off against a several debt.[99] Moreover, for statutory set-off what is required is identity of legal ownership of the claim and cross-claim; hence a debt due from a beneficiary cannot be set off at law against a claim by the trustee.[1] However, equity is more liberal and looks through to the beneficial title.[2]

7–44

(5) *Both claim and cross-claim must be subject to determination by the court*

The independent set-off mechanism cannot operate if the claim is to be tried in court proceedings but the proceedings on the cross-claim have been stayed and referred to arbitration pursuant to an arbitration agreement.[3]

7–45

(6) *The circumstances must not be such as would make it inequitable for the defendant to plead set-off*

Even where independent set-off would otherwise be available, it will be denied where there is an equity to prevent it, as where the rights, though legally mutual, are not equitably mutual[4] or where there is an express or implied agreement between the parties precluding set-off.[5]

7–46

---

below, para.7–68, n.8), for the maturity of the two debts at the time of commencement of proceedings is inherent in the language of the statute.

[98] *Briscoe v Hill* (1842) 10 M. & W. 735, *per* Parke B. at 738.

[99] *Vulliamy v Noble* (1817) 3 Mer. 593, *per* Lord Eldon L.C. at 618.

[1] *Tudor v Tudor* (1833) 4 B. & Ad. 745, *per* Littledale J. at 751. For the different rule prevailing in equity see below.

[2] In the days of the Statutes of Set-Off it gave the remedy by way of analogy with the Statute. See above, paras 7–04, 7–10.

[3] *Aectra Refining and Manufacturing Inc. v Exmar NV* [1994] 1 W.L.R. 1634.

[4] *Re Whitehouse & Co.* (1878) 9 Ch.D. 595, *per* Jessel M.R. at 597.

[5] As in the case of claims to freight. See below para.7–60.

Significance of independent set-off

7–47 Independent set-off has become of diminished importance with the expansion of transaction set-off. There is, however, one case in which recourse to the rules of independent set-off[6] is necessary, namely where the claim and cross-claim, whether arising under the same or separate transactions, are unconnected, so that the cross-claim does not satisfy the requirement of equity that it should be inseperably connected with the claim. So in an action for money due under a bill of exchange a liquidated sum payable to the defendant under a transaction unconnected with that for which the bill was given may, it is thought, be set off at law under the rules established by the Statutes of Set-Off[7] though it cannot be set off in equity.

5. TRANSACTION (EQUITABLE) SET-OFF

(i) General principles

Nature of transaction set-off

7–48 Transaction set-off is that form of equitable set-off which arises where the claim and cross-claim are closely connected. It is to be contrasted with the right of independent set-off given by equity by analogy with the Statutes of Set-Off as previously described. Historically transaction set-off was perceived as procedural in character, so that it operated not as a substantive defence but, like independent set-off, as a means of reducing the amount for which the plaintiff was entitled to judgment. However, this perception changed in the light of the decision of the Court of Appeal in *Hanak v Green*,[8] and it is now clear that transaction set-off provides a substantive defence and thus operates in diminution of liability.[9] What remains unclear is the manner of its exercise and the time as from which it takes effect.[10]

Prerequisites of transaction set-off

7–49 There are four general requirements for transaction set-off. The first three are well-established, the fourth has attracted a division of judicial opinion and

---

[6] Embodying rules previously applied under the Statutes of Set-Off, which required that both claim and cross-claim be legal, and those applied by equity by analogy with the Statute, which looked to beneficial rather than legal title. See above, paras 7–04, 7–10.

[7] See below para.7–57.

[8] [1958] 2 Q.B. 9.

[9] *BICC plc v Burndy Corp.* [1985] Ch. 232; *Federal Commerce and Navigation Ltd. v Molena Alpha Inc. (The Nanfri)* [1978] 1 Q.B. 927, affirmed on other issues [1979] A.C. 757.

[10] See below, paras 7–54 *et seq.*

awaits authoritative determination. Even where there would otherwise be a right of set-off it may be cut off, as regards future dealings, by receipt of notice of assignment[11] and may be excluded by agreement.[12]

(1) *The cross-claim must be inseparably connected with the claim*

The cross-claim must be inseparably connected with the claim, that is, so closely connected with the claim as to render it inequitable to allow the plaintiff to obtain judgment on his claim without giving credit for the cross-claim.[13] Earlier authorities referred to the requirement that the cross-claim "impeach" the claim but more recently this label has been discarded as unhelpful and replaced by the "inseparable connection" test.[14] The mere fact that the cross-claim arises out of the same transaction as the claim is not by itself sufficient to attract a right of transaction set-off; the claim and cross-claim must be so inseparably related that it would be an injustice to allow judgment for the claimant on the claim without deduction of the cross-claim.[15] Thus in an action by a solicitor for recovery of his costs the defendant may set off a claim for damages for negligence on the part of the solicitor which necessitated the work for which his bill was rendered[16]; a claim for negligence and breach of contract in the storage of a vehicle, as the result of which it was stolen, may be set off against a claim for storage charges[17]; a claim for damages for a landlord's failure to repair may be set off against rent payable under the lease[18]; and a claim for delay or defective workmanship by a builder against a liquidated sum payable under the building contract.[19] On the other hand, the balance allegedly payable under an unsettled account between the parties is not available as a set-off even if arising under the same transaction,[20] nor is set-off allowed in respect of a cross-claim for unliquidated damages for breach of contract against a sum payable under the contract for a performance unconnected with that to which the cross-claim

7–50

---

[11] See below, para.7–66.

[12] See below, para.7–69.

[13] *Rawson v Samuel* (1841) Cr. & Ph. 161; *Hanak v Green* [1958] 2 All E.R. 141; *The Teno* [1977] 2 Lloyd's Rep. 289; *British Anzani (Felixstowe) Ltd. v International Maritime Management (U.K.) Ltd.* [1979] 2 All E.R. 1063.

[14] *Bim Kemi v Blackburn Chemicals Ltd.* [2001] 2 Lloyd's Rep. 92, adopting the speech of Lord Brandon in B*ank of Boston Connecticut v European Grain and Shipping Ltd.* [1989] A.C. 1056 at 1102–1103.

[15] *Rawson v Samuel* (1841) Cr. & Ph. 161; *Government of Newfoundland v Newfoundland Ry. Co.* (1888) 13 App.Cas. 199 at 212; *Hanak v Green* [1958] 2 All E.R. 141 at 149.

[16] *Piggott v Williams* (1821) 6 Madd. 95.

[17] *Morgan & Son Ltd. v S. Martin Johnson & Co. Ltd.* [1948] 2 All E.R. 196.

[18] In *British Anzani (Felixstowe) Ltd. v International Marine Management Ltd.* [1980] Q.B. 137 Forbes J. held that the defendant tenant was entitled to set off such a claim even though it arose not under the lease but under a building agreement pursuant to which the lease was granted; *a fortiori* where the repairing covenant is contained in the lease.

[19] *D. Galambos & Son Pty. Ltd. v McIntyre* (1975) 5 A.C.T.R. 10; *Bim Kemi v Blackburn Chemicals Ltd.*, above.

[20] *Rawson v Samuel*, above; *Hill v Ziymack* (1908) 7 C.L.R. 352; *Bhogal v Punjab National Bank, The Times*, November 25, 1987.

relates.[21] However, it has to be said that English judges have tended to disregard this principle and to interpret the requirement of close connection more liberally than some of their Australian colleagues,[22] almost invariably allowing even unliquidated claims for damages, whether in contract or in tort, to be set off against a liquidated claim where the two claims arose under the same contract.[23] One of the few exceptions is claims to freight, where the courts have adhered to the well-settled rule, based on an implied term resulting from long-standing usage, that neither abatement nor set-off is permitted against a claim for freight unless otherwise agreed by the parties or by a contrary usage.[24]

7–51 Whilst the fact that the claim and cross-claim arise out of the same transaction is not *per se* sufficient to establish a transaction set-off, conversely it is not a barrier to set-off that the cross-claim arises out of a separate transaction; it is enough that it springs from transactions that are inseparably connected, so that the defendant has a claim to the protection of equity, and this is even if both claim and cross-claim are unliquidated.[25] So a builder sued for failure to carry out work properly under a building contract has been held entitled to set off a claim against the building owner on a *quantum meruit* for additional work done and even a claim for damages for trespass to his workmen's tools.[26] Similarly, a lessee sued for arrears of rent was allowed to set off (*inter alia*) a claim for damages for breach of the building agreement pursuant to which the lease was granted.[27] But where the two contracts are unconnected, transaction set-off is not available and the defendant will have to fall back on independent set-off or its equitable analogy, for which purpose it is necessary that both claims be liquidated.

A similar principle applies where rights under two unconnected contracts between the same parties become vested in the same assignee. For example, if D owes money to C under a loan contract and has a claim for unliquidated damages against C for defective workmanship under a separate building contract and C assigns its right under both contracts to T, then in a claim by T against D on the loan contract D cannot set off his cross-claim under the building contract. *A fortiori* no transaction set-off is available where the two unconnected contracts were made by the debtor with different parties. So if two suppliers of the same customer assign their debts to the same factoring company, the customer cannot, when sued by the factor, set off against the factor's claim as assignee of the first supplier an unliquidated cross-claim which the customer has against the second supplier, for this arises under a contract unconnected with that from which the factor's claim is derived. In both these

---

[21] *Re K.L. Tractors Ltd.* [1954] V.L.R. 505.

[22] See Meagher, Gummow & Lehane, Equity: *Doctrines and Remedies* (3rd ed.), para.3710; I. C. F. Spry, *Equitable Remedies* (6th ed.), pp.178–180.

[23] See, for example, *Hanak v Green*, above, n.13.

[24] See below para.2–60.

[25] *Bim Kemi AB v Blackburn Chemicals Ltd.* [2001] 2 Lloyd's Rep. 92.

[26] *Hanak v Green*, above, n.13. But the decision has not gone uncriticised. See n.22, above.

[27] *British Anzani (Felixstowe) Ltd. v International Marine Management (U.K.) Ltd.* [1980] Q.B. 137.

examples, if D's cross-claim had been liquidated instead of unliquidated he could have pleaded a independent set-off, for which no connection between the two claims is needed.

(2) *Cross-claim must be based on non-payment of money*

The second requirement is that the claim be for money or for relief based on the non-payment of money. It had at one time been thought that unless the claim was for money set-off was not available at all, even if the relief claimed was based on the non-payment of money, *e.g.* forfeiture or specific performance. However, in *BICC plc v Burndy Corp.*[28] the Court of Appeal held by a majority[29] that it sufficed that the claim there made for specific performance was based on the non-payment of money, and that if this requirement were satisfied there was no reason why set-off should not be pleaded as a defence to a claim for specific performance, whether the set-off was legal or equitable. In relation to equitable (transaction) set-off the majority view seems correct, for as Dillon L.J. cogently observed:

7–52

"I cannot see that it can make any difference in substance whether the claim for the other relief is joined in one action with the claim for payment to which the set-off is a valid defence, or whether only the other relief is claimed, leaving the claim to payment to be raised in a subsequent action or to be resolved by the application of the set-off."[30]

However, this cannot be true of legal (independent) set-off, which does not constitute a substantive defence, so that the claim and cross-claim maintain their independent existence until judgment.[31] Accordingly, in relation to this form of set-off Kerr L.J. was surely right in concluding that the defendant was not entitled to relief as a matter of right and that if relief was to be given it could only be because the court was entitled to take the existence of the cross-claim into account in exercising its discretion to refuse the equitable remedy of specific performance.

In the case of transaction set-off the ability to set off a money claim against non-monetary relief based on a default in payment is not confined to judicial relief but extends to set-off against a landlord's right of distress.[32]

---

[28] [1985] 1 All E.R. 417. As to financial instruments, see above, paras 1–40, n.41, and 6–41.
[29] Kerr L.J. dissented, holding that set-off could be asserted only as a defence to a claim for money and that if the claim was for non-monetary relief, such as specific performance, the existence of the cross-claim went only to the exercise of the court's discretion in equity.
[30] *ibid.*, at 425. It is not necessary that the right to payment shall have accrued due at the date of commencement of proceedings. See below para.7–68.
[31] *Stein v Blake* [1996] A.C. 243, per Lord Hoffmann at 251.
[32] *Eller v Grovecrest Investments Ltd.* [1995] Q.B. 272.

(3) *There must be mutuality*

7–53   Thirdly, the claims must be mutual, that is, due from the same parties in the same right.[33] It has sometimes been suggested that there is no requirement of mutuality for transaction set-off; but it would seem more accurate to say that equity, being concerned with beneficial interests rather than bare legal titles, construes the requirement of mutuality differently from that at law, so that where the plaintiff makes a claim as a bare trustee[34] the defendant may set off a debt due from the beneficiary,[35] and where it is the beneficiary who is sued he may set off a debt due from the claimant to the trustee and held on trust for him,[36] provided that, in accordance with the usual rule, the debt is closely connected with the claim that the defendant beneficiary can show equitable grounds for being protected against the claim.[37]

On the other hand, where a trustee enters into a contract, then unless he does so as agent of the beneficiary or otherwise negates his own liability he is personally liable to the other party[38] and cannot set off against that liability a debt due from the other party to the beneficiary, for whilst the benefit of a contract may be transferred or held on trust without the consent of the debtor the burden of a contract cannot be transferred without the consent of the creditor, so that there is no privity of contract between the other party and the beneficiary and thus no mutuality of claim and cross-claim. Similarly, where the defendant is sued by one who is a bare trustee for a beneficiary, the defendant cannot set off a cross-claim he has against another trustee for that beneficiary, for the claim is vested in the beneficiary but the liability on the cross-claim is the personal liability of the second trustee.[39] Again, a defendant cannot set off against his personal liability to the claimant a debt due from the claimant to the defendant in his capacity as trustee or personal representative,[40] and one who buys goods from a company after notice that a receiver has been appointed by debenture holders of the company cannot, when sued for the price, set off a claim arising against the company prior to the receiver's appointment, for the beneficial right to the

---

[33] *Middleton v Pollock* (1875) L.R. 20 Eq. 29.

[34] *Aliter*, where the claim is as trustee under an active trust or as executor or administrator of an unadministered estate, for until the beneficiary has acquired the right to terminate the trust or the administration of the estate has been completed the beneficiary has no interest in the assets (*Middleton v Pollock Ex p. Nugee* (1875) L.R. 20 Eq. 29).

[35] *Bankes v Jarvis* [1903] 1 K.B. 549. *Aliter*, where the trust is disputed and the assertion of the trust involves the taking of accounts to establish whether the alleged beneficiary does indeed have a cross-claim against the plaintiff (*Re Willis Percival & Co. Ex p. Morier* (1879) 12 Ch.D. 491; applied in *Bhogal v Punjab National Bank* [1988] 2 All E.R. 296).

[36] *Cochrane v Green* (1860) 9 C.B.N.S. 448.

[37] *Middleton v Pollock*, above, *per* Jessel M.R. at 36–37, criticising *Cochrane v Green*, above, for neglecting this qualification.

[38] See Halsbury's Laws of England (4th ed., 2000 reissue), Vol.48, para.976 and cases there cited; Ford & Hardingham, "Trading Trusts: Rights and Liabilities of Beneficiaries," in Equity and Commercial Relationships (P. D. Finn, ed.) 48 at 71.

[39] This point was taken in argument in *Bhogal v Punjab National Bank*, above, but was not discussed in the judgments, the respondents succeeding anyway on (*inter alia*) the separate ground mentioned above, n.35.

[40] *Middleton v Pollock Ex p. Nugee*, above.

price is vested not in the company but in the debenture holder for whose benefit the receiver concluded the sale contract.[41] Where an assignee of a debt in turn assigns it to another, the second assignee, though taking subject to equities affecting the first assignment,[42] is not affected by direct claims the debtor may have against the first assignee,[43] for the second assignee's claim is ultimately held in right of the original creditor, not of the first assignee, so that there is no mutuality of claim and cross-claim.

It is submitted that where one of the claims is vested in a single creditor and the other in joint creditors, set-off is no more available in equity than at law,[44] and that the cases commonly relied on to support a right of set-off in such a case[45] did not concern set-off in the true sense at all but were decided on different grounds.[46]

(4) *The cross-claim must be overtly asserted*

A question which has yet to be authoritatively determined is the manner in which the remedy of transaction set-off is to be exercised. There are at least three possible approaches. The first is that the set-off is automatic and self-executing, so that at the very moment the cross-claim comes into existence it operates to extinguish the claim *pro tanto*.[47] This approach has little to commend it, and even in legal systems which in theory adopt it, such as the French civil code,[48] courts have found it impracticable to apply the strict letter of the law and require set-off to be asserted.

7–54

---

[41] *N.W. Robbie & Co. Ltd. v Witney Warehouse Co. Ltd.* [1963] 3 All E.R. 613 (where the cross-claim was by an assignee, but the principle applies equally where there has been no assignment). Aliter, where the claim made by the receiver is not on a new contract concluded after his appointment but is a pre-receivership contract which the receiver is carrying out and the cross-claim arises under that contract (*Parsons v Sovereign Bank of Canada* [1913] A.C. 160; *Rather Iron Works Ltd. v Canterbury Precision Engineers Ltd.* [1974] Q.B. 1).

[42] Obviously in so far as the first assignee takes free from equities (*e.g.* because the debtor's cross-claim arose after notice of the assignment), the second assignee likewise takes free from equities. This was not spelled out in *The Raven* (below, n.43) since it did not arise on the facts of that case, where one assigned claim was subject to equities binding on the first assignee whilst as regards the other assigned claim there were no equities at all, merely a direct claim against the first assignor.

[43] *Banco Central S.A. & Trevelan Nagiation Inc. v Lingoss & Falce Ltd. (The Raven)* [1980] 2 Lloyd's Rep. 266; *Re Milan Tramways Co.* (1884) 25 Ch.D. 587. See further below para.167.

[44] Except where the joint debt is also due severally (*Fletcher v Dyche* (1787) 2 Term Rep. 32).

[45] *Ex p. Stephens* (1805) 11 Ves. 24; *Vulliamy v Noble* (1817) 3 Mer. 593.

[46] *Middleton v Pollock Ex p. Knight* (1875) 20 L.R. Eq. 515, where Jessel M.R. pointed out (at 518–523) that *Ex p. Stephens* was decided not on set-off but on the ground that the right of set-off the defendant debtor would have enjoyed if she had asserted it in due time was concealed from her by the fraud of the creditors, and that *Vulliamy v Noble* was not a case of set-off as between a single debt on one side and a joint debt on the other but turned on an agreement between the parties by which the proceeds of securities giving rise to the single debt were to be applied in discharge of the joint obligation, leaving the single creditor entitled to payment of the balance.

[47] This would not, of course, be the position in the case of independent set-off, where the set-off is purely procedural and the claim and cross-claim remain distinct until judgment. See above, para.7–36.

[48] CC art.1290.

There are sound practical reasons to reject automatic set-off[49] and to treat set-off as an equity which has to be asserted. First, both parties may wish to keep the claim and cross-claim separate. Secondly, there may be complications where a cross-claim is available against two or more claims, and the party having the cross-claim has an interest in deciding against which claim he wishes his cross-claim to be set off. Thirdly, the automatic extinction of an undoubted claim through a cross-claim not asserted by the respondent to the claim could mislead the claimant into believing that his claim was not in dispute and into exercising default remedies only to find later that he had no right to do so. Certainly there has been no English case in which a right of set-off has been held operative without being asserted at some stage. The need to assert a right of set-off has been well put by Dr Shelagh McCracken:

"It is not 'set-off' which of itself offers a defence—rather it is a consequence of a valid exercise of a right of set-off that the original obligation (or a part thereof) is no longer required to be performed."[50]

7–55   The second approach, then, is that set-off takes effect only from the time it is asserted (whether in or before proceedings), so that if before then the defendant's failure to meet the claim has triggered a right of self-help the plaintiff is entitled to treat the defendant as in default and to pursue his self-help remedy. English law does not appear to subscribe to this approach either, the courts taking the position that the assertion and establishment of a right of set-off demonstrates that to the extent of the set-off the party invoking it was never in breach of his own obligation.[51] The third approach is that the set-off has to be asserted in due time[52] but if so asserted it takes effect as from the time the right of set-off arose, so that it may retrospectively reduce or extinguish the claim. This appears to be the position in English law.

The time at which the right of set-off must be asserted depends upon whether the claimant institutes legal proceedings to enforce his claim or resorts to self-help measures. In the case of legal proceedings the right of set-off, like any other defence, must be properly pleaded, failing which the claimant is entitled to judgment on his claim. In the case of resort to self-help the position is less clear. The issue of retrospectivity becomes of crucial importance where a party, having asserted his right to payment without receiving any response indicating that the other party is relying on a set-off in respect of a cross-claim, proceeds to exercise a contractual self-help default remedy, such as termination of the contract, repossession of goods leased under the contract or acceleration of payment pursuant to an acceleration clause. Does the later assertion and establishment of a right of set-off extinguishing the claim invalidate the exercise of the default remedy so as to render

---

[49] The position is otherwise in insolvency set-off, where the set-off is automatic and self-executing. See below, paras 7–77 *et seq.*

[50] *The Banker's Remedy of Set-Off* (2nd ed.), p.121.

[51] *Federal Commerce & Navigation Co. Ltd. v Molena Alpha Inc. (The Nanfri)* [1978] Q.B. 927, *per* Lord Denning M.R. at 974; *BICC plc v Burndy Corp.* [1985] Ch. 232.

[52] See below.

it ineffective or, still worse, expose the claimant to a liability for conversion? The question was addressed by Lord Denning M.R. in *The Nanfri*[53] in the following terms:

"Again take the case where the contract gives a creditor a right to take the law into his own hands – to take a particular course of action if a sum is not paid – such as to forfeit a lease for non-payment of rent, or to withdraw a vessel for non-payment of hire. There the distinction between set off and cross-claim is crucial. When the debtor has a true set off it goes in reduction of the sums owing to the creditor. If the creditor does not allow it to be deducted, he is in peril. He will be liable in damages if he exercises his contractual right of withdrawal wrongly. But when the debtor has no set off or defence properly so called, but only a counterclaim or cross-action, then the creditor need not allow any deduction to be made. He can exercise his contractual right without fear; and leave the debtor to bring an action for damages on his counterclaim."[54]

The case postulated by Lord Denning is where the creditor "does not allow" the set-off to be deducted from his claim, which implies that the other party is asserting the right to deduct the amount of the set-off and is refused. That provides a sensible solution to the problem. If set-off is asserted before the creditor has resorted to self-help he should give credit for it before taking self-help measures and is precluded from taking such measures if the set-off extinguishes his claim. Where, on the other hand, the other party does not contest the claim on the ground that he has a right to deduct the amount of his cross-claim the creditor should be entitled to treat the other party as in default and to pursue his self-help remedies on the basis that the other party is electing to keep his cross-claim in existence and to utilise it in some other fashion, for example, in reduction of some other existing or future claim of the creditor. If the position were otherwise the creditor would have to suspend his self-help remedy indefinitely to await a possible future assertion of a right of set-off. Thus where the remedy for default in payment of an installment is to make the entire balance of the debt become due and payable, an acceleration before the assertion of a right of set-off should be considered effective so as to make the full balance of the debt payable, though the debtor would remain entitled to set off his cross-claim against that balance.

(5) *The circumstances must be such that it would be manifestly unjust to refuse to allow the set-off*

Since fairness is the principle underlying set-off, it will be applied only where it would be manifestly unfair or unjust to deny it. It will only be in unusual cases that this test will not be satisfied where the transaction giving rise to the **7–56**

---

[53] See above, n.51.
[54] [1978] Q.B. 927 at 974.

cross-claim is inseparably connected with the transaction giving rise to the claim.[55] Nevertheless it has been held to be appropriate in every case to give separate question to the question of manifest injustice.[56]

(ii) Particular types of transaction

Set-off against liability on a negotiable instrument

7-57   A negotiable instrument, such as a bill of exchange, a promissory note or a negotiable certificate of deposit, generates an autonomous payment obligation, a contract entirely distinct from that of the underlying transaction in respect of which is was given. The courts are extremely reluctant to allow a breach of the underlying contract to be set up as a defence to a claim on a negotiable instrument, for fear that this will adversely affect its marketability as the equivalent of cash. Hitherto almost all the reported decisions have been concerned with bills of exchange. The typical case in which the question arises is where a seller of goods who receives a bill of exchange as conditional payment of the price applies for summary judgment on the bill after its dishonour and the defendant seeks leave to defend on the ground that the seller committed a breach of the contract of sale, *e.g.* by delivering defective goods. There does not appear to be a reported case in which a set-off in the strict sense has been upheld. The authorities clearly establish that an unliquidated cross-claim cannot be set off against liability on a bill of exchange, so that where defective goods are accepted by the buyer, restricting his rights to a claim for damages for breach of warranty, these cannot be set off against liability on the bill but must be claimed in a separate action.[57] Still less is the defendant entitled to set off a claim for unliquidated damages arising under an entirely separate contract.[58] Refusal of set-off in these cases, though often described as a rule particularly applicable to bills of exchange, follows the general equitable rule that an unliquidated claim arising under one contract cannot be set off against a liquidated claim made on a separate and unconnected contract.[59]

---

[55] *Bim Kemi AB v Blackburn Chemicals Ltd.* [2001] 2 Lloyd's Rep. 92, *per* Potter L.J. at 201.

[56] *ibid.* In the next paragraph of his judgment, Potter L.J. put the matter slightly differently, saying that the judge at first instance was right to consider whether there were factors or circumstances which militated against the justice or fairness of recognising the right of set-off. This leaves open the question whether the onus is on the party asserting set-off to show, as a separate factor, that it would be manifestly unjust to refuse set-off, or on the party resisting set-off to show that to allow it would be unfair or unjust. It is thought that once the test of inseparable connection has been satisfied there is a presumption that it would be unjust to refuse set-off and it is for the claimant to show why it would be unfair or unjust to allow it.

[57] *James Lamont & Co. v Hyland Ltd.* [1950] 1 K.B. 585; *Brown Shipley & Co. Ltd. v Alicia Hosiery Ltd.* [1966] 1 Lloyd's Rep. 668; *Cebora S.N.C. v S.I.P. (Industrial Products) Ltd.* [1976] 1 Lloyd's Rep. 271; *Nova (Jersey) Knit Ltd. v Kammgarn Spinnerei GmbH* [1977] 1 W.L.R. 713; *Montebianco Industrie Tessili S.p.A. v Carlyle Mills (London) Ltd.* [1981] 1 Lloyd's Rep. 509.

[58] *Nova (Jersey) Knit Ltd. v Kammgarn Spinnerei GmbH*, above.

[59] See above, paras 7–50 *et seq.*

However, where the claimant is not a holder in due course[60] the defendant is entitled to plead total or partial failure of consideration as a defence to a claim on the bill where this gives him a right to recover a liquidated amount.[61] So if the buyer exercises a right to reject defective goods, with a consequent claim for recovery of the price as money paid on a total failure of consideration, he can set this up as a complete defence to a claim on a bill given for the price, whilst if he accepts some goods but exercises a right to reject the remainder he can defend an action on the bill as to that part of it which represents the price of the rejected goods.[62] In these cases, the buyer's cross-claim is not correctly described as a set-off; it is a substantive defence to a claim on the bill.

What remains unclear is whether there is a special rule in relation to negotiable instruments where the defendant's cross-claim does not arise out of the underlying transaction which represents the consideration for the bill but is a liquidated claim based on an unconnected contract, *e.g.* a claim for repayment of a loan made to the holder of the bill. Such a claim would not constitute a substantive defence, for it does not affect the consideration for which the instrument has been given, nor could it be asserted as a transaction set-off, the contract generated by the instrument being considered unconnected to the underlying contract. However, in the ordinary way it would be available as an independent set-off.[63] Is the usual rule displaced where the claimant's claim is based on a negotiable instrument? There seems no reason why it should be. Where the defendant's claim is liquidated, so that it can be seen from the outset to what extent it represents an offset to the claimant's claim, the defendant ought to be allowed to plead it by way of set-off even against a claim on a negotiable instrument.

Set-off against liability under other payment instruments

The negotiable instrument is only one form of autonomous payment instrument. Others include the irrevocable commercial credit, the performance bond or guarantee and the standby credit.[64] These differ from the negotiable

7–58

---

[60] Failure of consideration cannot be set up against a holder in due course. See Bills of Exchange Act 1882, s.38(2).

[61] *Forman & Co. v Wright* (1851) 11 C.B. 481; *Thoni GmbH & Co. KG v R.T.P. Equipment Ltd.* [1979] 2 Lloyd's Rep. 282.

[62] *ibid.*

[63] See above paras 7–36 *et seq.*

[64] The commercial credit is a primary undertaking issued by a bank to a beneficiary such as the seller under a related trade transaction undertaking to accept, pay or negotiate a draft, or pay without a draft, on presentation of specified documents. The bank is the first port of call for payment and the buyer or other party at whose request the credit is opened (the account party) cannot be called upon to pay unless the bank fails to honour the credit. A performance bond or guarantee is a credit designed to support non-monetary performance of a contract, as opposed to payment, and is intended to be called upon only if the account party defaults under the underlying contract, though the bank's liability to pay is not dependent on proof of actual default, merely on presentation of a demand with such other document, *e.g.* a certificate of default, as may be specified in the credit. A standby credit fulfils broader business functions than the performance bond or guarantee but is legally indistinguishable from it.

instrument in two respects. First, they are not negotiable, so that the question of holder in due course status does not arise. Secondly, they are considered enforceable by mercantile usage despite the fact that they are unsupported by consideration,[65] and accordingly they are not susceptible to challenge on the ground of failure of consideration. Like negotiable instruments, they would appear to be immune from transaction set-off arising from a claim under the underlying transaction, for they too are treated as autonomous contracts.[66] But the issuer of such a credit, bond or guarantee is entitled to plead a statutory set-off in the unusual case where there is an existing relationship between the issuer and the beneficiary and a liquidated sum is due to the issuer from the beneficiary under some separate account.[67]

Defence and set-off against rent

7–59   For many years the view prevailed among practitioners that a landlord was entitled to be paid his rent without deduction and that rent was not subject to the ordinary rules of abatement and set-off. It is now clear that this is not so, and that in principle no special treatment is accorded to a claim for rent.

Cross-claims by a tenant against his landlord which are available to be set up in answer to the landlord's claim for rent fall into one of two categories: those which constitute a substantive defence to the rent claim and those which can merely be pleaded by way of set-off. The distinction is theoretically of significance in that a defence which goes to the whole of the rent claim prevents the tenant from being in breach of his rent obligation under the lease, whereas a cross-claim by way of set-off is merely a countervailing claim, not a payment of rent as such, and its availability would not prevent the landlord from exercising a right of forfeiture for non-payment of rent, though in the ordinary way the court would obviously treat a set-off covering the whole of the arrears of rent as a ground for granting relief against forfeiture.[68]

There are at least three cases in which the tenant's cross-claim constitutes a substantive defence to the landlord's claim for rent:

(1)   Where the landlord has committed a breach of an obligation in the lease, or in another contract, and the performance of that obligation is expressly made a condition of the tenant's liability for rent;

---

[65] See Roy Goode, *Commercial Law* (2nd ed.), pp.986–987.
[66] *Discount Records Ltd. v Barclays Bank Ltd.* [1975] 1 W.L.R. 315; *Edward Owen Engineering Ltd. v Barclays Bank International Ltd.* [1978] 1 Q.B. 159; *United City Merchants (Investments) Ltd. v Royal Bank of Canada (The American Accord)* [1983] A.C. 168. *In Esso Petroleum Co. Ltd. v Milton* [1997] 1 W.L.R. 938 the Court of Appeal held by a majority (Simon Brown L.J. dissenting) that an obligation to pay by direct debit was governed by similar considerations, so that where the debtor cancelled the direct debit the creditor was entitled to summary judgment for the amount due to him without set-off.
[67] *Hong Kong and Shanghai Banking Corp v Kloeckner AG* [1990] 2 Q.B. 514.
[68] Under s.146 of the Law of Property Act 1925.

(2)   Where the landlord has failed to carry out a repairing covenant after receiving notice of disrepair and the tenant has expended money in having the repairs carried out himself[69];

(3)   Where at the request of the landlord money has been paid by the tenant in discharge of some obligation of the landlord connected with the demised premises.[70]

In case (1), the defence derives from the express condition precedent to the tenant's liability for rent. Case (2), which at first sight appears to be an application of the common law principle of abatement enunciated in *Mondel v Steel*,[71] is in fact founded on a quite separate principle, namely that the tenant's expenditure in carrying out the landlord's repairing obligations is equivalent to *pro tanto* payment of the rent.[72] This being the case, the defence does not depend on the tenant showing a diminution in the value of the premises by reason of the disrepair.[73] On the other hand, the tenant must show that the landlord has broken his covenant, by failing to repair after having had notice of disrepair.[74] Moreover, it is not sufficient that the tenant has incurred a liability for the cost of repairs; he must have actually paid for them.[75] There appears to be a division of judicial opinion as to whether the tenant must go further and show that the quantum of the expenditure has either been accepted by the landlord or held by a judgment or award as proper and reasonable, so that damages are not at large. No such requirement is mentioned in the judgment of Goff J., in *Lee-Parker v Izzet*,[76] whereas in the latter case of *British Anzani (Felixstowe) Ltd. v International Marine Management (U.K.) Ltd.*[77] Forbes J. considered that until such acceptance or award the tenant's cross-claim remained a matter of assessment and was thus unliquidated and could not be treated as equivalent to payment of the rent. Even if this be so, it is clear that the tenant has at least a set-off as regards his expenditure, although the proper quantum remains to be established.[78] Case (3) is likewise treated as equivalent to payment of rent, constituting a substantive defence to the extent of the payment.

Even where the tenant does not have a substantive defence, he is entitled to set off a cross-claim against rent in accordance with the equitable rules previously discussed. In particular, he may set off even an unliquidated claim for

---

[69] *Taylor v Beal* (1591) Cro. Eliz. 222; *Lee-Parker v Izzet* [1971] 3 All E.R. 1099; *British Anzani (Felixstowe) Ltd. v International Marine Management Ltd.* [1980] Q.B. 137.

[70] *Taylor v Beal*, above; *British Anzani (Felixstowe) Ltd. v International Marine Management Ltd.*, above.

[71] (1841) 8 M. & W. 858. See below, para.7–71.

[72] *Lee-Parker v Izzet*, above; *British Anzani (Felixstowe) Ltd. v International Marine Management Ltd.*, above.

[73] *ibid.*

[74] *ibid.*

[75] *ibid.*

[76] [1971] 3 All E.R. 1099.

[77] [1980] Q.B. 137.

[78] *ibid.*; *Melville v Grapelodge Developments Ltd.* (1980) 39 P. & C.R. 179.

damages where this is based on the lease itself or on an agreement which is closely connected with it, *e.g.* the building agreement under which the lease was granted.[79]

Set-off against freight and hire[80]

7–60   There is a well-settled rule that there can be no set-off against a claim for freight, which is payable without deduction.[81] However, in recent cases a distinction has been drawn between freight for the carriage of cargo and hire for the use of a vessel under a time charterparty. In the latter case, the charterer has been held entitled to make deductions for loss suffered through breakdown of machinery and speed reduction in the chartered vessel.[82] Indeed, the courts have said that the deduction need not be a completely accurate assessment of the charterer's loss; it suffices that it was a reasonable assessment made in good faith.[83] The judgments refer to this right of deduction as a set-off, but since it is exercisable even before proceedings it seems more accurate to regard it as an application of the common law doctrine of abatement enunciated in *Mondel v Steel*,[84] which, as we have seen, is not a set-off but a substantive defence.

Set-off against secured debt

7–61   The fact that a debt is secured by a mortgage does not preclude it from being subject to transaction set-off, whether for liquidated or unliquidated damages, in proceedings for recovery of the debt.[85] The rule that there cannot be set-off against a property claim is irrelevant here, for the set-off is not against the asset given in security but against the sum secured.

---

[79] For a good analysis, see F. D. Rose, "Deductions from freight and hire under English law," [1982] L.M.C.L.Q. 33.

[80] *British Anzani (Felixstowe) Ltd. v International Marine Management Ltd.*, above.

[81] *Aries Tanker Corp. v Total Transport Ltd.* [1977] 1 All E.R. 398.

[82] *Federal Commerce Navigation Ltd. v Molena Alpha Inc. (The Nanfri)* [1979] A.C. 757; *Santiren Shipping Ltd. v Unimarine S.A.* [1981] 1 All E.R. 340. But there is no right of deduction in respect of a cross-claim not based on deprivation of or prejudice in the use of the vessel (*Leon Corp. v Atlantic Lines & Navigation Co. Inc. (The Leon)* [1985] 2 Lloyd's Rep. 470).

[83] *ibid.*

[84] *ibid.*

[85] *TSB Bank v Platts* [1998] 2 B.C.L.C. 1. The position is otherwise where the mortgagee's claim is for possession. While the normal rule is that set-off is available even against a claim for non-monetary relief where it is based on default in payment (see *BICC v Burndy Corp.* [1985] 1 Ch. 232), a mortgagee is in a special position because of his legal estate to take possession immediately the mortgage has been executed and despite the absence of default (*National Westminster Bank plc v Skelton* [1993] 1 All E.R. 242; *Ashley Guarantee plc v Zacaria* [1993] 1 All E.R. 254). See also below, paras 7–82, 7–84 and 7–85.

6. THE EFFECT OF ASSIGNMENT ON INDEPENDENT AND TRANSACTION SET-OFF

Set-off by assignee

The assignee of a debt or other chose in action is entitled to plead it by way   **7–62**
of set-off to the same extent as if it had been vested in him from the beginning.[86] He cannot, however, set off against his creditor's assignee a debt
purchased by him after notice of assignment.[87]

Defences and set-off against assignee[88]

There are four distinct rules governing the debtor's defensive rights against an   **7–63**
assignee.

First rule: assignee takes subject to defences Since the assignee cannot   **7–64**
stand in any better position than his assignor, he takes subject to all substantive defences and rights of abatement open to the debtor against the
assignor, whether or not existing at the time the debtor received notice of
the assignment. This rule does not constitute any special protection for
the debtor against an assignee; it is simply an application of the principle
that *nemo dat quod non habet*: the assignor cannot transfer greater rights
than he himself possesses.

Second rule: assignee takes subject to equities It is a rule of equity that the   **7–65**
assignee takes "subject to equities." This rule is often treated as synony-
mous with the first but it is in fact a distinct rule[89] evolved by courts of
equity[90] to protect the debtor against injustice that might result from an
assignment. In the case of a statutory assignment this second rule is now
embodied in s.136 of the Law of Property Act 1925, under which the
assignment is effectual in law "subject to equities having priority over the
right of the assignee." In theory, therefore, the debtor might be able to set
off against an assignee cross-claims not available as a set-off against the

---

[86] *Bennett v White* [1910] 2 K.B. 643.
[87] *N. W. Robbie & Co. Ltd. v Witney Warehouses Ltd.* [1963] 3 All E.R. 613. This is merely a specific application of the wider rule that precludes an assignee from setting up new equities arising after notice of assignment. See below. For the purpose of this rule and others set out below a fixed charge and a floating charge which has crystallised are equated with an assignment.
[88] For a thought-provoking reappraisal of the rules, see Andrew Tettenborn, "Assignees, equities and cross-claims: principle and confusion" [2002] L.M.C.L.Q. 485.
[89] And is more restrictive. See para.7–66.
[90] Who prior to the introduction of statutory assignments in the Supreme Court of Judicature Act 1873 were the only courts prepared to recognise the assignability of choses in action, and imposed certain conditions for so doing. For the position where the contract itself excludes equities see below para.7–69.

assignor.[91] But with the wide view which English courts now have of transaction set-off it is not easy to visualise circumstances in which a debtor could have a right of set-off against an assignee which would not be equally available against the assignor.

7–66 *Third rule: receipt of notice of assignment fixes eligibility for set-off* This is that the debtor cannot set off against the assignee cross-claims arising after he has received notice of assignment.[92] The reason for this rule is obvious: to allow the debtor, by further voluntary dealings with the assignor after receipt of notice of assignment, to bring into existence further cross-claims and set them off against the debt assigned would enable him to cut down at will the value of the assigned debt to the detriment of the assignee. When he receives the notice of assignment the debtor knows that the debt is no longer held by the assignor; if despite this he goes on dealing with the assignor the risk is on him and he cannot put it upon the assignee. The following points should be noted in connection with this third rule:

(1) It is not sufficient that the cross-claim arises under a contract concluded between the assignor and the debtor before notice of assignment was given; it is necessary that a debt should actually have arisen in favour of the debtor under the contract before he received notice of the assignment of his creditor's claim.[93] On the other hand, it is immaterial that the debt has not yet fallen due for payment; it suffices that the obligation has become a *debitum in praesenti, solvendum in futuro*[94] as opposed, for example, to a purely contingent liability.

(2) The relevant date is not the assignment but the date on which the debtor receives notice of it. For this purpose notice of the existence of a floating charge does not affect the debtor's right to set up fresh equities, for a floating charge gives no rights over any particular asset until crystallisation,[95] and is thus not equated with an assignment. So a debtor who continues to deal with a company after notice that it has granted a floating charge is nevertheless entitled to set off a cross-claim arising before crystallisation of the charge,[96] or after

---

[91] Meagher, Gummow & Lehane, *Equity Doctrines and Remedies* (3rd ed.), para.3710. In *Abousaff v Abacus Cities Ltd.* [1981] 4 W.W.R. 660, the court held that the debtor cannot set off against the assignee a cross-claim which would not have been a valid set-off against the assignor, so that the debtor's unliquidated claim for damages against the assignor for breach of contract separate from and unconnected with that on which the assigned debt is based could not be set off against the assignee of the debt.

[92] *Roxburghe v Cox* (1881) 17 Ch.D. 520; *Re Pinto Leite & Nephews* [1929] 1 Ch. 221; *Business Computers Ltd. v Anglo-African Leasing Ltd.* [1977] 2 All E.R. 741.

[93] *ibid.*

[94] *ibid.*; *Christie v Taunton, Delmard, Lane & Co.* [1893] 2 Ch. 175.

[95] See above paras 4–03 *et seq.*

[96] *Biggerstaff v Rowatt's Wharf Ltd.* [1896] 2 Ch. 93.

crystallisation and before he has received notice of it.[97] But he cannot set off claims arising after he has received notice of crystallisation.[98]

(3) The rule does not apply at all where the cross-claim is not a mere set-off but a substantive defence to the claim or a right of abatement; nor does it apply even to a pure set-off where this is closely or inseparably connected with the claim, whether arising under the same contract or under different contracts.[99]

Fourth rule: no set-off for cross-claims against intermediate assignees The fourth rule, which has been criticised,[1] is that the assignee takes subject only to equities available against his assignor, not to cross-claims of the debtor against an intermediate assignee,[2] because what the second assignee is asserting is not the rights of the first assignee but those of the original creditor.[3] On the other hand, in the relations between the second assignee and the original creditor, the second assignee cannot acquire a better title to the debt than his predecessor, so that if the first assignment is void or voidable at the suit of the original creditor, the second will be similarly affected.[4] **7–67**

7. OTHER ASPECTS OF INDEPENDENT AND TRANSACTION SET-OFF

Pleading set-off

Set-off is pleaded by way of defence to the claimant's claim.[5] In the case of independent set-off the sum to be set off had to have accrued due to the defendant by at the time of commencement of the action,[6] but this requirement was later considered[7] to have been dispensed with by rules of court in relation to **7–68**

---

[97] *Business Computers Ltd. v Anglo-African Leasing Ltd.* [1977] 2 All E.R. 741.

[98] *ibid.*

[99] *Smith v Parkes* (1852) 16 Beav. 115; *Government of Newfoundland v Newfoundland Rly. Co.* (1888) 13 App.Cas. 199; *Business Computers Ltd. v Anglo-African Leasing Ltd.*, above, *per* Templeman J. at 748. As to non-assignable debts, see para.3–40.

[1] Andrew Tettenborn [2002] L.M.C.L.Q. 485 at 491.

[2] *Banco Central S.A. & Trevelan Navigation Co. v Lingoss & Falce Ltd. (The Raven)* [1980] 2 Lloyd's Rep. 266; *Re Milan Tramways Co.* (1884) 25 Ch.D. 587.

[3] *Re Milan Tramways Co.*, above, *per* Cotton L.J. at 593.

[4] *Barnard v Hunter* (1865) 2 Jur. N.S. 1213; *Southern British National Trust Ltd. v Pither* (1937) 57 C.L.R. 89. The principle that a contract cannot be avoided after an innocent third party has acquired an interest in the subject-matter does not apply where what are transferred are the contract rights themselves, as opposed to the goods or other property the subject of the contract.

[5] C.P.R. r.16.6. This may be done even if the defendant is also filing a Pt 20 claim, *e.g.* a counterclaim. So if the amount of the cross-claim exceeds the claim the defendant should plead set-off to the extent necessary to extinguish the claim and counterclaim any balance.

[6] *Richards v James* (1848) 2 Ex. 471.

[7] In *Wood v Goodwin* [1884] W.N. 17.

transaction set-off.[8] If the defendant sets up a cross-claim which was statute-barred at the date of commencement of the action,[9] the plaintiff may rely on the Limitation Act 1980 in his reply, thus negating the set-off. This is one of the factors distinguishing set-off from a substantive defence, which is not subject to the Limitation Act.[10]

Exclusion of set-off by agreement

7–69   It is open to the parties to contract out of the right of independent or trans-action set-off,[11] whether by issuing securities that are expressed to be free from equities,[12] or by providing that payment is to be made without deduction or set-off,[13] or by specifying deductions that a party can make from the other party's entitlement so as to exclude by implication other deductions, including set-off.[14] A contractual waiver of a right of set-off against an assignee is not against public policy[15] and is binding on the debtor[16] except where it is rendered void under the Unfair Contract Terms Act 1977.[17]

Set-off by and against the Crown

7–70   In general, set-off may be pleaded both by and against the Crown by virtue of the Crown Proceedings Act 1947. However, in proceedings by the Crown, the defendant cannot without leave of the court plead set-off against a claim for taxes, duties or penalties or rely by way of set-off on a claim for repayment of taxes, duties or penalties.[18] Further, without leave of the court no set-off can be pleaded by or against the Crown where:

---

[8] R.S.C. Ord. 18, r.9, which provided that "a party my in any pleading plead any matter which has arisen at any time, whether before or since the issue of the writ." This appears to have been overlooked in *Edmunds v Lloyd Italico* [1986] 2 All E.R. 249, where, in holding that transaction set-off was not available in respect of a payment made to the defendant after the commencement of the action, the court cited *Richards v James*, above, which was, however, a case of independent set-off. The C.P.R. do not incorporate any equivalent to R.S.C. Ord. 18, r.9, but it is assumed that the practice under that rule continues to apply.

[9] A claim by way of set-off is deemed to be a separate action commenced on issue of the plaintiff's writ (Limitation Act 1980, s.35).

[10] *Henriksens Rederi A/S v PHZ Rolimpex (The Brede)* [1974] Q.B. 233.

[11] But not set-off in insolvency. See below para.177.

[12] *Re Blakely Ordnance Co.* (1867) L.R. 3 Ch. 154; *Re Agra and Masterman's Bank* (1867) L.R. 2 Ch. 391; *Hilger Analytical Ltd. v Rank Precision Industries Ltd.* [1984] B.C.L.C. 301.

[13] *John Dee Group Ltd. v WMH(21) Ltd.* [1998] B.C.C. 972; *Coca-Cola Finance Corp. v Finsat International Ltd.* [1996] 3 W.L.R. 849.

[14] *Mottram Consultants Ltd. v Bernard Sunley & Sons Ltd.* [1975] 2 Lloyd's Rep. 197 (Lord Morris of Borth-y-Gest and Lord Salmon dissenting).

[15] *Coca-Cola Finance Corp. v Finset*, above.

[16] See cases cited at n.35, above.

[17] *Stewart Gill Ltd. v Horatio Myers & Co. Ltd.* [1992] 1 Q.B. 600.

[18] Crown Proceedings Act 1947, s.35(2)(g); R.S.C., Ord. 77, r.6, annexed as Sch.1 to the CPR. This rule was criticised by the Insolvency Law Review Committee as unfair to the taxpayer and the general body of creditors (Insolvency Law and Practice (Cmnd. 8558, 1982), para.1345) but it has remained unchanged.

(1) the Crown is sued or sues in the name of a government department and the subject-matter of the set-off does not relate to that department; or

(2) the Crown is sued or sues in the name of the Attorney-General.[19]

The effect of these restrictions is to displace the principle that the Crown is indivisible and to preclude set-off against taxes or as between two claims involving two different government departments except where leave is given by the court.

8. ABATEMENT

The common law doctrine of abatement

The old common law doctrine that promise and counter-promise were gener-   **7–71**
ally to be treated as independent, so that failure to perform the one did not excuse non-performance of the other, found its strongest expression in contracts of sale of goods. The buyer wishing to withhold payment because the goods were not up to warranty was met with the answer that the sole condition of his obligation to pay the price was the transfer of property to him, and that this having happened the contract was partially executed, with the result that the buyer could not unilaterally retransfer the property and treat the contract as discharged.[20] However, in due course the rigour of the rule was mitigated by allowing the defendant to set up his claim for damages for breach of warranty in diminution of the price, on the basis that by reason of the breach what was supplied to the defendant was reduced in value. The locus classicus for the description of this right of abatement is the judgment of Parke B. in *Mondel v Steel*[21]:

"Formerly, it was the practice, where an action was brought for an agreed price of a specific chattel, sold with a warranty, or of work which was to be performed according to contract, to allow the plaintiff to recover the stipulated sum, leaving the defendant to a cross action for breach of the warranty or contract . . . But after the case of *Basten v Butter*[22] a different practice, which had been partially adopted before in the case of *King v Boston*[23] began to prevail, and being attended with much practical convenience, has been since generally followed; and the defendant is now permitted to show that the chattel by reason of the non-compliance with the

---

[19] *ibid.*
[20] *Street v Blay* (1831) 2 B. & Ad. 456.
[21] (1841) 8 M. & W. 858. *Mondel v Steel* was not in fact the root decision (see *Street v Blay*, above and cases there cited) but provides the most detailed exposition of the doctrine of abatement.
[22] (1806) 7 East 479.
[23] (1789) 7 East 481.

warranty in the one case, and the work in consequence of the non-performance of the contract in the other, were diminished in value . . . [I]n all these cases of goods sold and delivered with a warranty, and work and labour, as well as the case of goods agreed to be supplied according to a contract . . . it is competent for the defendant, in all of those, not to set-off, by a proceeding in the nature of a cross action, the amount of damages which he has sustained by breach of the contract, but simply to defend himself by showing how much less the subject-matter of the action was worth, by reason of the breach of contract; and to the extent that he obtains, or is capable of obtaining, an abatement of the price on that account, he must be considered as having received satisfaction for the breach of contract, and is precluded from recovering in another action to that extent; but no more."[24]

In the case of contracts of sale of goods the doctrine of abatement was carried into what is now s.53(1)(a) of the Sale of Goods Act 1979.

Scope of the doctrine of abatement

7-72 The doctrine of abatement enunciated in *Mondel v Steel* does not extend to contracts generally. It is confined to a strictly limited group of contracts: sale of goods, other forms of supply of goods (*e.g.* by way of lease or hire-purchase) and contracts of work and labour.[25] Abatement for defective work may be pleaded even in answer to a claim by a builder for payment under an architect's interim certificate.[26] However, it is limited to reduction in value of the goods or work and cannot be pleaded to support other types of claim, such as damages for delay.[27]

Is abatement a substantive defence?

7-73 It is clear that abatement is a doctrine entirely distinct from set-off. In contrast to transaction set-off prior to 1873, it has always taken the form of a defence; it is limited to the amount by which the plaintiffs breach has diminished the value of his performance; and it is available to the defendant as a matter of right, not of judicial discretion. But is it a substantive defence or, like independent set-off, purely procedural? In *Gilbert-Ash (Northern) Ltd. v*

---

[24] (1841) 8 M. & W. 858, at 870–872.

[25] *Gilbert-Ash (Northern) Ltd. v Modern Engineering (Bristol) Ltd.* [1974] A.C. 689 at 717; *Aries Tanker Corp. v Total Transport Ltd.* [1977] 1 All E.R. 398, *per* Lord Wilberforce at 404. Contracts of employment may possibly be within the doctrine as well. See *Sim v Rotherham Metropolitan Borough Council* [1986] 3 All E.R. 387, where Scott J. found it unnecessary to decide the point, holding that the right to deduct was in any event given as a matter of set-off.

[26] *Gilbert-Ash (Northern) Ltd. v Modern Engineering (Bristol) Ltd.*, above, overruling a line of prior authority to the contrary.

[27] *Henrisken Rederi A/S v T.H.Z. Rolimpex (The Brede)* [1974] 1 Q.B. 233, *per* Lord Denning M.R. at 248; *Mellowes Archital Ltd. v Bell Projects Ltd.* (1997) 87 B.L.R. 26.

Modern Engineering (Bristol) Ltd.,[28] Lord Diplock entertained no doubt that it was the former:

"That it was no mere procedural rule designed to avoid circuity of action but a substantive defence at common law was the very point decided in *Mondel v Steel*."[29]

This statement[30] is not correct; it runs counter to the express words of the judgment of Parke B. in *Mondel v Steel*, where, referring to the statement of Lord Tenterden in *Street v Blay*[31] that the right to set up the damages for breach of warranty in diminution of the price was given "on the principle, it should seem, of avoiding circuity of action," Parke B. went on to say that in the opinion of the whole court this meant not that the plea was in the nature of a set-off but that "the sum to be recovered for the price of the article might be reduced by so much as the article was diminished in value, by reason of the non-compliance with the warranty; and that this abatement was allowed in order to save the necessity of a cross action."[32] The High Court of Australia has held in a majority decision that abatement is purely procedural and that the breach of warranty does not by itself work a reduction or extinguishment of the buyer's liability for the price,[33] and a similar ruling has been given in another Australian case.[34]

However, so far as English law is concerned Lord Diplock's statement has since received support from Hoffmann L.J. in *Aectra Refining and Marketing Inc. v Exmar NV*,[35] so that, as with transaction set-off, it must today be seen as a substantive defence. In relation to contracts of sale of goods the principle of *Mondel v Steel* is now embodied in s.53(1)(a) of the Sale of Goods Act 1979, which allow the buyer to treat any breach of condition on the part of the seller as a breach of warranty and set it up in diminution of the price.

Present significance of abatement

If the above analyses of the doctrines of set-off and abatement are correct, there is little need to rely on abatement at the present day since the ground is fully covered by the substantive defence of transaction set-off. That, indeed, was the view of Scott J. as expressed in his instructive judgment in *Sim v Rotherham Metropolitan Borough Council*.[36] What is needed is a definitive

7–74

---

[28] See above.
[29] [1974] A.C. 689 at 717.
[30] Which beguiled the writer in the first edition of this book.
[31] (1831) 2 B. & Ad. 456 at 462.
[32] *Mondel v Steel*, above, *per* Parke B. at 870. See to the same effect *Davis v Hedges* (1871) L.R. 6 Q.B. 687, *per* Hannen J. at 691.
[33] *Healing (Sales) Pty. Ltd. v Inglis Electrix Pty. Ltd.* [1969] A.L.R. 533. See in particular the judgments of Kitto J. at 541 and Windeyer J. at 547, 552.
[34] *Newman v Cook* [1963] V.R. 659.
[35] [1994] 1 WLR 1634 at 1650.
[36] [1986] 3 All E.R. 387 at 412, 413.

ruling as to whether abatement can ever be relied on as a substantive defence to defeat the exercise of a self-help remedy. We have previously seen that transaction set-off is available as a substantive defence is asserted in due time, and now that abatement too has come to be seen as a substantive defence it would seem that the same principles must apply.

9. INSOLVENCY SET-OFF: GENERAL PRINCIPLES

7-75   The focus in the passages which follow is on the rules of set-off applicable in the winding-up of companies, but similar considerations apply to the bankruptcy of individuals. It is to be noted that the rules governing insolvency set-off apply only to liquidation, not to administration, and that while an administrator order, and, indeed, the petition for such an order freezes the enforcement of security and the institution of legal proceedings, this does not freeze the remedy of set-off.[37]

The right of set-off in insolvency

7-76   The right of set-off in company liquidations is to be found in rule 4.90 of the Insolvency Rules 1986, which provides as follows:

"Rule 4.90 Mutual credit and set-off

(1)   This Rule applies where, before the company goes into liquidation, there have been mutual credits, mutual debts or other mutual dealings between the company and any creditor of the company proving or claiming to prove for a debt in the liquidation.

(2)   An account shall be taken of what is due from each party to the other in respect of the mutual dealings, and the sums due from one party shall be set off against the sums due from the other.

(3)   Sums due from the company to another party shall not be included in the account taken under paragraph (2) if that other party had notice at the time they became due that a meeting of creditors had been summoned under section 98[38] or (as the case may be) a petition for the winding up of the company was pending.

(4)   Only the balance (if any) of the account is provable in the liquidation. Alternatively (as the case may be) the amount shall be paid to the liquidator as part of the assets."[39]

---

[37] See R.M. Goode, *Principles of Corporate Insolvency Law* (2nd ed.), p.307, cited with approval by the Singapore Court of Appeal in *Electro-Magnetic (S) Ltd. v Development Bank of Singapore Ltd.* [1994] 1 S.L.R. 734.

[38] *i.e.* the meeting of creditors which a company is required to convene when convening its own meeting to pass a resolution to go into a creditors' voluntary winding-up.

[39] *i.e.* if the company's claim against the creditor exceeds the creditor's claim against the company.

Principles underlying insolvency set-off

Much doubt and controversy has surrounded the meaning of this rule and its **7–77** bankruptcy equivalent, s.323 of the Insolvency Act. As at what date is the account to be taken? If it is the liquidation or bankruptcy date, how is this to be done when at that date the creditor's claim against the company is purely contingent? Does liquidation automatically reduce the claims on both sides to a single balance so as to preclude a post-liquidation assignment of one such claim or is the position that such an assignment remains possible but takes effective subject to the equity of the bankruptcy set-off? These complex issues have now been resolved in two masterly analyses, by Hoffmann L.J. at first instance in *MS Fashions Ltd. v Bank of Credit and Commerce International SA (No. 2)*[40] and Lord Hoffmann (as he had now become) in *Stein v Blake*[41]:

> "Certain principles as to the application of these provisions have been established by the cases. First, the rule is mandatory ('the mandatory principle'). If there have been mutual dealings before the winding-up order which have given rise to cross-claims, neither party can prove or sue for his full claim. An account must be taken and he must prove or sue (as the case may be) for the balance. Secondly, the account is taken as at the date of the winding-up order ('the retroactivity principle'). This is only one manifestation of a wider principle of insolvency law, namely, that the liquidation and distribution of the assets of the insolvent company are treated as notionally taking place simultaneously on the date of the winding up order: see *In re Dynamics Corporation of America* [1976] 1 W.L.R. 757, 762, *per* Oliver J. Thirdly, in taking the account the court has regard to events which have occurred since the date of the winding up ("the hindsight principle"). The hindsight principle is pervasive in the valuation of claims and the taking of accounts in bankruptcy and winding up."[42]

The mandatory principle

Insolvency set-off is mandatory and cannot be excluded by agreement of the **7–78** parties. This was so held by a majority decision of the House of Lords in *National Westminster Bank Ltd. v Halesowen Presswork and Assemblies Ltd.*[43] The reason given is that the statutory provisions are considered to regulate matters of public interest in the orderly administration of the estate and are not purely a source of private rights enacted for the benefit of individual debtors of the estate having cross-claims against it. This majority ruling in *Halesowen*, though consistent with the imperative language of the set-off

---

[40] [1993] Ch. 425, affirmed [1993] Ch. 439.
[41] [1996] 1 A.C. 243.
[42] *MS Fashions Ltd. v Bank of Credit and Commerce International SA (No. 2)*, above, at 432–433.
[43] [1972] A.C. 785, Lord Cross dissenting. But see below, paras 6–35 *et seq.*

provision, constitutes an impediment to the reorganisation of companies in financial difficulty, a fact recognised in *Halesowen* but in the majority view requiring legislation to deal with it. The Insolvency Law Review Committee gave much thought to the matter, pointing out that it was a common practice for a company in difficulty, when negotiating a moratorium with its creditors, to agree to open a new bank account with its existing bankers and keep this in credit, the bank for its part undertaking not to set off existing indebtedness, so that the fund would be preserved intact for any liquidator and the bank would not receive a preference. The present law made it necessary for the company to open another account with a different bank.[44] The Committee concluded that there was no sound policy for maintaining the prohibition against contracting-out of insolvency set-off and good commercial reasons for reversing it, and they recommended legislation to that effect.[45] No steps have yet been taken to implement this recommendation.

The retroactivity principle

7–79   The effect of this principle is that the account between the company and the creditor asserting a right of set-off is considered to be taken as at the date of winding-up even though it is not taken, and in practice cannot be taken, until a later date. In other words, insolvency set-off is self-executing and, once the facts are known, operates automatically from the point of liquidation without the need for any procedural step.[46] It follows that it is not open to the creditor to assign his claim against the company prior to the taking of the account, for the claim must be treated as *ipso jure* ceasing to exist as a separate claim upon the company going into liquidation, the claim and cross-claim being then automatically combined by force of law to produce a single net debit balance due to or from the creditor. This net balance, if in favour of the company, is capable of assignment by the liquidator or, if in favour of the solvent party, by that party, at any time after the company has gone into liquidation, without the need to wait for the taking of accounts.[47] This follows from the fact that the ultimate quantification of claim and cross-claim and the striking of a balance take effect from the date of liquidation.

The hindsight principle

7–80   This is closely linked to the principle of retroactivity. The court looks at post-liquidation events to determine the state of account as at the date of liquidation. It applies in particular to the valuation of claims, whether these are made by way of set-off or otherwise. Contingent claims which crystallise into

---

[44] *Insolvency Law and Practice* (Cmnd. 8558, 1982), para.1341.
[45] *ibid.*, para.1342.
[46] *Stein v Blake*, above, *per* Lord Hoffmann at 254, 255, 258.
[47] *Stein v Blake*, above, *per* Lord Hoffmann at 258.

debts after the date of liquidation are brought into account as debts and may be revalued accordingly[48] with retrospective effect.[49] Similarly, amounts put in for existing but unliquidated claims may be adjusted if the claims become liquidated or are able to be more accurately valued in the light of post-liquidation events. It follows from the hindsight principle, as well as from the retroactivity principle, that an assignment of the net balance can be made at any time after the company goes into liquidation, whether or not the net balance has then been struck.

Conditions of application of insolvency set-off

In order for rule 4.90 to apply six conditions must be satisfied: **7–81**

(1) There must have been mutual credits, mutual debts or other mutual dealings between the parties;

(2) The mutual dealings must have taken place before the company goes into liquidation;

(3) The claims on both sides must be such as will in their nature terminate in debts;

(4) The claim by the solvent party must be one which would be admissible for proof at the time when it becomes necessary to ascertain the state of accounts between the company and the solvent party[50];

(5) The claim by the company must have matured as a debt by the time it becomes necessary to ascertain the state of accounts between the company and the solvent party;

(6) The person asserting the set-off must not have had notice, at the time the sum claimed by him became due, that a meeting of creditors had been summoned under s.98 of the Insolvency Act 1986 or that a petition for the winding up of the company was pending.

We shall examine each of these conditions in turn.

Mutual credits, mutual debts and other mutual dealings

The requirement of mutuality has two facets. First, the respective characters   **7–82**
of the claim and the cross-claim must be commensurate. This means that

---

[48] See Insolvency Rules 1986, r.4.86(1).
[49] Subject only to the qualification that revaluation does not disturb distributions of dividend already made, though any additional sum payable as the result of it will have priority in any future distribution.
[50] By this is meant the time when it is necessary for *any* purpose to ascertain the state of account, not necessarily any single point in time. See below, para.7–87.

claim and cross-claim must both be monetary claims or claims which a party is entitled to have reduced to money. So a person holding property as bailee or trustee for another cannot set off against his delivery or accounting obligation a money claim against the bailor or beneficiary. This rule is so strictly applied that even if the property held by the trustee is itself a money fund, the trustee is not permitted to set off his personal claim against the beneficiary, and if the beneficiary goes into liquidation the trustee must transfer the fund to the liquidator intact and is left to prove in the liquidation for his cross-claim.[51] However, there is no obligation to set-off against a money claim secured by a trust or charge.[52] Secondly, there must be mutuality of parties, that is, the claim and cross-claim must be between the same parties in the same right. So it is not possible to set off against a claim by the company in liquidation a cross-claim against a third party, even if prior to liquidation there had been a valid contractual set-off along these lines, for on winding-up any contractual set-off, so far as not already exercised, disappears. Again, a claim against the company in liquidation cannot be set off against a claim vested in the company as trustee for a third party. In determining mutuality the court will look at the benefit ownership of claim and cross-claim rather than the legal title, but will require clear evidence that that the beneficial interest is vested in someone other than the party holding the legal title.[53]

The mutual dealings must have preceded the liquidation

7–83   This is expressly stated in rule 4.90. However, it is not necessary that the dealings should have given rise to mutual *debts* prior to the winding-up. It suffices that the mutual dealing have created obligations which give rise to claims that can be set against each other at the time when it becomes necessary to ascertain the state of accounts between the parties.[54]

The claims on both sides much be such as will in their nature terminate in debt

7–84   Set-off is in principle confined to mutual money obligations, secured or unsecured.[55] The solvent party cannot rely on set-off to withhold property of the

---

[51] *National Westminster Bank plc v Halesowen Presswork and Assemblies Ltd.* [1972] A.C. 785, *per* Lord Kilbrandon at 821; *In re Mid-Kent Fruit Factory* [1896] 1 Ch. 567. The underlying principle appears to be that money held on trust is held for a particular purpose and cannot be applied for a different purpose, namely towards discharge of a cross-claim, without the consent of the person for whom it is held. Another way of reaching the same result is to say that a contract claim and a trust claim do not constitute mutual dealings.

[52] See above, para.7–61; below, para.7–84, n.55.

[53] *Bank of Credit and Commerce International SA v Prince Fahd Bin Salman Abdul Aziz Al-Saud* [1997] B.C.C. 63.

[54] *Stein v Blake* [1996] 1 A.C. 243.

[55] The fact that one of the debts is secured does not affect the right of the debtor to set off his own cross-claim against it; the effect of this is simply to reduce the amount of the secured obli-

company in his possession or control, whether as bailee or as bare trustee, and in the latter case this applies as much to a money fund held by the solvent party as bare trustee for the company as it does to tangible property so held. Accordingly if B, a bailee of goods owned by A Co., wrongfully sells the goods he cannot set off a debt due to him from the company against his obligation to account for the proceeds, for the company's claim to the proceeds is not a mere money claim in debt but a claim to ownership of the money fund which is enforceable as a proprietary claim in equity. Additional grounds for refusing a set-off are that a person cannot take advantage of his own wrong by converting another's property into money[56] and that a misappropriation is not a dealing.[57]

However, there are at least two apparent exceptions to the rule precluding set-off against property and trust moneys. First, if the property of the company in liquidation is subject to a lien or other security interest in favour of the solvent party the security carries through to the proceeds of sale and may be enforced by retention of the proceeds to the extent of the amount owing to the secured creditor. This is not a true set-off, merely a method of enforcing the security interest. Secondly, if property of the company is held by another with instructions or authority to convert it into money, then so long as that authority remains unrevoked at the time of liquidation the other party, on selling the property, can set off against his liability to account for the proceeds a debt owed to him by the company in liquidation, even if the sale does not take place until after winding up, provided that the proceeds are received by the claimant by the time it becomes necessary to ascertain the state of accounts between him and the company.

The taking of accounts under rule 4.90 of the Insolvency Rules is the principle established in *Rose v Hart*,[58] which has been said to constitute an anomalous exception to the rule that a money claim may not be set off against a proprietary claim and to the separate mutuality rule that trust funds are not susceptible to set-off.[59] But this is doubtful. The essence of the rule in *Rose v Hart* is the provision of mutual credits, the solvent party extending credit to the company in reliance on his prospective receipt of the proceeds of the

---

gation. See *MS Fashions Ltd. v Bank of Credit and Commerce International SA (No. 2)*, above, *per* Dillon L.J. at 446; *Re ILG Travel Ltd.* [1996] B.C.C. 21. There is a rather cryptic observation by Rose L.J. in *Re Bank of Credit and Commerce International SA (No. 8)* [1996] Ch. 245 at 258 that "[I]nsolvency is concerned with the distribution of the debtor's uncharged assets among his unsecured creditors. Trust property and security stand outside the scheme of distribution and the scope of insolvency set-off. Set-off ought not to prejudice the right of a secured creditor to enforce his security in any order he chooses and at a time of his choice." It is, of course, true that in principle a secured creditor is unaffected by a bankruptcy or liquidation and need not prove in competition with other creditors. However, he can enforce his security only for the amount due to him, and to the extent to which his claim is satisfied by the automatic set-off arising under r. 4.90 of the Insolvency Rules there is no longer a debt to be enforced (the same applies to set-off outside liquidation—see above, para.7–61). Another way of reaching the same result is to say that a contract claim and a trust claim do not constitute mutual dealings.

[56] *Smith v Bridgend County Borough Council* [2002] 1 A.C. 336.
[57] *Manson v Smith* [1997] 2 B.C.L.C. 161, *per* Millett LJ at 164.
[58] (1818) 8 Taunt. 499.
[59] Derham, *op cit.*, para.10.15.

company's property for which the company gives credit to him, and that the credits are such "as must in their nature terminate in debts."[60] Hence the true basis of the decision in *Rose v Hart* would seem to be that the person holding the company's property with instructions to convert it into money has implied authority, by virtue of their mutual dealings, to regard himself as a mere debtor for a sum equal to the proceeds, not as a trustee of the proceeds themselves, which he is free to treat as his own moneys.

7–85   The significance of the distinction is well established in decisions on reservation of title to goods under contracts of sale which authorise resale by the buyer but impose no express requirement that he is to account for the proceeds of sale. In such cases the court is likely to infer that the buyer is merely to be a debtor for the amount of the proceeds (or of such part of them as is necessary to discharge his price obligation), not a trustee.[61] A similar principle applies where the terms of the agreement between the parties impose on the solvent party a duty to hold the proceeds on trust for the company but entitle him to deduct sums due to him from the company. Such an agreement will be construed as creating a charge on the proceeds, so that the solvent party is not a bare trustee but one whose trust obligation applies only to the balance remaining in his hands after he has deducted from the proceeds the amount due to him.[62] The absence of a duty to keep the proceeds segregated from the solvent party's own moneys is not inconsistent with such a trust.[63] The position is otherwise where the solvent party is a bare trustee of the proceeds and thus has a duty to make them over to the company in liquidation without deduction.[64]

All this presupposes that the disposition of the company's property was authorised, for if it was not the person making it can hardly contend that he had authority to treat the proceeds as his own.[65] Moreover, as previously mentioned, a person cannot rely on his own wrongdoing to create a set-off or to serve as a mutual dealing. So if he never had authority to sell in the first place or his authority was revoked prior to the sale he will be a trustee of the entire proceeds and will have no right to set off his cross-claim against his duty to account.[66]

7–86   In the light of these considerations the decision of the Court of Appeal in the controversial decision in *Rolls Razor Ltd. v Cox*[67] is hard to justify. In that case the defendant was a self-employed salesman appointed by the plaintiffs to sell their washing machines in return for commission and was required by the terms of his appointment to hand over the proceeds without deduction.

---

[60] *Rose v Hart* (1818) 8 Taunt. 499, *per* Gibbs C.J. at 506.
[61] *Re Andrabell Ltd.* [1984] 3 All E.R. 407; *Hendy Lennox Ltd. v Grahame Puttick Ltd.* [1984] 2 All E.R. 152. See R.M.Goode, *Proprietary Rights and Insolvency in Sales Transactions* (2nd ed.), pp.99 *et seq.*
[62] *Re ILG Travel Ltd.* [1996] B.C.C. 21.
[63] *ibid.*
[64] *ibid.; Henry v Hammond* [1913] 2 K.B. 515.
[65] R.M. Goode, *op. cit.*, p.99.
[66] *Rose v Hart* (1818) 8 Taunt. 499; *Eberle's Hotels & Restaurant Co. Ltd. v Jonas* (1887) 18 Q.B.D. 459.
[67] [1967] 1 All E.R. 397.

The company also deducted a percentage of each week's commission to form a retention fund to which it could resort if the salesman defaulted in his obligations in regard to machines or proceeds. With the company having gone into liquidation, the defendant asserted a lien and a right to set off the commission and retention moneys due to him against the proceeds he had received of two washing machines sold for the company prior to liquidation and the value of (*inter alia*) an unsold table top still in his possession at the time of liquidation and seven tap-adaptors, not for sale, which he used in the demonstration of the machines. The Court of Appeal upheld this contention as regards the goods, and proceeds of goods, held for sale[68] (Winn L.J. dissenting as to the table top) on the ground that that while the defendant did not have a lien on the goods, there were mutual credits—by the company to the defendant in respect of the proceeds of sale and by the defendant to the company in respect of the retention fund—so that a right of set-off arose which the company had not been entitled to defeat by purporting to terminate the agent's authority to sell.

The majority decision is hard to justify. In the first place, the table top had not in fact been converted into money even after the winding-up, and in no previous case had a money claim been set off against an obligation to deliver unrealised property. Secondly, the defendant's contention that he was entitled to a lien on the goods was rejected, not merely because he was a mere agent, not a factor, but also because this was inconsistent with the terms of his agreement with the company requiring him to deliver up the goods on termination of the agreement. Surely it was equally inconsistent with the agreement that he should be allowed to sell the goods after termination of his authority and then deduct what was due to him from the proceeds. The decision in *Rose v Hart*[69] was specifically predicated on the assumption that the agent's authority to sell remained unrevoked up to the time of sale, and the same was true of the decision in *Palmer v Day*.[70] Nor could it be said that the defendant's authority to sell was irrevocable because it was coupled with an interest,[71] namely the right to look to the proceeds for payment of his commission, for this, too, was prohibited by the agreement. Accordingly it could not be said that there were mutual credits, and that being so the defendant's authority to sell had been effectively brought to an end by the company and would in any event have come to an end on the winding-up. The defendant was thus not a mere debtor but a trustee, who ought not to have been allowed to profit from his own act of conversion.[72] It is true that the set-off provisions are mandatory—a point relied on by Lord Denning M.R. to overcome the contract point—but they do not apply at all unless the test of mutuality is satisfied, and this is not the case where the claim on one side is to payment of money and on the other to delivery of property held on trust or to the

---

[68] But not the tap-adaptors held for use only.
[69] See above.
[70] [1895] 2 Q.B. 618.
[71] See *Bowstead and Reynolds on Agency* (17th ed.), paras 10–006 and 10–007.
[72] See above, para.7–84.

proceeds of property wrongfully converted. The present position has rightly been described as anomalous[73] and is a good illustration of hard cases making bad law.

Claim by solvent party must be of a kind admissible to proof at the relevant time

7–87   The solvent party cannot assert a set-off in respect of a claim which would not be admissible for proof at the time when it becomes necessary to ascertain the state of accounts between the parties. So a claim which is statute-barred cannot be used as a set-off,[74] nor can a claim which is so contingent as to be incapable of estimation by the liquidator.[75] The solvent party cannot avoid this result by deferring the lodging of his proof, for the statutory provisions as to the taking of an account do no depend on the lodging of a proof but apply at any point in time where the occasion arises for the taking of the account.[76]

Not all claims eligible for proof are also eligible for set-off. The requirement of mutuality must also be satisfied.[77]

No set-off where claim by company is contingent

7–88   Though a contingent claim by the solvent party may be proved, and therefore set off, if capable of estimation, the set-off rules are incapable of being applied where it is the company liquidation that has the contingent claim.[78]

No notice of winding-up meeting or petition when claim becomes due

7–89   Under rule 4.90(3) of the Insolvency Rules sums due from the company to another party are not to be included in the account of mutual dealings if that other party had notice at the time they became due that a meeting of creditors had been convened under s.98 of the Insolvency Act or (as the case may be) that a petition for winding-up was pending. The word "due" denotes an existing debt, whether or not payable in the future. So provided that the solvent party was without notice of the above facts when the debt was contracted, the fact that he later acquires notice before the debt matures does not debar him from having it brought into account. It is also clear that the assignee of a debt due from the company is precluded from setting it off

---

[73] Wood, *op. cit.*, para.9–304.

[74] *Pott v Clegg* (1847) 16 M. & W. 821.

[75] See Insolvency Rules 1986, rr.4.86, 13.12(3).

[76] *Stein v Blake* [1996] 1 A.C. 243.

[77] *Bank of Credit and Commerce Interntional SA v Prince Fahd Bin Salman Abdul Aziz Al-Saud* [1997] B.C.C. 63. See above, para.7–82.

[78] See below, para.7–92.

against his own indebtedness to the company if he had notice of the above facts at the time he took his assignment. This would seem to result not from rule 4.90(3), which focuses on the time the debt was contracted, not the time when it was assigned, but from a general principle of insolvency law preventing a debtor to the company from improving his position *vis-à-vis* other creditors by buying in claims against the company after notice of a formal act indicative of the company's inability to pay its debts[79] and more specifically from the fact that a person taking an assignment with notice of the company's impending solvency cannot be said to be giving credit to the company, so that the requirement of mutuality is not satisfied.

10. INSOLVENCY SET-OFF: SPECIAL SITUATIONS

(i) Set-off in relation to unmatured or contingent claims under executed contracts

The question addressed here is the extent to which unmatured or contingent claims arising under contracts wholly performed by the claimant may be set off by or against the solvent party.　　　　　　　　　　　　　　　　**7–90**

Unmatured or contingent claims by the solvent party

The effect of the statutory provisions for the admission to proof of unmatured debts at their face value[80] and of contingent claims at their estimated value is that as from the date of liquidation such claims are notionally converted into matured debts and are automatically set off against any matured debts owed by the creditor to the company. This, however, is subject to the rule against double proof which (*inter alia*) precludes a surety from proving or setting off his right of indemnity against the insolvent company until he has paid in full the amount of the guaranteed debt or such separate part of it as he has guaranteed.[81]　　　　　　　　　　　　　　　　**7–91**

Unmatured or contingent claims against the solvent party

In the converse case where it is the company in liquidation that has the contingent claim the rules set out above do not apply. This is because the liquidator has no right to accelerate the liability of the solvent party; the principle of acceleration applies only to claims *against* the company. We are again　　　**7–92**

---

[79] See *Re Eros Films Ltd.* [1963] Ch. 565.
[80] But discounted for the purpose of dividend distribution (Insolvency Rules 1986, r.11.13(2)).
[81] See below, para.8–23.

indebted to Hoffmann L.J. (as he then was) for the working out of the rights of the parties in this situation. The solvent party is entitled to prove for his claim in full without offset of the company's unmatured or contingent claim against him. If the latter claim matures into an immediately payable debt the liquidator can sue for it in the name of the company but the solvent party is entitled to set off against the liquidator the amount of his own cross-claim after giving credit for any dividend received.[82]

The collapse of the Bank of Credit and Commercial International SA gave rise to a number of actions concerning the effect of the insolvency rules where the bank had loaned money to a borrower and taken a security deposit of funds from a third party. In some cases this was underpinned by the third party's personal guarantee, in others it was not. In one case the guarantee contained a "principal debtor" clause which was held to impose on the surety the liability of a principal debtor for repayment. In working out the insolvency set-off rules it is necessary to distinguish three situations.[83] The first is where the depositor gives a personal guarantee which contains a principal debtor clause, so that his liability is not merely contingent. The second is where he gives a personal guarantee which does not contain a principal debtor clause and provides for payment on demand, so that his liability is contingent on demand being made. The third is where he gives no personal guarantee at all but merely deposits funds with the creditor as security for the loan to the borrower.

(1) Deposit reinforced by personal guarantee containing a principal debtor clause

7–93   In *MS Fashions Ltd v Bank of Credit and Commerce International SA (No. 2)*[84] the issue was concisely presented by Hoffmann L.J. in the following terms:

> "A bank advances money to a company. Repayment is guaranteed by a director who has a deposit account with the bank. As between himself and the bank, the director is expressed to be a principal debtor. On the insolvency of the bank, can the director set off his claim for return of his deposit against his liability to pay the company's debt, so that the debt is wholly or pro tanto extinguished? Or can the bank claim the whole debt from the company and leave the director to prove in the liquidation for his deposit?"[85]

---

[82] *MS Fashions Ltd. v Bank of Credit and Commerce International SA (No. 2)*, above, at 435.
[83] For an excellent discussion, see Richard Calnan, "The Insolvent Bank and Security Over Deposits" (1996) J.I.F.B.L. 185.
[84] [1993] Ch. 425.
[85] *ibid.*, at 430.

Hoffmann L.J. held that as a matter of construction the effect of the principal debtor clause was that the director was not merely making a deposit by way of security but was assuming a personal liability for repayment jointly and severally with the borrower company, or alternatively severally, that such liability was not merely contingent and that accordingly the liquidation of the bank resulted in an automatic set-off of the deposit against the liability, thus *pro tanto* extinguishing the indebtedness of the borrower company. It was therefore not open to the liquidator, as it would have been if there had been no principal debtor clause, to recover from the borrower without giving credit for the deposit, leaving the director to prove as an unsecured creditor for the amount of his deposit released from the charge as the result of the borrower's repayment.

On the finding of a personal guarantee as a matter of construction the result reached was inevitable. However, it has to be said that the evidence for a personal guarantee was decidedly tenuous; and the conclusion that the charge itself could be analysed as the creation of a personal liability not exceeding the amount of the deposit[86] is not sustainable, for it imports a personal liability where none is needed except, of course, for the purpose of arriving at the desired result! The Court of Appeal felt unable to agree with this conclusion in *Re Bank of Credit and Commerce International SA (No. 8)*[87] and Lord Hoffmann himself, in the subsequent appeal to the House of Lords,[88] acknowledged that it produced anomalous results and was based on the peculiar wording of the guarantee.

(2) *Deposit reinforced by personal guarantee payable on demand with no principal debtor clause*

In this situation the surety is not a principal debtor and in the absence of demand his liability is merely contingent. As we have seen, a contingent claim *by* the company in liquidation *against* the solvent party is not accelerated by the liquidation, so that unless demand is made, converting the contingent claim into a matured debt, no set-off can be invoked by the liquidator. In consequence the liquidator can avoid the independent set-off by refraining from making the requisite demand, thus maintaining the company's claim in full against the borrower without having to give credit for the sum that would have been treated as received from the surety in a balance of account had the set-off provisions been triggered. The lesson for liquidators is not to be too hasty in making demands on sureties!

7-94

---

[86] *ibid.,* at 431.
[87] [1996] Ch. 245; [1996] B.C.L.C. 204 *sub. nom. Morris v Agrichemicals Ltd.* See below, para.7-95.
[88] *Re Bank of Credit and Commerce International SA* [1998] A.C. 214 at 224-225.

(3) *Deposit not reinforced by any personal guarantee*

7–95 This was the situation in the BCCI case mentioned above, where the facts were otherwise very similar to those in *MS Fashions*. Money was deposited with the bank by way of non-recourse collateral security[89] for a loan to the principal debtor. The bank then went into liquidation. The liquidator declined to resort to the security deposit and sought repayment from the principal debtor without giving credit for the deposit, leaving the depositor to prove as an unsecured creditor. The borrower and the depositor contended that credit should be given for the deposit. Among the various grounds advanced were: that the depositor as a non-recourse surety had a right to pay off the debt and to have his deposit utilised for that purpose; that the liquidator's approach would expose the borrower to a double liability, namely to repay the loan and to indemnify the depositor against the loss of his deposit through the bank's insolvency; that the bank's inability to repay the deposit discharged the borrower *pro tanto* from liability by reason of the bank's "loss" of the security in becoming insolvent and its consequent inability to return it; and that the deposit was paid to the bank on trust to be applied for a particular purpose, namely discharge of the principal debt, for which it should be used by the liquidator.

The House of Lords,[90] affirming the decision of the Court of Appeal,[91] had no difficulty in rejecting all these arguments. In the absence of any personal guarantee by the depositor it was not possible to set off the deposit against the loan. The bank owed money to the depositor and the borrower owed money to the bank. The debts were therefore not due from the same parties, so that the mutuality which was essential to avoid a preference over other creditors was lacking. The proposition that the borrower was exposed to double liability was fallacious, since it rested on the assumption that the borrower was obliged to indemnify the depositor against the loss of his deposit, a proposition which was untenable. The surety's only right to indemnity was where he had paid off the principal debt. Nor could the principle relating to loss of securities by the creditor avail the borrower or depositor. The deposit had not been disposed of or the depositor's legal entitlement to repayment impaired; the position was simply that the bank was unable to repay. In any event there was no basis for saying that the loss of a security provided by a surety discharges the principal debtor; at best it would discharge the surety. Finally, there was no evidence to show that the deposit had been impressed with a purpose trust. The bank was a mere debtor.

It was recognised that this result produced the paradox that a surety who gave no personal guarantee was worse off than one who gave a personal guarantee and thus had his liability extinguished by set-off. But that was inevitable

---

[89] The Court of Appeal, approving the decision of Millett J. in *Re Charge Card Services Ltd.* [1987] Ch. 150, had held that it was conceptully impossible for a bank to take a charge over its own customer's credit balance and that the charge-back had purely contractual effect. The House of Lords had a different view. See above, para.3–12.

[90] Re *Bank of Credit and Commece International SA* [1998] A.C. 214.

[91] [1996] Ch. 245.

if injustice to the general body of creditors was to be avoided. The point here is that what the depositor was seeking to do was to avoid the consequences of the bank's insolvency so far as he was concerned by requiring the bank to utilise the deposit to pay off the debt. But the deposit was an asset of the bank which under the *pari passu* principle should be available for the general body of creditors. In the absence of any trust affecting it the depositor, as an unsecured creditor, had no right to give instructions to the liquidator as to the application of the deposit. By collecting repayment from the borrower the liquidator would cause the debt to be discharged, thus freeing the deposit from the security and entitling the depositor to repayment. In that situation the depositor should stand in the same position as other unsecured creditors.

(iii) Set-off in relation to executory contracts

It will be evident from the foregoing that where all the relevant contracts are executed and the claims on both sides are for money or are reducible to money insolvency set-off will rarely be a problem in English law. Set-off in relation to existing liquidated claims, even if payable in the future, is straightforward. Unliquidated claims and contingent are valued (so far as capable of estimation) and become treated as the equivalent of liquidated claims for purposes of proof and set-off. **7–96**

The one real danger zone is that occupied by executory contracts.[92] Where the contracts on both sides are still in force and executory at the time of winding-up the solvent party is exposed to the risk of cherry-picking by the liquidator, who may seek to enforce the contract that is profitable to the estate[93] while disclaiming the unprofitable contract[94] and leaving the solvent party to prove in the winding-up for damages. In principle such damages cannot be set off against the solvent party's liability under the other contract because of the principle that post-liquidation receipts derived from the activity of the liquidator and use of the company's resources do not belong to the company in its own right,[95] so that the requisite element of mutuality is lacking.[96] The solution is to provide in each contract that all executory contracts will automatically be rescinded, and the resulting money claims netted out, in the event of either party going into liquidation.

---

[92] See above, para.7–29.

[93] Which in principle he can do except where (a) the winding-up of the company can be regarded as a repudiatory breach; or (b) the court accedes to an application by the solvent party to rescind the contract under s.186 of the Insolvency Act 1986, which it will normally do only where the two contracts are so connected that it would be inequitable to allow the liquidator to enforce one contract if he is not prepared to procure the company's performance of the other.

[94] Under s.178 of the Act. See R. Goode, Principles of Corporate Insolvency Law (2nd ed.), pp.127 *et seq.*

[95] *Re Collins* [1925] Ch. 556; *Wilmot v Alton* [1897] 1 Q.B. 17.

[96] See Wood, *English and International Set-Off*, paras 5–97, 7–145 *et seq.*, for an exhaustive analysis with reference to typical transactions.

(iv) Preferential debts

7–97   Where the creditor is owed both preferential and non-preferential debts, a set-off available to the company in liquidation for less than the total amount due is not to be applied exclusively to the preferential debts (thus benefiting the estate) or exclusively to the non-preferential debts (thus preserving the creditor's priority intact) but is to be applied to the two sets of debt rateably.[97]

(v) Voidable preferences

7–98   No question of preference can arise where the creditor collects payment by exercise of a right of set-off, for this does not require the consent of the company at all, let alone a desire on its part to improve the creditor's position. Payment by the company into an overdrawn account with its bank is likewise not capable of being a preference where the payment does not exceed the amount of a credit balance held by the company on another account to which the bank could have resorted by way of combination of accounts if the payment in question had not been made, for the effect of the payment is *pro tanto* to reduce the available amount of set-off against the account in credit, so that the position of other creditors is unaffected. Where, by virtue of an agreement between a company and its directors, the company has a contractual right to set off against one director's credit balance amount due from another director, exercise of that right is not a preference of the first director, for it is for the company's benefit, not that of the first director.[98]

(vi) Specially protected transactions and arrangements

7–99   In order to promote market stability and reduce systemic risk, various types of transaction concluded on a market or through a recognised clearing house or settlement system enjoy special protection from insolvency rules. This has been discussed earlier.[99]

---

[97] *Re Unit 2 Windows Ltd.* [1985] 2 All E.R. 647. This would appear to apply equally to a combination of accounts not effected prior to the winding-up. See Tony Shea, "Statutory Set-Off", [1986] 3 J.I.F.B.L. 152, 154.

[98] *Re Exchange Travel (Holdings) Ltd (No. 3).* [1996] B.C.L.C. 524.

[99] See above, paras 6–35, 6–44 and 7–31.

VIII

Some Aspects of Suretyship Law

I now turn to my last topic, namely that of suretyship guarantees.[1] I wish to **8–01** consider, first, some aspects of the general law on such guarantees outside insolvency and then to discuss the rights of the creditor in respect of a guaranteed debt where the debtor, the surety or both become bankrupt. I use the term "bankrupt" to include the liquidation of a company, for although the bankruptcy rules of proof no longer apply as such to winding up[2] the rules governing guarantees on a winding up are in all material respects the same as those applicable in bankruptcy, except as otherwise stated below.

1. GENERAL PRINCIPLES[3]

The suretyship guarantee as an accessory contract

A suretyship guarantee is an undertaking to be answerable for the debt or **8–02** other default of another. The obligation is triggered by the default of the principal debtor. If the default is in payment of money, the surety's obligation is to pay what is due; if it is failure to perform a non-monetary obligation the surety has either to perform itself, if the contract so provides or permits, or to pay damages. The essential point is that a suretyship guarantee is an accessory contract, not a primary contract.[4] That is to say, the surety's

---

[1] The subject is bedevilled with problems of terminology. A traditional approach is to treat suretyship as covering both guarantees and indemnities (see, for example, Geraldine Andrews and Richard Millett, *Law of Guarantees* (3rd ed.), para.1.03). However, in modern banking and commercial usage the term "suretyship guarantee" denotes a guarantee triggered by default on the part of the principal debtor, by way of contrast to "demand guarantee", which denotes an independent, primary undertaking (see below). The suretyship guarantee is also contrasted with the contract of indemnity, which is also a primary undertaking but differs from a demand guarantee in that typically it is an undertaking to cover the creditor's loss rather than an undertaking to pay a specified amount or maximum amount, so that the liability on an indemnity is unliquidated whereas that on a demand guarantee is liquidated.

[2] See above para.7–75.

[3] The leading English textbook on guarantees is Andrews and Millett, *op. cit.* See also *Rowlatt on Principal and Surety* (4th ed.); Phillips & O'Donovan, *The Modern Contract of Guarantee* (3rd ed.); and K. P. McGuinness, *The Law of Guarantee*.

[4] The typical bond given by an insurer in relation to a construction contract whereby the bond is expressed to become void if the contractor fulfils its obligations is a suretyship bond, not an

obligations are co-terminous with those of the principal debtor, his liability does not arise until the principal debtor has made default and anything which nullifies, reduces or extinguishes the liability of the principal debtor has the same effect on the liability of the surety.[5] This cardinal principle may, of course, be qualified or displaced by the terms of the guarantee.

The question whether and in what conditions a surety may invoke a right of set-off which the debtor has against the creditor remains controversial. In principle, a transaction (or equitable) set-off available to the debtor should equally be available to the surety since this operates as a substantive defence.[6] By contrast, it is generally considered that an independent (or statutory) set-off exercisable by the debtor is not available to the surety since this is a procedural defence which arises from a transaction independent of that to which the guarantee relates[7] and takes effect only at the point of judgment for any balance.[8] Against this it has been argued that any form of set-off, including independent set-off, is available so long as the debtor is joined in the proceedings.[9] But it may be questioned on what basis the debtor should be forced to have his right of independent set-off exercised in favour of the surety when it has nothing to do with the guaranteed debt.

The suretyship guarantee is to be distinguished from the demand guarantee and the standby letter of credit, which are primary undertakings and are payable solely on presentation of a written demand and other specified documents and, in the case of a demand guarantee governed by the ICC's Uniform Rules for Demand Guarantees, a statement that the principal is in breach and the respect in which it is in breach.[10] Demand guarantees and standby credits are, like documentary credits, independent of the underlying transaction, so that in the absence of clear evidence of fraud the issuer has to pay even if there has been no default in performance by the principal (the debtor of the obligation). For the beneficiary to make a demand when there has been no default may well be a breach of its obligation to the principal but that is of no concern to the issuing bank, which has entered into a separate engagement to pay on presentation of documents and is not concerned

---

independent obligation to pay the amount of the bond, and accordingly loss must be proved (*Trafalgar House Construction (Regions) Ltd. v General Surety & Guarantee Co. Ltd.* [1996] A.C. 199. The distinction between primary and accessory obligations is not always easy to draw. See, for example, the decision of the Court of Appeal in *Actionstrength Ltd. v International Glass Engineering In.Gl.En Spa* [2002] 1 W.L.R. 566, which reversed the decision of the judge at first instance. There was an unsuccessful appeal to the House of Lords [2003] U.K.H.C. 17, but not on the characterisation of the guarantee.

[5] See Andrews and Millett, *op. cit.*, paras 1.05, 6.18 *et seq*; Phillips & O'Donovan, *op. cit.*, pp.215 *et seq.*

[6] See above, paras 7–02, 7–48.

[7] See John Phillips, "When should the guarantor be permitted to rely on the principal's set-off" [2001] L.M.C.L.Q. 383; Philip R. Wood, *English and International Set-Off*, paras 10–216, 10–227.

[8] See above, para.7–36.

[9] S.R. Derham, *Set-Off* (3rd ed.), paras 18.10, 18.26.

[10] Art.20. See Georges Affaki, *ICC Uniform Rules on Demand Guarantees: A User's Handbook to the URDG*; Roy Goode, *The ICC Uniform Rules for Demand Guarantees.*

with the underlying contract or with non-documentary factors. The present chapter is confined to suretyship guarantees.

Requirement of evidence in writing

Contracts of guarantee are one of the few remaining contracts which under the Statute of Frauds are unenforceable unless evidenced in writing signed by or on behalf of the surety.[11] The statute does not apply to demand guarantees and standby letters of credit, which as stated above are independent payment undertakings and are in principle enforceable whether or not there has been default in performance of the underlying contract. **8–03**

Unilateral and bilateral guarantees

The typical guarantee is a unilateral contract, *i.e.* there is a promise by one party only, the surety. The creditor does not usually undertake to the surety that he will make an advance to the debtor; it is merely agreed that *if* the creditor makes an advance, the surety guarantees repayment. In contract law terms, the surety's promise is a continuing offer which is to be accepted by the offeree's conduct in making the advance, until which time there is no contract and the surety can revoke the guarantee unless this otherwise provides.[12] The fact that the prospective creditor may have committed itself to the prospective debtor to make an advance is irrelevant, for it remains the case that until the advance is made there is no acceptance of the surety's offer and no contract of guarantee. However, if the consideration for the guarantee is indivisible, or entire, it is not necessary that the advance should be made in full in order for the surety to become bound. It is established that an offer to be accepted by performance ceases to be revocable once performance has begun.[13] So if the surety guarantees a prospective advance of £100 and in reliance on this the creditor commits itself to make such an advance but initially advances £40 as a first payment, the guarantee becomes irrevocable and the surety is committed not only for that advance but for further advances up to the balance of £60.[14] The position is otherwise if the consideration is divisible, as where the advance is to be made by five instalments of £20 each. In such a case each advance constitutes a separate acceptance and the surety can revoke his guarantee as to future instalments. **8–04**

Where the guarantee is expressed to be given in consideration of the prospective creditor's agreeing with the creditor to make advances, the surety becomes committed to the creditor at the same time as the latter incurs a binding commitment to the prospective debtor, for that is the act of

---

[11] Statute of Frauds 1677, s.4. As to estoppel, see the House of Lords decision above, n.4.
[12] *Offord v Davies* (1862) 12 C.B.N.S. 748.
[13] *Errington v Errington* [1952] 1 K.B. 290.
[14] If the creditor fails to fulfil its obligations the surety is not liable (*Errington v Errington*, above).

acceptance. If, by the terms of the guarantee, the prospective creditor also undertakes *with the surety* to make advances to the prospective debtor the guarantee is a bilateral contract and the surety becomes bound immediately.

Continuing guarantees

8–05   Similar considerations apply to a continuing guarantee, that is, a guarantee which is given not for a fixed advance but for all the debtor's obligations from time to time or for continuing advances on a current account, so that the surety in effect guarantees the ultimate debit balance.[15] In this case there is a separate acceptance of the surety's continuing offer each time an advance is made, so that the surety becomes committed as to all such advances but remains free to revoke the guarantee as to future advances.[16] A guarantee of obligations arising under a continuing contract between the debtor and the creditor, such as a factoring agreement, is impliedly terminated by the termination of the principal contract, since there are no future obligations under that contract to which the guarantee is capable of attaching, and this remains the case even if that contract is later restored. Accordingly in the absence of a fresh guarantee the surety's liability is limited to the obligations of the debtor under the principal contract prior to its termination.[17] Unless the guarantee is so revoked by notice to the creditor or is terminated by some legal event such as the surety's bankruptcy, the surety's liability continues until the debtor's account has been closed and the ultimate debit balance then struck and discharged.

The surety's ability to revoke a continuing guarantee is on the assumption that the consideration is divisible so that each advance is to be treated as a separate acceptance. Where, however, in reliance on the guarantee the creditor commits itself to allow the debtor a drawing facility up to a stated amount, then upon the first drawing being made the surety ceases to be able to revoke the guarantee even though the contract is unilateral, for the stipulated performance of an indivisible obligation has begun. The same applies to other types of indivisible obligation. For example, in *Lloyd's v Harper*[18] a father whose son was a candidate for underwriting membership of Lloyd's guaranteed all obligations of the son incurred in that capacity. The father later died and the question was whether notice of his death operated to revoke the guarantee. The Court of Appeal, upholding the decision of the trial judge, held that it did not. In contrast to the position in *Coulthart v Clementson*,[19] the consideration was an entire consideration given once and for all and there was no basis for limiting its scope to the lifetime of the surety or for treating the guarantee as revocable.

---

[15] See below.

[16] *Coulthart v Clementson* (1879) 5 Q.B.D. 42.

[17] *Silverburn Finance (UK) Ltd. v Salt* [2001] 2 All E.R. (Comm) 438.

[18] (1880) 16 Ch.D. 290.

[19] See above.

As before, if the creditor commits itself to the surety to give the drawing facility the guarantee is a bilateral contract and takes effect so as to bind the surety immediately.

So long as a continuing guarantee remains in force, the order of receipts **8–06** and payments passing through the debtor's account is of little significance, for the surety's indebtedness relates not to a specific drawing by the debtor but to a balance of account, and the rule in *Clayton's Case*[20] does not apply. The position is otherwise where an event occurs which causes the guarantee to come to an end. Unless the guarantee otherwise provides,[21] termination of the guarantee fixes the moment at which the debit balance must be struck. The surety is not answerable for future drawings or advances. It is therefore important that the creditor should freeze the debtor's account when the guarantee comes to an end, and place all future receipts to the credit of a separate account.[22] If this is not done, or the rule in *Clayton's Case* otherwise excluded, further sums paid to the credit of the principal debtor's account will go in reduction of the earliest indebtedness first—that is, the indebtedness covered by the guarantee—whilst new drawings will be outside the guarantee. *Clayton's Case* thus has the effect of converting guaranteed indebtedness into non-guaranteed indebtedness, since the amount of the former is reduced by each payment to the credit of the account.

Although in principle a continuing guarantee of a current account is revocable at any time as to future advances, this is subject to any contrary provision in the guarantee. Bank guarantees commonly provide for a period of three months' notice to be given to terminate a continuing guarantee. Such a provision not only ensures that the bank is covered for transactions in course of processing at the time the notice is received but also provides the bank and the debtor with an opportunity to procure a substitute security. Nevertheless several questions may arise. If the bank makes further advances during the currency of the notice, are these covered by the guarantee? *Prima facie* they are. Doubts have been expressed as to whether a bank which knows that its surety wishes to end the guarantee acts equitably in allowing further advances during the period of the notice, but in the ordinary way there seems no reason for equitable intervention. The parties have agreed on a specified period of notice, the surety's liability does not crystallise until the end of that period,[23] and to allow the surety to treat his liability as crystallised on receipt

[20] (1816) 1 Mer. 527. See below.
[21] As in *Westminster Bank Ltd. v Cond* (1940) 46 Com. Cas. 60, where a clause in the guarantee was held effective to exclude the rule in *Clayton's Case* despite the fact that pursuant to the clause the bank made no break in the account.
[22] In the absence of an effective appropriation of the payment by the debtor to the existing account, the creditor is entitled to open a new account for the crediting and debiting of receipts and payments unless the guarantee otherwise provides (*Re Sherry* (1884) 25 Ch.D. 692). But it is sensible to follow the usual practice of providing for this specifically in the guarantee (or otherwise excluding the operation of the rule in *Clayton's Case*), so as to avoid the possibility of an appropriation by the debtor to the existing account.
[23] *Bank of Credit and Commerce International SA v Simjee*, unreported, July 3, 1996, CA; *National Westminster Bank plc v French*, unreported, October 20, 1977, Goff J.; *Morrison v Barking Chemicals Co Ltd.* [1919] 2 Ch. 325.

of the notice rather than on its expiry would enable him to call on the debtor to discharge the liability before expiry of the notice, which would be inconsistent with the bargain made by the parties.[24] A further question, deriving from the fact that a surety is not liable to pay until demand has been made, is whether the effect of expiry of the notice is simply to crystallise the surety's liabilities at that time or whether it is necessary that demand be made before such expiry. In *National Westminster Bank plc v Hardman*[25] the Court of Appeal held that the surety was discharged if demand for payment was not made before expiry of the notice. The court may have felt that it was impelled to this result by the wording of the guarantee, which was expressed to remain in force until determined (*inter alia*) by notice but it runs counter to the commercial sense of the transaction. Moreover, since the liability did not crystallise until expiry of the notice it is hard to see how demand could have been made prior to that time. In *Bank of Credit and Commerce International SA v Simjee*[26] the Court of Appeal held, in relation to a somewhat differently worded guarantee, that no cause of action against the surety would arise until demand but that the demand could only relate to such of the obligations of the debtor at the time of expiry of the notice as still remained unperformed at the time of the demand. Expiry of the notice crystallised the surety's obligations but the guarantee continued in force as regards those obligations and there was no reason why demand could not be made thereafter. What these cases show is the importance of clarity in the drafting of continuing guarantees.

Limited guarantees

8–07   A guarantee may be limited in duration or in amount. I do not propose to say anything about guarantees limited in duration except to point out again the necessity of stating clearly what the specified time limit means. I have seen several guarantees in which it is provided that "this guarantee shall cease to have effect two years after the date thereof." Many years ago, when proferred such a guarantee by an overseas bank, I asked what it meant. Was it restricted to obligations maturing before the expiry of the period or did it cover obligations incurred before expiry though maturing afterwards?[27] Did the creditor have to make a demand within the two-year period? Issue a writ within that period? Serve the writ before the lapse of the two years? Or get a judgment within that time? I received a reply stating that in their 150 years of banking no one had ever raised the point. Nevertheless, they accepted my amendment!

---

[24] *Morrison v Barking Chemicals Co Ltd.*, above.
[25] [1988] F.L.R. 302.
[26] See above.
[27] For a detailed discussion, see Phillips & O'Donovan, *op. cit.*, pp.374–375. For similar issues in relation to the termination of continuing guarantees, see above, para.8–06.

Equal care needs to be taken in drafting a guarantee under which the surety's liability is to be limited in amount. In particular, it is necessary to distinguish the guarantee of a fixed sum, or of a part of an indebtedness, from the guarantee of the entire indebtedness with a limit of liability. If the debtor is to be advanced £10,000, a guarantee of £5,000 of the indebtedness may appear to be the same as a guarantee of the whole advance with a limit of liability of £5,000; but in law there is all the difference in the world. In the former case, the guaranteed part of the debt is treated as if it were a separate debt, so that on paying the £5,000 the surety discharges that notional separate debt and, unless otherwise provided by the guarantee, becomes entitled to share rateably in securities held by the creditor for the full indebtedness[28] and takes over the right to prove in the debtor's bankruptcy as regards the part so paid.[29] Where, on the other hand, the surety guarantees the whole indebtedness but with a limit of liability to £5,000, then whilst he cannot be sued for more than £5,000, the guaranteed indebtedness remains indivisible and the surety cannot take over securities or prove in the bankruptcy unless he discharges the entire indebtedness.[30]

Guarantees given at request of debtor and guarantees not so given

A distinction is also to be drawn between the case where the guarantee is given at the request of the debtor himself, in order to enable him to get the loan, and the case where it is given solely by arrangement between the creditor and the surety. Hire-purchase provides a neat illustration of the two forms of guarantee. A decides to acquire a car on hire-purchase through his local motor dealer, D, the hire-purchase agreement being concluded through the medium of D with a finance house, F. F may stipulate that A is to furnish a surety, and A arranges for his father, B, to guarantee his liability. F may also have an arrangement with the dealer, D, by which D undertakes recourse in respect of all transactions introduced by him. A is not involved in the furnishing of such a guarantee; indeed, it is extremely unlikely that he will know of it.

8–08

The importance of the distinction between the two forms of guarantee lies in the fact that where a guarantee is given at the debtor's request, he impliedly undertakes to indemnify the surety against all payments the latter has to make, whereas one who gives a guarantee without reference to the debtor has no right of indemnity as such, merely a right to be subrogated to the creditor if and when he, the surety, has discharged the full indebtedness.

---

[28] *Goodwin v Gray* (1874) 2 2 W.R. 312.
[29] *Re Sass* [1896] 2 Q.B. 12.
[30] *ibid.*

Nature of the surety's undertaking

8-09   The surety, in entering into the guarantee, undertakes responsibility for payment of the principal indebtedness and for performance of all other obligations of the debtor to which the guarantee relates. Of course, so far as the surety is concerned, liability for breach of those other obligations has to be converted into monetary terms. The surety's liability applies not merely to the debtor's primary payment obligation but also to any secondary liability for damages which the debtor may incur as the result of repudiating the principal contract. This was affirmed by the House of Lords in *Moschi v Lep Air Services Ltd.*[31]:

> The appellant guaranteed the obligations of a company under an agreement by which the company undertook to discharge his existing indebtedness to the respondents by weekly instalments. The company having repeatedly failed to pay the instalments due, the respondents treated the default as a repudiation and terminated the agreement. The appellant's contention that this discharged him from liability under the guarantee as being the equivalent of an unauthorised variation of the agreement, was rejected. The House of Lords held that the appellant's true liability as surety was not for payment of the instalments as such but for performance of the company's obligations, so that the cause of action against the appellant was not in debt but in damages, and this covered the company's secondary liability resulting from its repudiation of the agreements, as well as its primary liability for payment of the instalments.

Plainly the appellant's contention would have made a nonsense of the guarantee, and the result of the case is to be applauded. However, one has to treat with a degree of caution the rather sweeping statements in the speeches that a claim against a surety sounds in damages, not in debt and that on acceptance of a repudiatory breach all debt claims become converted into damages claims. The first proposition is based on Lord Diplock's historical analysis of old forms of pleading which has no relevance to modern pleading.[32] The second proposition is true as regards future liabilities but is manifestly not the case as regards accrued indebtedness. It is trite law (to use one of Lord Diplock's favourite expressions) that termination for breach does not affect accrued liabilities nor, by the same token, does it change their character. In *Lep* itself, for reasons which are not clear, the claim seems to have been exclusively for damages, instead of being for payment of the accrued instalments and damages for the value of the lost future performance, and on this basis the surety's liability would equally be a damages liability. But it is evident that where a surety guarantees the payment of liquidated sums due under a contract which is later terminated for the debtor's repudiatory breach, then while

---

[31] [1973] A.C. 331. See to the same effect the decision of the House of Lords in *Hyundai Heavy Industries Co. Ltd. v Papadopoulos* [1980] 2 All E.R. 29.
[32] See Roy Goode, *Commercial Law* (2nd ed.), pp.833–834.

the claim for the lost value of future instalments is a damages claim the claim for accrued indebtedness remains a claim in debt for which the surety is liable.

In a subsequent decision of the House of Lords in *Hyundai Heavy Industries Co. Ltd. v Papadopoulos*[33] the majority of the House was in no doubt that the decision in *Lep* as to the character of the claim related to future sums payable, not to sums already accrued, and that nothing in that case was intended to displace the well-established principle, reiterated in *Chatterton v Maclean*,[34] that acceptance of a repudiatory breach does not affect accrued liabilities.   **8–10**

In the recent decision in *Hampton v Minns*,[35] in which, curiously, there was no reference to *Papadopolous*, the deputy High Court judge nevertheless reached the correct conclusion that the surety's obligation in that case was a debt obligation and as such was outside the scope of s.1 of the Civil Liability (Contribution) Act 1978 and s.10 of the Limitation Act 1980. The learned judge drew a distinction between a promise by the surety to pay if the debtor did not pay and a promise to procure performance by the debtor. I would draw the distinction somewhat differently and look at the nature of the performance required of the debtor. To the extent that this is an obligation to pay an ascertained sum of money the surety's obligation is to procure the debtor to make that payment or else pay himself and therefore is an obligation sounding in debt, not in damages. The characterisation ought not to depend on fine verbal distinctions between "pay" and "perform". If the performance required is the payment of a liquidated sum, then accrual of the payment obligation creates a debt due from the debtor and accordingly a debt due from the surety if the debtor defaults. It is only obligations unmatured at the date of termination for breach that become converted into damages, and this for the simple reason that because of the termination the innocent party is no longer able to tender the performance that will earn him the future money entitlements. The distinction between a claim for debt and a claim for damages is significant in that in the latter case the creditor has to prove his loss and is required to take reasonable steps to mitigate his damage whereas in the case of a debt claim the right to payment has accrued and neither proof of loss nor a duty to mitigate comes into consideration.

Rights of the surety against the debtor

Where the guarantee was given at the request of the debtor, express or implied, the surety has a right to be indemnified by the debtor for liability incurred and payments made under the guarantee, and in particular is entitled to recoupment for each payment under the guarantee as it is made.[36]   **8–11**

---

[33] [1980] 2 All E.R. 29.

[34] [1951] 1 All E.R. 761.

[35] [2002] 1 W.L.R. 1.

[36] *Davies v Humphreys* (1840) 6 M. & W. 153. At law, the surety cannot claim this indemnity before payment. In equity, however, he may seek an order for indemnity on incurring the

Whether or not the debtor requested the surety to give the guarantee, the surety is entitled, on discharging the indebtedness, to be subrogated to the creditor's rights against the debtor and any securities held by the creditor.[37] For the purpose of protecting the surety, the guaranteed debt is considered notionally to remain in force and any securities given are likewise deemed to continue for the benefit of the surety notwithstanding that he has discharged the debt. As previously indicated, where the whole indebtedness is guaranteed, the right of subrogation arises only on complete payment of the debt; partial payment gives no right to *pro rata* subrogation. The position is otherwise where the surety guarantees only part of the debt and then pays that part.

Finally, a surety is entitled, like anyone else, to purchase the debt from the creditor and to enforce it as assignee on giving notice of assignment to the debtor.

Rights of the surety against a co-surety

8–12   Contribution rights exist between sureties in the same degree. One of two sureties who has paid more than his proportionate share of the indebtedness is entitled to recover the excess from his co-surety.[38] However, a co-surety, that is, a surety on the same level as the surety claiming contributions, is to be distinguished from one who may be termed a sub-surety, that is, who merely guarantees the obligations of the surety and undertakes no liability except on the surety's default. Contribution cannot be claimed from a sub-surety, for he is entitled to be indemnified by the surety for whom he gives his sub-guarantee.[39] The latter may have a right of set-off in respect of a cross-claim against the overpaying surety, but set-off cannot be asserted against a surplus payable to the overpaying surety from the proceeds of security which he acquired by subrogation as the result of his payment of the debt.[40]

---

liability to pay as the result of the debtor's default, and the requisite order may be made even though, in the case of a guarantee callable on demand, the demand has not been made (*Thomas v Nottingham Incorporated Football Club Ltd.* [1972] Ch. 596). The form of order in such cases is a declaration that the surety is entitled to be exonerated from liability, by payment by the debtor, and a direction to the debtor to pay or secure the debt (*ibid.; Tate v Crewdson* [1938] Ch. 869; *Watt v Mortlock* [1964] Ch. 84).

[37] This is so whether or not the surety knew of the existence of the securities when giving his guarantee, and applies to securities taken by the creditor after as well as before the guarantee (*Forbes v Jackson* (1882) 19 Ch.D. 615).

[38] *Deering v Earl of Winchelsea* (1787) 2 Bos. & Pul. 270. For the various methods of ascertaining the contribution in different situations, see Andrews and Millett, *op. cit.*, para.12.12; *Rowlatt on Principal and Surety* (4th ed.), pp.152 *et seq.*; Phillips & O'Donovan, *op. cit.*, pp.549 *et seq.*

[39] *Scholefield Goodman & Sons v Zygnier* [1986] A.C. 562.

[40] *Brown v Cork* [1985] B.C.L.C. 363. For a criticism of the decision, see Derham, *op.cit.*, paras 8.40, 8.41.

Creditor's duty of care in the management of securities

As stated above, one of the rights enjoyed by a surety who pays off the debt **8–13** is to be subrogated to securities held by the creditor. It follows that any act or omission of the creditor which impairs those securities (*e.g.* by failing to perfect them by registration) or which leads to their being realised at less than a proper price potentially injures the surety's interests.[41] A question much ventilated in the cases is whether a mortgagee owes a duty of care to the mortgagor, and in consequence to any surety, in the management of the securities. In *Downsview Nominees Ltd. v First City Corporation*[42] the Privy Council adopted a very restricted view of the mortgagee's obligations, holding that while a mortgagee owes a duty to take reasonable care to obtain a proper price there is no general duty to use reasonable care in dealing with the assets given in security. However, *Downsview*, though of persuasive value, is not binding on English courts. Shortly prior to *Downsview*, which had followed an earlier decision of the Privy Council in *China and South Sea Bank Ltd. v Tan Soon Gin*,[43] Sir Donald Nicholls V.C. had protested that he had difficulty in seeing why the mortgagee's duties should be considered so narrowly confined.[44] Since then a series of cases has affirmed that a mortgagee owes not merely a duty of good faith in the exercise of his powers but a general duty of due diligence,[45] and that this duty, which is owed not in contract or tort but in equity, extends to all those who have an interest in the equity of redemption, including sureties.[46]

There are other duties owed by the creditor to the surety, for example, not to vary the principal contract or grant the debtor a release or an extension of time without the consent of the surety. These are discussed below.

What is interesting is that so far there appears to have been no case in which it was necessary to establish a positive duty on the creditor to the surety actionable in damages. Rather the effect of failure to hold the securities unimpaired has been to release the surety from its obligations to the extent of the impairment. In Hohfeldian terms,[47] the surety's "rights" have so far been conceived as immunities and the creditor's breach of "duties" as imposing disabilities rather than as conferring an independent cause of action. However, one can readily envisage situations in which relief from liability would not be enough, as where the surety meets a demand for payment

---

[41] Whether in fact it does so depends on the circumstances. The diminished value of the security may still be sufficient to ensure that the surety is recouped. Alternatively the debtor may be solvent, so that surety can recoup himself without the need to rely on the security.

[42] [1993] A.C. 295.

[43] [1990] 1 A.C. 536.

[44] *Palk v Mortgage Services Founding plc.* [1993] Ch. 330 at 338.

[45] *Medforth v Blake* [2000] Ch. 86; *Yorkshire Bank plc v Hall* [1999] 1 All E.R. 879; *Burgess v Auger, Burgess v Vanstock Ltd.* [1998] 2 B.C.L.C. 478. For an earlier decision of the Court of Appeal to similar effect, though grounding the duty in negligence, see *Standard Chartered Bank Ltd v Walker* [1982] 3 All E.R. 938;

[46] *Burgess v Auger, Burgess v Vantock Ltd.*, above.

[47] See W. N. Hohfeld, *Fundamental Legal Conceptions*.

in full and then discovers that the security to which he has acquired rights by subrogation is worthless because it was not duly registered and has been displaced by a subsequent encumbrance. In that situation, can he recover any resultant loss in an action for damages for breach of the equitable duty? In principle, there seems no reason why he cannot. Damages (or equitable compensation) may be awarded for breach of the equitable duty of care and skill in just the same way as at law for negligence.[48]

The crucial question is the extent of the defence. Does the creditor's culpable behaviour discharge the surety entirely or only to the extent of the prejudice he has suffered? The answer to this question depends on whether the conduct in question constitutes the breach of a non-promissory condition of the guarantee,[49] in which case the surety is wholly discharged irrespective of whether he has suffered loss, or is merely a breach of the equitable obligation to respect the surety's interests (so far as is consistent with the protection of the creditor's own interests), in which case the surety is discharged only to the extent of his loss.

Grounds of discharge of the surety

8–14 The law is very protective of sureties. I have already mentioned that the surety's liability is tailored to that of the principal debtor, so that where the principal contract is void, voidable[50] or unenforceable or is discharged by the debtor's acceptance of the creditor's repudiatory breach[51] the surety is free from liability.[52] In addition, great importance is attached to the surety's rights of subrogation against the principal debtor and co-sureties. Accordingly any culpable act or omission of the creditor which alters or affects those rights is likely to discharge the surety, wholly or in part. As mentioned earlier, the exact impact of the creditor's improper behaviour on his rights against the surety depends on whether such behaviour constitutes a breach of an implied condition of the contract of guarantee itself or whether it merely infringes the equitable right of the surety not to have his interests wantonly disregarded. In the former case the surety is discharged completely, irrespective of whether he has suffered prejudice. Into this category fall, first,

---

[48] *Bristol and West Building Society v Mothew* [1998] Ch. 1, *per* Millett L.J. at 17, citing with approval the judgment of Ipp J. in *Permanent Building Society v Wheeler* (1994) 14 A.C.S.R. 109 at 157. For a comprehensive discussion of equitable damages, see I.C.F. Spry, *Equitable Remedies* (6th ed.), Chap.7.

[49] As to the possibility of a promissory condition, see below.

[50] And avoided. See Andrews and Millett, *Law of Guarantees* (3rd ed.) para.6.24.

[51] A non-repudiatory breach does not of itself discharge the surety (*National Westminster Bank Ltd. v Riley* [1986] B.C.L.C. 268).

[52] He is also discharged, of course, where the creditor commits a repudiatory breach of the contract of guarantee (*Ankar Pty. Ltd. v Westminster Finance (Australia) Ltd.* (1987) 70 A.L.R. 641) or fails to observe a non-promissory condition of the contract. This is a matter of general contract law, not a particular feature of the law relating to guarantees, though it is given particular force in guarantee law by the fact that it is an implied condition of the guarantee contract that no alteration will be made in the terms of the principal contract without the surety's consent. See below.

those cases where the creditor fails to provide the consideration for which the guarantee was expressed to be given,[53] and, secondly, all cases where the creditor, without the consent of the surety, varies the terms of the principal contract, so altering the basis of the surety's undertaking to guarantee the debtor's obligations. So even if he suffers no loss the surety is fully discharged where, for example, the creditor releases the debtor,[54] concludes a binding agreement to give the debtor an extension of time for payment without reserving his rights against the surety,[55] releases the security, wholly or in part[56] or otherwise varies the terms of the agreement with the debtor without the surety's consent and in a manner capable of prejudicing him. In effect, the maintenance of the terms upon the basis of which the surety gave his guarantee is a condition of the guarantee, and as in the case of any other breach of condition the court will not concern itself with the extent of the prejudice suffered as a result of the breach but will regard the breach as entitling the surety to regard himself as discharged.[57]

By contrast, where the creditor, without altering the basis of the bargain so far as the surety is concerned, carelessly impairs the surety's position, *e.g.* by failing to register a security or by realising it at an undervalue through careless acts or omissions, the surety is discharged only to the extent of his resultant loss.[58]

Exclusion of duty of care and other grounds of discharge from liability

Almost invariably, standard-term guarantees contain provisions excluding **8–15** the above rules. Typically, the guarantee will provide that the creditor's rights against the surety shall not be prejudiced or affected by the grant of any time or indulgence to the debtor or a co-surety or by the creditor's failure to take, perfect or hold unimpaired any security taken from the debtor or a co-surety. At common law such provisions are generally effective. An example is furnished by the decision of the Supreme Court of Canada in *Bauer v Bank of Montreal*[59]:

> The creditor, a bank, failed to register a bill of sale taken from the debtor, who later became bankrupt, thereby rendering the bill of sale void. In the result, the goods comprised in the bill remained part of the debtor's estate in bankruptcy and were not available to the surety. The bank successfully

---

[53] *Scott v Forster Pastoral Co Pty Ltd.* (2000) 35 A.C.S.R. 294; *Ankar Pty Ltd v National Westminster Finance (Aust) Ltd* (1987) 162 C.L.R. 549 (failure to give notice of events to the surety as provided by the guarantee).

[54] *Commercial Bank of Tasmania v Jones* [1893] A.C. 313.

[55] *Webb v Hewitt* (1857) 3 K. & J. 438; *Swire v Redman* (1876) 1 Q.B.D. 536.

[56] *Pledge v Buss* (1860) John 663.

[57] *Smith v Wood* [1929] 1 Ch. 14.

[58] *Skipton Building Society v Stott* [2001] Q.B. 261; *Brueckner v Satellite Group (Ultimo) Pty Ltd* [2002] N.S.W.S.C. 378; *Wulff and Billing v Jay* (1872) L.R. 7 Q.B. 756.

[59] (1980) 110 D.L.R. (3d) 424.

relied on a clause in the guarantee which allowed it to abstain from perfecting any security interest.

The Supreme Court of Canada, upholding the decision of the Ontario Court of Appeal, rejected the surety's arguments (1) that the clause was an exemption clause to be construed *contra proferentem*; and (2) that it was unenforceable as unusual, onerous and unreasonable, and gave judgment for the bank.

Another technique used to protect the creditor from rules which discharge the surety, wholly or in part, is the "principal debtor" clause, by which the surety's obligations are expressed to be incurred as principal debtor. Such clauses are generally effective to insulate the creditor from the discharging effects of granting time or improperly releasing securities.[60] But it does not follow that the guarantee is to be treated for all purposes as an indemnity or other form of independent undertaking. It is necessary to construe the guarantee according to its terms. So if the surety gives a guarantee of "the moneys hereby secured" and part of such moneys are irrecoverable as a penalty, that part is equally irrecoverable from the surety despite the use of a principal debtor clause.[61]

The efficacy of such clauses is subject to the provisions of the Unfair Contract Terms Act 1977 as regards exclusion or limitation of liability in a guarantee by a consumer or a guarantee on standard written terms of business, and to the more wide-ranging provisions of the Unfair Terms in Consumer Contract Regulations 1999[62] as regards a guarantee by a consumer.

2. BANKRUPTCY

8–16   I now turn to the impact of bankruptcy[63] on the rights of creditor and surety. The possibilities I shall canvass are the bankruptcy of the debtor, the bankruptcy of the surety and the bankruptcy of both debtor and surety. I shall conclude with a brief analysis of the circumstances in which a guarantee may be set aside on the surety's insolvency as a transaction at an undervalue.

If the subject of fixed and floating charges seemed complicated, and the cases difficult to analyse, the going becomes harder still when we come to look at the case law on the impact of bankruptcy on suretyship guarantees. For some reason, conflicting authorities and obscure reasoning seem endemic in the earlier bankruptcy cases, and not infrequently one finds in the

---

[60] *National Westminster Bank plc v Riley* [1986] B.C.L.C. 268.
[61] *Citicorp Australia Ltd v Hendry* (1985) 4 N.S.W.L.R. 1. See also the decision of Lloyd J. in *General Produce Co v United Bank Ltd* [1979] 2 Lloyd's Rep. 255. For a useful discussion of the question, see Jaya Prakash, "The 'principal debtor' clause in a guarantee—some traps for the unwary" (1997) 3 Singapore Law Rev. 650.
[62] SI 1999/2083.
[63] This should be read as including winding-up except as otherwise indicated.

literature two quite inconsistent propositions placed one after the other, each being duly supported by authority, yet without a hint in the later case that it marks a departure from the earlier.

So anyone going into this field does so at his peril. I have done my best to reconcile the apparently irreconcilable, to extract a consistent principle from seemingly conflicting cases and to discover and express a rational policy basis for some of the rules I shall later be discussing. That said, I must caution you that bankruptcy law is one of the most technical and, in some respects, one of the most arbitrary branches of law, and that in the absence of a definitive ruling from the courts the answers to some questions remain conjectural.

(i) Bankruptcy of the debtor

Three questions in particular arise where the debtor becomes bankrupt. **8–17** First, on the assumption that the contract of guarantee is not vulnerable under bankruptcy law, to what extent do sums received by the creditor from the surety or from the realisation of security given by the surety or from a third party reduce the amount for which the creditor is entitled to prove or to maintain a proof already lodged? Secondly, in what circumstances does a payment by the debtor to the creditor prior to the debtor's bankruptcy constitute a voidable preference of the surety? Thirdly, what is the impact of the debtor's insolvency on the position of the surety?

Receipts from surety or third party: the general rule

The general rule is that sums received from the surety, or from the realisation **8–18** of security taken from the surety, do not have to be deducted by the creditor from the amount of his proof, whether received before or after the bankruptcy has occurred[64] and, in the latter case, whether before or after proof, so long as the creditor does not receive in total more than 100 pence in the pound. At first sight it seems surprising that the creditor should not have to give credit at least for sums received from the surety prior to the bankruptcy. But the rule has a sound policy base. It is a well settled principle of equity that until the creditor has received payment of the guaranteed debt in full the surety cannot prove in the insolvent debtor's estate for a sum paid by him to the creditor, the reason being that he has, expressly or by implication,

---

[64] *Ellis v Emmanuel* (1876) 1 Ex.D. 157; *Re Sass* [1896] 2 Q.B. 12; *Ulster Bank Ltd. v Lambe* [1968] N.I. 161; *Re an Arranging Debtor No. A. 1076* [1971] N.I. 96; *Westpac Banking Corp. v Gollin & Co. Ltd.* (1987) Aug. 13, Tadgell J. (Supreme Court of Victoria). In the last three decisions the court declined to follow an earlier Scottish decision, *McKinnon's Trustee v Bank of Scotland* [1915] S.C. 411, in which it had been held that the creditor had to give credit for pre-bankruptcy payments received from the surety. It seems clear that whatever the position under Scottish law, *McKinnon* does not represent English law. I am indebted to the late Mr C. R. Craigie, then a member of the New South Wales Bar, for a detailed note of the *Westpac case*.

undertaken to be responsible for the full sum guaranteed, including whatever remains due to the creditor after receipt of dividends by him out of the bankrupt's estate, and thus has no equity to prove for his right of reimbursement in competition with the creditor.[65] If the creditor were required to give credit for a pre-bankruptcy part payment by the surety, neither of them could prove for the amount of such payment and the general body of creditors would thus be unjustly enriched. Similarly, sums received by the creditor before the bankruptcy from the realisation of security furnished by the surety are not deductible in computing the amount for which he can prove.[66] A fortiori credit need not be given for sums received after bankruptcy and before proof, still less for receipts after proof. To make assurance doubly sure it is common for guarantees to empower the creditor to place sums received from the surety which do not fully discharge the guaranteed debt to the credit of a suspense or "securities realisation" account.[67] But this procedure, though sensible as a matter of accounting practice, is not essential to enable the creditor to maintain his proof for the full sum owing to him.

The same is true where the creditor receives payment from a complete stranger. There is thus a general rule that only a payment by or on behalf of the party primarily liable (in the case under discussion, the bankrupt) has to be taken into account; payments from other sources are disregarded. As will be seen, a similar rule applies in the case where it is the surety who is bankrupt.

The same principle applies where the surety has guaranteed the whole indebtedness with a limit of liability. Since the guarantee covers the ultimate balance, the surety has no equity to prove in competition with the creditor until payment has been made in full, even though his liability under the guarantee is limited to a lower amount which he has paid.[68]

I have said that partial payments by a surety do not reduce the amount for which the creditor can prove. By partial payments I mean payments of less than the total indebtedness to which the guarantee relates. If the creditor has misguidedly taken a guarantee covering only part of the debt, as opposed to a guarantee of the full indebtedness with a limit of liability, then on paying that part the surety becomes entitled to lodge a proof himself in respect of

---

[65] See cases cited above, n.64. A separate rule against double proof prevents the surety and the creditor from proving for the same debt, so that the creditor's right to prove for the whole debt without giving credit for a part payment received from the surety precludes both a proof for that payment by the surety and a set-off. See para.8–23.

[66] It may be noted that for the purpose of bankruptcy a creditor is considered secured only where he holds security over an asset of the debtor. Security taken from a third party such as a surety does not fall to be treated as a security in the treatment of proofs in bankruptcy. This reflects the policy of bankruptcy law that security should be brought into account only where, if given up, it would augment the debtor's estate (see *Re Dutton, Massey & Co.* [1924] 2 Ch. 199).

[67] The effect of such a payment is to provide the creditor with a fund to which he can resort when he chooses. The payment constitutes a deposit by the surety which is withdrawable only if the creditor receives 100p in the pound. The creditor is entitled to appropriate the deposit in or towards the discharge of the principal indebtedness, but until he makes an appropriation the deposit does not constitute a payment of any part of the debt (*Commercial Bank of Australia v Official Assignee of the Estate of Wilson* [1893] A.C. 181).

[68] *Re Rees* (1851) 17 Ch. 1.

the part so paid[69]; and since two creditors cannot separately prove for the same debt—this is the so-called rule against double proof—it follows that the creditor must reduce his proof (even if already lodged) by the amount paid by the surety in discharge of his guarantee. As stated earlier, the part of the indebtedness guarantee is treated as a separate debt for the purpose of the rules as to proof by a surety.

Receipts from surety or third party: negotiable instruments

For reasons which are not clear, negotiable instruments constitute an excep- **8–19** tion to the general rule.[70] Where, for example, the creditor is the holder of a bill of exchange accepted by the debtor and drawn or indorsed by a third party (whose position is thus analogous to that of a surety[71]), then although the creditor can prove in the debtor's bankruptcy for the full amount of the bill whilst concurrently pursuing a claim to full payment against the third party, yet if before lodging his proof against the debtor the creditor receives part payment from the third party he must reduce his proof by the amount of the payment.[72] Where, on the other hand, the payment is not received from the third party until after the creditor has lodged his proof, he can keep his proof for the full amount of the debt and need not give credit for the sum received.[73] The moral is obvious. Where one of the parties liable to you on a bill of exchange becomes bankrupt, lodge your proof as fast as you possibly can, and until then defer steps to recover from the other parties.

Preference of surety

Payments made or property transferred by a debtor prior to bankruptcy may **8–20** in certain conditions be voidable on bankruptcy as a preference not only of the creditor but of a surety. Common cases are where an insolvent debtor reduces or discharges his loan account in order to procure the release of a relative or friend who has furnished a guarantee, and where moneys are paid into a debtor company's overdrawn account not simply because this is the natural depository of cheques and other sums paid to the company but with a view to reducing or extinguishing the suretyship liability of a director. The Insolvency Act 1986 makes separate provision for the avoidance of preferences in bankruptcy and in the administration or winding up of a company, and whilst the two are dealt with in almost identical fashion there are certain differences in detail which necessitate distinct treatment.

---

[69] *Re Sass* [1896] 2 Q.B. 12, *per* Vaughan Williams J. at 15.
[70] *Re Blackburne* (1892) 9 Morr. 249; *Re Houlder* [1929] 1 Ch. 205.
[71] *Duncan, Fox & Co. v North & South Wales Bank* (1880) 6 App.Cas. 1; *Re Conley* [1938] 2 All E.R. 127, *per* Lord Greene M.R. at 133.
[72] *Re Blackburne*, above.
[73] *Re London, Bombay & Mediteranean Bank* (1874) L.R. 9 Ch.App. 686; *Re Houlder*, above.

(1) *Bankruptcy*

8–21   The statutory provisions as they affect sureties apply where an individual is adjudged bankrupt and he has at a relevant time given a preference to a surety, that is, has done anything or suffered anything to be done which puts the surety in a better position in the event of the debtor's bankruptcy than the surety would have been in if that thing had not been done.[74] The typical act of preference of a surety is a payment by the debtor to the creditor which reduces the surety's liability under his guarantee. The term "preference" (which replaced the phrase "fraudulent preference" in the Bankruptcy Act 1914) is somewhat misleading, since whilst the earlier legislation was concerned with the preference of the surety over other creditors at the time of the payment or other act of preference, the new provisions apply where the surety's position is thereby improved on the debtor's bankruptcy, regardless whether the effect of the payment or other act in question was to favour the surety over other creditors at the time it was made or done. Where a preference is established the court is given wide powers to restore the status quo,[75] and in the case of preference of a surety these include an order providing for any surety whose obligations to any person were released or discharged (in whole or in part) by the giving of the preference to be under such new or revived obligations to that person as the court thinks appropriate.[76]

In order for a preference to fall within the statutory provisions two conditions must be satisfied. First, in giving the preference the debtor must have been influenced by the desire to put the surety in a better position, in the event of the debtor's bankruptcy, than that in which he would otherwise have been.[77] Secondly, the preference must have been given at a "relevant time," that is, at a time in a specified period ending with the day of presentation of the bankruptcy petition on which the debtor is adjudged bankrupt, and the debtor must have been insolvent[78] at that time or have become insolvent in consequence of the preference.[79] Where the surety is an associate of the debtor[80] the period is two years; in other cases, it is six months.[81] The surety's exercise of a right of set-off is not a preference, for it does not involve the debtor's consent.

---

[74] Insolvency Act 1986, s.340(1), (3).

[75] *ibid.*, ss.340(2), 342. See R. Goode, *Principles of Corporate Insolvency Law* (2nd ed.), pp.372 *et seq.*

[76] *ibid.*, s.342(1)(e).

[77] *ibid.*, s.340(4). This is presumed where the surety was an associate of the debtor at the time (*ibid.*, s.340(5)).

[78] For this purpose the debtor is insolvent if he is unable to pay his debts as they fall due or the value of his assets is less than the amount of his liabilities, taking into account his contingent and prospective liabilities (*ibid.*, s.341(3)).

[79] *ibid.*, s.341.

[80] As defined in s.435 of the Act.

[81] *ibid.*, s.341(1).

(2) *Administration or winding up*

Similar provisions apply where the debtor is a company against which an **8–22** administration order is made or which goes into liquidation,[82] but with the following modifications:

(a) Instead of "associate" the provisions refer to a person connected with the company[83] otherwise than by reason only of being its employee[84];

(b) A "relevant time" is a time in the period of six months (or in the case of a connected person, two years) ending with the "onset of insolvency" (as defined by s.240(3) of the Act) or at a time between the presentation of a petition for an administration order and the making such order on that petition[85];

(c) Instead of having to show that the debtor company was insolvent at the time of or in consequence of the preference, the liquidator or other office-holder attacking the preference has the much easier task of showing that at the time of or in consequence of the preference the company was unable to pay its debts within the meaning of s.123 of the Act.[86]

Proof by the surety

(1) *In respect of the guaranteed debt*

Since the creditor is entitled to maintain his proof for the full amount of the **8–23** debt existing at the date of the receiving order without giving credit for part payment by the surety, and since there cannot be a double proof in respect of the same debt, it follows that the surety himself has merely a contingent right to prove against the debtor's estate in respect of the guaranteed debt and cannot lodge a proof until the creditor has been paid in full.[87] As previously pointed out, the position is otherwise where the surety has guaranteed only part of the debt and paid that part.[88] However, where the right to indemnity is not by virtue of a liability incurred under a contract of guarantee *stricto sensu* but is that of a drawer or indorser under a bill of exchange, then if the drawer or indorser makes part payment to the holder before the latter has proved in the acceptor's bankruptcy, the maker of the

---

[82] *ibid.*, ss.238 (the ingredients of which are attracted by ss.239(1)) and 239–241.

[83] As defined by s.249 of the Act.

[84] *ibid.*, s.240(1)(a).

[85] *ibid.*, s.240(1).

[86] *ibid.*, s.240(2), which is much wider than the definition in s.341(3).

[87] *Re Fenton* [1931] 1 Ch. 85. Set-off is thus precluded. See Insolvency Rules 1986, r.4.90.

[88] See above para.8–18. But his right to prove in competition with the creditor may be excluded by the terms of the guarantee. See, below, para.8–24.

payment can forthwith prove for it, for as mentioned earlier[89] the holder has to deduct such payment in calculating the amount of his proof, so that the problem of double proof does not arise.

(2) *In respect of an independent liability of the debtor*

8–24   The rule against double proof does not, of course, apply to a debt owed to the surety independently of that which he has guaranteed. If, for example, the surety has lent the debtor money, this is quite distinct from the debt to which the guarantee relates, and the surety is entitled to prove for it.

Most forms of bank guarantee provide that the surety is not to prove in competition with the bank until the bank's claim has been paid in full, the intention being to prevent the banker's dividend from being watered down by the surety's own claim. The non-competition clause has been standard for decades; I have myself settled countless forms of guarantee incorporating it. But one night, while lying in the bath, I was struck by the fact that the clause, far from protecting the interests of the creditor, is positively inimical to those interests, for its effect is to benefit not only the creditor himself but all other unsecured creditors. To prohibit the surety from proving for an independent liability is thus not wisdom but folly, for it prevents the creditor from getting the benefit of a double dividend. What the well-drawn guarantee ought to provide is that the surety *shall* prove in the bankruptcy (with a power of attorney to the creditor to lodge a proof in the surety's name) and shall account to the creditor for any dividends he receives, to the amount necessary to discharge his guarantee liability, meanwhile holding such receipts on trust for the creditor. Where such a provision is contained in two or more guarantees given to different creditors, then presumably the creditor holding the guarantee which is first in time prevails.

Is a trust of the dividends registrable as a charge on book debts? In my view, no. In the first place, the debt is not the dividend itself but the proved indebtedness which has given rise to the dividend. Secondly, the dividend payable in a bankruptcy or winding up is not a debt at all, for it is not recoverable by action against the trustee in bankruptcy or liquidator.[90] The remedy of a creditor who does not receive a declared dividend is to apply to the court to require the trustee or liquidator to perform his statutory duties.[91]

Surety's subrogation to creditor's rights

8–25   Upon paying the guaranteed debt in full the surety becomes subrogated to the rights of the creditor.[92] Accordingly (1) the creditor is account-

---

[89] See above para.8–19.
[90] *Prout v Gregory* (1889) 24 Q.B.D. 281; *Spence v Coleman* [1901] 2 K.B. 199.
[91] *ibid.*
[92] Both in equity and under s.5 of the Mercantile Law Amendment Act 1856.

able to the surety for any further dividends received from the bankrupt's estate[93]; (2) the surety succeeds to securities held by the creditor; and (3) to the extent to which the creditor was a preferential creditor (whether directly or by subrogation to a preferential creditor), the surety becomes a preferential creditor for the like amount.[94]

Example 1

S gives a guarantee in respect of D's liability for rates or taxes. D becomes bankrupt and S pays the rates or taxes in question. To the extent to which these were preferential, S ranks as a preferential creditor.[95]   **8–26**

Example 2

S guarantees D Company's overdraft with C Bank. D Company goes into liq-   **8–27** uidation by reason of insolvency. Part of its indebtedness to C Bank represents advances to pay wages which, if unpaid at the date of liquidation, would have ranked as preferential debts.[96] The bank, having advanced the wages, is by statute subrogated to the preferential claims of the employees concerned.[97] S later pays off the bank, and thus becomes subrogated to the bank's own subrogatory rights in respect of the wages. S can therefore prove as a preferential creditor to the extent to which the wages advanced by the bank were preferential.

Impact of debtor's bankruptcy on surety's liability

(1) In general, liability is unaffected

The bankruptcy of the principal debtor does not as a general rule affect the   **8–28** creditor's rights against the surety. The creditor may lodge a proof in the bankruptcy for the full outstanding balance of the debt and simultaneously sue the surety to judgment, and enforce such judgment to the extent to which the creditor has not received a dividend from the estate.[98] Even the discharge of the debtor does not affect the surety's liability. This is expressly provided by s.281(7) of the Insolvency Act 1986.

---

[93] *Re Sass* [1896] 2 Q.B. 12.
[94] *Re Lamplugh Iron Ore Co. Ltd.* [1927] 1 Ch. 308.
[95] *ibid.*
[96] Under the Insolvency Act 1986, s.386 and Sch.6.
[97] *ibid.* Sch.6, para.11.
[98] For the position where the surety also becomes bankrupt, see below, para.8–34.

(2) *Interest accruing after bankruptcy order*

8–29 Some care needs to be taken in regard to the interest clause in the guarantee. If interest is expressed to be payable "so long as any amount is due from the debtor," the right to charge interest to the surety apparently terminates with the debtor's bankruptcy, at which point the debt ceases to be legally recoverable from him.[99] This result can be avoided by stipulating that interest is to run against the surety "until payment" of the amount due from the principal debtor.[1]

(3) *Invalidation of securities*

8–30 What is the position of the surety where a debit balance on the debtor's account is cleared with a payment or the proceeds of a security which is later avoided, *e.g.* as a preference under s.239 of the Insolvency Act 1986 or as a floating charge given by an insolvent company within s.245 of the Act or void for want of registration under s.395 of the Companies Act 1985? In the case of a preference the answer to this question, which was obscure under the previous law, is given by ss.239(3) and 241 of the Act. By s.239(3) the court is required to make such order as it thinks fit for restoring the position to what it would have been if the company had not given the preference. Without prejudice to the generality of this provision s.241 empowers the court to make an order providing for any surety or guarantor whose obligations were released or discharged (in whole or in part) by the giving of the preference to be under such new or revived obligations to the creditor as the court thinks appropriate.[2] The court may also order security to be provided for the discharge of any such obligation and for the obligation to be charged on any property, the security or charge to have the same priority as that released by the giving of the preference.[3] The effect of these provisions is to enable the court to restore the status quo existing before the giving of the preference. But unless and until it does so the preference by which the guaranteed debt was settled operates to discharge the surety and to release any security furnished by him to support his guarantee.

   Where security subject to a floating charge—whether crystallised or uncrystallised—is realised and the proceeds utilised to discharge the debt, the surety is discharged and any security furnished by him is extinguished. The fact that the charge later becomes liable to avoidance for non-registration or on any other ground is irrelevant, for it is settled law that if the charge is enforced or payment collected prior to an event such as liquidation which

---

[99] *Re Moss* [1905] 2 K.B. 307.
[1] *Re Fitzgeorge* [1905] 1 K.B. 462.
[2] s.241(1)(e).
[3] s.241(1)(f).

avoids the charge, its effect is spent and its subsequent avoidance has no impact on the rights of the parties.[4]

(ii) Bankruptcy of the surety

It is now necessary to consider the converse situation where the debtor is still **8–31** solvent (or at any rate not in bankruptcy or winding up), whilst the surety has become bankrupt, and to examine questions arising in relation to proof by the creditor[5] and by a co-surety.

Proof by creditor

As in the case of the bankruptcy of the principal debtor, it is necessary to **8–32** distinguish payments made by the principal debtor as the party primarily liable from those made by a third party such as a co-surety or a stranger. The creditor is required to deduct from the amount of his proof against the surety's estate sums received from the principal debtor prior to submission of the proof,[6] but not sums received after the proof has been submitted.[7] On the other hand payments received from a co-surety or other party not primarily liable for the debt do not have to be deducted even if received before proof.[8] The creditor cannot, of course, receive more than 100p in the pound.

Where the surety has guaranteed only part of the debt, then whether a payment by the principal debtor is to be attributed to the guaranteed part of the indebtedness or to the rest of the debt is a matter of appropriation as between debtor and creditor, and the surety's trustee has no right to require the payment to be applied in reduction of the part of the debt covered by the guarantee.[9]

Again, negotiable instruments are a special case. A creditor proving against a surety on a negotiable instrument must credit sums received before proof

---

4 See above para.5–69.
5 For a discussion of the creditor's right to set off actual and contingent claims under the guarantee against sums due to the surety, see above para.7–91. The setting aside of a guarantee as a transaction at an undervalue is considered below paras 8–36 *et seq.*
6 *Re Blakeley* (1892) 9 Morr. 173; *Re Amalgamated Investment & Property Co. Ltd.* [1985] 1 Ch. 349. Note that the relevant date for taking account of payments by the principal debtor is the date the proof is submitted, not the date it is admitted (*Re Amalgamated Investment & Property Co. Ltd.*, above).
7 *ibid.*
8 *Re Blackburne* (1892) 9 Morr. 249; *Re Houlder* [1929] Ch. 205.
9 This is merely a particular application of the general rule that a surety has no right to dictate to what debt a payment by the debtor to the creditor should be appropriated (*Re Sherry* (1884) 25 Ch.D. 692).

from any party liable on the bill, whether or not he is the party primarily liable on the bill,[10] but sums received after proof need not be deducted.[11]

Proof by co-surety

8–33 A co-surety who has paid more than his due proportion of the debt cannot prove for his right of contribution in the estate of the bankrupt surety until the creditor has been paid in full, for the creditor himself has the prior right of proof and the rule against double proof prevents the co-surety from proving for the same debt. However, once the co-surety has paid in full he becomes subrogated to the rights of the creditor[12] and can prove in his name, or take over his proof if already lodged, for the full amount of the debt, not merely the amount of the contribution to which he is entitled, so long as he does not receive in total more than 100p in the pound.[13]

(iii) Bankruptcy of both debtor and surety

The general rule

8–34 Where both debtor and surety become bankrupt, the creditor is in general entitled to maintain a proof in both estates for the full amount of the debt, and is not obliged to reduce his proof in one estate so as to give credit for dividends declared or received in the other,[14] so long as he does not receive *in toto* more than 100p in the pound.

Negotiable instruments

8–35 Where the debtor and the surety are both liable on a negotiable instrument, as where the debtor is the acceptor and the surety is the drawer or indorser of a bill of exchange held by the creditor, a different rule applies. In this case, when proving against one estate the creditor must give credit for sums received or dividends declared (whether or not paid) from the other estate before he lodged his proof in the former estate,[15] though he is not obliged to revise his proof lodged in one estate where the receipt from or declaration of

---

[10] *Re Blackburne*, above. The party primarily liable on a bill is the acceptor or, in the case of an accommodation bill, the drawer.

[11] *ibid.; Re London, Bombay & Mediterranean Bank* (1874) 9 Ch.App. 686.

[12] Both in equity and by virtue of s.5 of the Mercantile Law Amendment Act 1856.

[13] *Re Parker, Morgan v Hill* [1894] 3 Ch. 400.

[14] The same principle applies here as where only one of the parties is insolvent. See *Re Rees* (1881) 17 Ch.D. 98; *Re Sass* [1896] 2 Q.B. 12; and above para.8–18.

[15] *Cooper v Pepys* (1741) 1 Atk. 107; *Re Stein Ex p. Royal Bank of Scotland* (1815) 2 Rosa 197; *Re Houghton* (1857) 26 L.J.Bcy. 58.

dividend in the other estate does not take place until after the lodging of the proof in the first estate.[16]

Finally, mention must be made of the rule in *Ex p. Waring*.[17] Under this rule, where a bill is accepted for the accommodation of the drawer and the latter deposits money with the acceptor to meet the acceptances, then if the drawer and the acceptor become insolvent the holder of the bill is entitled to have the amount so deposited paid to him. The theory appears to be that as the deposit was made for the specific purpose of covering the acceptor's liability under the bill, it is impressed with a trust for that purpose and cannot be treated as an asset in the acceptor's estate.[18] In lodging his proof of debt, the holder must give credit for any sums received under the rule.[19]

3. VULNERABILITY OF GUARANTEE AS TRANSACTION AT UNDERVALUE

The statutory provisions

Where a company in administration or liquidation has at a relevant time[20] **8–36** entered into a transaction at an undervalue and is at that time unable to pay its debts as they fall due[21] or becomes unable to do so in consequence of the transaction, the Insolvency Act 1986 confers wide powers to restore the status quo.[22] Similar provisions apply on the bankruptcy of an individual.[23] It would seem that the giving of a guarantee is capable of constituting a transaction at an undervalue for the purpose of these provisions, though their application to guarantees is not free from difficulty.

What constitutes a transaction at an undervalue

A company enters into a transaction with a person at an undervalue if: **8–37**

    (a)   the company makes a gift to that person or otherwise enters into a transaction with that person on terms that provide for the company to receive no consideration; or

---

[16] *Re Fothergill* (1876) 3 Ch.D. 445; *Re London, Bombay & Mediterranean Bank* (1874) L.R. 9 Ch.App. 686.
[17] (1815) 19 Ves. 345.
[18] *Ex p. Dever (No. 2)* (1885) 14 Q.B.D. 611.
[19] *Re Barned's Banking Co.* (1875) L.R. 10 Ch. 198.
[20] For the meaning of this see above para.8–21.
[21] Within the meaning of s.123 of the Act.
[22] Insolvency Act 1986, ss.238, 240, 241.
[23] *ibid.*, ss.339, 341, 342.

(b) the company enters into a transaction with that person for a consid-
     eration the value of which, in money or money's worth, is signifi-
     cantly less than the value, in money or money's worth, of the
     consideration provided by the company.[24]

The general notion is clear enough. If a company makes a payment, transfers
an asset or provides services or other things and receives in exchange either
nothing at all or something less than the value of what it parts with or provides, it enters into a transaction at an undervalue. But how do the provisions
apply in relation to a guarantee, which does not at the time it is given involve
a payment, transfer or provision of any kind by the surety, merely the
incurring of a contingent obligation to pay?

Guarantee as a transaction at an undervalue[25]

8–38   Let us take a typical case where a company gives a guarantee in respect of
advances to be made to its parent by a third party. The giving of the guarantee confers a benefit on the creditor, and the advance of funds by the creditor to the parent may be expected to benefit the subsidiary in facilitating its
support and development by the parent, but the value of the benefit in each
case may be difficult to estimate. This brings us to a fundamental problem in
applying the statutory provisions to a guarantee. Whether a transaction is a
transaction at an undervalue has presumably to be tested as at the time it is
entered into, not the time when performance of the obligations incurred
under it is demanded or effected. So in deciding whether a guarantee gives
rise to a transaction at an undervalue the act which constitutes the transaction is the giving of the guarantee, not the creditor's subsequent call under
the guarantee or payment by the surety in response to such a call; and the
time as at which the benefit conferred by the creditor by the guarantee falls
to be valued is the time the surety becomes bound by the guarantee,[26] not the
time when payment under it is demanded or made. Similarly, the benefit
derived by the surety from the prospective provision of funds to its parent

---

[24] *ibid.*, s.238(4). The comparable provision in bankruptcy is s.339(3).

[25] See generally R. Goode, *Principles of Corporate Insolvency Law* (2nd ed.), pp.363–368.

[26] This will depend on the circumstances. Where the consideration for the guarantee is the creditor's counter-promise to make advances to the parent, the contract of guarantee is bilateral
and comes into effect by the exchange of the promise and counter-promise. More commonly,
however, the creditor makes no promise of any kind to the surety, and the consideration for
the latter's promise is the actual making of the advance by the creditor. In such a case the contract of guarantee is unilateral and comes into existence only when the creditor accepts the
surety's offer by making the advance, until which time the document is legally inoperative and
the surety is free to withdraw from his guarantee. For this purpose it is immaterial that the
guarantee is under seal, since as a purely accessory engagement it is intended to come into
effect only on the furnishing of consideration by the creditor. See K. P. McGuinness, *The Law
of Guarantee*, para.4.62. It follows from the above that the apparent difficulty of valuing a
guarantee at the time it is given and before the creditor has either made his advance or undertaken to the surety to make it cannot arise, for until then the guarantee is not legally operative
at all.

must be valued at the date of the guarantee, not at the date the funds are actually provided to the parent or the date when the surety receives a benefit as the result of their provision. Hence the task is to assess the present value of the contingent right conferred on the creditor by the guarantee and then determine whether this is significantly greater than the present value of the contingent benefit to be received by the surety from the advance to the parent. The onus of showing this lies on the liquidator or other office-holder seeking to impeach the transaction.

The benefit conferred on the creditor by the giving of the guarantee varies inversely with the strength of the parent. If the parent is solvent and there is little likelihood of default the guarantee has a correspondingly low value to the creditor. We cannot say that it has no value, for the guarantee relates to the future, and though the parent may be solvent when the guarantee is given it does not follow that it will still be solvent when repayment falls due. On the other hand, even if there is some prospect of default the value of the guarantee is not necessarily the full value of the debt, for against this must be set whatever part of the debt is likely to be recoverable from the parent as debtor and from any security furnished by the parent. It follows that whilst the benefit to the surety of an advance made to the parent will usually be considerably less than the amount of the advance, it will not necessarily be less or "significantly" less than the benefit conferred on the creditor by the guarantee.

The practical problems involved in valuing the contingent benefits received by the creditor on the one hand and the surety on the other, coupled with the fact that the onus is on the office-holder to prove an undervalue and the availability of the statutory defence referred to below, mean that in the ordinary way a guarantee is unlikely to be held a transaction at an undervalue unless there is both a serious risk of default and no benefit to the surety, as where the guarantee is taken to support an advance already made to the parent which the latter is unlikely to be able to repay.

Defence in respect of bona fide business transactions

Even where it is established that the guarantee is a transaction at an under- **8–39** value, the court cannot exercise its powers of adjustment if it is satisfied:

(a) that the company which entered into the transaction did so in good faith and for the purpose of carrying on its business; and

(b) that at the time it did so there were reasonable grounds for believing that the transaction would benefit the company.[27]

---

[27] Insolvency Act 1986, s.238(5). There is no comparable provision for bankruptcy.

Powers of court

8–40   Where the guarantee constitutes a transaction at an undervalue and the statutory defence referred to above is not available the court may make such order as it thinks fit for restoring the position to what it would have been if the company had not entered into the transaction[28] and without prejudice to the generality of this power may include in such an order provision for any of the matters listed in s.241(1) of the Act, subject to the restrictions imposed by s.241(2).[29]

---

[28] *ibid.*, s.238(3). The comparable provision in bankruptcy is s.339(2).
[29] The bankruptcy equivalent is to be found in s.342(1), (2).

324

INDEX